1 & 2 PETER/ JUDE

A Commentary in the Wesleyan Tradition

*New Beacon Bible Commentary

1 & 2 PETER/ JUDE

A Commentary in the Wesleyan Tradition

Daniel G. Powers

BEACON HILL PRESS
OF KANSAS CITY

ISBN 978-0-8341-2513-1

Printed in the United States of America

Cover Design: J.R. Caines
Interior Design: Sharon Page

Library of Congress Cataloging-in-Publication Data

Powers, Daniel G.
1 & 2 Peter/Jude / Daniel G. Powers.
p. cm. — (New beacon Bible commentary)
Includes bibliographical references.
ISBN 978-0-8341-2513-1 (pbk.)
1. Bible. N.T. Peter—Commentaries. 2. Bible. N.T. Jude—Commentaries. I. Title. II. Title: First and Second Peter/Jude. III. Title: First and Second Peter. IV. Title: Jude.
BS2795.53P69 2010
227'.9207—dc22

2010019781

10 9 8 7 6 5 4 3 2 1

DEDICATION

For my parents, Richard and Shirley Powers,
who have exemplified so well what it means
to "follow in his steps" (2 Pet 2:21)

With love,
Your son
Dan Powers

COMMENTARY EDITORS

CONTENTS

GENERAL EDITORS' PREFACE

The purpose of the New Beacon Bible Commentary is to make available to pastors and students in the twenty-first century a biblical commentary that reflects the best scholarship in the Wesleyan theological tradition. The commentary project aims to make this scholarship accessible to a wider audience to assist them in their understanding and proclamation of Scripture as God's Word.

Writers of the volumes in this series not only are scholars within the Wesleyan theological tradition and experts in their field but also have special interest in the books assigned to them. Their task is to communicate clearly the critical consensus and the full range of other credible voices who have commented on the Scriptures. Though scholarship and scholarly contribution to the understanding of the Scriptures are key concerns of this series, it is not intended as an academic dialogue within the scholarly community. Commentators of this series constantly aim to demonstrate in their work the significance of the Bible as the church's book and the contemporary relevance and application of the biblical message. The project's overall goal is to make available to the church and for her service the fruits of the labors of scholars who are committed to their Christian faith.

The *New International Version* (NIV) is the reference version of the Bible used in this series; however, the focus of exegetical study and comments is the biblical text in its original language. When the commentary uses the NIV, it is printed in bold. The text printed in bold italics is the translation of the author. Commentators also refer to other translations where the text may be difficult or ambiguous.

The structure and organization of the commentaries in this series seeks to facilitate the study of the biblical text in a systematic and methodical way. Study of each biblical book begins with an ***Introduction*** section that gives an overview of authorship, date, provenance, audience, occasion, purpose, sociological/cultural issues, textual history, literary features, hermeneutical issues, and theological themes necessary to understand the book. This section also includes a brief outline of the book and a list of general works and standard commentaries.

The commentary section for each biblical book follows the outline of the book presented in the introduction. In some volumes, readers will find section ***overviews*** of large portions of scripture with general comments on their overall literary structure and other literary features. A consistent feature of the commentary is the paragraph-by-paragraph study of biblical texts. This section has three parts: ***Behind the Text***, ***In the Text***, and ***From the Text***.

The goal of the ***Behind the Text*** section is to provide the reader with all the relevant information necessary to understand the text. This includes specific historical situations reflected in the text, the literary context of the text, sociological and cultural issues, and literary features of the text.

In the Text explores what the text says, following its verse-by-verse structure. This section includes a discussion of grammatical details, word studies, and the connectedness of the text to other biblical books/passages or other parts of the book being studied (the canonical relationship). This section provides transliterations of key words in Hebrew and Greek and their literal meanings. The goal here is to explain what the author would have meant and/or what the audience would have understood as the meaning of the text. This is the largest section of the commentary.

The ***From the Text*** section examines the text in relation to the following areas: theological significance, intertextuality, the history of interpretation, use of the Old Testament scriptures in the New Testament, interpretation in later church history, actualization, and application.

The commentary provides ***sidebars*** on topics of interest that are important but not necessarily part of an explanation of the biblical text. These topics are informational items and may cover archaeological, historical, literary, cultural, and theological matters that have relevance to the biblical text. Occasionally, longer detailed discussions of special topics are included as ***excurses.***

We offer this series with our hope and prayer that readers will find it a valuable resource for their understanding of God's Word and an indispensable tool for their critical engagement with the biblical texts.

Roger Hahn, Centennial Initiative General Editor
Alex Varughese, General Editor (Old Testament)
George Lyons, General Editor (New Testament)

ACKNOWLEDGMENTS

Most of my doctoral work focused on Paul's letters. So I felt privileged but anxious when the Centennial Initiative Committee invited me to write a commentary on 1 and 2 Peter and Jude. But what a joy to rediscover these unique writings! My mind and my spirit have been challenged and renewed from this academic and devotional exercise.

I am grateful to Nazarene Bible College for granting me a sabbatical leave during the fall trimester of 2008 to complete the initial draft of the commentary. I appreciate the encouragement and support I received from the administration, faculty, and students of NBC, especially from my friend and colleague Tom King. Special thanks should go to NBC's librarian, Ann Attig, who tracked down several elusive resources.

Thirty years ago I submitted to the careful and insightful tutelage of Frank Carver at Point Loma College as a college freshman. As my subsection editor in this project, Frank has similarly guided my work again in this commentary. I have deep gratitude for his invaluable assistance, both thirty years ago and now.

My wife and children are probably even happier than I am that this project has now been completed. Thank you, Thomas, Kimberly, Marcus, and David, for your patience and encouragement. Mieke, my wife, is my greatest supporter and helper. Since we first met, you have always been my "Dutch treat." *Dank je, Mieke. Ik hou van jou!*

Finally, "to the only God our Savior be glory, majesty, power and authority, through Jesus Christ our Lord, before all ages, now and forevermore!" (Jude 25).

—Daniel G. Powers

ABBREVIATIONS

With a few exceptions, these abbreviations follow those in *The SBL Handbook of Style* (Alexander 1999).

General

A.D.	anno Domini
B.C.	before Christ
ca.	circa
ch	chapter
chs	chapters
ed(s).	editor(s), edited by
e.g.	*exempli gratia*, for example
esp.	especially
etc.	*et cetera*, and the rest
i.e.	*id est*, that is
ktl.	etc. (in Greek transliteration)
LXX	Septuagint (Greek translation of the OT)
MT	Masoretic Text (Hebrew OT)
n.	note
n.d.	no date
NT	New Testament
OT	Old Testament
Repr.	reprinted
s.v.	*sub verbo*, under the word
trans.	translator
vol(s).	volume(s)
v	verse
vv	verses

Modern English Versions

GNT	Good News Translation
JB	Jerusalem Bible
KJV	King James Version
NAB	New American Bible
NASB	New American Standard Bible
NEB	New English Bible
NIV	New International Version
NJB	New Jerusalem Bible
NLT	New Living Translation
NRSV	New Revised Standard Version
REB	Revised English Bible
RSV	Revised Standard Version

Print Conventions for Translations

Bold font	NIV (bold without quotation marks in the text under study; elsewhere in the regular font, with quotation marks and no further identification)
Bold italic font	Author's translation (without quotation marks)

Behind the Text:	Literary or historical background information average readers might not know from reading the biblical text alone
In the Text:	Comments on the biblical text, words, phrases, grammar, and so forth
From the Text:	The use of the text by later interpreters, contemporary relevance, theological and ethical implications of the text, with particular emphasis on Wesleyan concerns

Old Testament

Gen	Genesis
Exod	Exodus
Lev	Leviticus
Num	Numbers
Deut	Deuteronomy
Josh	Joshua
Judg	Judges
Ruth	Ruth
1—2 Sam	1—2 Samuel
1—2 Kgs	1—2 Kings
1—2 Chr	1—2 Chronicles
Ezra	Ezra
Neh	Nehemiah
Esth	Esther
Job	Job
Ps/Pss	Psalm/Psalms
Prov	Proverbs
Eccl	Ecclesiastes
Song	Song of Songs/ Song of Solomon
Isa	Isaiah
Jer	Jeremiah
Lam	Lamentations
Ezek	Ezekiel
Dan	Daniel
Hos	Hosea
Joel	Joel
Amos	Amos
Obad	Obadiah
Jonah	Jonah
Mic	Micah
Nah	Nahum
Hab	Habakkuk
Zeph	Zephaniah
Hag	Haggai
Zech	Zechariah
Mal	Malachi

(Note: Chapter and verse numbering in the MT and LXX often differ compared to those in English Bibles. To avoid confusion, all biblical references follow the chapter and verse numbering in English translations, even when the text in the MT and LXX is under discussion.)

New Testament

Matt	Matthew
Mark	Mark
Luke	Luke
John	John
Acts	Acts
Rom	Romans
1—2 Cor	1—2 Corinthians
Gal	Galatians
Eph	Ephesians
Phil	Philippians
Col	Colossians
1—2 Thess	1—2 Thessalonians
1—2 Tim	1—2 Timothy
Titus	Titus
Phlm	Philemon
Heb	Hebrews
Jas	James
1—2 Pet	1—2 Peter
1—2—3 John	1—2—3 John
Jude	Jude
Rev	Revelation

Apocrypha

Bar	Baruch
Add Dan	Additions to Daniel
Pr Azar	Prayer of Azariah
Bel	Bel and the Dragon
Sg Three	Song of the Three Young Men
Sus	Susanna
1–2 Esd	1–2 Esdras
Add Esth	Additions to Esther
Ep Jer	Epistle of Jeremiah
Jdt	Judith
1–2 Macc	1–2 Maccabees
3–4 Macc	3–4 Maccabees
Pr Man	Prayer of Manasseh
Ps 151	Psalm 151
Sir	Sirach/Ecclesiasticus
Tob	Tobit
Wis	Wisdom of Solomon

OT Pseudepigrapha

Apoc. Mos.	*Apocalypse of Moses*
As. Mos.	*Assumption of Moses*
2 Bar.	*2 Baruch (Syriac Apocalypse)*
3 Bar.	*3 Baruch (Greek Apocalypse)*
4 Bar.	*4 Baruch (Paraleipomena Jeremiou)*
1 En.	*1 Enoch (Ethiopic Apocalypse)*
2 En.	*2 Enoch (Slavonic Apocalypse)*
3 En.	*3 Enoch (Hebrew Apocalypse)*
4 Ezra	*4 Ezra*
Sib. Or.	*Sibylline Oracles*
T. 12 Patr.	*Testaments of the Twelve Patriarchs*

Josephus

Ant.	*Jewish Antiquities*
J.W.	*Jewish War*

Ancient Classical Writings

Meteor.	Aristotle, *Meteorologica*

Philo

Mos.	*On the Life of Moses*

Apostolic Fathers

Ign. *Eph.*	Ignatius, *To the Ephesians*

Secondary Sources: Journals, Series, and Reference Works

ABD	*Anchor Bible Dictionary* (see Freedman)
BDAG	*A Greek-English Lexicon of the New Testament and Other Early Christian Literature* (see Bauer)
BSac	*Bibliotheca Sacra*
EvQ	*Evangelical Quarterly*
ExpTim	*Expository Times*
Int	*Interpretation*
JBL	*Journal of Biblical Literature*
JETS	*Journal of the Evangelical Theological Society*
JSNT	*Journal for the Study of the New Testament*
NIDNTT	*New International Dictionary of New Testament Theology* (see Colin Brown)
NTS	*New Testament Studies*
RB	*Revue Biblique*
SBLDS	Society of Biblical Literature Dissertation Series
SBLMS	Society of Biblical Literature Monograph Series
TDNT	*Theological Dictionary of the New Testament* (see Kittel)
TNTC	Tyndale New Testament Commentaries
WesTJ	*Wesleyan Theological Journal*
WTJ	*Westminster Theological Journal*
ZNW	*Zeitschrift für die Neutestamentliche Wissenschaft*

Greek Transliteration

Greek	***Letter***	***English***
α	*alpha*	*a*
β	*bēta*	*b*
γ	*gamma*	*g*
γ	*gamma nasal*	*n* (before γ, κ, ξ, χ)
δ	*delta*	*d*
ε	*epsilon*	*e*
ζ	*zēta*	*z*
η	*ēta*	*ē*
θ	*thēta*	*th*
ι	*iōta*	*i*
κ	*kappa*	*k*
λ	*lambda*	*l*
μ	*my*	*m*
ν	*ny*	*n*
ξ	*xi*	*x*
ο	*omicron*	*o*
π	*pi*	*p*
ρ	*rhō*	*r*
ρ	initial *rhō*	*rh*
σ/ς	*sigma*	*s*
τ	*tau*	*t*
υ	*upsilon*	*y*
υ	*upsilon*	*u* (in diphthongs: *au, eu, ēu, ou, ui*)
φ	*phi*	*ph*
χ	*chi*	*ch*
ψ	*psi*	*ps*
ω	*ōmega*	*ō*
`	rough breathing	*h* (before initial vowels or diphthongs)

Hebrew Consonant Transliteration

Hebrew/ Aramaic	***Letter***	***English***
א	*alef*	ʾ
ב	*bet*	*b*
ג	*gimel*	*g*
ד	*dalet*	*d*
ה	*he*	*h*
ו	*vav*	*v* or *w*
ז	*zayin*	*z*
ח	*khet*	*ḥ*
ט	*tet*	*ṭ*
י	*yod*	*y*
כ/ך	*kaf*	*k*
ל	*lamed*	*l*
מ/ם	*mem*	*m*
נ/ן	*nun*	*n*
ס	*samek*	*s*
ע	*ayin*	ʿ
פ/ף	*pe*	*p*
צ/ץ	*tsade*	*ṣ*
ק	*qof*	*q*
ר	*resh*	*r*
שׂ	*sin*	*ś*
שׁ	*shin*	*š*
ת	*tav*	*t*

BIBLIOGRAPHY

Achtemeier, Paul J. 1996. *1 Peter.* Hermeneia. Edited by E. J. Epp. Minneapolis: Fortress.

Aland, Kurt, ed. 1965. *The Authorship and Integrity of the New Testament.* London: SPCK.

Allen, Joel S. 1998. A New Possibility for the Three-clause Format of Jude 22-23. *NTS* 44:133-43.

Argyle, A. W. 1974. Greek among the Jews of Palestine in New Testament Times. *NTS* 20:87-89.

Balch, David L. 1981. *Let Wives Be Submissive. The Domestic Code in 1 Peter.* SBLMS 26. Chico, Calif.: Scholars.

Ball, Charles S. 1966. First and Second Peter. Pages 241-308 in vol. 6 of *The Wesleyan Bible Commentary.* Grand Rapids: Eerdmans.

Barclay, William. 1960. *The Letters of James and Peter.* The Daily Study Bible. Philadelphia: Westminster.

Barker, Glenn W., William L. Lane, and J. Ramsey Michaels. 1969. *The New Testament Speaks.* New York: Harper and Row.

Barnes, Albert. 1962. *Barnes' Notes on the New Testament: Complete and Unabridged in One Volume.* Edited by Ingram Cobbin. Repr. Grand Rapids: Kregel.

Barnett, Albert E. 1957. Exposition in *The Second Epistle of Peter.* Pages 166-206 in vol. 12 of *The Interpreter's Bible* 12. Edited by G. A. Buttrick. Nashville: Abingdon.

Bartchy, S. Scott. 1992. Slavery (Greco-Roman). Pages 65-73 in vol. 6 of *ABD.*

Bartlett, David L. 1998. The First Letter of Peter: Introduction, Commentary, and Reflections. Pages 229-319 in vol. 12 of *New Interpreter's Bible.* Nashville: Abingdon.

Bassett, Paul M. 1978. The Fundamentalist Leavening of the Holiness Movement, 1914-1940. The Church of the Nazarene: A Case Study. *WesTJ* 13:65-85.

Bauckham, Richard J. 1983. *Jude, 2 Peter.* Word Biblical Commentary 50. Nashville: Nelson.

Bauer, William, W. F. Arndt, F. Wilbur Gingrich, and Frederick W. Danker. 2000. *A Greek-English Lexicon of the New Testament and Other Early Christian Literature.* 3d ed. Chicago: University of Chicago Press.

Bauernfeind, Otto. 1964a. *Aretē*. Pages 457-61 in vol. 1 of *TDNT.*

______. 1964b. *Aselgeia*. Page 490 in vol. 1 of *TDNT.*

Bauman-Martin, Betsy J. 2004. Women on the Edge: New Perspectives on Women in the Petrine *Haustafel*. *JBL* 123:253-79.

______. 2007. Speaking Jewish: Postcolonial Aliens and Srangers in First Peter. Pages 144-77 in *Reading First Peter with New Eyes: Methodological Reassessments of the Letter of First Peter.* Edited by Robert L. Webb and Betsy Bauman-Martin. Library of New Testament Studies, 364. London: T. & T. Clark.

Beare, Francis Wright. 1961. *The First Epistle of Peter: The Greek Text with Introduction and Notes*. 2d ed. Oxford: Blackwell.

Beasley-Murray, G. R. 1965. *The General Epistles: James, 1 Peter, Jude, 2 Peter.* Bible Guides 21. New York: Abingdon.

Best, Ernest. 1971. *1 Peter.* New Century Bible. Somerset: Oliphants.

Beyer, Hermann W. 1964a. *Allotriepiskopos*. Pages 620-22 in vol. 2 of *TDNT.*

______. 1964b. *Eulogētos*. Page 764 in vol. 2 of *TDNT.*

Bigg, Charles. 1905. *A Critical and Exegetical Commentary on the Epistles of St. Peter and St. Jude.* The International Critical Commentary. New York: Charles Scribner's Sons.

Blum, Edwin A. 1981a. 1 Peter. Pages 209-54 in vol. 12 of *The Expositor's Bible Commentary.* Edited by Frank E. Gaebelein. Grand Rapids: Zondervan.

______. 1981b. 2 Peter. Pages 257-89 in vol. 12 of *The Expositor's Bible Commentary.* Edited by Frank E. Gaebelein. Grand Rapids: Zondervan.

______. 1981c. Jude. Pages 381-96 in vol. 12 of *The Expositor's Bible Commentary.* Edited by Frank E. Gaebelein. Grand Rapids: Zondervan.

Boismard, M. E. 1956. Une Liturgie Baptismale dans la Prima Petri. *RB* 63:182-208.

______. 1957. Une Liturgie Baptismale dans la Prima Petri. *RB* 64:161-83.

Bonhoeffer, Dietrich. 1959. *The Cost of Discipleship.* 2d ed. Repr. New York: Macmillan.

Boobyer, G. H. 1958. The Verbs in Jude 11. *NTS* 5:45-47.

Bornemann, W. 1919. Der erste Petrusbrief—eine Taufrede des Silvanus? *ZNW* 19:143-65.

Braun, Herbert. 1968. *Planaō* Pages 228-53 in vol. 6 of *TDNT.*
Bray, Gerald, ed. 2000. *James, 1-2 Peter, 1-3 John, Jude.* Ancient Christian Commentary on Scripture 11. Downers Grove, Ill.: InterVarsity.
Bromiley, Geoffrey W. 1985. *Theological Dictionary of the New Testament: Abridged in One Volume.* Grand Rapids: Eerdmans.
Brown, Colin, et al., eds. 1971-78. *The New International Dictionary of New Testament Theology.* 3 vols. Translated, with additions and revisions, from Theologisches Begriffslexikon zum Neuen Testament. Edited by Lothar Coenen, et al. by a team of translators. Grand Rapids: Zondervan.
Brown, Raymond E., Karl P. Donfried, and John Reumann, eds. 1973. *Peter in the New Testament.* Minneapolis: Augsburg.
Brox, Norbert. 1979. *Der erste Petrusbrief.* Evangelisch-Katholischer Kommentar zum Neuen Testament. Zurich: Benziger.
Büchsel, Friedrich. 1964. *Apoginomai.* Page 686 in vol. 1 of *TDNT.*
______. 1967. *Lytroō.* Pages 349-51 in vol. 4 of *TDNT.*
Bultmann, Rudolf. 1964a. *Agalliaomai.* Pages 19-21 in vol. 1 of *TDNT.*
______. 1964b. *Dēloō.* Pages 61-62 in vol. 2 of *TDNT.*
Callen, Barry L., and Richard P. Thompson, eds. 2004. *Reading the Bible in Wesleyan Ways: Some Constructive Proposals.* Kansas City: Beacon Hill Press of Kansas City.
Calvin, John. 1948. *Commentaries on the Catholic Epistles.* Translated and edited by John Owen. Geneva: n.p., 1551. Repr. Grand Rapids: Eerdmans.
Carlston, Charles Edwin. 1961. Transfiguration and Resurrection. *JBL* 80:233-40.
Carver, Frank G. 1987a. Biblical Foundations for the "Secondness" of Entire Sanctification. *WesTJ* 22/2:7-23.
______. 1987b. *The Cross and the Spirit: Peter and the Way of the Holy.* Kansas City: Beacon Hill Press of Kansas City.
Chang, Andrew D. 1985. Second Peter 2:1 and the Extent of the Atonement. *BSac* 142:52-63.
Charles, J. Daryl. 1991. Literary Artifice in the Epistle of Jude. *ZNW* 82:106-24.
Christensen, Michael J., and Jeffrey A. Wittung, eds. 2007. *Partakers of the Divine Nature: The History and Development of Deification in the Christian Traditions.* Grand Rapids: Baker Academic.
Clowney, Edmund P. 1988. *The Message of 1 Peter: The Way of the Cross.* The Bible Speaks Today. Edited by John R. W. Stott. Downers Grove, Ill.: InterVarsity.
Cranfield, C.E.B. 1958. The Interpretation of 1 Peter iii.19 and iv. 6. *ExpTim* 69:369-72.
______. 1960. *I and II Peter and Jude: Introduction and Commentary.* The Torch Bible Commentaries. London: SCM.
Cullmann, Oscar. 1953. *Peter: Disciple—Apostle—Martyr.* London: SCM.
Dana, Harvey E., and Julius R. Mantey. 1927. *A Manual Grammar of the Greek New Testament.* Toronto: Macmillan.
Daube, David. 1947. Appended Note: Participle and Imperative in 1 Peter. Pages 467-88 in *The First Epistle of St. Peter,* by Edward Gordon Selwyn. London: Macmillan.
Davids, Peter H. 1990. *The First Epistle of Peter.* The New International Commentary of the New Testament. Grand Rapids: Eerdmans.
Dearman, J. Andrew. 1985. Amen. Page 29 in *HarperCollins Bible Dictionary.* Rev. ed. Edited by P. J. Achtemeier, et al. 3d ed. San Francisco: HarperCollins.
Deissmann, Adolf. 1978. *Light from the Ancient East.* Rev. ed. Translated by Lionel R. M. Strachan. Grand Rapids: Baker.
Delling, Gerhard. 1964. *Hēmera.* Pages 943-53 in vol. 2 of *TDNT.*
______. 1968. *Pleonexia.* Pages 266-74 in vol. 6 of *TDNT.*
Drane, John. 1999. *Introducing the New Testament.* Rev. ed. Oxford: Lion.
Dunham, Duane A. 1983. An Exegetical Study of 2 Peter 2:18-22. *BSac* 140:40-54.
Dunn, James D. G. 1977. *Unity and Diversity in the New Testament: An Inquiry into the Character of Earliest Christianity.* Philadelphia: Westminster.
du Toit, A. B. 1974. The Significance of Discourse Analysis for New Testament Interpretation and Translation: Introductory Remarks with Special Reference to 1 Peter 1:3-13. *Neotestamentica* 8:54-80.
Earle, Ralph. 1984. *Word Meanings in the New Testament.* Vol. 6. Kansas City: Beacon Hill Press of Kansas City.
Earle, Ralph, Harvey J. S. Blaney, and Carl Hanson, eds. 1955. *Exploring the New Testament.* Kansas City: Beacon Hill Press.
Easton, Burton Scott. 1932. New Testament Ethical Lists. *JBL* 51:1-12.

Ehrman, Bart D. 2003. *Lost Scriptures: Books That Did Not Make It into the New Testament.* Oxford: Oxford University Press.
Elliott, John H. 1976. The Rehabilitation of an Exegetical Step-Child: 1 Peter in Recent Research. *JBL* 95:243-54.
______. 1981. *A Home for the Homeless: A Sociological Exegesis of 1 Peter, Its Situation and Strategy.* Philadelphia: Fortress.
______. 1992. First Epistle of Peter. Pages 269-78 in vol. 5 of *ABD.*
Ellis, E. Earle. 1978. Prophecy and Hermeneutic in Jude. Pages 221-36 in *Prophecy and Hermeneutic in Early Christianity: New Testament Essays.* Wissenschaftliche Untersuchungen zum Neuen Testament 18. Tübingen: Mohr.
Erdman, Charles R. 1919. *The General Epistles: An Exposition.* Philadelphia: Westminster.
Feinberg, John S. 1986. 1 Peter 3:18-20, Ancient Mythology, and the Intermediate State. *WTJ* 48:303-36.
Filson, Floyd V. 1955. Partakers with Christ: Suffering in First Peter. *Int* 9:400-412.
Finlan, Stephen, and Vladimir Kharlamov, eds. 2006. *Theosis: Deification in Christian Theology.* Eugene, Oreg.: Wipf and Stock.
Fischel, H. A. 1973. The Uses of Sorites (*Climax, Gradatio*) in the Tannaitic Period. *Hebrew Union College Annual* 44:119-51.
Foerster, Werner. 1964. *Eirēnē*. Pages 400-417 in vol. 2 of *TDNT.*
______. 1971a. *Asebēs*. Pages 185-91 in vol. 7 of *TDNT.*
______. 1971b. *Eusebeia*. Pages 175-85 in vol. 7 of *TDNT.*
Foh, Susan T. 1979. *Women and the Word of God: A Response to Biblical Feminism.* Phillipsburg, N.J.: Presbyterian and Reformed.
Fornberg, Tord. 1977. *An Early Church in a Pluralistic Society: A Study of 2 Peter.* Lunn: Gleerup.
France, R. T. 1977. Exegesis in Practice: Two Samples. Pages 252-82 in *New Testament Interpretation: Essays on Principles and Methods.* Edited by I. Howard Marshall. Grand Rapids: Eerdmans.
Freedman, David Noel, ed. 1992. *The Anchor Bible Dictionary.* 6 vols. New York: Doubleday.
Fuhrman, Eldon R. 1967. The Second Epistle of Peter. Pages 311-18 in vol. 10 of *Beacon Bible Commentary.* Kansas City: Beacon Hill Press of Kansas City.
Gamble, Harry Y. 1992. Canon: New Testament. Pages 852-61 in vol. 1 of *ABD.*
Gilmour, Michael J. 2001. Reflections on the Authorship of 2 Peter. *EvQ* 73:291-309.
Goodspeed, Edgar J. 1954. Enoch in 1 Peter 3:19. *JBL* 73:91-92.
Green, Michael. 1987. *The Second Epistle General of Peter and the General Epistle of Jude: An Introduction and Commentary.* Rev. ed. TNTC 18. Grand Rapids: Eerdmans.
Grudem, Wayne A. 1988. *The First Epistle of Peter: An Introduction and Commentary.* TNTC 17. Grand Rapids: Eerdmans.
Grundmann, Walter. 1965. *Kakopoios*. Pages 485-86 in vol. 3 of *TDNT.*
Gundry, Robert H. 1964. The Language Milieu of First-Century Palestine. *JBL* 83:404-8.
______. 1967. "Verba Christi" in I Peter: Their Implications Concerning the Authorship of I Peter and the Authenticity of the Gospel Tradition. *NTS* 13:336-50.
Guthrie, Donald. 1970. *New Testament Introduction.* 3d ed. Downers Grove, Ill.: InterVarsity.
Hanson, Anthony. 1982. Salvation Proclaimed: I. 1 Peter 3:18-22. *ExpTim* 93:100-105.
Harrington, Daniel J. 2003. *Jude and 2 Peter.* Sacra Pagina, 15. Collegeville, Minn.: Liturgical Press.
Harrison, Everett F. 1964. *Introduction to the New Testament.* Grand Rapids: Eerdmans.
Hart, J. H. A. 1979. The First Epistle General of Peter. Pages 1-80 in vol. 5 of *The Expositor's Greek Testament.* Repr. Grand Rapids: Eerdmans.
Heeren, Achille van der. 1911. Peter, Epistles of Saint. Pages 752-55 in vol. 11 of *The Catholic Encyclopedia.* New York: Robert Appleton.
Hemer, C. J. 1978-79. The Address of 1 Peter. *ExpTim* 89:239-43.
Hiebert, D. Edmond. 1984a. A Portrayal of False Teachers: An Exposition of 2 Peter 2:1-3. *BSac* 141.255-65.
______. 1984b. Directives for Living in Dangerous Days: An Exposition of 2 Peter 3:14-18. *BSac* 141:330-40.
______. 1984c. *First Peter: An Expositional Commentary.* Chicago: Moody.
______. 1984d. The Necessary Growth in the Christian Life: An Exposition of 2 Peter 1:5-11. *BSac* 141:43-54.
______. 1984e. The Prophetic Foundation for the Christian Life: An Exposition of 2 Peter 1:19-21. *BSac* 141:158-68.

Hill, D. 1982. "To Offer Spiritual Sacrifices . . ." (1 Peter 2:5): Liturgical Formulations and Christian Paraenesis in 1 Peter. *JSNT* 16:45-63.

Hillyer, Norman. 1992. *1 and 2 Peter, Jude.* New International Biblical Commentary 16. Peabody, Mass.: Hendrickson.

Hoffmann, E. 1986. Hope, Expectation. Pages 238-44 in vol. 2 of *NIDNTT.*

Homrighausen, Elmer G. 1957. Exposition in The First Epistle of Peter. Pages 86-159 in vol. 12 of *The Interpreter's Bible.* Edited by G. A. Buttrick. Nashville: Abingdon.

Hort, Fenton John Anthony. 1898. *The First Epistle of St. Peter, I:1—II:17: The Greek Text with Introductory Lecture, Commentary, and Additional Notes.* London: Macmillan.

Houwelingen, P. H. R. van. 1988. *De tweede Trompet: De authenticiteit van de tweede brief van Petrus.* Kampen: Kok.

______. 1993. *2 Petrus en Judas: Testament in tweevoud.* Commentaar op het Nieuwe Testament. Kampen: Kok.

Howe, Frederic R. 2000a. The Christian Life in Peter's Theology. *BSac* 157:304-14.

______. 2000b. The Cross of Christ in Peter's Theology. *BSac* 157:190-99.

Hunter, Archibald M. 1957. Introduction and Exegesis in The First Epistle of Peter. Pages 75-159 in vol. 12 of *The Interpreter's Bible.* Edited by G. A. Buttrick. Nashville: Abingdon.

Jamieson, Robert, A. R. Fausset, and David Brown. 1870. *A Commentary, Critical and Explanatory, on the Old and New Testaments.* Vol. 2. Repr. Hartford: Scranton.

Jeremias, Joachim. 1964a. *Akrogōniaios*. Page 792 in vol. 1 of *TDNT.*

______. 1964b. *Anthrōpinos*. Pages 366-67 in vol. 1 of *TDNT.*

______. 1967. *Lithos.* Pages 268-80 in vol. 4 of *TDNT.*

Johnson, Dennis E. 1986. Fire in God's House: Imagery from Malachi 3 in Peter's Theology of Suffering (1 Pet 4:12-19). *JETS* 29:285-94.

Johnstone, Robert. 1978. *The First Epistle of Peter: Revised Text, with Introduction and Commentary.* Repr. Minneapolis: James Family.

Kelly, J. N. D. 1969. *A Commentary on the Epistles of Peter and Jude.* Harper's New Testament Commentaries. New York: Harper and Row.

Kittel, Gerhard, and Gerhard Friedrich, eds. 1964-76. *Theological Dictionary of the New Testament* (TDNT). 10 vols. Translated and edited by Geoffrey William Bromiley. Grand Rapids: Eerdmans.

Kleist, James A. 1957. The Epistle to Diognetus. Pages 135-47 in vol. 6 of *Ancient Christian Writers.* Edited by Johannes Quasten and Joseph C. Plumpe. London: Longmans, Green and Co.

Klijn, A. F. J. 1967. *An Introduction to the New Testament.* Translated by M. van der Varhorst-Smit. Leiden: Brill.

Knox, John. 1953. Pliny and 1 Peter: A Note on 1 Peter 4:14-16 and 3:15. *JBL* 72:187-89.

Kümmel, Werner Georg. 1975. *Introduction to the New Testament.* Rev. ed. Translated by Howard Clark Kee. Nashville: Abingdon.

Latourette, Kenneth Scott. 1975. *A History of Christianity. Volume 1: Beginnings to 1500.* Rev. ed. New York: Harper and Row.

Leaney, A. R. C. 1967. *The Letters of Peter and Jude.* Cambridge Bible Commentary. Cambridge: University Press.

Lee, E. Kenneth. 1962. Words Denoting "Pattern" in the New Testament. *NTS* 8:166-73.

Leighton, Robert. 1972. *Commentary on First Peter.* Grand Rapids: Kregel.

Lodahl, Michael. 2004. *All Things Necessary to Our Salvation: The Hermeneutical and Theological Implications of the Article on Holy Scripture in the Manual of the Church of the Nazarene.* San Diego: Point Loma Press.

Lohse, Eduard. 1991. *Die Entstehung des Neuen Testaments.* 5th ed. Kohlhammer theologische Wissenschaft 4. Stuttgart: Kohlhammer.

Luther, Martin. 1990. *Commentary on Peter and Jude.* Repr. Grand Rapids: Kregel.

Macknight, James. 1969. *A New Literal Translation from the Original Greek of All the Apostolic Epistles, with a Commentary, and Notes.* Vol. 5. Repr. Grand Rapids: Baker.

Martin, Ralph P. 1978. *New Testament Foundations: A Guide for Christian Students. Volume 2: The Acts, the Letters, the Apocalypse.* Grand Rapids: Eerdmans.

Martin, Troy W. 1992. *Metaphor and Composition in 1 Peter.* SBLDS 131. Atlanta: Scholars Press.

Mayor, Joseph B. 1978. *The Epistle of St. Jude and the Second Epistle of St. Peter.* London: Macmillan and Company, 1907. Repr. Minneapolis: Klock and Klock.

McCormick, K. Steve. 1991. Theosis in Chrysostom and Wesley: An Eastern Paradigm on Faith and Love. *WesTJ* 26:38-103.

Metzger, Bruce M. 1994. *A Textual Commentary on the Greek New Testament*. 2d ed. Stuttgart: Deutsche Bibelgesellschaft.
Michaelis, Wilhelm. 1967. *Epoptēs*. Pages 373-75 in vol. 5 of *TDNT*.
Michaels, J. Ramsey. 1967. Eschatology in 1 Peter III.17. *NTS* 13:394-401.
______. 1988. *1 Peter.* Word Biblical Commentary 49. Nashville: Nelson.
Michel, Otto. 1967. *Oikos*. Pages 119-31 in vol. 5 of *TDNT.*
Mitchell, Stephen. 1992. Galatia. Pages 870-72 in vol. 2 of *ABD*.
Moffatt, James. 1928. *The General Epistles: James, Peter, and Judas.* The Moffatt New Testament Commentary. London: Hodder and Stoughton.
Moo, Douglas J. 1996. *2 Peter and Jude.* The NIV Application Commentary. Grand Rapids: Zondervan.
Morris, Leon. 1965. *The Apostolic Preaching of the Cross.* London: Tyndale.
Moule, C. F. D. 1956. The Nature and Purpose of 1 Peter. *NTS* 3:1-11.
Mounce, Robert H. 1982. *A Living Hope: A Commentary on 1 and 2 Peter.* Grand Rapids: Eerdmans.
Neyrey, Jerome H. 1980. The Form and Background of the Polemic in 2 Peter. *JBL* 99:407-31.
______. 1993. *2 Peter, Jude.* The Anchor Bible 37c. New Haven, Conn.: Yale University Press.
Nicholson, Roy S. 1967. The First Epistle of Peter. Pages 253-309 in vol. 10 of *Beacon Bible Commentary.* Kansas City: Beacon Hill Press of Kansas City.
Oepke, Albrecht. 1964. *Grēgoreō*. Pages 338-39 in vol. 2 of *TDNT.*
Perkins, Pheme. 1995. *First and Second Peter, James, and Jude.* Interpretation: A Bible Commentary for Teaching and Preaching. Louisville, Ky.: John Knox.
Peterson, Eugene H. 2006. *Eat This Book: A Conversation in the Art of Spiritual Reading.* Grand Rapids: Eerdmans.
Picirelli, Robert E. 1975. The Meaning of "Epignosis." *EvQ* 47:85-93.
Polkinghorne, G. J. 1969. *The First Letter of Peter. A New Testament Commentary.* Edited by G. C. D. Rowley. Grand Rapids: Zondervan.
Powers, Daniel G. 2001. *Salvation through Participation. An Examination of the Notion of the Believers' Corporate Unity with Christ in Early Christian Soteriology.* Contributions to Biblical Exegesis and Theology 29. Leuven: Peeters.
Quell, G. 1967. *Eklegomai*. Pages 144-76 in vol. 4 of *TDNT.*
Rees, Paul S. 1962. *Triumphant in Trouble: Studies in 1 Peter.* Westwood, N.J.: Revell.
Reicke, Bo. 1964. *The Epistles of James, Peter, and Jude.* Anchor Bible 37. Garden City, N.Y.: Doubleday.
Rengstorf, Karl Heinrich. 1964a. *Apostolos.* Pages 407-45 in vol. 1 of *TDNT.*
______. 1964b. *Doulos*. Pages 261-79 in vol. 2 of *TDNT.*
Robertson, Archibald Thomas. 1933. *Word Pictures in the New Testament*. Vol. 6: *The General Epistles and the Revelation of John*. Nashville: Broadman.
______. 1934. *A Grammar of the Greek New Testament in the Light of Historical Research*. Nashville: Broadman.
Rogers, Cleon L., Jr., and Cleon L. Rogers III. 1998. *The New Linguistic and Exegetical Key to the Greek New Testament*. Grand Rapids: Zondervan.
Rogers, Edward. 1959. *That They Might Have Life.* Great Neck, N.Y.: Channel.
Rowston, Douglas J. 1975. The Most Neglected Book in the New Testament. *NTS* 21:554-63.
Schaff, Philip. 1977. *The Creeds of Christendom*. Vol. 2. New York: Harper and Brothers, 1877. Repr. Grand Rapids: Baker.
Schelkle, Karl Hermann. 1970. *Die Petrusbriefe, der Judasbrief.* 3d ed. Herders theologischer Kommentar zum Neuen Testament. Freiburg: Herder.
Schlier, Heinrich. 1964. *Hypodeigma*. Pages 32-33 in vol. 2 of *TDNT.*
Schmidt, Karl Ludwig. 1965. *Kaleō*. Pages 487-91 in vol. 3 of *TDNT.*
______. 1985. *Diaspora*. Pages 156-57 in *Theological Dictionary of the New Testament: Abridged in One Volume.* Edited by Geoffrey W. Bromiley. Grand Rapids: Eerdmans.
Schmitz, Ernst Dieter. 1976. Knowledge. Pages 390-406 in vol. 2 of *NIDNTT.*
Schrenk, Gottlob. 1964a. *Eudokeo*. Pages 738-42 in vol. 2 of *TDNT.*
______. 1964b. *Hypogrammos*. Pages 772-73 in vol. 1 of *TDNT.*
______. 1967. *Eklektos*. Pages 181-92 in vol. 4 of *TDNT.*
Schweizer, Eduard. 1974. *Psychē*. Pages 637-56 in vol. 9 of *TDNT.*
Selwyn, Edward Gordon. 1947. *The First Epistle of St. Peter.* 2d ed. London: Macmillan.
Snodgrass, Klyne R. 1977. I Peter II.1-10: Its Formation and Literary Affinities. *NTS* 24:97-106.
Stählin, Gustav. 1965. *Isos*. Pages 343-54 in vol. 3 of *TDNT.*
______. 1967. *Mythos*. Pages 762-95 in vol. 4 of *TDNT.*

Stein, Robert H. 1976. Is the Transfiguration (Mark 9:2-8) a Misplaced Resurrection Account? *JBL* 95:79-96.

Strachan, R. H. 1979. The Second Epistle General of Peter. Pages 81-148 in vol. 5 of *The Expositor's Greek Testament.* Repr. Grand Rapids: Eerdmans.

Strathmann, H. 1967. *Laos*. Pages 29-57 in vol. 4 of *TDNT.*

Unnik, W. C. van. 1954. The Teaching of Good Works in 1 Peter. *NTS* 1:92-110.

______. 1956. A Classical Parallel to 1 Peter ii.14 and 20. *NTS* 2:198-202.

Verbrugge, Verlyn D., ed. 2000. *New International Dictionary of New Testament Theology: Abridged Edition.* Grand Rapids: Zondervan.

Vincent, Marvin R. 1946. *Word Studies in the New Testament.* Vol. 1. Grand Rapids: Eerdmans.

Walls, Andrew F. 1979. The Canon of the New Testament. Pages 629-43 in vol. 1 of *The Expositor's Bible Commentary.* Edited by Frank E. Gaebelein. Grand Rapids: Zondervan.

Watson, Duane F. 1998a. The Letter of Jude: Introduction, Commentary, and Reflections. Pages 473-500 in vol. 12 of *New Interpreter's Bible.* Nashville: Abingdon.

______. 1998b. The Second Letter of Peter: Introduction, Commentary, and Reflections. Pages 323-61 in vol. 12 of *New Interpreter's Bible.* Nashville: Abingdon.

Webb, Robert L. Intertexture and Rhetorical Strategy in First Peter's Apocalyptic Discourse: A Study in Sociorhetorical Interpretation. Pages 72-110 in *Reading First Peter with New Eyes: Methodological Reassessments of the Letter of First Peter.* Edited by Robert L. Webb and Betsy Bauman-Martin. Library of New Testament Studies, 364. London: T. & T. Clark.

Webb, Robert L., and Betsy Bauman-Martin, eds. 2007. *Reading First Peter with New Eyes: Methodological Reassessments of the Letter of First Peter.* Library of New Testament Studies, 364. London: T. & T. Clark.

Welch, Reuben R. 1973. *We Really Do Need Each Other: A Call to Community in the Church.* Nashville: Nelson.

Wesley, John. 1966. *A Plain Account of Christian Perfection, as believed and taught by the Reverend Mr. John Wesley from the year 1725 to the year 1777.* Repr. Kansas City: Beacon Hill Press of Kansas City.

______. 1979a. Preface to *Sermons on Several Occasions.* Vol. 5 in *The Works of John Wesley.* 3d ed. London: Wesleyan Methodist Book Room, 1872. Repr. Kansas City: Beacon Hill Press of Kansas City.

______. 1979b. Sermon LXXXV: On Working Out Our Own Salvation. Pages 506-13 in vol. 6 of *The Works of John Wesley.* 3d ed. London: Wesleyan Methodist Book Room, 1872. Repr. Kansas City: Beacon Hill Press of Kansas City.

______. 1981. *Explanatory Notes upon the New Testament.* London: Wesleyan-Methodist Book Room, n.d. Repr. Kansas City: Beacon Hill Press of Kansas City.

Westcott, Brooke Foss. 1974. *The Epistle to the Hebrews: The Greek Text with Notes and Essay.* Repr. Grand Rapids: Eerdmans.

Wheaton, David H. 1970. 2 Peter. Pages 1249-58 in *The New Bible Commentary.* Rev. ed. Edited by D. Guthrie and J. A. Moyter. Grand Rapids: Eerdmans.

Whiston, William, trans. 1957. *The Life and Works of Flavius Josephus.* New York: Holt, Rinehart and Winston.

Wilder, Terry L. 2004. *Pseudonymity, the New Testament, and Deception.* Lanham, Md.: University Press of America.

Wolters, Al. 1990. "Partners of the Deity": A Covenantal Reading of 2 Peter 1:4. *Calvin Theological Journal* 25:28-44.

Wright, N. T. 2008. *Surprised by Hope: Rethinking Heaven, the Resurrection, and the Mission of the Church.* New York: HarperCollins.

Wynkoop, Mildred Bangs. 1972. *A Theology of Love: The Dynamic of Wesleyanism.* Kansas City: Beacon Hill Press of Kansas City.

Zodhiates, Spiros. 1992. *The Complete Word Study Dictionary: New Testament.* Chattanooga, Tenn.: AMG.

I PETER

INTRODUCTION

Peter is without question the most prominent of the disciples of Jesus. In every list, Simon Peter appears first (Mark 3:13-19; Matt 10:1-4; Luke 6:12-16; Acts 1:13). He was the first to confess to Jesus, "You are the Christ" (Mark 8:29). He was one of the inner circle of disciples (with James and John) present at the transfiguration (Mark 9:2-8) and whom Jesus asked to pray with him in Gethsemane (Mark 14:32-42). The young man in white at the empty tomb told the women to report the resurrection to "his disciples and Peter" (Mark 16:7). And Paul notes that Jesus appeared to Peter first out of all the disciples (1 Cor 15:5).

Based on Peter's prominent role, one would expect any letters associated with Peter to play an equally significant role among the NT canonical writings. But this has not been the case. In the history of the church there has been a "disconcerting pattern of benign neglect" (Elliott 1976, 243) of the Epistles of Peter.

The cause of this neglect could be as simple as the relative brevity of the two Epistles of Peter. Or it could be as complex as the biased perception that 1 and 2 Peter do not measure up to the greater theological and literary standards of the larger Pauline Epistles. This inattention is unfortunate, because 1 Peter contains significant theology and pastoral care. Wherever the church has undergone suffering, 1 Peter has proven to be extremely relevant. Suffering is not usually a popular or attractive theme. But if Jesus and Paul are correct, the church will suffer. Whenever that occurs, 1 Peter stands as a source of comfort and guidance. In transforming ways, Peter connects the suffering of the Christian to the sufferings of Jesus.

A. Authorship

The letter claims to be written by "Peter, an apostle of Jesus Christ" (1:1). The reference in 2 Peter to "my second letter to you" (3:1) reinforces the Petrine claim for 1 Peter, especially since no other Epistle is associated with him.

The historical attestation for Petrine authorship is strong. Irenaeus (ca. 140-202), the first writer to quote passages from 1 Peter, identified Peter explicitly as the author. Likewise, Tertullian (ca. 155-225) and Clement of Alexandria (ca. 150-215) cited passages from the letter and named Peter as the author. Various scholars have observed, however, that there are "numerous certain echoes" of 1 Peter in even earlier writings (Elliott 1992, 269). For instance, *1 Clement* (ca. 96), Polycarp's letter *To the Philippians* (ca. 120-140), and Justin Martyr (ca. 150-160) seem to be familiar with the letter. Eusebius of Caesarea (ca. 260-340) sums up the majority viewpoint of the early church in his *Ecclesiastical History:* "Of Peter one epistle, known as his first, is accepted, and this the early Fathers quoted freely, as undoubtedly genuine, in their own writings" (Bray 2000, xvii). Thus, the internal and external evidence in support of Petrine authorship is strong.

Many modern scholars, however, take exception to the idea that Peter is the actual author of 1 Peter. Many pseudonymous writings were created between the second century B.C. and the second century A.D. Most of these falsely ascribed writings were credited to well-known individuals, such as the Apostle Peter. Writings such as the *Gospel of Peter,* the *Apocalypse of Peter,* and the so-called *Letter of Peter to Philip* have all been proven to be pseudonymous writings. They were attributed to Peter as a token of honor and respect to his legacy. Many scholars contend that 1 and 2 Peter should be added to this same list of deutero-Petrine writings. There are five basic grounds for refuting Petrine authorship (Lohse 1991, 133).

1. *Lack of familiarity with Jesus.* The letter does not demonstrate a familiarity with the earthly Jesus or his teachings such as would be expected from a close disciple.

2. *Theological development.* The theological stance of the letter seems to belong to the postapostolic period.

3. *The Greek is too good.* The literary quality of 1 Peter is too refined and elegant for a Galilean fisherman.

4. *Too much dependence on Paul.* The letter reflects too much dependence upon Pauline language and thought.

5. *Time period after Peter's death.* First Peter addresses a situation in the church that depicts a time period after Peter's death.

These objections to Petrine authorship cannot be taken lightly. And yet a rebuttal can be offered for each.

1. Lack of Familiarity with Jesus

This objection is extremely subjective. It presupposes that the letter must contain a certain number of references to the earthly Jesus before it can be considered authentic. The letter does, in fact, contain various allusions to sayings and teachings of Jesus. But they are less obvious than might be found in a gospel, because they have been applied specifically to the situation of his audience. Ironically, many of the scholars who deny Petrine authorship of 1 Peter because of its *lack of familiarity* with the earthly life and teachings of Jesus also deny the Petrine authorship of 2 Peter because it demonstrates *too much familiarity* with Jesus. This objection is too subjective to be compelling.

One must not forget that "the purpose behind the writing of the epistle was not to comment on the life and teaching of Christ, but to encourage believers in the midst of trial and suffering" (Harrison 1964, 383). Peter's reflection upon his personal experiences with Jesus is subordinate to his greater concern for the welfare and encouragement of his struggling hearers. First Peter was written to comfort and guide a church struggling with persecution, not to provide personal anecdotes and information about the life of Jesus.

Reflections of Jesus' Teaching in 1 Peter

Contrast between perishable things of earth and imperishable things in heaven	1 Pet 1:4 Luke 12:33
Blessing and happiness to the one who does not see and yet believes in Christ	1 Pet 1:8 John 20:29
Christian experience described as new birth	1 Pet 1:3; 2:2 John 3:3, 7
Belief in God through Christ	1 Pet 1:21 John 14:1, 6
Command to love one another	1 Pet 1:22 John 13:34-35; 15:12
Jesus identified as the rejected stone that becomes the capstone	1 Pet 2:4, 7 Mark 12:10; Matt 21:42
Call to live exemplary lives before other people in order to cause praise to God	1 Pet 2:12 Matt 5:16

Live as free persons without giving cause for offense	1 Pet 2:13-17 Matt 17:26-27
Jesus is the shepherd and his followers are his sheep	1 Pet 2:25; 5:2, 4 John 10:11, 14
Blessing comes to those who suffer for doing what is right	1 Pet 3:14 Matt 5:10
Be sober and watchful in the last days	1 Pet 5:8-9 Mark 14:38; Matt 26:40-41

(Gundry 1967, 337-44)

2. Theological Development

The letter is characterized by "traditional material," such as hortatory, confessional, and poetic (hymnic) material, instead of biographical or anecdotal material from the life and teaching of Jesus (Lohse 1991, 133). First Peter displays more affinity with the so-called deutero-Pauline letters (Colossians, Ephesians, 1 and 2 Timothy, Titus) than with the generally accepted Pauline letters (Brox 1979, 51). This affinity provides evidence for some that 1 Peter must have been written after Peter's death.

This argument is as subjective as the first. First, there is no consensus that Colossians, Ephesians, and the Pastorals are all deutero-Pauline. Second, how "doctrine developed in the first century and a half of the church's existence [is] in large measure conjectural" (Bartlett 1998, 230).

The attempt to deny Petrine authorship on the basis of such conjecture is hardly convincing. This is especially true when the writings of Peter are scrutinized by a "Pauline model" for theological development. Since Paul is the NT's most prolific writer, other epistles are inevitably compared and assessed against Paul's letters. But "the Gentile/Jewish controversies so central to Paul seem to have faded to the background" in 1 Peter (Bartlett 1998, 230). The assumption of Bartlett (and others) that Peter's and Paul's theology, controversies, and concerns will be the same is unfounded. Peter and Paul obviously viewed ethnic tension in strikingly different ways (see Gal 2:11-16). Accordingly, it is inappropriate to judge the theological development and themes of Peter on the basis of Paul. Subjectivity and conjecture make this objection unconvincing.

3. The Greek Is Too Good

Some argue that the polished Greek grammar and style of 1 Peter could not have been produced by a simple fisherman such as Peter, whose first language was Galilean Aramaic. In Acts 4:13 the Sanhedrin considered Peter and John "unschooled, ordinary men."

Does "unschooled" indicate that Peter and John were uneducated and illiterate (so Beare 1961, 28)? Or, does the underlying Greek term indicate "no more than that Peter and John were unversed in rabbinic lore" (so Martin 1978, 332). The members of the Sanhedrin were surprised that they were able to speak so eloquently, despite their lack of formal rabbinic training. The description says nothing about their cultural background or linguistic expertise.

The idea that a Galilean like Peter could not be conversant and even skilled in Greek has been challenged recently. Robert Gundry observes that "scholars have always recognized that Galilean Jews, farther removed from the center of Judaism, closer to gentile areas like the Decapolis, and located on the Via Maris trade route, were more Hellenized than Judean Jews" (1964, 406-7).

There is strong archaeological evidence that Greek was highly influential throughout all of Palestine in the first century, not just Galilee. "Proof now exists that all three languages in question—Hebrew, Aramaic, and Greek—were commonly used by Jews in first century Palestine" (Gundry 1964, 405). Argyle concurs:

> To suggest that a Jewish boy growing up in Galilee would not know Greek would be rather like suggesting that a Welsh boy brought up in Cardiff would not know English. . . . There is greater readiness now than there was formerly to admit that Jesus and his disciples, all of whom were Galileans (Acts 2:7), were bilingual, speaking Greek as well as Aramaic. (1974, 88-89)

The notion that Peter was incapable of composing the kind of Greek found in 1 Peter is an unsubstantiated assumption.

Even if Peter's language skills were deficient, the polished Greek language and style of the letter could be accounted for by the use of an amanuensis. The author notes in 5:12 that he has written the letter "with the help of Silas" (lit., ***through Silas;*** see commentary on 5:12). Some argue that this merely identifies Silas as the one who delivered the letter. But it seems more likely that it identifies him as the trusted scribe who actually penned the letter on Peter's behalf. Incidentally, Silas is mentioned as Paul's co-sender of both Thessalonian letters. Admittedly, there is no indication of how involved he was in the actual writing of these letters.

It is possible that Peter's use of an amanuensis may explain the language and style of this letter. But there is no compelling reason to deny the language and style of this letter to Peter himself. There is strong evidence of the far-reaching usage of Greek in Palestine among Jews. Thus, "the linguistic argument can no longer be used with confidence" against Petrine authorship (Argyle 1974, 89).

4. Too Much Dependence on Paul

The alleged dependence of 1 Peter on the language and thought of Paul is supposedly most evident in Romans and Ephesians. The influence of Romans is found in 1 Pet 2:13-17, where the Christian's responsibility to the state is discussed (Rom 13:1-7). The similarity with Ephesians is limited to several doxological and liturgical formulas (see Achtemeier 1996, 16-17). W. C. van Unnik demonstrates that the relationship between Peter's and Paul's writings is "not one of dependence but of parallelism" (1954, 93). Such studies have seriously undermined the supposed scholarly consensus.

Recently, many attribute the similarities between 1 Peter and the Pauline writings to "a shared tradition working independently on the two writers" (Kelly 1969, 14). As recipients of a common Christian tradition, both Peter and Paul applied the teachings of this tradition to their specific audiences in similar, yet distinctive, ways. The alleged dependence on Paul's letters is not convincing evidence against the Petrine authorship of 1 Peter.

5. Time Period After Peter's Death

This argument assumes that the suffering mentioned in 1 Peter reflects the official, empire-wide persecution of Christians that did not occur until after Peter's time. Beare (1961, 14-15), for example, argues that the reference to "criminal" (4:14-15) indicates that the letter was written after Christianity was considered to be a crime. At the earliest, Christianity was outlawed throughout the Roman Empire during the reign of Trajan (A.D. 98-117). Thus, some contend that 1 Peter represents a period well after Peter's death (ca. A.D. 64).

The assumption that 1 Peter reflects officially sanctioned government persecution of Christians is hardly justified by the text of the letter. If Christianity was facing such persecution, it is difficult to explain why the author called upon his audience to be submissive to the government (2:13-14) and to "honor the king" (2:17). Moreover, the language of persecution in 1 Peter runs parallel with the persecution language of other NT writings (Moule 1956, 9). As a result, "it is now the majority view that the Roman Empire did not initiate any sort of official anti-Christian policy that could have prompted the suffering of which 1 Peter speaks" (Bauman-Martin 2007, 159).

From the beginning, heralds of the Christian message faced hostility and violent opposition in various places. This kind of persecution would not have been unusual for believers in Asia Minor. Peter describes the persecution facing his readers as "grief in all kinds of trials" (1:6). It ranged from "insults" (2:23; 4:14), to malicious speech (3:16), and even death (3:17-18). This language does not depict "formal or government persecution, but rather informal, social persecution that has arisen as a result of changes in their social relationships due to their conversion to the Christian faith (e.g., 4:3-4)" (Webb 2007, 88). Nonetheless, nothing about the depiction of the persecution in 1 Peter precludes a situation during Peter's lifetime.

This commentary assumes the traditional Petrine authorship of 1 Peter. There is no evidence that compellingly denies Peter as author. As Michaels observes, "The traditional view that the living Peter was personally responsible for the letter as it stands has not been, and probably in the nature of the case cannot be, decisively shaken" (1988, lxvi-lxvii). The case for Petrine authorship is about as strong as one could expect for an ancient writing. There will always be doubts. But this letter can be regarded as an authentic writing of the Apostle Peter himself.

B. Audience

The recipients of 1 Peter are explicitly identified as believers "scattered throughout Pontus, Galatia, Cappadocia, Asia and Bithynia" (1:1). These regions are located in an area known as Asia Minor.

Peter's letter presupposes a Christian presence in this region. But what we know of the evangelization of these five areas remains highly speculative. Jews from three of the regions—Pontus, Cappadocia, and Asia—were present in Jerusalem at the first Christian day of Pentecost (Acts 2:9). The gospel may have been preached in these regions by believers who returned from Jerusalem after Pentecost. Asia (with Ephesus its capital) and Galatia were evangelized by Paul (Acts 13—19; Gal 1—2). Aside from Paul's deterred attempt to evangelize Bithynia in Acts 16, there are no NT references to missionary activity in Bithynia. Thus, one can only speculate as to who brought the Christian message there and when.

If little is known about the evangelization of these provinces, even less is known about Peter's connection to them. Early Christian tradition does not trace the locations or the extent of Peter's travels. Eusebius notes in *History of the Church* (3.1) that Peter "seems to have preached" in these regions. But his reference is probably no more than an allusion to 1 Peter, not of a known journey through the region. Believers in Galatia were undoubtedly familiar with Peter (see Gal 2:8, 11-14). But it is impossible to know whether they knew Peter personally or by reputation only. Peter's apparent familiarity with the readers "has been used as an argument against Petrine authorship, but not much can be built upon it since the knowledge is not circumstantial, and in any case we are almost wholly in the dark about Peter's movements" (Kelly 1969, 41).

The order in which the regions are listed has attracted considerable attention from scholars. Most surprising is the separation of Pontus and Bithynia, the first and last regions listed. The two were recognized as a single Roman province since 64 B.C. Thus, was the author ignorant of the geographical regions of Asia Minor (Brox 1979, 25-26)? Or, did some other consideration regulate the sequence?

Most scholars have accepted F. J. A. Hort's suggestion that the order was determined by the anticipated route of travel by the bearer of the letter (1898, 157-84; see Hemer 1978-79, 239). The messenger probably began his mission in Pontus and visited a circle of churches, returning to Bithynia, not far from where he began. This course was well-known in this period. Josephus (*Ant.* 16.21-23) indicates that Herod the Great followed this route in 14 B.C. with Marcus Agrippa.

With few exceptions, the early church fathers believed Peter wrote his first letter to Jewish Christians (Bray 2000, 65). The idea of a Jewish audience was shared by many subsequent scholars, including Calvin and Wesley. Some of the letter has a strong Jewish character. The opening description of the readers as part of the *Diaspora* is just one example (1:1). Another factor supporting a Jewish audience is the prevalent usage of OT quotations throughout the letter. The author also applies OT descriptions to the audience otherwise used exclusively for Jews (2:9). Moreover, as "an apostle to the Jews" (Gal 2:8), it would seem more natural for Peter to write to a Jewish audience.

Despite this internal and external evidence, it is more probable that 1 Peter was written to a Gentile audience. Peter's ministry was certainly not limited to Jews (see Acts 10—11). And Peter's description of his readers with terminology formerly used exclusively for the Jews may indicate that he understood these terms to be spiritually fulfilled in the church.

The strongest evidence in favor of a predominantly Gentile audience is provided by various statements in the letter that seem to be irreconcilable with a Jewish audience. Hiebert summarizes these statements well:

> The recipients are described as those who had been called "out of darkness into his marvelous light" (2:9), who once "were no people, but now are the people of God" (2:10). Their life before their conversion was described as "the time of your ignorance" (1:14), but as believers they had been redeemed from their "vain manner of life handed down from your fathers" (1:18). They were warned against heathen practices from which they had been delivered (4:3-4). If they had been Jews, their pagan neighbors would not have thought it "strange" that they no longer indulged in those pagan sins (4:4). The women are spoken of as having *become* daughters of Sarah (3:6) through conversion. Such statements

> clearly refer to Gentile Christians whom Peter considered strangers in an alien environment. (1984c, 16)

While there may have been some Jews represented in the congregations to which Peter wrote (Grudem 1988, 38; Kelly 1969, 4), it is virtually certain that the letter was addressed to a predominantly Gentile audience.

C. Place and Date

The letter claims to have been written from "Babylon" (5:13). But what is the meaning and location of this "Babylon"?

1. Some argue that "Babylon" refers to a city by this name in Egypt that housed a Roman colony (Klijn 1967, 157-58). There is a Coptic tradition that Peter wrote his letter from Egypt. But there is no record of any Christian influence there in the first century. And it is highly improbable that Peter would not have distinguished this obscure city from the more famous Babylon in Mesopotamia.

2. A second possibility is that 5:13 contains a reference to Mesopotamian Babylon. The problem with this suggestion is that the one-time empire capital located in today's Iraq had become a small and obscure place. Strabo (died A.D. 19) wrote, "The greater part of Babylon is so deserted that one would not hesitate to say . . . 'The Great City is a great desert'" (*Geography* 16.1.5; cited in Grudem 1988, 33). Furthermore, there is no mention of missionary activity in this Babylon in early Christian history.

3. The third and most probable suggestion is that "Babylon" is a figurative reference to Rome. Rome was often identified with Babylon in both Christian tradition (Rev 14:8; 17:5, 18; 18:2) and in Jewish tradition (*Sib. Or.* 5:143, 159; *2 Bar.* 11:1; 67:7). Why would Peter use a cryptic description of Rome in his letter? Cullmann asserts that a "typological use of geographical names" was fairly common in ancient Christian literature (1953, 83). "Babylon" is most likely a metaphorical reference to Rome.

> Indeed, no other metaphor could so well describe the city of Rome, rich and luxurious as it was, and given over to the worship of false gods and every species of immorality. Both cities had caused trouble to the people of God, Babylon to the Jews, and Rome to the Christians. (Van der Heeren 1911, 753)

"Babylon" would be a very fitting pseudonym for Rome.

The date of 1 Peter is irrevocably dependent upon the question of authorship. The discussion often revolves around the question of the kind of persecution alluded to in the letter. Those who deny Petrine authorship tend to date the letter during the time of Domitian (A.D. 81-96) or the time of Trajan (A.D. 98-117). We know that Christians experienced persecution during their reigns.

The persecution described in the letter could have transpired during the reign of Nero. Peter was eventually martyred on Nero's orders (Eusebius, *Ecclesiastical History* 3.1.2-3). If Peter was the author, it was probably written from Rome sometime before Nero's persecution of Christians began, that is, between A.D. 62 and 64.

D. Genre and Unity of the Letter

First Peter obviously resembles the style of Paul's letters. It contains an opening salutation identifying its author and audience (1:1-2*a*). This is followed by a greeting (1:2*b*), a thanksgiving (1:3*a*), the body of the letter (1:3*b*—5:11), personal greetings (5:12-14*a*), and a closing benediction (5:14*b*).

Nonetheless, some have suggested that 1 Peter can be classified better as a different genre. Two of the more popular suggestions attempt to connect the genre to sermonic material or baptismal liturgy (see Martin 1978, 336-44). While these suggestions are interesting and enlightening, they are unconvincing. The letter includes a number of traditional themes and forms (see Davids 1990, 11-14). But the author freely adapts this material to fit his purpose and the situation of his audience. The genre of 1 Peter, then, is best described as a circular letter intended to be read in various churches in Asia Minor.

Some scholars have challenged the unity of the letter. Is 1 Peter a single document or a composite of two earlier documents (see Achtemeier 1996, 58-62)? There is a noticeable break between 4:11 and 4:12. After the doxology in 4:11, the letter resumes with an intensified discussion of current suffering (vv 12-19). This transition causes some to contend that 1 Peter consists of two earlier writings: 1:3—4:11 and 4:12—5:11.

A doxology, however, does not necessarily mark the conclusion of a letter (see Rom 11:33-36; Eph 3:20-21). Although the references to suffering are more specific in 1 Pet 4:12-19, the same theme of sharing in the suffering of Christ binds both sections of the letter. First Peter may plausibly be regarded as a single, unified letter.

E. Purpose of the Letter

The purpose of 1 Peter is expressed succinctly in 5:12: "I have written to you briefly, encouraging you and testifying that this is the true grace of God." On this basis, the letter had a twofold purpose: exhorting the audience and testifying to the truth they have been taught.

First, the hortatory character of 1 Peter is one of its most prominent features. This is especially evident in the many imperatives employed throughout. First Peter was not written primarily to expound upon theological truths or doctrines. It was written to encourage believers to remain faithful and courageous in the midst of persecution and suffering for Christ's sake. This encouragement was rooted in the theologically rich understanding of the suffering, death, and resurrection of Jesus.

Second, Peter wrote this letter to reassure his readers that their faith was true. Despite the opposition and persecution they faced, they are fundamentally right in their faith and in their Christlike behavior. Peter insisted that Christ was the ultimate litmus test by which the motivation, orientation, and conduct of every person will be measured. One's orientation to Christ—either acceptance or rejection—will determine one's ultimate destiny. Thus, despite the opposition and rejection they were experiencing for the sake of the gospel, Peter assured them that faithful allegiance to Christ, the living Stone, was the true path to salvation and victory, now and always.

F. Themes of the Letter

First Peter is not a theological treatise, yet it incorporates many theological ideas and lessons.

1. Proto-Trinitarian

One noticeable feature is the proto-Trinitarian perspective of the divine Godhead. Each person of the Godhead is recognized for his function within the lives of believers.

God is affirmed as the Creator of all things (4:19) and the Judge of the living and the dead (4:5). He is recognized as the Father of Jesus Christ (1:3) and the Father of all believers (1:17). As the Holy One, God calls his followers to be holy, even as he is holy (1:15-16).

The letter displays a high Christology. Peter accepts the preexistence of Christ as the one "chosen before the creation of the world" (1:20). Christ is Isaiah's Servant of Yahweh (2:22-24) and the true paschal Lamb (1:19). Through his resurrection he is exalted to the right hand of God, exercising supremacy over all creation (3:22).

Human salvation is intimately connected to believers' faith in and identity with Christ. Those who will be saved are obedient to Christ (1:2), reborn and saved through his resurrection (1:3; 3:21), and rebuilt "into a spiritual house" and "a holy priesthood" as they come to Christ (2:5). They are called to follow Christ's example (2:21) and to "participate in the sufferings of Christ" (4:13; see vv 13-16) as they eagerly await his imminent appearance when they will share in his glory and grace (1:7, 13; 5:4, 10).

The Holy Spirit is portrayed as the "Spirit of Christ," who actively pointed the OT prophets to the future suffering and glory of Christ (1:11). In the present age the Holy Spirit sets apart believers to God (1:2) and energizes those who proclaim the gospel (1:12). He is the "Spirit of glory and of God," who rests on those who are persecuted because of their faith in Christ (4:14).

Peter portrays the believers' salvation as intricately tied to the threefold work of God the Father, Jesus Christ, and the Holy Spirit. It would be premature to describe Peter's portrayal of the divine Godhead as a doctrinal Trinity. But the interrelated yet distinct work of each personality is portrayed in a way that foreshadows later Trinitarian understanding.

2. Suffering

Suffering is also a central theme. The occasion of 1 Peter was the suffering of believers for the sake of Christ. Peter responds to this by correlating the suffering of believers with the sufferings of Christ. And he does this in a uniquely NT manner. Like Paul, Peter teaches that "the sufferings of Christ are ours" (2 Cor 1:5 NASB; see 2 Cor 4:7-12). Filson observes, "We often tend to regard Christ's sufferings as the means by which we escape suffering. He suffered for us, so we will not have to suffer. This idea does not come from the NT church" (1955, 404).

In alignment with other NT teachings (e.g., John 15:18-25; 2 Cor 1:3-7; Phil 1:29; 1 Thess 3:2-4), Peter does not perceive suffering as something "strange" in the believers' lives. Rather, suffering is a natural part of following Christ (4:12). Although suffering is caused by the devil (5:8-9), Peter is confident that suffering has its place in the plan and purpose of God. Suffering for the sake of Christ works to refine and purify believers (1:7; 4:12-13). Moreover, just as God used the sufferings of Christ to make salvation for believers possible (3:18), the exemplary suffering of believers could have a redemptive effect on unbelievers (2:12; 3:1-2).

Suffering is not inevitable for believers (1:6), and yet every Christian must be ready to face it (1:7; 4:1). Thus, the concern of the letter is not *if* believers will face suffering but *how* they should react to it. Christ is used as the supreme example. Like Christ, believers are to react to suffering in three ways. First, they should not respond with hate or retaliation (2:21-24; 3:9). Second, they are to meet suffering with a spirit of submission (2:13—3:6; 5:6). And third, they are to persist in doing good (1:15; 2:12-15, 20, 24; 3:6, 11, 13, 17; 4:2, 17, 19).

This exhortation to do what is good is repeatedly emphasized. The motivation for doing what is right is multifaceted. Believers should continue to do what is right despite their unjust suffering because: (1) they are blessed when they do this (3:14; 4:14); (2) this is what God has called them to do (1:15; 2:20-21); (3) their good conduct under the stress of suffering may draw unbelievers to salvation (2:12; 3:1-2); and, (4) Christ suffered unjustly and believers should follow his example (2:20-21; 3:17-18).

3. Holiness

Holiness is another strongly emphasized theme. Holiness is not only spiritual in nature but essentially ethical in nature as well. Holiness of life is a natural byproduct and result of one's holiness of heart. The importance of holiness is envisioned in three areas of the believers' life: personal, social, and communal.

Personal holiness is the foundational tenet of the letter. One of Peter's first imperatives is the command, "Just as he who called you is holy, so be holy in all you do" (1:15). "Through the sanctifying work of the Spirit" (1:2) believers are described as "self-controlled" (1:13), "holy" (1:15), "purified" (1:22), and free from "all malice and all deceit, hypocrisy, envy, and slander" (2:1). The supreme hallmark of holiness in the lives of believers is expected to be their love for others (1:22). In this way, holiness affects both the believers' relationship to God and to other people.

Peter expected personal holiness to flow automatically into social holiness. Whereas 1:13—2:10 deals with the believers' call and experience of personal holiness, 2:11—4:11 focuses upon social holiness in terms of their relationship to non-Christians. For God's sake believers were to obey the law of the land by submitting themselves to the government (2:13-14) and the king (2:13, 17). They were also to submit to their masters or husbands, even if they were unfair, cruel, or unbelieving (2:18-20; 3:1-2).

Peter was concerned that Christians should not offend unbelievers (2:11-12, 15; 3:15-16). The motivation for social holiness was twofold:

> On the one hand, there is an *imitatio Christi* theme (2:21; 3:18—4:2). Christians act as they do because they model their behavior on that of Christ. On the other hand, there is the threat of judgment (4:12, 17). The suffering is a test of faith, so it would be wise not to fail. (Davids 1990, 18)

The presupposition is that personal holiness will affect daily behavior, which extends into social relationships.

Personal holiness also leads to communal holiness; it affects the believers' relationships with one another. These were to be marked by love, hospitality, service according to gifts, servant leadership, and humility (4:7-11; 5:1-7). These virtues were important because they led to unity within the Christian community.

The purpose of communal holiness was twofold. First, the integrity and uprightness of believers' relationships with each other would make their lives easier, because they were innately good (4:8-10). Second, their exemplary relationships with each other were to keep the community together in the face of societal opposition and suffering (5:1-5). Holiness was to be the keystone of the believers' defense and response to the constant threat of suffering in a hostile society.

COMMENTARY

I. GREETING: 1 PETER 1:1-2

BEHIND THE TEXT

Three names are associated with the Apostle Peter: Simon, **Peter**, and Cephas. *Simon* was undoubtedly the Jewish name given him at birth. **Peter**/*Cephas* was the nickname Jesus gave him at Caesarea Philippi when he confessed that Jesus was the long-awaited Messiah (see Matt 16:13-16; Mark 8:27-30; Luke 9:18-20; John 1:42). **Peter** is adapted from the Greek word *Petros; Cephas* transliterates the Aramaic. Both names mean "rock."

In the earliest NT writings, Peter was consistently named *Cephas* (Gal 1:18; 2:9, 11, 14; 1 Cor 1:12; 3:22; 9:5; 15:5). But as the church became increasingly Greek-speaking, *Cephas* was displaced by the Greek name **Peter**. All four Gospels refer to him as either *Peter* or *Simon Peter.* All three names of the apostle are given in John 1:42, "Jesus looked at him and said, 'You are Simon son of John. You will be called Cephas' (which, when translated, is Peter)." The use of **Peter** in this letter probably reflects the Gentile background of his audience.

IN THE TEXT

■ 1 **Peter** begins his letter in the basic pattern customary of all ancient Greek letters: "A to B, greetings." Here, the name **Peter** is qualified by a short description of his office: **an apostle of Jesus Christ.**

Apostle means ***one who is sent out***—a ***"messenger"*** or ***"envoy"*** of another (BDAG, 122). In the NT, the word always signifies that the person "is sent, and sent with full authority" (Rengstorf 1964a, 421). Despite variation in the use of the term in the NT, one common feature stands out: The person designated an **apostle** was always an eyewitness of the resurrected Jesus and was personally commissioned by him (Rengstorf 1964a, 431).

Peter qualifies easily as an **apostle.** Peter not only was sent out with authority to preach and heal (see Mark 6:7; Matt 10:1; Luke 9:1-2) but also was one of the first witnesses of the risen Christ. He was personally commissioned by Jesus to spread the gospel (see John 21:15-19; Matt 28:16-20). Unlike Paul, Peter's authority as an apostle was never challenged.

Peter's authority was derived from and commissioned by **Jesus Christ** himself. Peter was "a messenger of Christ sent into the world with authority to carry out the will of the one who sent him" (Davids 1990, 45-46). **An apostle of Jesus Christ** expresses the nature of Peter's authority as not inherent but borrowed. His authority was derived from Christ himself. His letter carries a message and an authority that supersedes the mere words or message of a man named Peter. They portray the message and authority of Christ himself.

In contrast to the concise depiction of the author, the identification of the audience is expansive. Peter calls them **God's elect, strangers in the world, scattered throughout** several Roman provinces in Asia Minor. Although **God's** is not in the Greek text, the NIV appropriately adds it for clarity.

Election

The term **elect** (*eklektois*) has often been mistakenly interpreted to mean privilege without responsibility. This is certainly not the way the word was intended or used by biblical authors.

The Bible does not normally use "election" in an individualistic sense. Apart from kings, it is rare for the divine choices to refer to individuals in the OT (Quell 1967, 152). **Elect** (or ***chosen***) was regularly used by the people of Israel to express their conviction that they were God's special people, singled out from among the nations (see Deut 4:37; 7:6; 14:2; Ps 105:6; Isa 45:4; Kelly 1969, 40).

Furthermore, election does not necessarily imply "the rejection of what is not chosen, but giving favor to the chosen subject, keeping in view a relationship to be established between the one choosing and the object chosen" (Zodhiates 1992, 544). The purpose of the choice is almost always determined by some kind of commission (e.g., 2 Sam 21:6; Ps 105:43; Isa 42:1; 65:22 LXX). "Such election can only meaningfully retain its validity in the fulfillment of that service" (Verbrugge 2000, 174).

As a result, the underlying idea of election in the OT expresses both privilege and responsibility. The prophets insist that responsibility always accompanies election (see Amos 7:10-15; Jer 7:22-26; 28; 37—38). Ultimately, election as responsibility develops into the concept of election as mission. "This development of the belief in election into the concept of witness to the truth of God is to be regarded as the consummation of the OT message of salvation" (Quell 1967, 168). Thus, the nation of Israel is God's elect, but they are elected for a special purpose; namely, to be witnesses to the nations that Yahweh is God (see Isa 42:1; 43:10).

Significantly, in the OT divine election was understood to be a unique characteristic of the people of Israel. But in the NT divine election applied to all faithful persons (i.e., the church) who had placed their faith in Jesus Christ (see Mark 13:20; Luke 18:7; 1 Cor 1:27-30; Jas 2:5; 2 John 1). "All the privileges which had once belonged to Israel now belong to the Christian Church" (Barclay 1960, 196).

This idea is expressed strongly in 1 Peter. Peter transfers to Gentile believers "the hallowed language appropriate to God's own people" (Kelly 1969, 40). The faithful recipients of Peter's letter are referred to as **God's elect** (1:1). They are linked to the Choice Stone (i.e., Christ) as a chosen community (2:4-5); they are called a "chosen people" (*genos eklekton;* 2:9).

The broadened application of the notion of **God's elect** in the NT to include the church is characterized by three qualifications, summarized by Schrenk:

- The NT finds the basis of election in Christ and has in view a universal community, not just a single nation.
- It discerns in election the eternal basis of salvation that is never separated from responsibility and decision.
- Far from viewing election as preferential treatment, the NT relates it strictly to mission in service to the divine purposes for the universe. (Quoted in Quell 1967, 192)

The terms **God's elect** (*eklektois*), **strangers in the world** (*parepidēmois*), and **scattered** (*diasporas*) are typically reserved exclusively for the people of Israel. But Peter assigns Gentile believers the same divine privileges and prerogatives Israel enjoyed. It is not that Christian believers have replaced Israel as the "true" people of God, as some suggest (see Ball 1966, 249). Rather, the identity of God's chosen people has been expanded to include Christian believers, regardless of their ethnic heritage.

God's elect and **strangers in the world** are closely associated in this passage. The terms portray a vivid contrast in both relationship and status. "One expresses a relationship to God, the other a relationship to human society. One denotes a privileged group (before God), the other a disadvantaged group (in society)" (Michaels 1988, 6). Peter's depiction of his audience as **God's**

elect must have been encouraging. Although scattered like exiles, they were, in fact, God's favored, select people.

Parepidēmois, **strangers in the world** or ***sojourners,*** describes Peter's audience as people who are "**staying for a while in a strange or foreign place, *sojourning, residing temporarily*"** (BDAG, 775). Used rarely in the Bible (NT: 1 Pet 1:1; 2:11; Heb 11:13; LXX: Gen 23:4; Ps 38:13), the term "connotes one who is merely passing through a territory, with no intention of permanent residence" (Kelly 1969, 41). Some interpreters take **strangers** in a sociological sense, identifying Peter's audience as immigrants in Asia Minor (see Elliott 1981). Most, however, take this figuratively. They were spiritual sojourners in the world. As **strangers,** they were temporary residents of this world. They had "a deeper attachment and a higher allegiance in another sphere" (Beare 1961, 49).

Achtemeier proposes another explanation for **strangers** deserving consideration:

> Used of Christians, it describes the fact that because of their unwillingness to adopt the mores of their surrounding society, they can expect the disdainful treatment often accorded exiles (e.g., 1 Pet 4:3–4). It refers for that reason less to the notion of Christians disdaining the temporal because of their longing for their eternal, heavenly home, with its implications of withdrawal from secular society, than to the notion that despite such treatment, they must nevertheless continue to practice their faith in the midst of those who abuse them (e.g., 2:12; 3:9, 15*b*–16; 4:19). (1996, 81)

Epistle to Diognetus

An anonymous letter to Diognetus from the second century A.D. eloquently describes Christians as temporary residents of this world:

> Christians are not distinguished from the rest of mankind by either country, speech, or customs; . . . Yet while they . . . conform to the customs of the country in dress, food, and mode of life in general, the whole tenor of their way of living stamps it as worthy of admiration and admittedly extraordinary. They reside in their respective countries, but only as aliens. They take part in everything as citizens and put up with everything as foreigners. . . . They find themselves in the flesh, but do not live according to the flesh. They spend their days on earth, but hold citizenship in heaven. (Kleist 1957, 138-39)

Peter's audience consisted of people who were elect, strangers, and **scattered** (*diasporas*). *Diaspora*, like *eklektos*, normally referred to Jews living outside the land of Israel. It is so used twelve times in the LXX, and only twice in the NT outside 1 Peter (John 7:35 and Jas 1:1). It typically describes the scattering of Israel among the Gentiles, which came as punishment from God (e.g., Deut 28:25; Jer 13:13-14; 34:17-22; Dan 12:2). In 1 Peter the notion of divine punishment is completely absent. Peter uses this term to describe all Christians who, like exiled Israel, lived as aliens in their surrounding culture.

As ***scattered exiles,*** however, members of the *Diaspora* cherished the hope that "they [would] eventually come to their true home, the heavenly Jerusalem" (see Eph 2:19; Phil 3:20; Heb 11:13; 13:14; Best 1971, 70). The term **scattered** is closely associated with **strangers.** But the focus of each word can be differentiated: "The one word looks to the land in which the recipients were strangers, the other to the land which is their true home" (Schmidt 1985, 157).

The juxtaposition of the three words—**elect, strangers,** and **scattered**—is striking. Nowhere else in Christian or Jewish literature are these descriptions connected. Perhaps their new status as **scattered** and **strangers** was directly related to their election. As **God's elect,** Christian believers were called away from their former way of life and allegiances. First Peter is "an epistle from the homeless to the homeless" (Michaels 1988, 9). Regardless of their geographical location, these Christian believers had no earthly home. Their election set them apart. The letter specifically addressed believers who temporarily resided in **Pontus, Galatia, Cappadocia, Asia and Bithynia.**

Pontus is a Greek word meaning "sea." It could refer to the Black Sea. In the NT, Pontus indicates a province of Asia Minor along the southern shore of the Black Sea from Bithynia to Armenia. Luke mentioned inhabitants from Pontus as being present at the day of Pentecost when the Holy Spirit was poured out upon the believers (Acts 2:9).

Map of Asia Minor

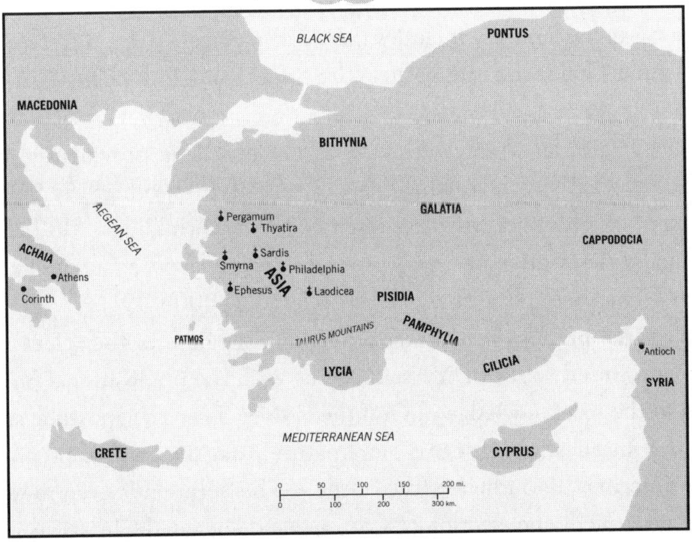

Galatia was located in north central Asia Minor. It was named for its dominant ethnic group, the Gauls. They were a Celtic tribe from Western Europe that migrated to Asia Minor during the third century B.C. Galatia can refer to the Celtic territory to the north or to the Roman province, which included non-Gauls living further south. Scholars disagree as to the identity of the "Galatians" addressed in Paul's Epistle (see Mitchell 1992, 871). In 1 Peter, **Galatia** undoubtedly refers to the Roman province.

Cappadocia is an isolated interior region of eastern Asia Minor north of the Taurus Mountains, east of Lake Tatta, south of Pontus, and west of the Euphrates River. Cappadocia became a Roman province in the first century A.D. Acts 2:9 mentions Jewish pilgrims from Cappadocia and Asia at the first Christian Pentecost.

Asia sometimes refers to the Old Persian Empire. But by NT times, **Asia** usually indicated the Seleucid kingdoms, whose rulers were called "the kings of Asia" (see 1 Macc 8:6). The last Seleucid ruler willed his kingdom to Rome, which called this new province **Asia.** Asia was early evangelized by Christian missionaries (see Acts 19—20).

Bithynia is a Roman province in northwest Asia Minor. Bithynia is bordered to the east by Pontus and to the north by the Black Sea. The NT mentions no Christian missionary activity in Bithynia, despite Paul's efforts (Acts 16:7).

Scholars speculate as to the why these regions are mentioned in this order, especially since Pontus and Bithynia were considered a single Roman province after 64 B.C. Most believe the order reflects the travel itinerary of the one who would deliver the letter (see Introduction).

■ **2** Three prepositional phrases emphasize how the readers have become what they are. Each phrase includes the work and agency of a different person of the triune God: God the Father, the Spirit, and Jesus Christ. As Howe observes:

> The Trinitarian framework here is obvious. The providential plan of God the Father, the setting apart or sanctifying work of the Spirit, and the death of Jesus Christ (represented by the sprinkling of the blood) are equally descriptive of God's provision for believers as "chosen sojourners." The three phrases are closely related. (2000b, 191)

All three prepositional descriptions in v 2 relate to the "elect" in v 1, the "apostle" in v 1, or both. Verse 2 begins with the prepositional phrase **according to the foreknowledge of God the Father.** Since the apostolic status of Peter is not in question, it seems more natural that the triad of prepositional phrases describes his audience (the "elect"). This solution is even more probable because the divine election of scattered and alienated Christians is one of the main issues of the letter. Peter encourages his readers with this threefold reminder of God's salvific activity in their lives.

First, they **have been chosen according to the foreknowledge of God the Father. Foreknowledge** (*prognōsin*) is found only here and in Acts 2:23 where Peter explains Christ's death in his Pentecost sermon as being according to the "foreknowledge of God" (NRSV). Divine **foreknowledge** does not emphasize God's ability to know things in advance. Instead, it emphasizes that what occurs happens **according to** (*kata*) his plan.

Divine **foreknowledge** does not imply a lack of personal responsibility on the part of believers. On the contrary, Peter reminds them that God's provision for them should enable their **obedience to Jesus Christ.** He says "nothing . . . about the certainty that they will be brought from their present exile to the New Jerusalem" (Best 1971, 71). In fact, in 4:15-19 and 5:9-12 Peter implies that their ultimate salvation depends upon their response to their present predicament.

The reminder that they **have been chosen according to the foreknowledge of God the Father** underscores three important truths:

First, their salvation has been made possible by divine initiative. God is consistently portrayed in the Bible as the Author of salvation. It was always God's plan, even "before the foundation of the world" (Eph 1:4 NRSV; 2 Thess 2:13-14), to provide salvation to humanity through Christ's death and resurrection and the Holy Spirit's conviction and cleansing. The church's "origin lies, not in the will of the flesh, in the idealism of men, in human aspirations and plans, but in the eternal purpose of God. . . . To remember this has always a steadying and strengthening effect" (Cranfield 1960, 30).

Second, their present predicament is not by accident or divine oversight. In fact, it is because they were chosen by God that they are now **strangers . . . scattered** (v 1) throughout Asia Minor. Their struggles and trials have not surprised or stymied God. On the contrary, what they are facing fits within the foreknowledge and eternal purposes of God.

Third, God is their **Father.** God is the Father of Jesus in the Trinitarian formula of v 2. But as the source of the "new birth" in v 3, he is also the Father of Christians. God is intimately and caringly involved in their lives. In the midst of their suffering, they are objects of God's loving, fatherly concern.

The second prepositional phrase of v 2 emphasizes the means by which God works in believers' lives. Their election and ultimate salvation take place **through the sanctifying work** (*hagiasmōi*) **of the Spirit.** *Hagiasmos*, a noun of action, carries a twofold connotation: consecration and cleansing. It is difficult to distinguish the two. By setting believers apart for God's use, the Spirit transforms their lives morally. Here and in 1:15-16, "Peter declares holiness of heart and life to be God's criterion for His people" (Ball 1966, 250).

This **sanctifying work** is performed through the agency of the Holy Spirit (a subjective genitive). That is, the Spirit sanctifies believers. But this sanctification requires human cooperation. Sanctification "is, on the one hand, a divine act (see 1 Cor 1:30), practically synonymous with the call itself, and, on the other, a moral implication of that call and (in part at least) a human responsibility" (Michaels 1988, 11).

The Spirit set believers apart as God's chosen people. As a result, they are forgiven of their past sins and transgressions. But the Spirit continues his sanctifying work, cleansing their lives and making them holy.

The purpose (*eis*, ***for***) of the divine Spirit's activities is **for obedience** (*hypakoēn*) **to Jesus Christ.** *Hypakoē* "conveys the picture of listening and submitting to that which is heard" (Hiebert 1984c, 39). In 1 Peter, **obedience** (1:2, 14, 22) repeatedly reminds believers of their own role in their election and sanctification.

The Greek of v 2 does not specify to whom or what obedience is required. The NIV, along with the NASB and the NRSV, connects the genitive **Jesus Christ** (*Iēsou Christou*) to **obedience** as well as to **sprinkling by his blood.** Thus, they translate the phrase as **obedience to Jesus Christ and sprinkling by his blood.** But this implies that *Iēsou Christou* is an objective genitive—believ-
1:2 ers obey **Christ.** This may be true, but the more natural sense in Greek is to connect **Jesus Christ** to **sprinkling** and not to **obedience.**

Peter's reference to "obedience to the truth" (NRSV) in 1:22 is significant here. **Obedience** as "obeying the truth" invites believers to submit to the saving grace of God and the sanctifying work of the Spirit made possible by Christ's death. That is, they should obey because of all God has done to save them. The promise of salvation requires a response of obedience.

"Obedience to the truth" (NRSV) requires more than mental assent to what God says. It calls for conformity of one's conduct to God's commands. Obedience to God's initiative requires believers to turn away from their former way of life opposed to his will and purposes. They submit themselves to the eternal plan of God by trusting Jesus Christ. Such obedience not only is a change of attitude toward God but also requires a decisive change of action and behavior. This change is made possible by the triune God: the Father's foreknowledge, the Spirit's sanctifying work, and the Son's atoning death. But the possibility becomes a reality only as believers accept and obey God.

The third prepositional phrase of v 2 speaks of ***sprinkling with the blood of Jesus Christ.*** This imagery is derived from the OT. In Exod 24, God confirms the covenant between himself and Israel. After Moses reads from the

Book of the Covenant, the people respond, "We will do everything the LORD has said; we will obey" (v 7). In response, Moses takes half of the blood of the sacrifice and sprinkles it on the altar. Then he sprinkles the other half on the people. Moses explains, "This is the blood of the covenant that the LORD has made with you in accordance with all these words" (v 8).

Peter does not explicitly refer to "covenant" here. But the obvious parallels with Exod 24 suggest that he had covenant in mind. Whereas the old covenant was ratified by the sprinkling of the blood of bulls, the new covenant is ratified by the ***sprinkling with the blood of Jesus Christ.*** The violent death of Christ on behalf of sinners offers saving benefits to all who will receive them. Undoubtedly, Gentile believers are included among God's chosen people.

Peter emphasizes both human responsibility (**obedience**) and divine provision (***the sprinkling with the blood of Jesus Christ***). Clearly, obedience is essential for human salvation. "To belong to God is to obey Jesus Christ" (Moffatt 1928, 91). True believers are revealed, not through their philosophical declaration of trust and ultimate security, but by their willingness to follow and obey the Savior's call and commands.

The emphasis on **obedience** is balanced by the assurance of divine enablement. The word order—first **obedience,** then **sprinkling**—may suggest the continuing availability of Christ's atonement. If so, **obedience . . . and sprinkling** implies "that God's plan for them is not obedience marred by unforgiven sin but obedience whose failings are cleansed by the blood of Christ" (Grudem 1988, 54).

The letter's salutation appears in the final clause of v 2: **Grace and peace be yours in abundance.** The typical Greek greeting in most ancient letters was *chairein,* which means ***"welcome, good day, hail (to you),"*** or ***"greetings"*** (BDAG, 1075; see Acts 15:23; 23:26; Jas 1:1). Like Paul, Peter substitutes the word *charis* (**grace**), which is derived from the same root as *chairein.* This wordplay extends not only greetings to his audience, but more importantly, God's **grace.** In the NT **grace** signifies the undeserved, loving favor of God for sinners supremely revealed through Jesus Christ.

Peace (*eirēnē*) is derived from the customary Hebrew greeting *shalom. Shalom* is much richer in its content than the English or Greek words for **peace.** Both "peace" and *eirēnē* convey the notions of tranquillity due to the absence of war and dissension. *Shalom,* however, also conveys the "sense of well-being and salvation" (Foerster 1964, 411).

Peter's greeting includes the full range of the blessings of God. **Grace** in the NT refers to all of God's blessings available to believers through Christ. **Peace** in the OT refers to all God's blessings to Israel. This Christian greeting prays that both gifts—**grace and peace**—may be enjoyed by the audience, and **in abundance** (*plēthyntheiē; "in ever greater measure,"* BDAG, 826).

FROM THE TEXT

Proto-Trinitarian Theology. The NT does not teach a specific doctrine of the Trinity. The ecumenical consensus developed over several centuries. Nonetheless, the foundation of Trinitarian theology is embedded in the language and thought of the NT. This is clearly illustrated in the opening verses of 1 Peter. Peter reflects upon his readers' salvation, assured by the foreknowledge of God the Father, by the atoning death of Jesus Christ, through the sanctifying work of the Holy Spirit. Hunter writes:

> This is as yet "the trinity of experience," out of which sprang the later dogma. The early Christians found by experience that they could not express all that they meant by the word "God" till they had said, "Father, Son, and Spirit." (1957, 90)

Other NT passages similarly anticipate the later doctrine of the Trinity (e.g., Matt 28:19; 2 Cor 13:14; Eph 4:4-6; Jude 20-21). But 1 Pet 1:2 is unique. Not only are the three persons of the Godhead mentioned, but each is recognized as playing an equally important role in salvation.

The Expanded People of God. Peter freely applies terms and descriptions to Gentile Christians typically reserved for Israel alone. He describes them as **God's elect** and **scattered** (*diasporas*) people. But he also borrows language and imagery from God's covenant with Israel to describe the reality of Christians' relationship with God (**sprinkling**).

Yet, if Peter perceives Gentile Christians as replacing Israel as God's chosen people, he gives no indication of it. Rather, without any explanation or reserve, he simply equates the experience of the Christian believers with their Jewish counterparts "as if they were a strange new kind of Jew" (Michaels 1988, 13). This message for disenfranchised and pressured Christians of every ethnic group in any era inspires encouragement. The history of God's saving activities on behalf of his chosen people is the heritage of every Christian believer through Christ.

Resident Aliens. Peter writes to Christian believers who are ***scattered strangers in the world.*** The reality of this kind of existence seems to go back to Jesus' prayer that his followers would not be *"of* the world" even though they are *"in* the world" (John 17:13, 14, emphasis added). But what does it mean practically to be "resident aliens" in the world? The forms of application of this concept may vary within different cultural, social, and historical eras. Peter's words would seem to call Western believers, who enjoy a greater amount of religious freedom, to live in a uniquely Christian way.

The faith in Christ of the original readers of this Epistle had already led to their estrangement from their society and culture. This often led to their public and programmatic persecution. For embattled and oppressed believers of every era, Peter's letter offers encouragement and hope in the face of persistent opposition.

Sanctification. Peter refers specifically to the sanctifying work of the Spirit in the lives of all believers. He considers sanctification a normal part of believers' experience, which goes hand in hand with God's eternal plan for their salvation and the atoning death of Jesus Christ for sinners.

The word that Peter uses for sanctification (*hagiasmos*) "refers not only to the activity of the Holy Spirit in setting man apart unto salvation and transferring him into the ranks of the redeemed, but also to enabling him to be holy even as God is holy" (Zodhiates 1992, 70). It has always been God's purpose, through Jesus Christ, not only to redeem sinful humanity but also to transform the lives of sinful people into his likeness (see 2:21).

The sanctifying work of the Holy Spirit is both a finished result and an ongoing process. The Spirit sets believers apart for God and also cleanses and purifies their character to conform to God's purpose and will. The inherent elements of this sanctifying are twofold. Sanctification is a work the Spirit does *in* believers, cleansing them from moral evil. But it is also a work he does *through* them, enabling them to live daily in holiness and obedience to the will of God.

Believers should resist a reading of the Bible or a theology that insinuates that a person is "saved in principle but not in fact" (Wynkoop 1972, 56). This is why John Wesley insisted that sanctification is found in the intersection of being "renewed in the image of God 'in righteousness and holiness'" as well as "loving God with all our heart, and mind, and soul" (1966, 41). Not only is God's plan of salvation through Christ realized through the Spirit's work of setting believers apart for heaven, but equally important is the Spirit's work of making earthbound believers holy here and now, demonstrated by their obedience to God.

II. PRAISE TO GOD FOR SALVATION: 1 PETER 1:3-12

BEHIND THE TEXT

After the opening salutation, most ancient letters contain a thanksgiving or blessing on behalf of the recipients. The thanksgiving section often introduces many of the major themes of the letter. This is certainly true in 1 Peter. Its thanksgiving touches upon the major themes of salvation, suffering, and hope. These receive deliberate attention in subsequent sections of the letter.

The thanksgiving of 1 Peter can be divided into three main sections. The first (1:3-5) expresses praise to God for the hope-filled assurance of salvation through the resurrection of Jesus Christ. The second section (vv 6-9) reflects upon the believers' joy and perseverance despite the testing of their faith through suffering. The third (vv 10-12) reminds the audience of the great privilege their salvation through Christ represents, since it has been long anticipated and foretold by the prophets of old.

Some interpreters divide the thanksgiving according to the Trinitarian reference in the opening greeting (v 2; see du Toit 1974, 68). They presume that the first section (vv 3-7) focuses upon the Father; the second (vv 8-9) speaks about Jesus Christ; and the third section (vv 10-12) reflects upon the work of the Holy Spirit. Multiple references to Jesus Christ in the second and third sections undermine this analysis. Nonetheless, the recurrence of Trinitarian references to God in these verses closely connects the thanksgiving to the opening greeting. Peter's Trinitarian emphasis makes it clear that he perceives salvation to be intimately tied to the work of God as Father, Son, and Holy Spirit.

Many interpreters have attempted to identify the rite of baptism standing behind 1 Peter. Thus, it has been portrayed as a baptismal sermon (Lohse 1991, 132), liturgy (Boismard 1956, 182-208; Boismard 1957, 161-83; Kelly 1969, 46), discourse (Beare 1961, 52), or homily (Bornemann 1919, 146). Despite these efforts, there is no compelling evidence within 1 Peter to connect this letter to baptism. There is only one overt reference to baptism in the letter (3:21). The reference to "sprinkling" in v 2, as the discussion in the preceding section demonstrates, alludes to the covenant ceremony in Exodus rather than to baptism.

Support for a baptismal theme is often sought in the references to "new birth" in 1:3, 23, and 2:2. The absence of any mention of water or washing within these verses, however, disqualifies these as references to baptism. While the terms *regeneration* and *baptism* may be theologically related, they are hardly identical or interchangeable. The attempts to connect 1 Peter to baptism are unfounded. "Such similarities [are] more apparent than real" (Achtemeier 1996, 93).

IN THE TEXT

■ **3** In the first section of his thanksgiving, Peter offers a blessing of **praise** (*eulogētos*) **to the God and Father of our Lord Jesus Christ.** In the NT *eulogētos* is never used of humans (Beyer 1964b, 764; see 2 Cor 1:3; Eph 1:3). The word literally means ***speak well of someone.*** But its NT usage as a blessing is derived "from the LXX translation of the OT form of praise of God, 'Blessed (i.e., praised) be Yahweh'" (Verbrugge 2000, 218). The object of this praise is **the God and Father of our Lord Jesus Christ.** Even though the praise is theocentric, the focus is clearly christocentric. The nouns **God** and **Father** are inseparably united by a single definite article (*ho*).

The relationship between God and Jesus is significant for Peter's audience because of their new birth. Jesus died and was resurrected so they might be reborn into salvation. By this means, the God of Jesus becomes their God;

and the Father of Jesus, their Father. The blessing is formally derived from the OT, but thoroughly Christian in its content.

Peter praises **God** because **he has given us new birth.** *Anagennēsas* (**has given . . . new birth**) means ***"beget again"*** or ***"cause to be born again"*** (BDAG, 59). This verb is found in the Bible only in 1 Pet 1:3 and 23. The root verb *gennaō* ("give birth") often has a female as its subject. Of course, God is beyond gender—God is neither male nor female. But the imagery of God as both a merciful Father and a mother giving birth to children is a reminder that believers owe their entire existence to God.

Although the term *anagennaō* is unique to 1 Peter, a similar concept appears in the Gospel tradition (see Mark 10:14-15; Matt 19:28; John 1:12-13; 3:3-8). Close parallels also occur in Paul (see "new creation": Gal 6:15; 2 Cor 5:17).

The notion of a new beginning through a new birth with the infusion of divine life was also a "widespread idea in the ancient world. It was present in the mystery religions and in Judaism" (Rogers and Rogers 1998, 566). Thus, the idea of **new birth** was probably familiar to Peter's audience, even though they were not Jews.

While **new birth** is closely connected to faith and obedience (vv 2, 5, 7, 8), it cannot be earned or merited. Rather, the impetus for the new birth is God's **great mercy** (see Exod 34:6; Ps 25:6; Dan 9:18). Ultimately, this perspective on the mercy of God prompts this doxology. The connection of **new birth** with **mercy** is important. The **new birth** of believers created their status as "scattered strangers" in the world. Peter reminds them that this was a result of God's *mercy,* and so a blessing, not a curse. For believers undergoing persecution, this was important. 1:3

The remainder of vv 3-5 signals the goal of the believers' new birth by a threefold use of the preposition *eis,* **into.** By virtue of his great grace, God has birthed believers **into a living hope** (*eis elpida zōsan,* v 3), "into an inheritance" (*eis klēronomian,* v 4), and ***into a prepared salvation*** (*eis sōtērian hetoimēn,* v 5). The NIV obscures this triple use of *eis.* The NRSV and NASB also translate the third *eis* as "for." But the repetition of *eis* marks three explicit benefits of the believers' new birth.

First, believers are reborn **into a living hope.** In the NT **hope** "always relates to a future good" (Vincent 1946, 630). Peter qualifies this hope as a *living* hope. The contrast is not between the "living" hope of Christianity and the "dead" hopes of Judaism. It is more likely the disparity of the Christians' living hope with the defeated, empty, and false hopes of the pagan religions from which they were converted. "Living hope as a fundamental religious attitude was unknown in Greek culture" (Hoffmann 1986, 239). Ultimately, pagan worshippers had to stand without hope before the hostile forces of guilt and death.

But Christian believers possess a living hope **through the resurrection of Jesus Christ from the dead.** Christian hope is not just wishful thinking, optimism about the future. Christian hope is **living** precisely because Jesus Christ is alive. "There is a clear parallel here between the new birth of Christians and the resurrection of Jesus Christ. Both move from death to life; thus the resurrection of Jesus is the grounds for the new life of the believer" (Bartlett 1998, 250). Because of Jesus' resurrection from the dead, Christian believers have **a living hope.** It is not empty and futile because the resurrection of Christ has destroyed the power of death. The Christian Savior who makes new life and new birth possible is the resurrected and living Lord (see Rom 8:11; 2 Cor 4:13—5:10).

The past, present, and future intersect in this concept of **hope.** Peter reminds his persecution-plagued audience that their living present and future hope are founded upon the victorious resurrection of Jesus Christ in the past. This hope does not back down in the face of death, persecution, or hardship. This hope is living, not only because it lives on in the face of difficult circumstances, but because it gives life to those who hope.

■ **4** Second, believers are reborn **into an inheritance.** There are two plausible backgrounds for the term **inheritance.** The underlying Greek word is used almost two hundred times in the LXX. Many of these instances refer to Canaan, the promised land God gave Israel after the Exodus. Some see **inheritance** as reflecting the OT theme of God's gift (of the Promised Land) to his chosen people. This corresponds with Peter's description of believers as God's chosen people and his practice of reapplying Jewish terms and descriptions to his Gentile-Christian audience in these opening verses.

The other possible background of **inheritance** may be within other NT passages and the sayings of Jesus in the Gospel tradition. Christians are often described as "inheriting" the kingdom, eternal life, or the like (see Matt 5:5; 19:29; 25:34; Mark 10:17; Luke 10:25; 18:18; 1 Cor 6:9-10; 15:50; Gal 5:21; Heb 1:14; 6:12). Michaels claims that "it is likely that Peter's thought is still being shaped by the traditional saying of Jesus about rebirth that seems to underlie [John 3] v 3: 'Unless you are born again, you will not inherit the kingdom of heaven'" (1988, 20).

While this suggestion may appear attractive, "inheritance" is found nowhere in the context of Jesus' "born again" discourse in John 3. It seems more probable that Peter is again using the rich language and imagery of the OT to depict the results of the believers' new birth.

Three striking adjectives describe this **inheritance.** It is **an inheritance that can never perish, spoil or fade.** "The accumulated adjectives recall various images employed to describe it—and emphasize the fact that it is eternal and spiritual" (Hart 1979, 42). Each of the adjectives in Greek begins with an alpha-privative, a prefix roughly equivalent to un- or non- in English.

The first adjective (*aphtharton;* ***"imperishable, incorruptible, immortal";*** BDAG, 155) indicates a sharing "in the very nature of God and in the eschatological [future] reality he will establish" (Achtemeier 1996, 95-96). Cranfield claims that the adjective connotes "cannot be ravaged." In secular contexts *phthartos* referred to "an army laying waste to the land" (1960, 38). The land of Israel had often been ravaged by invading armies. The inheritance of reborn believers is not subject to such death, decay, or disintegration.

The second adjective (*amianton*) conveys the idea that the inheritance is morally free of and "unsusceptible of any stain" (Jamieson, Fausset, Brown 1870, 499). Achtemeier sees this again as sharing "in the undefiled nature of God himself" (1996, 96).

The third adjective (*amaranton*) refers to the fading glory of flowers. But the glory and beauty of this inheritance is unfading; it will never grow dim.

The combined thrust of these three adjectives is that, unlike other inheritances or earthly goods, this heritage is secure and everlasting. "The inheritance is untouched by death, unstained by evil, unimpaired by time" (Beare 1961, 57-58). This is the glorious nature of the believers' inheritance.

Peter assures his readers that this inheritance is **kept in heaven for you** (see Matt 6:19-20; 1 Cor 15:52-54). The spiritual nature of this inheritance is affirmed by the reference to **heaven.** The perfect participle **kept** "indicates a completed past activity (by God) with results that are continuing in the present: God himself has 'stored up' or 'reserved' this inheritance for all believers and it continues to be there, 'still reserved' for them" (Grudem 1988, 57).

Peter's original audience, facing more persecution, had undoubtedly been injured already, both physically and materially. But their eternal inheritance would survive the darkest and most punishing times. Preserved for them in heaven, this inheritance was immune to the evil and vindictive forces of this world.

■ **5** Believers are also reborn ***into a prepared salvation.*** The complicated Greek construction makes this third result of the new birth difficult to recognize in many English translations. The preposition *eis,* however, makes it clear that this was Peter's intention.

Before identifying the last goal of the believers' new birth, Peter inserts a strong message of encouragement. The eternal inheritance kept in heaven is ***for you who are being guarded by the power of God.*** Not only is the inheritance safe (v 4), but the believers themselves are being guarded by the power of God (v 5).

The word ***guarded*** is borrowed from military language. It conveys the idea of a sentinel placed on duty to protect a valued asset or position. Peter implies that believers will undoubtedly continue to find themselves under attack by their enemies. But they were being guarded and kept safe by nothing less than the power of God.

The present tense of the participle ***being guarded*** indicates that God's protection is continually present. Peter could assure his audience that their divine protection was not sporadic or incidental. Rather, they were being guarded steadily and constantly by nothing less formidable than **God's power.**

The protection of believers is experienced **through faith** (*dia pisteōs*). **Faith** is not merely intellectual assent. **Through faith** believers completely commit themselves to Jesus Christ. Wesley observes that faith is that "through which alone salvation is both received and retained" (1981, n.p.). The shielding power of God assures believers that they will be able to withstand the pressures that surround them. But Peter reminds his audience that God guards believers who continually trust him. "The power from without corresponds to the faith within" (Hort, quoted by Selwyn 1947, 125).

Believers are being kept and guarded for (*eis*) a **salvation that is ready to be revealed in the last time.** Within the NT, **salvation** (*sōtēria*) can be oriented to the past (e.g., Rom 8:24), present (e.g., 1 Cor 1:18; 1 Pet 1:9), or future. In the future, believers will participate fully in the glorious vindication and salvation of Christ. Only at that time will they come into the full possession of their heavenly inheritance with its fullness of life and its open vision of God (e.g., Rom 8:18-25; Phil 3:20-21).

Peter's reference to **in the last time** (*en kairōi eschatōi*) indicates that he envisions the future salvation of believers. Everything is in place and ready for the final salvation of believers, which Peter envisions as occurring soon (4:7). That this salvation has been made **ready** (*hetoimēn*) reinforces the certainty of their eternal, heavenly reward. On that day, the salvation into which believers have been reborn will be revealed. Peter tells his readers that they "stand on the threshold of their inheritance; its unveiling is both imminent and certain" (Michaels 1988, 23).

■ **6** In the second section of his thanksgiving (1:6-9), attention is shifted from the benevolence and certainty of God's blessings to the readers' present response to God's blessings: **In this you greatly rejoice.** It is most likely that **in this** refers to the entire content of the previous three verses (Selwyn 1947, 126). Thus, the rebirth, hope, inheritance, salvation, faith, and imminence of the end are being called to mind to prompt the believers' joy.

The verb **rejoice** (*agalliaomai*) is found only in the Bible and in the writings of the early church. It appears three times in 1 Peter (1:6, 8; 4:13). The intense joy of Christians implies an outward expression of that joy. This involves "a jubilant and thankful exultation" (Bultmann 1964a, 20) because of God's help. Here **rejoice** is most naturally interpreted as an indicative verb (see v 8)—a statement, rather than a command (an imperative as in the GNT and NLT; see Martin 1992b, 307-8).

Believers exult in the blessings of God despite their **grief in all kinds of trials.** The verb translated **suffer grief** (*lypeō*) denotes "both physical and emotional pain" (Verbrugge 2000, 344; e.g., Matt 26:37-38; 2 Cor 2:5). In the letter's references to suffering (see 2:19-21; 3:17-18; 4:1), physical pain or persecution seems to dominate. But emotional pain often accompanies physical pain.

The expression **all kinds of trials** (*poikilois peirasmois*) is the same phrase Jas 1:2 uses, "Consider it pure joy, my brothers, whenever you face trials of many kinds." The word *peirasmois,* **trials,** contains the dual ideas of testing and temptation. Peter is not thinking of the future possibilities of suffering alone. He has in mind the concrete and perhaps necessary (*ei deon;* ***if it is necessary***) persecution that believers have faced and will continue to face. The Greek word sometimes depicts God's testing of believers. But Peter's tone throughout this letter indicates that their suffering and **trials** are not caused by God. God is not the source of their grief; but their suffering does fall within the provision of God's work within the lives of Christian believers (v 7).

Despite the severity of their suffering, Peter offers encouragement to his audience by reminding them that their suffering is only **now for a little while** (*oligon*). *Oligon* can be interpreted in three ways:

First, it could mean that they had suffered for only a short time. This interpretation may be rejected since the focus of this passage is decidedly geared toward the future. In 5:10, where *oligon* appears again, the future orientation of his encouragement is obvious.

Second, *oligon* might refer to the expected duration of their suffering. That is, it would not last very long. This meaning, preferred by many (Achtemeier 1996, 101; see NRSV, NIV, NASB), has this advantage: It reinforces the mention in v 5 that their "salvation . . . is ready to be revealed."

Third, *oligon* could refer to the degree or extent of their suffering. It is comparatively small, considering the future "eternal glory in Christ" (5:10) they will experience (see Rom 8:18; 2 Cor 4:17). Early in the eighth century, the Venerable Bede wrote that Peter "stresses the fact that this is only 'for a little while,' because once we have entered our eternal reward, the years we spent in suffering here below will seem like no time at all" (cited in Bray 2000, 71).

It is difficult to decide whether the duration or the degree of their suffering is Peter's emphasis. Peter may have had both ideas in mind. In contrast to their suffering **now for a little while,** believers are reminded that the reward of their faith is both imminent and eternal.

The believers' exultation is juxtaposed between the future reality of God's blessings (v 5) and the present reality of their grievous trials (v 6). Because of the apparent incongruity of joy and suffering, many church fathers used the future tense in quoting 1 Pet 1:6, 8 (Martin 1992, 60-61). They could only envision the joy of believers as being postponed until the coming of Christ on the Last Day. That is, believers *will* rejoice then.

But this is the central paradox of the Christian faith. Christians can have victory and joy despite suffering and persecution. Paul reflects this attitude in 2 Cor 6:10. There he describes believers as "sorrowful, yet always rejoicing; poor, yet making many rich; having nothing, and yet possessing everything." Calvin writes that "the faithful know by experience, how these things can exist together. . . . Hence they experience sorrow from evils; but it is so mitigated by faith, that they cease not at the same time to rejoice" (1948, 32). Peter underscores the fact that the joy of the believers is not offset by the difficulties and trials of the day.

■ **7** Peter addresses the topic of suffering directly in this verse, a theme he will revisit before he concludes the letter (see 3:13-17; 4:12-19; 5:9-10). The NIV adds **These have come** to the direct **so that** (*hina*) in order to begin a new sentence. Peter explains the beneficial result of the believers' suffering: Through suffering, the faith of believers is **proved genuine.** As a result, **praise, glory and honor** will be theirs **when Jesus Christ is revealed.**

Some interpret v 7 as explaining the *reason* for the believers' suffering instead of its *result.* This presumes that suffering and trials (*peirasmois,* v 6) are actually caused by God in order to test the genuineness of the faith of believers. Thus, an essential part of God's *foreknowledge* (v 2) would be his foreordination of a destiny of suffering for believers (see Bartlett 1998, 251). But this is not the focus of Peter's treatment. Suffering is not presented as an inherent part of God's perfect, predestined plan for the world. Rather, Peter encourages his readers by reminding them that suffering is under God's control but not part of God's ideal world.

God is moving history toward its rightful conclusion. Suffering is often a visible element of this progression.

> But that does not mean that suffering itself is good, that its agents are good, or that God wants us to suffer. It does mean that in a world in rebellion against God, created as this world has been with the various spiritual and human forces (with their freedom to choose) in it, it is the

best way in God's mercy and hidden wisdom for him to work out his good plan. Suffering may not be God's desire, but it is not outside his sovereignty. (Davids 1990, 56)

In other words, God does not cause the suffering believers face. But he will use that suffering to benefit and refine their life and faith.

Peter identifies two ways suffering and trials can benefit believers. First, their persistence in the midst of suffering demonstrates that their faith is **genuine.** Second, their patience in suffering will result in **praise, glory and honor when Jesus Christ is revealed.**

Peter uses the analogy of the refining of gold, common in his day, to illustrate the benefit of suffering. Just as gold is refined by fire—purified and proven authentic, so the faith of believers is purified and **proved genuine** by trials. But unlike gold, which can ultimately be consumed and perish in the refining fire, the faith of believers is of much greater worth. It will endure the refining fire of present suffering and receive an eternal reward when **Christ is revealed.**

Praise, glory and honor are attributes "which belong to God himself and which he alone can give" (Achtemeier 1996, 102). Peter does not say believers can earn these through their heroic deeds in the midst of suffering. Rather, these rewards are the result of their *genuine faith,* which is proven and demonstrated through their steadfastness in suffering. These awards will be granted when Jesus Christ is "revealed in the last time" (1:5). 1:7

Suffering in I Peter

There are four sections in I Peter that deal specifically with suffering:

1. suffering grief in various trials (1:6-7)
2. unjust suffering of slaves (2:18-25)
3. suffering due to the public confession of faith (3:13-18)
4. suffering "fiery trials" for the faith (4:12-19)

The unjust suffering of slaves in ch 2 seems to be out of character with the other suffering material in chs 1, 3, and 4. These refer to suffering brought on by one's confession of faith. In ch 2 Peter comforts slaves to endure courageously their suffering at the hands of unjust masters. However, the model of Christ Peter uses (2:21) implies that these slaves suffer as a result of their confession of faith. Thus, the encouragement offered unjustly suffering slaves is probably more closely related to that in chs 1, 3, and 4 than often thought.

Peter never tries to explain how believers can avoid suffering through prayer, greater faithfulness, or more godly behavior. Rather, he calls them to *endure* suffering. Suffering is not presented as divine punishment or as part of some foreordained divine plan. Rather, suffering results from the believers' identity with Christ, who also suffered and died. Suffering is not perceived as a punishment, but as an inherent feature of one's faith in Christ.

> First Peter interprets the suffering of Christians in at least these ways: (1) Suffering can provide for the refining of faith (1:6-7). (2) The one who suffers imitates Christ, who also suffered unjustly, not only as Christians' redeemer but also as their example (2:21-25; 3:17-18; 4:13; 5:13). (3) Suffering is not only the result of human bad will but also is a consequence of the power of the devil (5:8). (4) Nonetheless, part of the power of Christ's resurrection was his power to proclaim victory over the forces of evil (3:18-20). Therefore, by implication, Christians know that those who cause their suffering will also finally be judged and defeated. (5) Suffering for being a Christian is itself a sign that the end of history is at hand (4:12-16). (6) When Christ does return, those who have suffered for their faith will receive the reward of eternal glory, and the Spirit, which is the firstfruits of that glory, already is given to the faithful who suffer (1:7; 2:11; 4:13; 5:4, 10-11). (Bartlett 1998, 252)

■ **8-9** Peter explains why believers can rejoice greatly despite their present suffering and trials (v 6). The cause for their joy is twofold. It is because of their (1) present relationship with Jesus Christ (v 8) and (2) secure hope in a future salvation (v 9).

Peter's readers **have not seen** Jesus and **do not see him now.** And yet they love Jesus and believe in him. That they **have not seen him** suggests a contrast between Peter and his audience. Unlike Peter and the other apostles, they had never seen Jesus. This contrast implies that the author of this letter was an eyewitness of Jesus' earthly ministry. This argues for authentic Petrine authorship.

A second contrast is made between the believers' lack of visual experience and their love and faith in Christ. The notion that faith outweighs sight in the experience of believers is a recurrent theme in the NT (see John 20:29; 2 Cor 4:18; 5:7; Heb 11:1, 3). What sustains believers in their trials is not a visual recollection of Jesus, but the fact that they **love him** and **believe in him.** Both of these verbs are in the present tense. This indicates a continual or regular activity. Believers rejoice, not because of perceptual experience, but because of their sustained relationship of love and faith in Jesus Christ.

This love and faith fills them with **an inexpressible and glorious joy.** The word **inexpressible** denotes a divine mystery that surpasses the capabilities of speech and thought. Even though these verses explain believers' joy, their joy defies all human explanation or comprehension. In their focus on Christ, not their present circumstances, they experience this joy. Thus, the first cause of believers' joy in suffering is their present, ongoing relationship with Christ, which is characterized and sustained by faith and love.

The second cause of their great joy is that believers are **receiving the goal of** their **faith, the salvation of** their **souls** (v 9). Every experience in the lives of believers, whether good or bad, demonstrates the genuineness of their faith (see v 7). As a result, they rejoice greatly even during difficult trials and suffering. This is because all these experiences lead to the ultimate **goal** (*telos*) of their faith. The word *telos* is used to describe the outcome, the goal, or the consummation of their faith. The *telos* of believers is specifically **the salvation of** their **souls**.

The word **soul** (*psychē*) is not used here in a Greek philosophical sense. It does not differentiate some kind of dichotomy between the body and the soul. Rather, "the 'soul' is used in the Semitic biblical sense of 'self' or 'person'" (Blum 1981a, 221). Thus, *psychē* refers to the salvation of the entire person, not simply the deliverance of only a higher or spiritual element of that person, to the neglect of the person's body.

Throughout the NT, salvation embraces a person's entire being. The Greek notion that salvation entails the soul's escape from entrapment within the body is alien to the biblical authors. The salvation Christ brings to believers always includes the redemption of humans in their wholeness (see 1 Thess 5:23).

The reference to **salvation** in conjunction with the word *telos* (**goal**) means that Peter is talking about the full possession of all the blessings of salvation that will be consummated only in the last day. Throughout vv 6-9 there is a contrast between the believers' present trials and their future hope and glory in Christ.

When Peter emphasizes that believers **are receiving** the goal of their faith—salvation—he uses the present tense again. The final consummation of their salvation will not occur until the last day when their salvation will be revealed by Christ (v 5). Nevertheless, believers already participate in salvation. Salvation is a process that develops and is authenticated in believers' lives through the events of their lives.

> The process described in v 9 is the entire process of growth in the Christian life, the process of appropriating in one's own life more and more of the blessings of salvation. This process happens, Peter says, as Christians continually believe in Christ and continually rejoice because of that personal trust in him. Such day by day faith and joy produces an unexpected benefit: continual growth toward Christian maturity. (Grudem 1988, 67)

■ **10-11** In the last section of this thanksgiving (1:10-12), Peter reflects further upon the salvation believers enjoy. The spiritual blessings they already enjoy are blessings OT prophets and even angels longed to perceive. Within the complicated structure of vv 10-11, Peter's audience is instructed on several points concerning their salvation.

First, the prophets of old foretold the **grace that was to come to you.** Here **grace** is essentially a synonym of *salvation* (Michaels 1988, 41). Peter did not specifically identify which prophets he had in mind. But he evidently refers to the OT prophets. "Both the language of v 11 (. . .), which indicates that the prophets in question preceded Christ, and the contrast between the words of the prophets (vv 10-11) and the proclamation of the gospel (v 12), point rather to OT than NT prophets" (Achtemeier 1996, 108; but see Selwyn 1947, 259-68). With other NT writers, Peter held the OT to be prophetic of Christ (e.g., Matt 13:16-17; Luke 24:25-27; John 5:39; Acts 7:52; 17:2-4).

These prophets **searched intently and with the greatest care.** Peter does not specify which prophetic passages he referenced. We could surmise that Peter thought of Isaiah's prophecies concerning the suffering Servant of the Lord (e.g., Isa 52:13—53:12). But other messianic prophecies are equally possible, including passages from the historical books of the OT and the Psalms (see Clowney 1988, 56-59). Peter alludes not only to prophecies foretelling Christ's sufferings but also to Christ's glories. With deliberate vagueness, Peter allows an almost limitless supply of OT passages to parade through his readers' imagination from their knowledge of biblical and postbiblical history (see Michaels 1988, 40).

Second, these anonymous prophets longed to discover **the time and circumstances** of Christ's coming. Many people past and present have yearned to discover an insight into the timetable of God. Peter stresses that his audience lived in a privileged era. Far from being underprivileged, they were living in the day of prophetic fulfillment. Regardless of the severity of their own sufferings, they lived in a time for which the OT prophets had yearned.

Third, **the Spirit of Christ** was the one who **predicted the sufferings of Christ and the glories that would follow.** Only here and in Rom 8:9 is the Holy Spirit identified as the "Spirit of Christ" (see v 12). This phrase has a twofold significance: (1) It reflects the NT idea that Christ is the one who sends the Holy Spirit (John 14:26; 20:22). (2) It denotes that the Holy Spirit witnesses to Christ and represents Christ (John 15:16-17; Acts 1:8). The **Spirit of Christ . . . predicted the sufferings** and **glories** of Christ through the prophets.

The **sufferings of Christ** are mentioned often in this letter (2:21; 4:13; 5:1, 9) because they parallel the sufferings of Peter's audience. He deliberately refers to **sufferings** first, and to **glories** second. "The order is critical: the glories follow the sufferings. Neither Christ nor his people receive the crown of glory without the crown of thorns" (Davids 1990, 63-64).

■ **12** The prophets longed to witness the events the Spirit of Christ revealed to them. And yet **it was revealed to them** (divine passive: ***by God the Holy Spirit***) **that they were not serving themselves** but the generation in which Peter's audience lived. They lived in a privileged time! The same Holy Spirit who inspired the prophetic predictions inspired **those who have preached the gospel to** contemporary believers. The message they received through Peter and other preachers was not communicated incorrectly. The messages of OT prophets and NT preachers are both safeguarded by the Holy Spirit, who was **sent from heaven.**

The last phrase of v 12—**even angels long to look into these things**—again reminds the audience of their privilege of living in the era of prophetic fulfillment. The verb **long to look** (*parakypsai*) means literally "to stoop down near or by something, bend forward or near in order to look at something more closely" (Zodhiates 1992, 1108).

Angels

There is a Jewish tradition that implies that angels are superior to humans in their knowledge of God's acts and plans of redemption for humanity (Dan 7:16; Zech 1:9; *1 En.* 1:2; 72:1). There was an equally widespread tradition that angels lacked such knowledge (Mark 13:32; Rom 16:25; 1 Cor 2:8-9; Eph 3:10; *1 En.* 16:3; *2 En.* 24:3). The latter tradition seems to be implied here.

The reference to angels insinuates nothing about their activities or authority. It emphasizes instead their intense interest in what had transpired through Christ and what was transpiring in the lives of suffering Christian believers.

> Though the world may think such Christians insignificant and worthy of pity or scorn (see 3:14-16; 4:4), angels—who see ultimate reality from God's perspective—find them objects of intense interest, for they know that these struggling believers are actually the recipients of God's greatest blessings and honored participants in a great drama at the focal point of universal history. (Grudem 1988, 73)

Despite their suffering, Peter reminds his readers that they are a privileged people.

FROM THE TEXT

Several poignant truths emerge in the thanksgiving section of 1 Pet 1:3-12.

Regeneration. Peter reiterates the notion that believers have been "reborn" into the Christian faith. The life of faith in Jesus Christ marks an entirely new existence for believers. It is a new beginning, a new dawn, a new era in their lives.

Believers today can identify with the notion that initiation into the Christian faith is an experience that can be likened to a rebirth. "Born again" believers readily recognize the radical change that faith and obedience to Jesus Christ implies.

Peter adds two important concepts to the normal perception of what Christian rebirth entails. First, his original readers were "scattered strangers" in the world. Their rebirth by faith in Jesus Christ came with painful side effects. It was a costly faith; it marked them socially and religiously as outcasts and outsiders in their world. Regardless of the joy and peace believers today associate with their Christian rebirth, they should never forget that it can also result in difficulty and pain.

Second, Peter reminds believers of the marvelous blessings accompanying their new birth. God has mercifully rebirthed believers into a living hope, an eternal inheritance, and a prepared salvation. Some believers might be tempted to think their conversion is the goal of the Christian life. But Peter reminds them that born-again believers enjoy victory over past sins, a living and sustaining hope for the present, and a glorious future inheritance—final salvation through Christ. Thus, conversion is not the end of our spiritual journey; indeed, it is only the beginning.

III. EXHORTATIONS FOR GOD'S HOLY PEOPLE: 1 PETER 1:13—2:10

A. Call to Holiness (1:13—2:3)

BEHIND THE TEXT

With v 13, the tone of the letter changes from a description of the certainty of the believers' hope for salvation (indicative verbs) to an exhortation for believers (imperative verbs) to live lives appropriate of such a great salvation.

The alternation between the indicative and the imperative moods "points to the fact that in this letter, as in early Christian proclamation in general, the imperative grows out of the indicative" (Achtemeier 1996, 115). The implications are twofold: First, the grace and hope believers receive from God through the resurrection of Jesus Christ (1:3) obligates them to live accordingly. Second, the reality of God's grace and hope empowers believers to fulfill the imperative of Christlikeness.

First Peter is a letter of exhortation (see 2:11; 5:1, 12). This is clearly demonstrated by the specific instructions that are given (see 2:18—3:7; 5:1-5) and the frequent use of imperatives. There are thirty-six imperatives in the Greek text. Many English translations presume even more imperatival verbs. This is due to the grammatical assumption that adverbial participles associated with imperative verbs express commands. Beare notes that Peter "is exceptionally fond of using the participle as an imperative" (1961, 71). The assumption that Greek adverbial participles may be translated with English imperatives has been seriously challenged by David Daube (1947, 467-88) and others. Unless the context specifically demands it, this commentary does not assign imperatival force to adverbial participles.

First Peter 1:13—2:10 has two main sections. The first (1:13—2:3) articulates a call to holiness. The second (2:4-10) describes the new building of God's people. Some scholars include 2:1-3 with 2:4-10. But 2:1-3 fits better with 1:13-25 because it provides specific instructions as to how believers are to live holy lives (1:15).

The first section consists of four subdivisions:

1. Command to be holy (1:13-16)
2. Justification and motivation for holiness (1:17-21)
3. Demonstration of holiness by loving one another (1:22-25)
4. Reiteration of the call to holiness (2:1-3)

IN THE TEXT

1. Command to Be Holy (1:13-16)

■ **13 Therefore** marks the transition from thanksgiving in 1:3-12 to exhortation in 1:13—2:3. After Peter has established the basis for the hope of salvation through Christ, he quickly calls his readers to make this hope a reality in the way they conduct their daily lives.

The main verb of v 13 is the first imperative of the letter: **set your hope** (*elpisate*). Two participles, taken by the NIV as imperatives, precede this main verb. The first participle (**prepare your minds for action**) is in the aorist tense. This describes an event that *precedes* the action of the main verb. The second participle (**be self-controlled**) is in the present tense. It describes an event that *accompanies* the action of the main verb.

Thus, v 13 can be translated: ***Therefore, after you have prepared your minds for action and while you are self-controlled, set your hope fully on the grace to be given you when Jesus Christ is revealed.***

The first participle (***after you have prepared your minds for action***) literally means: "*when you have girded the loins of your mind*" (BDAG, 62). To "gird" (*anazōnnymi*) is used metaphorically, indicating believers' preparedness for action. The underlying imagery is vivid. It was customary for a man to tuck the front of his robe into his belt in order to free up his arms and legs for quick action or fast running (see 1 Kgs 18:46; Exod 12:11; Jer 1:17; Luke 17:8). The expression is equivalent to our "roll up your sleeves" or "tighten your belt" (Earle 1984, 68).

The reference to the mind (*dianoias*) "doubles the metaphor" (Calvin 1948, 44). By attributing loins—the center of a person's bodily strength—to the mind, the metaphor does not emphasize physical strength. Instead, it emphasizes strong mental activity in terms of "mental resolve or preparation" (Davids 1990, 66). In other words, Peter invites his readers to get ready for an exercise in serious thought.

The second participle (**be self-controlled,** *nēphontes*) literally means ***being sober.*** The present tense designates an ongoing or continuing attitude of levelheadedness. Peter uses the same word in 4:7 and 5:8 to call his readers to spiritual alertness for praying and resisting the devil.

These two participles provide the background for Peter's call for believers to **set** their **hope fully on the grace to be given** them. **Set your hope** recalls the theme of "living hope" from v 3. The aorist tense strikes "a more urgent, insistent note than the present would: not just 'hope,' but 'fix your hope purposefully'" (Kelly 1969, 66). The force of this insistent hope is strengthened by the adverb **fully** (*teleiōs*), occurring only here in the NT. Christian hope is not halfhearted or lukewarm. It is vibrant, insistent, and focused.

The focus of believers' **hope** is the **grace** that will be given **when Jesus Christ is revealed.** Christian hope is based on what Christ has already done (his death and resurrection; 1:2-3) and the confident expectation of his second coming (1:13). This hope prompts a reorientation of believers' lives.

■ **14** The hope of believers causes them to act **as obedient children.** The word **children** echoes the theme of "new birth" (1:3). As people reborn with God as their Father, believers are characterized by obedience.

The present participle **do not conform** (*mē syschēmatizomenoi*) represents an ongoing action that corresponds in time with the imperative **be holy** in v 15. It is best understood as subsidiary and preparatory to the leading command for holiness. "Thus while the participle carries imperatival force . . . , it is to be construed not so much as a further command but as the way by which becoming holy is to be accomplished: you are to be holy by not conforming to former ways" (Achtemeier 1996, 120).

The verb *syschēmatizomai* (**conform**) is found only here and in Rom 12:2 in the NT. In both instances, believers are called to reorient their lives to conform to the will of God, not to the expectations of people around them.

Peter urges his audience to shun their former way of life as characterized by **ignorance** and **evil desires. Ignorance** (*agnoiai*) typically describes the morally misguided lives of non-Jews. It reinforces the evidence that his audience consisted primarily of Gentiles. Peter has in mind here the more universal ignorance of those who do not know the true God. Such **ignorance** "is not primarily an intellectual but a moral and religious defect, nothing less than rebellion against God" (Michaels 1988, 58).

Those who are ignorant of God are shaped by their **evil desires** (*epithymiai*). *Epithymiai* can be either positive or negative (see Rom 6:12). Here it is clearly conceived negatively. It refers to "all kinds of self-seeking, whether directed toward wealth, power, or pleasure" (Michaels 1988, 56). Empowered by the confident hope of the grace of God through Christ, believers are enjoined to abandon the destructive grasp of their former ignorance and sinful desires.

■ **15** In contrast to the negative prohibition of v 14, Peter articulates the positive command to holiness in v 15: **Just as he who called you is holy, so be holy in all you do.**

The basis for Peter's command to **be holy** is found in God himself: "The holiness of God is the supreme motive for [human] holiness" (Nicholson 1967, 271). Believers are called to be holy because the one who called them to be his people is holy. People everywhere "will imitate the God whom they worship. They will form their character in accordance with his" (Barnes 1962, 1402). Since God's character and nature is holy, the people he calls should display his character and nature.

Holy (*hagios*) carries the double meaning of "set apart to sacred use" and "morally pure, blameless in heart and life" (Zodhiates 1992, 70). The description of believers as "strangers" (1:1, 17) emphasizes the "set apartness" of the Asian Christians within their culture and society. The ritual sense of holiness (i.e., "set apart") is certainly represented in this command. But the holiness to which believers are called carries primarily an ethical and moral force. The ethical nature of this command to be holy is explicitly expressed by the inclusion of the phrase **in all you do** (*anastrophēi*).

Anastrophē is derived from a verb meaning ***to move about, to turn about.*** It is a favorite word in Peter's writings (1:15, 18; 2:12; 3:1, 2, 16; 2 Pet 2:7; 3:11). It is used to depict one's conduct, behavior, or lifestyle. It covers "all actions, thoughts, words, and relationships" (Howe 2000a, 306-7). Peter invites his readers to be holy in everything they do, both in attitude and action.

The call to holiness is overwhelmingly inclusive. There is no aspect of believers' lives that does not fall under the command to be holy. "The church fails of impressiveness in the world largely because there is not enough difference between the people inside and those outside to strike a contrast" (Homrighausen 1957, 103). This sad state of affairs might be remedied if believers would heed Peter's command: **Be holy in all you do.**

■ **16** Christians should be holy because **it is written: "Be holy, because I am holy"** (citing Lev 11:44-45; 19:2). **Be holy, because I am holy** is the theological refrain that echoes throughout the Holiness Code contained in Lev 17—26. The many references to God's holiness in the OT "all come down to this in finality: God is holy and the passion of his heart, held in poignant focus at Calvary, is the creation of a family of children who will in fact be like him" (Rees 1962, 37). When the holy God calls people into his presence, he calls them to be holy, even as he is holy.

2. Justification and the Motivation for Holiness (1:17-21)

Peter provides a threefold justification for his demand for holiness. He identifies the basis for Christian holiness (v 17*a*), issues another call to live such lives (v 17*b*), and explains the redemption that should motivate this kind of life (vv 18-21). All three elements are intertwined as evidenced by the fact that vv 17-21 form a single sentence in Greek.

■ **17** The opening *kai* (***and***) ties vv 17-21 closely with the preceding verses. The climax of v 17 is found in the imperatival command: **live your lives as strangers here in reverent fear.** It reiterates the injunction in v 15 to "be holy in all you do." Believers are urged to live a life different from non-Christians—as **strangers**—because they **call on a Father who judges each man's work impartially** (v 17*a*).

The word translated **call** (*epikaleisthe*) means literally "'***to call upon***' or '***appeal***' to someone" (BDAG, 373). The present tense portrays an ongoing habit of calling upon God for help. This may highlight the importance of habitual prayer (Blum 1981a, 224). But the main emphasis is that believers' prayers call upon the Father as one **who judges each man's work impartially.**

Impartially (*aprosōpolēmptōs*) is found only here in the NT. But the idea that God does not show favoritism in his judgment is found often (see Acts 10:34; Rom 2:11; Gal 2:6; Eph 6:9; Col 3:25). Likewise, the notion that God judges everyone's work recurs throughout the NT (see Matt 16:27; Rom 2:6; 1 Cor 3:13; 2 Cor 5:10; Gal 6:7-9; Rev 20:12-13; 22:12).

Peter is careful to balance the perception of God as **Father** with the reality that he is also the Judge. Although God was their Father, believers were not to presume that disobedience and sin would go unnoticed or undisciplined. Their behavior is not inconsequential. **The Father . . . judges** each one's work **impartially.** If Christians "call God Father, they should remember his character and not allow familiarity to be an excuse for evil" (Davids 1990, 70).

Peter and God's Impartiality

Many scholars challenge the historical reliability of Luke's accounts in Acts. But it is striking to observe the intersection of Peter's words in Acts 10:34-35 with this passage in 1 Pet 1:17. In both passages, there is an emphasis upon impartiality, a reference to reverent fear (*phoboumenos, phobos*), and an emphasis on right living. Some interpret these parallels as evidence for Petrine authorship. "The internal evidence for St. Peter's authorship of the Epistle is borne out and amplified when we compare it with the speeches attributed to the Apostle in Acts" (Selwyn 1947, 33).

Believers are urged to live their lives in a manner worthy of the holy God who called them to be his people. The imperative **live your lives** (*anastrophēte*) rearticulates the call to "be holy in all you do" (*anastrophē;* v 15). The tense of the imperative is aorist, which "conveys a sense of urgency" to the command (Kelly 1969, 72).

Live your lives is qualified by the phrases **as strangers** and **in reverent fear.** The Greek phrase underlying the word **strangers** is literally: ***during the time*** (*chronon*) ***of your sojourning.*** Time on earth is temporary. Thus, Peter urges believers to live "as aliens residing in a strange land" (Hiebert 1984c, 89).

Christians should also live **in reverent fear** (*en phobōi*). *Phobos* carries a double meaning: ***"terror, fear"*** or ***"reverence, respect"*** (BDAG, 1062). Here, in the context of conformity to God's will, it has the force of "reverence." The phrase *en phobōi* stands emphatically at the beginning of the Greek clause, identifying **reverent fear** as the outstanding character trait of the Christian life. "Fear of displeasing our Father is the obverse side of loving him" (Grudem 1988, 82). Quickened by a reverential respect for their Heavenly Father, who is also their impartial Judge, believers are urged to live in a manner consistent with the holy nature of God himself.

■ **18-19** The foundation for holiness is the redemptive work of Christ: **For you know . . . you were redeemed . . . with the precious blood of Christ. For you know** (*eidotes*) is often used to remind Christians of standardized teaching (see Rom 5:3; 6:9; 1 Cor 15:58; 2 Cor 1:7; 4:14; 5:6). Peter reminded his audience of teaching they had already received (1:25).

The message of vv 18-19 hangs on the main verb **you were redeemed** (*elytrōthēte*). The verb "redeem" (*lytroō*) means "to free by money payment" or "to free by ransom" (Büchsel 1967, 349, 351). The word often described the manumission of slaves or the freeing of hostages with a price or "ransom" (see Morris 1965, 11-27, 39). Used in contrast with such a ransom involving **silver** and **gold** in v 18, the verb at first glance might seem to carry the meaning ***you were ransomed,*** and the price was **the precious blood of Christ.**

But this interpretation has problems. **You were redeemed** is used in the passive voice. And there is no explicit or implicit indication as to whom the price is paid. "Patristic theology spoke of it [ransom] as paid to the devil," but "there seems to be no trace of this in the New Testament" (Best 1971, 89). Moreover, ransom prices were typically identified in the genitive case, but both **silver** and **gold** and **blood of Christ** are in the dative. The dative case seems to identify the means by which the redemption takes place (instrumental means), not the ransom price that was paid.

You were redeemed probably conveys the simple notion of deliverance instead of the idea of ransom. Redemption refers to costly liberation. *Lytroō* ("to redeem") is used over one hundred times in the LXX. There, instead of conveying the idea of a ransom, the term "weakened, especially in the later literature, into the less precise idea of *deliverance,* not necessarily by payment of a ransom, but also by an act of power" (Beare 1961, 77; see Westcott 1974, 296). Thus, **the precious blood of Christ** does not identify a ransom price, but the great cost of Christ's self-sacrifice making possible the deliverance of believers.

Believers were delivered **from the empty way of life handed down to you from your forefathers.** Peter emphasizes once again the necessity of distinctive behavior by believers in contrast to their social and cultural milieu. The description of their former way of life as **empty** (*mataia: **worthless, futile, useless***) reinforces the perspective that Peter's audience was predominantly Gentile. It is unlikely that Peter would describe the traditions of the Jewish people with such a denigrating term. Their rejection of this **empty way of life** caused them to be viewed as "strangers." But the power of Christ's self-sacrifice enabled them to continue to reject any conformity (1:14) to the pervading culture with a steady hope (1:13).

The final phrase describes Christ as **a lamb without blemish or defect.** This description draws upon a variety of OT images. These include the lamb metaphor in the description of the Suffering Servant in Isa 53, the theme of deliverance from slavery in the Passover story, the "faultless and flawless" character of the lamb in the sacrificial system generally, and certain Jewish and early Christian traditions about the young ram offered as a sacrifice in place of Isaac in Gen 22 (Michaels 1988, 66).

This description reinforces the call to moral and ethical purity in the believers' lifestyle. Repeatedly and in a variety of ways, Peter underscores the expectation that the lives of true believers will be distinguished by holiness, by both the separateness and the blamelessness of their conduct.

Substitutionary Atonement?

Peter's statement in 1:18-19 that Christians are **redeemed . . . with the precious blood of Christ** has caused some commentators to conclude that he is describing salvation within the framework of substitutionary atonement (e.g., Hiebert 1984c, 92; Grudem 1988, 84). A careful examination of the background of the term "redeem," however, does not justify this conclusion. The general idea of "deliverance" is more descriptive of the usage of the term "redeem" in the LXX.

Moreover, the reference to the **blood of Christ** may stress life as much as or more than death. Within the sacrificial language of the OT, blood is not representative of death, but of life (Lev 17:14). The sacrificial undertones of Peter's language would seem to emphasize the "life-giving" blood of Christ. This is consistent with the emphasis of ch 1 on the *resurrection* of Christ accentuating his *life* more than his death.

These repeated references to Christ's resurrection stress, rather than an idea of substitutionary atonement, Peter's conception of salvation as made possible by the believers' participation by faith in the resurrected life of Jesus Christ (Powers 2001, 232-34). The deliverance of believers is accomplished through the life-giving power of Christ to believers demonstrated by God's resurrection of Christ from the dead.

1:18 20 ■ **20** God's decision to redeem believers through Christ was not made in haste or as a contingency plan occasioned by human sinfulness. Rather, Christ **was chosen before the creation of the world. Was chosen** (*proegnōsmenou*) means literally ***known beforehand.*** This foreknowledge was "an act of God in eternity past whereby he determined that his Son would come as the Savior of the world" (Grudem 1988, 85).

The use of the Greek *men . . . de* construction creates a vivid contrast. Whereas salvation through Christ was only **revealed in these last times** for the sake of believers, God foreordained salvation through Christ **before the creation of the world.**

Three important concepts are used in v 20 to bolster the courage of Peter's readers. First, God's plan for the salvation of believers through Christ dates back to time immemorial. Even before the creation of the world, God predestined Christ to be the Savior. A plan laid down so long in advance would not be quickly abandoned or revised.

Second, this verse implies Christ's preexistence. One's salvation is only as strong as the Savior on whom it is founded. The salvation of Christians is founded in Christ (1:21), who was preexistent even before the creation of the world in the presence of God the Father.

Third, it was **for your sake** that Christ was chosen. The description of Christ here is "not so much to provide further information about him and his relationship to God . . . as it is to emphasize that all of this occurred for the sake of the people of God" (Achtemeier 1996, 132). The realization that God's plan of salvation through Christ was **for your sake** provides the motivation for believers to obey God's call to "live . . . as strangers" (v 17) and "be holy, because [God is] holy" (v 16).

■ **21** It was **through** Christ **you believe in God, who raised him from the dead and glorified him.** For Peter, the foundation of salvation is the resurrection of Christ. Salvation is only *through Christ* (see Acts 4:10-12), whom God **raised . . . from the dead** and **glorified.** The reference to Christ's glorification encompasses his ascension into heaven, his reception of glory and honor from the Father, and his session at the right hand of God (see Phil 2:9-11; Eph 1:20-23).

As the one who raised Christ from the dead and glorified him, God is the living God. He imparts life to that which seems dead and hopeless. As a direct result, **your faith and hope are in God.** With the repeated reference to **hope,** vv 13-21 can be viewed as an *inclusio.* This is a literary framing device in which the same word or phrase stands at the beginning and the end of a section. **Hope** functions as literary bookends for Peter's exhortation in vv 13-21.

In v 13 Peter began to exhort his readers to "set [their] hope fully on the grace to be given" to them at the appearance of Christ. And he ends in v 21 by affirming that God's power to raise Christ from the dead is the foundation of the believers' faith and **hope** in him. **Hope . . . in God** is emphasized as the ultimate source and end of Christian faith.

There is a new element offered in this repetition of **hope.** It is the implication that the God who raised Jesus from the dead and glorified him will also raise and glorify those who believe and place their hope in him (Michaels 1988, 70).

3. Demonstration of Holiness by Loving One Another (1:22-25)

Peter urges his readers to demonstrate their obedience to God by loving **one another deeply.** As always in the NT, obedience to and love for God are not limited to personal and spiritual life. Rather, true love and obedience to God penetrate daily life and keenly affect the relationship of believers with others (see Mark 12:28-31 and parallels).

■ **22** The emphasis of this section is on the command to **love one another deeply.** This imperative is surrounded by two participial phrases (vv 22, 23) that undergird the injunction.

The NIV renders the first participial phrase as **Now that you have purified yourselves by obeying the truth so that you have sincere love for your brothers.** The Greek participle *hēgnikotes* (***having purified***) is a verbal cognate of *hagios* ("holy") used in the command, "Be holy, because I am holy" (v 15). Thus, the command to **love one another** in v 22 is intimately related to the command for personal holiness articulated in v 15.

The phrase **now that you have purified yourselves** can be interpreted as referring to either conversion or growth in moral purity subsequent to conversion. If it refers to conversion, then **obeying the truth** pertains to "believing the gospel." If it refers to growth in moral purity, then it refers to obedience to God's commands in daily living. Both the context of the call to holiness (v 15) and the linguistic usage strongly favor the latter interpretation (see Grudem 1988, 87-88).

The perfect tense of ***having*** **purified yourselves** indicates a completed event in the past with continuing consequences. In our judgment ***having*** **purified yourselves** refers to the subsequent work of sanctification rather than to conversion. If we are correct, this is a clear reference to both the crisis event of sanctification as a completed event in the past and to the continuing growth and process of sanctification.

Believers undergo this purification **by obeying the truth.** Some find an allusion to baptism in this reference to purification, but this is not readily
1:22 apparent. Instead, the reference to purification echoes the call to holiness (*hagios*) in v 15. Obedience is a recurrent theme in ch 1 (vv 2, 14, 22). It reinforces Peter's message that salvation has both spiritual and ethical implications. Obedience does not effect or earn purification. But Peter asserts that it is more than simply a human attitude. It is active and behavioral, as the resulting command concerning **love for your brothers** implies.

The result of **obeying the truth** is the ***genuine*** (*anypokriton:* "unhypocritical") ***love for your fellow believers*** (*philadelphia*). In secular Greek, *philadelphia* refers to the natural love between brothers and sisters, although it was sometimes used in a wider sense to mean "love of one's fellow countrymen" (Zodhiates 1992, 1444). In the NT, it is always used as an important description of the affection between spiritual brothers and sisters in the faith (see Rom 12:10; 1 Thess 4:9; Heb 13:1; 1 Pet 1:22; 2 Pet 1:7). Peter understands brotherly affection to be a natural byproduct of believers' purification and obedience to the truth of the gospel.

Despite the evidence of ***brotherly love*** (*philadelphia*) among his readers, Peter urges them to **love one another deeply, from the heart.** The manuscript evidence is divided as to whether or not "pure" (*katharos*) should be added to describe the **heart** (KJV: "pure heart"). Scribes tended to expand their texts by adding such adjectives (see Michaels 1988, 72 n. d). Since this is probably such a secondary addition, most recent translations omit the adjective (NIV, NASB, NRSV).

The seemingly redundant parallelism of **love** in this verse demonstrates its importance for Peter. Having affirmed the genuine brotherly affection of believers, he urges them to love one another even more. "Peter's point is that having purified their souls for the express purpose of displaying genuine affection for each other, they must do exactly that" (Michaels 1988, 75).

One cannot miss the central role of love in the **purified** life. "The holy life is first simply and continually letting God in Christ love us to the depth of our need . . . and in turn sharing that love with others" (Carver 1987a, 20).

■ **23** The second participle explains why believers must "love one another" (v 22): because they **have been born again . . . through the living and enduring word of God.**

You have been born again (*anagegennēmenoi*) is a perfect participle. It underscores the fact that the new birth of Peter's audience was a completed event with ongoing consequences. That is, their new birth resulted in continuing and growing love for one another. He contrasts their natural birth and their spiritual rebirth. Their natural birth was the fruit of **perishable seed.** But their new birth was the result of a seed that is **imperishable.** It is imperishable because the new birth is founded upon the **living and enduring word of God.**

Word of God alludes either to the spoken word of God (as in the proclamation of the gospel) or to the written word of God (as in the Bible). Peter quotes Isaiah in vv 24-25, referring to "the word that was preached" in v 25. Thus, both the spoken and the written word of God are probably included.

Peter reminds his readers that their new birth was not the result of a human, philosophical argument or persuasive form of logic. Rather, the new birth is founded on nothing less solid or permanent than the **word of God** that is written in the Scriptures and preached to them.

■ **24-25** The eternal nature of the "word of God" (v 23) is affirmed by a quotation from Isa 40:6-8. Unlike human life that **withers** and falls like the **grass** and **flowers of the field**, the **word of the Lord** (*rhēma kyriou*) **stands forever.** Davids writes:

> Thus Scripture itself proves that God's word, which is the word by which they were reborn, cannot be superseded. And, adds Peter, if by any chance he has not been clear, it is this word which was announced as good news when the gospel was preached to them and they were converted. (1990, 79)

Instead of *logos* as in v 23 Peter, influenced by Isa 40:8, employs *rhēma* to refer to the same reality.

4. Reiteration of the Call to Holiness (2:1-3)

The structure and language of 2:1-3 resemble 1:14-15. In both passages:

- A participial phrase describes the negative aspect of holiness (1:14: ***not conforming*** "to the evil desires you had"; 2:1: ***ridding* yourselves of all malice**).
- An imperative expresses the positive aspect of holiness (1:15: "be holy in all you do"; and 2:2: **crave pure spiritual milk, so that . . .**).
- The simile in both passages employs the imagery of new birth (1:14: "as obedient children"; 2:2: **Like newborn babies**).

■ 1 The main emphasis of 2:1-3 is captured in an imperative verb: "crave pure spiritual milk" (v 2). The participle **rid yourselves** (*apothemenoi*) borrows its imperatival force from the main verb in v 2. But it is not an imperative form. Literally, *apothemenoi* should be translated ***after you have rid yourselves.*** Like several other NT authors, Peter uses the verb to describe vices Christians must avoid or abandon (see Rom 13:12-13; Eph 4:22, 25-32; Col 3:8; Heb 12:1; Jas 1:21).

Believers are instructed to ***put away*** five vices. Each vice would be especially detrimental to interpersonal relationships. The first two vices are singular nouns—**malice** and **deceit,** representing "general attitudes disruptive of community life." The last three are plural nouns: **hypocrisy, envy, and slander,** denoting "practical expressions" of evil (Kelly 1969, 83).

Malice (*kakian*) "is the most general word for evil and wickedness" (Barclay 1960, 224). This is heightened by the adjective **all** (*pas*). *Kakia* gathers up "in one comprehensive term" the others that follow (Beare 1961, 87). It describes the perversity out of which all the other vices arise.

Deceit (*dolon*) specifically connotes cunning or treachery. Originally, *dolos* identified the ***bait*** used in fishing. But it came to be used metaphorically for the attitude of those who use deception to take advantage of others (Hiebert 1984c, 111). **Deceit** is also preceded by the adjective **all**—thus, every kind of deception.

Originally, **hypocrisy** (*hypokriseis*) described the behavior of an actor playing a role obscuring his true identity. This gradually acquired the negative connotations of "a man who all the time is concealing his real motives, a man who meets you with a face which is very different from his heart, and with words which are different from his real feelings" (Barclay 1960, 225).

Envy (*phthonous*) describes the demeanor of those who "wish better for oneself than for the other" (Achtemeier 1996, 144).

The final vice is **slander of every kind** (*pasas katalalias*). *Katalalia* is literally ***evil speech.*** It depicts the practice of "habitual disparagement of others" (Achtemeier 1996, 144). This kind of derogatory and undermining attitude of criticism continually finds fault in others, usually behind their backs. **All** (*pasas*) in conjunction with the plural form of this noun emphasizes that all manifestations of this vice must be eliminated.

Malice, deceit, hypocrisy, envy, and **slander** would be most apt to disrupt and destroy the mutual love to which Peter calls his readers in 1:22. Before spiritual growth can occur, such habits and attitudes must be stripped away.

■ **2** Some have questioned whether **like newborn babies** indicates immaturity among Peter's readers. Those who portray this letter as a baptismal homily contend that **newborn babies** depicts new converts who had just undergone baptism (see Cranfield 1960, 61). But "the point of comparison is not the smallness or innocence of a baby, but its strong and instinctive longing for a mother's milk" (Michaels 1988, 86). Peter urged his readers to cultivate a passion for **pure spiritual milk** in the same way newborn babies single-mindedly crave the nourishment of milk.

Crave is the only imperative verb in the passage. If it is not the letter's central imperative (so Snodgrass 1977, 97), it is certainly important. It uniquely emphasizes the positive orientation of actively seeking what will make them grow as believers (see Pss 42:1; 84:2).

Crave (*epipothēsate*) can be translated as ***yearn, long for, crave, or desire strongly.*** It is the verbal cognate of the noun *epithymia* ("desire"). Peter's wordplay calls for his audience to abandon their old lives dominated by the destructive passions of evil desires (*epithymias;* 1:14) in favor of nourishing cravings.

Believers are to **crave pure spiritual milk.** Elsewhere in the NT the **milk** metaphor is used pejoratively (1 Cor 3:1-3; Heb 5:11—6:2). But there is no negative connotation of **milk** here. "The point here is not that the readers are to advance beyond the stage of immature Christians. Rather, the point is that their desire for such milk is to be as constant and unrelenting as the infant's desire for its milk" (Achtemeier 1996, 146). This nourishment is modified by two adjectives: **pure** (*adolon*) and **spiritual** (*logikon*).

Adolon, "without deceit" and so "honest," is obviously the opposite of the vice **deceit** (*dolon*) in v 1. Believers should hunger for virtue. There is nothing crafty or deceitful about this milk; it is **pure** and ***"unadulterated"*** (BDAG, 21).

Logikon literally means "logical or reasonable" (Zodhiates 1992, 923). But it can be used "in contrast to 'literal'" (BDAG, 598). This is the sense intended here. The **milk** recommended to Christians is not literal milk, but figurative milk. It is a milk that "fits"—the proper nourishment for Christians. In v 3 the metaphor morphs to refer to tasting the Lord (see v 3). Thus, **spiritual** is an accurate option (see Rom 12:1).

Scholars differ as to precisely what **milk** refers. It could allude to the gospel (Selwyn 1947, 154) or to "the sustaining life of God given in mercy to his children" (Michaels 1988, 89). The preceding context suggests that **milk** refers to the word of God (1:23, 25; Davids 1990, 83; anticipated by Wesley 1981, n.p.).

The nourishing word of God enables Christians to **grow up in** their **salvation.** "Only as Christians feed on God's Word will they grow. Nothing can substitute for it" (Nicholson 1967, 279). Just as babies with no appetite for their mother's milk cannot grow, so Christians can only grow into mature believers by satisfying their craving for the knowledge and truth of God's word.

■ **3** With clear dependence on the first line of Ps 34:8, Peter offers the reason why believers can and should crave this milk: **you have tasted that the Lord is good.** The first word in the Greek of v 3 is *ei,* literally "if" (NASB, NRSV). But the NIV correctly takes the particle to assume here "the actuality of the condition" (Achtemeier 1996, 148)—**Now that** . . .

Some contend that **tasted** alludes to the eating and drinking of the Lord's Supper. But it is more likely that **tasted** continues the imagery of milk from v 2. Although **the Lord** refers to Yahweh in Ps 34, here Peter applies it to Jesus Christ (see 2:4). As believers contemplate the goodness of Christ, which they have **tasted** through their redemption and new birth, they are urged to "crave" and drink fervently from the "pure spiritual milk." This milk consists not merely of divine instructions, but of the experience of Christ himself.

FROM THE TEXT

Be Holy. Some contemporary Christians question the fairness of the command to be holy as God is holy. How is this possible given the troubles and pressures of modern society (see Perkins 1995, 37)? Peter's call to **be holy in all you do** (v 15) targeted an audience that knew more than its share of "trials and tribulations." Yet Peter urged them to be holy anyway. Some try to delay the necessity of fulfilling this daunting command. They try to interpret the NT calls to holiness as only a future ideal. They imagine that believers will somehow "inherit" holiness in heaven or on the day of Christ's return (Erdman 1919, 77-78).

Others attempt to relegate the injunction to **be holy** to merely an inner attitude of the heart. As the Holy One who cannot tolerate sin or impurity, God calls us into his presence as his children. Just as a child imitates and follows the example of an earthly father, so believers are called to imitate and follow the holy example of their Heavenly Father: **Be holy, because I am holy.** Earle writes: "An inward holiness which does not manifest itself outwardly will stand the test of neither God nor man" (1955, 401).

Salvation is provided by the death and resurrection of Jesus Christ. Because God raised Jesus from the dead, believers have reason to hope that redemption, forgiveness, and the power for holy living can be theirs (1:21).

The death of Jesus Christ shows just how far God's love will go to save fallen humanity. And it demonstrates how seriously he takes sin.

God's resurrection of Christ from the dead demonstrates his determination to empower his people to overcome the power of sin and death (see Rogers 1959, 10-11). The call to holiness within the daily life and conduct of believers cannot be understood on the basis of the death of Christ alone (see Powers 2001, 231-36). Only through the transforming power of the resurrection is God's impossible command to **be holy** possible: "The one who calls you is faithful and he will do it" (1 Thess 5:24).

The Word of God. Peter claims the new birth of believers depends on the **word of God** (1:23-25). In 1 Peter, this refers to both the proclamation of the gospel and the written Word of God, the Bible. The implications for evangelism are noteworthy. Exemplary lives and persuasive techniques are essential for presenting the gospel to unbelievers—but neither will bring them new life. It takes the powerful **word of God** empowered by the Holy Spirit and applied to their lives.

One essential characteristic of vital and growing Christians is their attraction to the word of God. It is only natural that believers who have **tasted** the goodness of Christ should **crave** the pure spiritual milk found in the Bible (2:1-3). As important as Christian fellowship and public worship are, they can never take the place of Bible study. Scripture is the necessary nourishment of believers who want to grow "in faith, love, holiness, unto the full stature of Christ" (Wesley 1981, n.p.). Any hope to spark a revival of spiritual growth and Christlikeness in our churches and society today will begin with a renewed hunger for the Word of God.

Christian Community. The call to lives of holiness and Christlikeness is a call to community. The sanctification of God's people is not centered in God alone (**Be holy, because I am holy;** 1:16) nor in personal purity alone (**Now that you have purified yourselves;** 1:22). Holiness is demonstrated in the building of a community of believers (**love one another deeply, from the heart;** 1:22). In an increasingly individualistic society, it is easy to imagine that Christianity and holiness are individual pursuits.

But this is not so. "Love for God, purity of self, love for the brother and sister in Christ are all essential ingredients of the community of living hope that 1 Peter seeks to build" (Bartlett 1998, 261). The mutual love of believers is the defining trait of the people of God and the distinguishing mark of true holiness.

> Love is commanded and if we are going to talk about love, we have to move out of the level of liking and emotion and feeling and warmth to the level of the will—a posture, a stance, an attitude, a frame of mind,

> a life's direction toward others that is conditioned by our understanding of God's self-giving in Jesus. (Welch 1973, 103)

Only as members of the *people of God* can believers become the *persons of God* he intended.

Putting Vices Aside. The importance of Christian community for spiritual life and growth is reinforced by the specific vices Peter commands his readers to strip away. Spiritual maturity is possible only when believers eliminate relationally fatal attitudes and habits like **malice, deceit, hypocrisy, envy,** and **slander** from their lives. These attitudes are not only detrimental to Christian community but also equally destructive to the spiritual growth and salvation of individual believers.

B. The New Building of God's People (2:4-10)

BEHIND THE TEXT

Peter shifts to a building metaphor to describe the kind of people that believers are to become. Apparently, the concept of spiritual growth introduced in vv 1-3 prompted the image of a building.

To accommodate this new imagery, in v 4 the image of Christ shifts. No longer described as milk, Christ is now presented as a **living Stone.** It is upon the foundation of Christ, the living Stone, that believers as a community are built into a **spiritual house.** Thus, Peter moves from soteriology to Christology to ecclesiology. He has moved from describing salvation to a description of Christ who made salvation possible, to a description of the saved community—the church. Curiously, Peter never uses the word "church" (*ekklēsia;* three times in Matthew; frequent in Acts, the Pauline letters, and Revelation; twice in Hebrews; once in James; three times in 3 John).

This passage focuses on a series of OT passages using stone imagery. Nowhere else in the NT are the stone images of Isa 28:16; Ps 118:22; and Isa 8:14 brought together in one setting. But since other NT passages use stone imagery, some scholars assume that Peter was dependent on one of these (e.g., Rom 9:25-33; Eph 2:14-22; or the Qumran text 1QS 8.4-10). None of these suggestions is convincing (see Snodgrass 1977, 98-103).

Peter's stone imagery is probably the result of two factors: "(1) direct knowledge of the Biblical text on the part of the author which included personal study; (2) the adaptation of traditional material for the author's own purposes" (Snodgrass 1977, 103). The stone sayings in 2:4-10 may well be Peter's own creation, as he reflected on the relevance of these OT passages to Christ and the church.

The four parts to this section include:

1. Christ, the living Stone (2:4)
2. The church: from living stones to a spiritual house (2:5)
3. Christ, the cornerstone (2:6-8)
4. The church: God's new people (2:9-10)

IN THE TEXT

1. Christ, the Living Stone (2:4)

■ **4** Verses 4-5 form one sentence in the Greek, with several striking changes in focus. The imagery quickly shifts from a "milk" metaphor (v 3) to a building metaphor with Christ as the **living Stone** (v 4) to Christians as "living stones" as part of the spiritual building (v 5), and then to Christians as holy priests "offering spiritual sacrifices acceptable to God" (v 5). Throughout these dramatic shifts, Christ remains the foundational figure of the entire passage. The passage begins (***to whom*** [*pros hon*]) and ends with Christ.

The role of believers is described in the opening words of the passage: **you come to him.** The present participle *proserchomenoi*, **Come**, describes the approach of believers to Christ as an ongoing activity or relationship. This verb "does not refer to the believers' initial commitment to Christ for salvation, but to the voluntary, repeated, or habitual coming of believers to Christ for sustenance and fellowship" (Hiebert 1984c, 119). God's spiritual house is built upon the sustained relationship of Christ with believers, who continually come to him for direction and guidance.

Christ is imaged as the **living Stone** (*lithon*). The adjective **living** (*zōnta*) earlier describes the "hope" of believers (1:3) and the "word of God" (1:23). Both are sources of life (i.e., *life-giving*). Similarly, Christ, the **living Stone,** *gives life* to believers who also become "living stones" by virtue of their relationship with him.

Lithos (**stone**) is the usual word for a dressed stone—one that has been shaped with tools, whether precious stones or those used in constructing a building. "It is to be distinguished from *petros*, a loose stone lying on field or roadside, and from *petra*, a rock, or simply rock in contrast with e.g. sand or metal" (Selwyn 1947, 158).

Some commentators suggest that **living Stone** was inspired by Peter's meditation upon the name given him by Christ (Matt 16:18; John 1:42; see Gundry 1967, 346). But this seems unlikely, since the name Peter (*Petros*) is different from the word used for **Stone** here.

The description of Christ as a **living Stone** seems paradoxical at first sight. To associate "stone" and "living" seems oxymoronic, self-contradictory. The NT frequently uses "stone" as a "metaphor for a lifeless thing, to be contrasted with God (Acts 17:29), with Abraham's children (Matt 3:9; Luke 3:8), or with human beings who can praise God (Luke 19:40)" (Michaels 1988, 98). Did Peter employ this term to depict the resurrected life of one who was "dead as a stone"? As a description of the one God raised from the dead (1:3, 21), the **living Stone** is a vivid and appropriate description of the resurrected Christ (compare the slain lamb standing in Rev 5:6).

Three adjectives describe Christ as the **living Stone: rejected** (by men), **chosen** (by God), and **precious** (to God). All three terms are found in the OT passages Peter will quote in 2:6-8.

2. The Church: From Living Stones to a Spiritual House (2:5)

■ **5** As a result of coming to Christ, believers become **living stones.** They, in turn, **are being built into a spiritual house.** The same phrase describing Christ in the singular in v 4 describes the community of believers in the plural in v 5—**living stones.** The opening words of v 5, ***Even you yourselves,*** emphasize the striking irony of their existence. Although rejected by humans as "strangers in the world" (1:1), believers are precious to God.

The corporate nature of the Christian community is again evident. Believers are not pictured as individual stones, but as a corporate unity—**living stones** connected together, collectively **being built into a spiritual house.**

The indicative verb **are being built** (*oikodomeisthe*) could be construed as an imperative: ***let yourselves be built.*** But this seems unlikely, given the intention of 2:4-10. This "is not moral instruction but a description of the church" (Best 1971, 101). Believers are not urged to *become* **a spiritual house;** they *are* **a spiritual house.**

Christians constitute the **spiritual** (*pneumatikos*; compare *logikon,* "spiritual" in 2:2) **house.** The house is **spiritual** because believers belong to the Spirit (*pneuma*) and the Spirit brings the house into existence. As **a spiritual house** the Christian community is the temple wherein God may be found. Peter implies a proto-Trinitarian understanding of God establishing the church (see 1:2).

Believers are constructed into **a spiritual house** for one purpose: to become **a holy priesthood.** The emphasis of **priesthood** (*hierateuma*) is not on the office, but on the people who function as priests. **Holy** recalls the demand for holiness in 1:15. By calling believers **a holy priesthood,** Peter reminds them that their existence as God's chosen people depends not only on their election but also on their obedience to God. "Whoever fills the office of this priesthood must certainly be holy. Whoever is not holy does not possess it" (Luther 1990, 93).

As **a holy priesthood,** believers offer **spiritual sacrifices acceptable to God.** These are "surely a reference to the whole shape of the faithful life—the life of holiness" (Bartlett 1998, 265). Paul urged his readers in Romans to offer their "bodies as living sacrifices, holy and pleasing to God" (Rom 12:1). Peter had in mind a similar idea. As a **holy** priesthood, believers offer the **spiritual sacrifices** of their own lives, holy and pleasing **to God through Jesus Christ.**

This offering is deemed acceptable to God for two reasons:

- First, because it is **spiritual** (*pneumatikos*)**.** The sacrifices belong to the Spirit (*pneuma*) and are prompted by the Spirit.
- Second, because the sacrifice is offered **through Jesus Christ.** Everything believers do—their worship, praise, deeds of love; in fact, the whole of their Christian life—fits into this broad meaning of sacrifice (see Hill 1982, 60-61).

Peter's description of all believers as **a holy priesthood** provides the basis for the Protestant doctrine of the "priesthood of believers." All believers are **a holy priesthood,** endowed with the privilege and responsibility of offering their lives to God in behalf of others.

In Peter's mixed metaphor, believers are both the stones of the new temple of God and the priests who offer sacrifices there. One image transitions to the other naturally and effortlessly. As Peter describes the church, the images pile up. Christ, the living Stone, enables believers to become living stones. Such stones make spiritual houses. Houses set apart for the worship of God become temples. In such temples priests offer spiritual sacrifices. This collection of images beautifully describes Peter's audience as the new people of God (1:13-15).

3. Christ, the Cornerstone (2:6-8)

BEHIND THE TEXT

The quotations in vv 6-8 appear in the reverse order of the topics introduced in v 4. The focus in v 4 shifts from humanity's rejection of Christ the living Stone to God's election and acceptance of the stone. In vv 6-8 the focus moves from God's election of the cornerstone to humanity's rejection of the stone. The following chiastic (X-shaped or envelope) structure is evident:

A. Stone rejected by humanity (v 4)

    B. Stone elected and chosen by God (v 4)

        C. Believers are stones chosen by God (v 5)

    B'. Stone elected and chosen by God (v 6)

A'. Stone rejected by humanity (vv 7, 8)

In such structures, the main point is found in the central element: Believers are divinely chosen living stones (v 5).

■ 6 Peter cites OT passages utilizing stone imagery. The description of Christ as the stone in vv 6-8 rests on three quotations of which the first (Isa 28:16) refers to the saving significance of the stone (Christ) for the community, while the other two (Ps 118:22; Isa 8:14) refer to the fact that it entails perdition for unbelievers (Jeremias 1967, 277).

Some scholars are uncertain as to the specific source of Peter's quotations (Achtemeier 1996, 159; Selwyn 1947, 163). Perhaps he conceived of this threefold combination of texts himself and added his interpretation at the end.

Peter cites Isa 28 to identify the stone as **a chosen and precious cornerstone** (*akrogōniaion*). The combination of the adjective *akron*, ***high point,*** and the noun *gōnia*, ***corner,*** has led some interpreters to take *akrogōnios* to refer to a ***"capstone"*** (BDAG, 40)—the culmination of a building's construction. However, the **cornerstone** is the foundation stone upon which the entire building rests for support. The significance of Christ for believers is supplied in the second half of the quotation: **and the one who trusts in him will never be put to shame.** Despite the suffering that identification with Christ may bring, he will never disappoint or fail those who trust in him.

■ 7-8 With the stone metaphor, Peter creates a striking contrast between believers and unbelievers. For those **who believe, this stone is precious. Believe** is a present tense verb, denoting the ongoing activity of trusting in Jesus Christ. True faith is not a one-time profession but a persistent way of life. Genuine believers keep trusting in and obeying Christ. Thus, they **will never be put to shame** or ***disappointed*** (v 6; see BDAG, 517 s.v. *kataischynō*).

In Mediterranean society, the opposite of shame and disgrace was honor and favorable recognition. Consequently, for true believers **this stone is precious** (*timē*), that is, ***valuable and honored.*** Just as Christ is "precious" (*entimon*) to God (2:4), he is **precious** (*timē*) to believers. Believers share God's perspective on Christ. Others may reject him, but God and believers honor him.

Peter completes the contrast between believers and unbelievers by citing Ps 118:22 and Isa 8:14. Psalm 118:22 demonstrates "that those who rejected Christ have been proven exactly wrong by God's exaltation of him to the place of greatest prominence, the head of the corner" or the capstone (Grudem 1988, 105).

Not only are unbelievers wrong in their assessment of Christ, but Isa 8:14 demonstrates that they are offended by him as well. Christ is **a stone** (*lithos*) **that causes** unbelieving **men** and women **to stumble and a rock** (*petra*)

that makes them fall. There is a "superficial difficulty" in the double portrayal of Christ as the **stone.** The same **stone** that occupies a place of honor in the building blocks the path of unbelievers. Christ trips and hampers those who reject him. But "the double image is necessary and true. Christ is too great to be neglected or avoided" (Beare 1961, 99).

In the final phrase of v 8, Peter explains why unbelievers stumble. First, they stumble **because they disobey the message.** The verb **disobey** is in the present tense. Unbelievers continuously disobey the message of Christ. As long as they persist in stubborn disobedience, they will stumble and fall.

Second, unbelievers stumble and disobey because that is **what they were destined** to do. The implications of this are problematic. Some find "double predestination" within this passage. Namely, God not only foreordained some people to be saved but also foreordained others to disobey and be condemned.

But this is not the only plausible reading of the text. **Were destined** (*etethēsan*) or "were . . . appointed" (NASB) is the same verb used in the quotation in v 6: "See, I lay [*tithēmi*] a stone in Zion." Thus, vv 6-8 form a single unit of thought:

> The matching verbs do not represent two distinct "appointings" but one with a twofold result. . . . In the single act of raising Jesus from the dead (1:3, 21), God has laid the "choice and precious Stone" that means honor and vindication for those who believe, but stumbling and shame for the disobedient. (Michaels 1988, 107)

By establishing the resurrected Christ as the cornerstone or capstone of the temple for his new people, God offers two contrasting human destinies: salvation for those who accept Christ through faith, and destruction for those who reject Christ. In both cases, the ultimate destiny of human beings depends on their personal relationship with Christ. Some were not destined to reject and disobey Christ. But for those who do, destruction is their divinely appointed destiny. God did not arbitrarily decide beforehand that certain individuals should be lost. Their own decisions determine their destiny. Their persistent rejection and disobedience to Christ brings destruction in its train. As Oecumenius commented on 1 Pet 2:8 in the sixth century: "God is not to be held responsible for this, for no cause of damnation can come from him who wants everyone to be saved. It is they who have made themselves into vessels of wrath, and unbelief has followed naturally from that" (cited in Bray 2000, 87).

4. The Church: God's New People (2:9-10)

■ **9** Peter concludes this section of the letter with a fourfold description of the people of God. They are **a chosen people, a royal priesthood, a holy nation,**

a people belonging to God. Each expression is built around a singular noun. This reinforces that believers are a collective unity. All four nouns are introduced by the emphatic **But you** (*hymeis de*). This refocuses attention on the contrast between believers and unbelievers (v 8). All four descriptions were first applied to Israel in Exod 19:6 or Isa 43:20-21.

The phrase **chosen people** (*genos eklekton*) is from Isa 43:20. *Genos* means ***species, type, or kind.*** It designates a family or race of people based on their common origin. It echoes the theme of new birth in 1:3, 14, 23; and 2:2.

This is the last time the word **chosen** (*eklekton*) is used in this letter. But it plays an important role in Peter's understanding of the people of God (1:1; 2:4, 6). Because of their identification with Christ, believers enjoy the status of **chosen people.** Christ constitutes them corporately as an ***elect species*** of people before God. Just as Israel traced their identity and election through Abraham, believers are a "new people" who trace their identity and election through Jesus Christ.

The phrases **royal priesthood** and **holy nation** are borrowed verbatim from Exod 19:6 in the LXX. There they identify Israel as God's people. Peter boldly describes believers with terms formerly reserved for Israel alone.

Believers were called "a *holy* priesthood" in v 5 (emphasis added); now they are **a royal priesthood** (emphasis added). As a **priesthood,** believers possess the special privileges of priests. They enjoy a unique closeness to God
2:9 as they perform holy service in his honor in behalf of others. They are **royal** by virtue of their service to Christ the King. "Every believer has both a royal function derived from Christ's kingship and a priestly one derived from His priesthood" (Kelly 1969, 98).

Believers also constitute **a holy nation. Nation** (*ethnos*) denotes a group of people who share common customs, laws, and practices. Their common identity with Jesus Christ has made believers one **nation,** despite their different ethnic and geographical roots. **Holy** describes them as ***set apart*** for God in their conduct and service.

The final description of believers as **a people belonging to God** is from Isa 43:21. **People** (*laos*) may be used to refer to people as united (Strathmann 1967, 33). First, *laos* underscores the solidarity of a group of people. Second, in the OT *laos* is "a specific term for a specific people . . . to emphasize the special and privileged religious position" of Israel "as the people of God" (Strathmann 1967, 32). This sense of ownership finds explicit expression in the phrase **belonging to God** (*eis peripoiēsin*; i.e., ***intended for possession***). Believers are people claimed by God as his special possession.

Each element of this fourfold description poignantly portrays the body of believers. The perspective of God stands in contrast with that of the world.

"The issue for the people of 1 Peter is their status in the eyes of God versus their status in the larger world in which they are despised exiles" (Bartlett 1998, 267). The world may see them as exiles and strangers, stumbling and straying, but God considers them his special people, precious and elect.

The purpose of believers' special position is **that** they **may declare the praises of him who called** them **out of darkness into his wonderful light.** God redeemed believers, not for their personal enjoyment, but so they could glorify him. **Declare** (*exangeilēte*) is found only here in the NT. But it is used repeatedly in the OT to ***tell forth*** or to ***announce*** God's praise (see Pss 9:14; 71:15; 73:28; 79:13; 107:22; 119:13, 26). Believers were **called out of darkness into his wonderful light.** They witness to God's deliverance by proclaiming his word (1:25; 3:15) and by the holiness of their lives (1:15; 2:11—3:7).

■ **10** Peter concludes with an allusion to Hos 1—2. As a result of the deliverance and salvation of his Gentile audience, Peter notes the irony. Those who **were not a people** have now become **the people of God.** And those who **had not received mercy** have now **received mercy.** As Gentiles, Peter's readers had not always enjoyed this favored status. Furthermore, their status could not be attributed to their own merit. Rather, they have become a special people only by virtue of God's mercy revealed in Jesus Christ.

FROM THE TEXT

Corporate Identity and Unity of Believers. Peter describes the new people of God collectively rather than individually. The **spiritual house** of God is not constructed like a mosaic, consisting of individual and isolated stones oblivious to the existence of other stones. Instead, the new "temple" is constructed from the collective unity of believers as **living stones.** Peter's true interest was in the corporate identity and unity of the believers.

> The free lance Christian, who wishes to be a Christian but is too superior to belong to the visible Church on earth in one of its forms, is simply a contradiction in terms. Everywhere the Bible presupposes a people of God. That is every bit as true of the New Testament as of the Old. The Scriptures know nothing of an individual piety that is out of touch with the living body of God's people. (Cranfield 1960, 63)

Priesthood of Believers. Peter clearly establishes the background for the doctrine of the priesthood of believers. All believers are depicted as **a holy priesthood** for the purpose of **offering spiritual sacrifices acceptable to God through Jesus Christ** (2:5). As such, the old boundaries separating "priest" and "congregation" are wiped away. Through Christ, all believers enjoy direct access to God.

But with the privileges of this special priesthood comes the responsibility to be **holy.** Believers are not **holy** because they belong to the priesthood of believers. They belong to the priesthood of believers only because they are **holy.** Obedience to the call to holiness underscores Peter's teaching of the priesthood of all believers.

God's Chosen People. The fourfold description of Christians in 2:9 emphasizes that they enjoy the privilege of being God's chosen people. Old Testament language describes Christian believers as God's chosen and elect people. This is not to suggest that the church has replaced Israel (see Achtemeier 1996, 167). Peter is noticeably silent regarding the relationship between the church and Israel.

Paul's discussion in Rom 9—11 indicates that Israel cannot be easily dismissed from its elect status. God has not turned his back on Israel; rather, "God's gifts and his call are irrevocable" (Rom 11:29). Nonetheless, both 1 Pet 2:4-10 and Rom 9—11 insist that union with Christ is a prerequisite for experiencing the covenant blessings of God for both Jews and Gentile believers. Salvation is never gained by virtue of one's ethnic, national, or other identity. It is the reward of an ongoing personal relationship with God through Christ.

Peter's depiction of believers in 2:4-10 reminds his Gentile audience that salvation and divine favor are not the result of human merit or inherent goodness. They reveal God's mercy through the death and resurrection of Jesus Christ.

IV. THE LIFE OF GOD'S PEOPLE: 1 PETER 2:11—3:12

BEHIND THE TEXT

In v 11 the focus of the letter shifts dramatically. The previous section (1:13—2:10) consisted of theological teaching with occasional practical application. By contrast, this section is mostly practical with a few brief theological points. That is, here Peter spells out the ethical implications of being God's holy people within a hostile world. In the previous section, he exhorted his audience to "be holy" (1:15), "love one another" (1:22), and to trust God (1:13, 17, 21). Here, Peter instructs them on the practice of holiness and trust in God in real life situations.

First Peter 2:18—3:7 offers guidance on Christian conduct in the home. Luther called such lists of domestic duties *Haustafeln*—German for "household tables." The *Haustafeln* in 1 Peter are structurally similar to those in Eph 5—6 and Col 3. In each, guidelines are given to slaves, husbands, and wives. Paul's lists also include directives to parents, children, and masters.

Peter's ethical teachings can be divided into two major arenas: life in the world (2:11-17) and life at home (2:18—3:7). The general principle for behavior in the world is presented in 2:11-12. Explicit instructions for civic duties are explained in vv 13-17. The directives for behavior in the home are broken down into instructions for slaves (2:18-25), wives (3:1-6), and husbands (3:7). In 3:8-12, Peter concludes his discussion of the everyday life of God's people with a series of practical directions for the entire Christian community.

IN THE TEXT

A. Living as God's People in the World (2:11-17)

■ **11** Peter addresses his readers as "beloved" (*agapētoi;* NASB), a word rarely found in non-Christian Greek literature (Achtemeier 1996, 173). This word is used frequently and broadly within the NT (e.g., Rom 12:19; 1 Cor 10:14; 2 Cor 7:1; Heb 6:9; Jas 1:16, 19; 2 Pet 3:1; 1 John 2:7; 3:2; Jude 3). It may have been the usual term for addressing a Christian congregation in sermons (Cranfield 1960, 69). The term is particularly fitting here since love was emphasized in 1:22 as the characteristic quality of God's holy people. The word ***beloved*** (NIV: **dear friends**) carries a double connotation. It expresses Peter's personal affection for his readers as well as the love God has for all of them.

The word *parakalō* (**I urge you**) often introduces ethical teaching. This instruction applies the theological considerations of the previous section. Literally, *parakaleō* means to ***"call to one's side."*** But here it connotes ***"urge, exhort, encourage"*** (BDAG, 764-65). By using this term, Peter does not so much command his readers as appeal to their own sense of how they should behave in light of God's acceptance of them as his holy and chosen people. The first step toward a holy lifestyle is the sober realization and contemplation of God's act of deliverance through Jesus Christ.

The readers are addressed **as aliens and strangers in the world** (see 1:1, 17). These believers live in a place that is not their true home. Peter uses words originally applied to these Christians as terms of derision and scorn to contrast their lifestyle from that of unbelievers. Since this world is not their home, believers should not live as if they were part of the world. Rather, **as aliens and strangers in the world,** they should **abstain from sinful desires, which war against** their **soul.**

Abstain means literally ***"be distant"*** or ***"keep away"*** (BDAG, 102-3). Its present tense denotes an ongoing activity: Christians must constantly abstain from sinful desires (compare 1:14). A contrast is drawn between the flesh and the soul, against which these desires battle. The phrase **sinful desires** means literally ***fleshly desires*** or ***desires of the flesh*** (*sarkikōn epithymiōn*).

Obviously, "flesh" and "soul" are opposites in this passage. But Peter does not presume the Greek philosophical notion that the body is inherently evil and spirit is inherently good. Rather, the term "flesh" refers to human self-centeredness, life apart from God. As such, any **desire** that does not conform to the will of God is "fleshly" or **sinful.** Peter uses the term "flesh" here in essentially the same general way as Paul (see Rom 8:3-8; 1 Cor 3:1-3 NASB). "Flesh" here does not refer only to blatantly "sinful" activities. Even good and wholesome activities can become an obstacle in the lives of believers. Thus, it applies to anything that can compromise their relationship with God.

"This is the only NT passage where *psychē* (soul) plainly stands in antithesis to *sarx* (flesh)" (Schweizer 1974, 653). The juxtaposition of these terms makes it tempting to interpret them in the conventional way of distinguishing soul and body as different parts of human nature. But we must resist. In 1:9 *psychē* denotes "the whole man as a self or person" (Cranfield 1960, 72).

Peter's instruction, then, is for believers to make it a practice to abstain habitually from any desires that do not conform to the holy character of God. They must avoid "fleshly" desires because they undermine (*strateuontai*; "**do military service**" [BDAG, 947] or ***wage war against***) the very essence of the human "personhood" to which God called them as his elect people.

To actualize their calling as God's holy and chosen people in their daily lives, believers must abstain from thoughts or actions that might attack and threaten that calling. This is the general principle that underlies all of Peter's specific ethical instructions in this passage.

■ **12** While v 11 concerns the inner spiritual principle for the believers' lives, v 12 concerns the outward conduct required of believers. As always, personal holiness precedes and must result in social righteousness.

Verses 11 and 12 form one sentence in the Greek. A present participle in v 12 connects the instructions of these two verses. A literal translation would be: ***I urge you to abstain . . . having good behavior*** (*anastrophēn*) ***among the pagans.***

In 1:15, the behavior (*anastrophēi*) of Christians was described as "holy"; here it is described as **good** (*kalēn*). In 1:15 and 17, Peter emphasized that behavior was the arena in which believers practiced their holiness and reverence to God. In 2:12, the emphasis "is on conduct that can be seen and appreciated as 'good' (*kalē*) even by fellow citizens who are not believers in Christ" (Michaels 1988, 117).

There is no tension between the descriptions of their conduct as **good** and **holy.** The difference lies in the perspective of the observers. The conduct God and believers consider **holy** should be considered **good** by their pagan neighbors. "Doing good" is one of the principles underlying many of Peter's ethical instructions (see 2:12, 15-16, 20; 3:1-2, 6, 13, 16; van Unnik 1954, 99-104).

The purpose of this "good" lifestyle is so that unbelievers **may see** the **good deeds** of believers **and glorify God on the day he visits us.** This may be expected even though unbelievers may initially **accuse** them **of doing wrong.** Early Christians were often falsely accused on political grounds as enemies of the state, on religious grounds as atheists, and on ethical grounds as introducing unlawful customs (see Ball 1966, 260). Peter urges Christians to live in such a way as to refute such false accusations.

The expression **on the day he visits us** (***in a day of visitation***) can refer either: (1) to some intermediate day of intervention at which time unbelievers will be converted by virtue of their observation of the lifestyle of the believers or, (2) to the last day of judgment (that is, "the day of visitation"; see Isa 10:3; Jer 6:15; Luke 1:68; 19:44; Wis 3:7-8; *1 Clem.* 1:3). Most interpreters take this phrase to refer to the Last Judgment (see Michaels 1988, 120; Achtemeier 1996, 178). But the context of this verse seems to favor the former meaning. Thus, Peter refers to an indefinite "day of inspection." Then unbelievers will finally (collectively or individually) recognize the legitimacy of the message and lifestyle of believers and come to salvation themselves (Grudem 1988, 116-17). Peter calls his readers to **live such good lives** that unbelievers will be led to conversion by their good example.

Verses 11-12 are programmatic for the rest of the letter. Peter identifies the general principle that must underlie the conduct of believers in every aspect of their lives, whether in the community or at home. Even in the midst of suffering, this general principle should be the guiding rule of believers' lives: Christians living in an unbelieving and hostile world must avoid sinful desires and continuously maintain an exemplary lifestyle. As a result, unbelievers will be saved and God will be glorified.

■ **13-14** Peter offers explicit instructions as to how this general principle should be lived out, first, in the public arena (2:13-17) and, second, in the privacy of one's home (2:18—3:7). The instructions for the home are further divided into instructions for slaves (2:18-25) and for spouses (3:1-7). Submission is the recurring theme of this section. Note the repetition of the imperative verb **submit yourselves** (***be submissive***) in 2:13, 18; and 3:1—at the beginning of each of these three subdivisions.

In the first section (2:13-17), the readers are enjoined to submit themselves **to every authority instituted among men** (*pasēi anthrōpinēi ktisei*). That is, "Submit yourselves ***to every human creature***" (see Jeremias 1964b, 366). This translation is bolstered by Peter's reference to the **king** and **governors,** not institutions, as that to which his readers must submit (vv 13-14). Thus, the principle is established that "the redeemed Christian life must not be self-assertion or mutual exploitation, but the voluntary subordination of oneself to others (see Rom 12:10; Eph 5:21; Phil 2:3)" (Kelly 1969, 108-9).

The theological justification for this submission is **for the Lord's sake.** The believer is not submissive and obedient to a government for the sake of the government, but for the sake of the Lord. Christ gave an example of submission during his earthly ministry—a point Peter will reflect upon in greater length in 2:21-24. And so it is *for his sake* that believers submit.

This phrase also limits submission, "for submission can never be to anything that [the Lord] does not will" (Davids 1990, 99). Where the will of a government might conflict with God's will, the phrase **for the Lord's sake** reminds believers that their ultimate allegiance is to Christ alone.

In vv 13*b*-14, Peter identifies two civic authorities as examples of those to whom his readers were to be submissive: **to the king, as the supreme authority, or to governors, who are sent by him.** The word **king** (*basilei*) was the title used by people in the East to designate the "Emperor" (see Deissmann 1978, 362). Likewise, the word **governors** (*hēgemōsin*) was often used for rulers the emperor appointed to carry out his commands in the various regions of the empire (see Matt 27:2; Acts 23:24).

The phrase **who are sent by him** probably does not refer to God, but to the emperor. It was the emperor who sent out **governors** throughout the empire (Achtemeier 1996, 183). The purpose of governors explains the purpose of civil governments. Peter briefly defines this purpose as **to punish those who do wrong and to commend those who do right.** Most civil governments seem more adept at punishing wrongdoers than at commending those who do right. And yet Peter (and Paul in Rom 13:1-4) identifies both the positive and negative roles of those given civil authority.

■ **15-16** The point of these two verses is simply put: Believers should subordinate themselves to others in order to silence their critics (v 15) and honor God (v 16).

Verse 15 offers two reasons why such submission and good deeds are needed. First, **it is God's will** (see v 13: "for the Lord's sake"). Second, it will **silence the ignorant talk of foolish men.** This undoubtedly refers to the false accusations of wrongdoing mentioned in v 12. In the LXX the **foolish** (*aphronōn*) designates "the arrogant unbeliever who sets himself up against truth and right" (Kelly 1969, 111).

Good deeds will **silence** (*phimoun;* "tie shut" or to ***"muzzle";*** BDAG, 1060) baseless slanderous talk. The winsome lives of believers will prove the accusations against them foolish and false.

Verse 16 contains no main verb: ***As free, and not using freedom as a cover-up for evil, but as servants of God.*** The verse undoubtedly intends to describe the lifestyle of those who do God's will by doing good.

Believers are free to do the will of God. Such freedom can never serve **as a cover-up for evil.** For illustrations of how professing Christians might abuse freedom as an excuse for morally and ethically irresponsible behavior, see 1 Cor 5:1-2; 6:12-20; 2 Pet 2; and Jude 4.

In v 16, the opening phrase **as free men** and the final phrase **as servants of God** appear to be oxymoronic. But this is not a contradiction. They capture the paradox of the Christian life. Michaels writes, "Christians are free from all that bound them in the past, but at the same time they are slaves of God committed to full and unqualified obedience (see Rom 6:18, 22)" (1988, 128). Freedom from the past enables Christians to serve God, to be what God originally intended humans to be.

■ 17 Peter's instructions for life in the world conclude with four vibrant imperatives. The first is in the aorist tense. The other three are present imperatives. Because of this, some consider the first command the main statement and the others specific applications of the first. But all four imperatives probably carry the same force, to be understood within a chiastic (X-shaped, envelope) structure:

A. Honor everyone

B. Love the brotherhood of believers

B'. Fear God

A'. Honor the king

The imperatives in A and A' use the same verb root (*timaō; **honor*** or ***show respect***), which connects the two. Thus, A and A' define the proper attitude of believers toward those "outside" the Christian community. Likewise, B and B' identify the attitude believers must have for "insiders." Christians must love one another deeply and reverence God. Peter earlier called for brotherly love and reverence of God in 1:22 and 1:17.

Note the subtle but apparent contrasts within these four injunctions.

- First, the attitude required of believers toward God versus the king: While the king should be given proper respect (*timate*), God alone should be feared (*phobeisthe*). The honor due the king (*timate*) is no different from that due to every person (*timēsate*).
- Second, the attitude required of believers toward every person versus brothers and sisters of the faith: Whereas every person should be treated with proper respect (*timēsate*), fellow believers should be loved deeply (*agapate*). Believers should respect every person and civic au-

thority. But their highest priority and responsibility is toward God and other believers.

FROM THE TEXT

The Life of Holiness. Peter calls believers to **abstain from sinful desires, which war against your soul** (2:11). They must resist any kind of human desire that would prevent them from being the kinds of persons God created them to be. As **aliens and strangers** in a transient world, believers must remember that they are true citizens in an everlasting kingdom. Christians must beware of allowing the finite outlook of their social world to hijack their values, ambitions, or activities. Even interests that are not inherently sinful can divert our attention from serving God and living holy lives.

When the interests and values of this world threaten to defeat our reborn selves, they become sinful. They contradict the kind of person believers have become in Christ. The essence of holiness is Christlikeness. When believers pursue the world's values instead of Christ's, they violate the command to **be holy, because** God is **holy** (1:16).

Christians must resist sinful desires and maintain an exemplary pattern of life. This fleshes out God's command to **be holy, because I am holy.** Holiness is not simply an attitude of the heart; it must be an orientation of one's life. Holiness of heart and life is not simply for the believer's own sake. Peter's instructions have a decidedly evangelistic concern. Holy living can be compelling and redemptive for unbelievers. An exemplary Christian life is one of the best strategies for evangelism.

Early in the eighth century, the Venerable Bede wrote, "It often happens that pagans who once reviled the faith of Christians, because they had abandoned their gods, stop doing so after they see what a holy and pure life they lead in Christ" (cited in Bray 2000, 91). The great fourth-century preacher John Chrysostom similarly endorsed the evangelistic power of a truly Christian lifestyle: "There would be no more heathen if we would be true Christians" (cited in Latourette 1975, 99).

Christians and Politics. What is the responsibility and role of Christians within civic and political affairs? Most Christians agree that this question is of great importance. Few agree on the answers, sometimes taking opposite views. Some think government should be controlled by Christians in some form of a theocracy. Others sincerely believe true Christians should avoid involvement in the government.

Finding the "right" answer is complicated by the fact that the NT writers themselves take diverse perspectives on the relationship between believers and the government. The book of Acts tacitly affirms the leadership and wisdom of Rome. It seems confident that the leaders of the empire will rule favorably toward the new Christian movement. In contrast, Revelation portrays the empire as the Babylonian harlot, who drinks "the blood of the saints" (17:5-6).

Within this wide array of perspectives, 1 Peter occupies a mediating position. Civic authorities are not divinely established authorities who must be obeyed (contrast Rom 13:1-7). Nor are they blood-thirsty adversaries (contrast Revelation). Rather, civic authorities are simply a "given." Government exists to punish wrongdoers and commend those who do good. Thus, the emperor should be respected, as every person should be.

Within the turbulent arena of politics, where extreme viewpoints seem to be the rule, Peter's mediating position is refreshing. Political discussions, even among believers, are seldom civil, but instead devoid of mutual courtesy and respect. Into this maelstrom of passionate debate and partisan disagreement, Peter interjects a calming voice.

B. Living as God's People in the Home (2:18—3:7)

BEHIND THE TEXT

Peter's first set of instructions for the home pertains to slaves. Slavery in the first-century Mediterranean world was unlike American slavery before the Civil War. Slavery through kidnapping, for example, was virtually eliminated by the Roman Empire in the first century B.C. While there are some similarities, the differences are vast and significant. Bartchy elaborates on these differences:

> Racial factors played no role; education was greatly encouraged (some slaves were better educated than their owners) and enhanced a slave's value; many slaves carried out sensitive and highly responsible social functions; slaves could own property (including other slaves!); their religious and cultural traditions were the same as those of the freeborn; no laws prohibited public assembly of slaves; and (perhaps above all) the majority of urban and domestic slaves could legitimately anticipate being emancipated by the age of 30. (1992, 66)

Slavery was a widespread and basic foundation for the propagation of ancient Greco-Roman society. When Peter was writing this letter, "Slaves constituted better than 50 percent of the population of major cities" (Mounce 1982, 34).

The quality of life of slaves depended almost entirely upon the character and mood of their owners. "Greco-Roman slave systems and legal frameworks gave slave owners much room to be cruel or compassionate" (Bartchy 1992, 69). For good or ill, slave masters owned the bodies of the slaves as well as their work. This is the social context of the slavery that Peter addresses in this section of his letter (see Achtemeier 1996, 190-93).

IN THE TEXT

I. Instructions for Slaves (2:18-25)

a. Submission (2:18-20)

■ 18 Peter first addresses the **slaves.** Similar household guidelines can be traced back as far as Plato and Aristotle. They were perpetuated by Stoics and Hellenistic Jews in the NT era (Balch 1981, 25-56). But slaves are never specifically mentioned in pre-Christian domestic codes. Peter may have devoted so much space to slaves "because a large proportion, perhaps the bulk, of his correspondents belonged to this class" (Kelly 1969, 115).

The general principle of submission to every person (2:13) is repeated with specific reference to slaves: **Slaves, submit yourselves to your masters with all respect.** The word for **slaves** here, *oiketai,* is somewhat rare (elsewhere in the NT only in Luke 16:13; Acts 10:7; Rom 14:4). It refers explicitly to "household servants." Such slaves probably belong somewhere between the *doulos,* a servile bond-slave, and the *diakonos,* a voluntary servant. Household slaves "were more exposed to suffering from the vices and bad tempers of their masters, than those in the field" (Macknight 1969, 462). But there is little evidence that they experienced more suffering than other slaves.

The verb translated **submit yourselves** is a participle. Its imperatival force depends on the context provided by 2:13, where believers are exhorted to submit to every human creature. Slaves are to submit themselves to their masters **with all respect** (*en panti phobōi*). The word *phobos* can be translated with **respect** or ***fear.***

The context suggests that Peter summoned slaves, not to reverence their masters, but to submit to them out of reverence (*phobos*) for God. Believers are to fear God alone, and not any human (3:6, 14). Thus, **with all respect** (= ***with all fear***) provides the spiritual motivation for slaves to submit to their masters. This interpretation is strengthened in v 19 by the mention of God as the reason for enslaved believers to endure unjust punishment from their masters.

Masters could be either **good** (*agathois*) or bad. Peter exhorted Christian slaves to submit themselves **not only to those who are good and considerate** (*epieikesin, **"gentle, kind, courteous, tolerant,"*** BDAG, 371), **but also to those who are harsh** (*skolios, **"crooked, unscrupulous, dishonest"*** [BDAG, 930]). Crooked masters not only physically abused their slaves but were "also dishonest regarding pay, working conditions, expectations, etc." (Grudem 1988,

126). Motivated by the reverential fear of God, Christian slaves were to submit to their masters—fair or unfair, kind or cruel, just or unjust.

■ **19-20** Justification (**For,** *gar*) for this difficult command is provided here. The phrase **it is commendable** translates the word *charis*, usually translated "grace" in the NT (see 1:2). The same word appears again at the end of v 20 (**this is commendable before God;** *charis para theōi*). Although *charis* typically refers to God's freely given favor, here it means "credit"—"that which counts with God or that with which God is pleased" (Michaels 1988, 139). Jesus used the word *charis* with this meaning in Luke 6:32-35. God is pleased with slaves who bear **up under the pain of unjust suffering.**

The phrase **because he is conscious of God** provides the spiritual basis for Christian slaves to submit. The ***credit*** or ***commendation*** believers seek is not from people but from God. Peter does not expect a Stoic endurance of suffering motivated by personal tenacity and self-awareness. Rather, he calls for Christian slaves to endure unjust suffering because they know God and desire to please him.

Verse 20 reiterates v 19 more explicitly, specifying **a beating** as an example of the unjust suffering slaves might have to **endure.** Here, the word **credit** translates *kleos* (contrast v 19), its only occurrence in the NT. This synonym for *charis* means ***"fame"*** or ***"glory"*** (BDAG, 547). It is closely related to the word ***commendation*** (*epainos*) in 2:14 (van Unnik 1956, 199). There is no glory for enduring a beating for doing wrong. There is only credit **if you suffer for doing good and you endure it.**

The last phrase, **this is commendable** (*charis*) **before God,** repeats *charis* as ***credit.*** The reference to God reinforces Peter's advocacy of accepting suffering, not for its own sake. Suffering is commendable only when it results from being "committed to God's will . . . [D]evotion to him overrides personal comfort" (Blum 1981a, 235).

Peter did not write to perpetuate or facilitate the social structure of slavery. Rather, he encouraged slaves to endure unjust suffering for the sake of the Lord in order to catalyze the hopes and intentions mentioned in 2:12 and 15. Namely, believers were to live such exemplary lives that the baseless accusations of unbelievers would be silenced and they would be brought to conversion. This explains why the spiritual motivation behind the endurance of unjust suffering is emphasized so prominently.

Slaves were to endure unjust suffering ***out of the reverential fear of God*** (v 18), because they were **conscious of God** (v 19), and because **this is commendable before God** (v 20). Apart from this motivation, suffering is simply suffering. But when unjust suffering is endured for the sake of God and his will, it becomes an evangelistic tool.

Peter includes no admonition to owners in his domestic code (contrast Eph 6:9; Col 4:1). Perhaps he perceived the position of slaves as representative of all believers. Their status was typical of Christian "aliens and strangers in the world" (2:11). He describes all believers as "God's slaves" in 2:16 (see Achtemeier 1996, 192). His directive to slaves was applicable to all believers. "In the midst of circumstances that provide a vulnerable life, the slave is to live in a way irreproachable either to humans or to God." Thus, slaves serve "as a paradigm for the way Christians, as vulnerable in society as the slaves are in their household, are to live in the midst of hostile surroundings" (Achtemeier 1996, 194).

b. Example of Christ (2:21-25)

BEHIND THE TEXT

Peter's discussion of the endurance of unjust suffering leads naturally to the example of Christ. Ultimately, the life of Jesus—including his death and resurrection—is the foundation for all NT ethics. Although the context pertains to slaves, the example of Christ is relevant to every Christian who suffers injustice.

The fourth Servant Song of Isa 53 forms the framework for Peter's depiction of the suffering of Jesus. This is evident not only in the quotation of Isa 53:9 in 1 Pet 2:22 but in other phrases borrowed from this Servant Song (e.g., "he bore our sins/infirmities" [1 Pet 2:24/ Isa 53:4]; "by his wounds you/we are healed" [1 Pet 2:24/ Isa 53:5]; "we/you like sheep have gone astray" [1 Pet 2:25/ Isa 53:6]).

Some interpreters have argued that 1 Pet 2:21-25 is derived from an early Christian hymn based on Isa 53. But the arguments are not compelling (see Michaels 1988, 136-37). It is more likely that Peter created these reflections based on his contemplation of Isa 53 in light of the passion of Christ.

Peter's excursus on the suffering of Christ has a twofold purpose. First, Christ is lifted up as an example of the endurance of unjust suffering (vv 21-23). Second, the sufferings of Christ remind his audience of the saving benefits of his passion (v 24). He reminds those suffering that their salvation was a result of the obedience of Christ, which led him to suffer and die on their behalf. This was intended to reinforce their motivation to exemplify Christ in their own suffering, even if unjust.

IN THE TEXT

(1) Christ as the Model (2:21-23)

■21 Peter provides a christological foundation for the endurance of unjust suffering. This is a part of Christian vocation: **to this you were called.** The example of Christ in the following verses demonstrates that the demonstrative pronoun **this** does not refer to slavery per se, but to unjust suffering. Suffering in the lives of Christians is not an accident or glitch in the plan of God. It is part and parcel of their calling. The verb **you were called** (*eklēthēte*) is a divine passive. That is, God is implicitly identified as the one who calls Christians to suffering.

The verb for **called** (*kaleō*) typically refers to God's saving call in Christ. It is "a technical term for the process of salvation" (Schmidt 1965, 489). The immediate goal of God's calling is holiness (1:15). The specific application of the call to holiness within the context of 2:21 is the call to do good, even when it means suffering.

Christians are called to endure unjust suffering **because Christ suffered for** them. This statement is similar to the early creedal statement: "Christ died for you/us" (1 Thess 5:10; 1 Cor 15:3; 2 Cor 5:14, 15; Rom 5:6, 8; 14:15). Peter adapted the creedal statement by changing "died" to "suffered" to make it more applicable to his audience's context (see Achtemeier 1996, 198).

The significance of Christ's suffering and death is that they were **for you** (*hyper hymōn*). Christ suffered and died *on behalf of* believers, for their *benefit*. Rather than some forensic substitution, the phrase *hyper hymōn* presupposes "an existing solidarity or unity between Christ and the believers" (Powers 2001, 142). This fits seamlessly into Peter's use of this adapted creedal formula here.

The solidarity between Christ and believers is made explicit in Peter's explanation of Christ suffering **for you.** He did so to leave **you an example, that you should follow in his steps.** The suffering of believers is modeled after the exemplary suffering of Christ. He is **an example,** *hypogrammon* (only here in the NT). The term was used to describe the model children would use to trace the letters of the alphabet (Schrenk 1964b, 772). As children learned to write by following an existing pattern, so believers were to trace the pattern of Christ in their lives in order to realize their call to holiness.

Peter added that believers were to **follow in his steps. Steps** (*ichnesin*) can mean *"footsteps"* or ***"footprint***[s]" (BDAG, 485). Some consider this as a call to imitate Christ. But this plea "is not that slaves should attempt to reproduce all the particular details of Christ's passion." It is that they should "move in the direction he is going" (Kelly 1969, 120). This is a call to discipleship—to follow after him. Peter is clear: The suffering of Christ is not efficacious for those who only observe the call of Christ. His suffering is efficacious only for those who obey him. In Augustine's apt words, "Christ's passion profits none but those who follow in his footsteps" (cited in Bray 2000, 94-95).

■22-23 Christ's response to unjust suffering was the pattern (v 21, *hypogrammon*) of behavior believers were to follow. Peter underscores the innocence of Jesus by citing Isa 53:9. This text certainly testifies to the sinlessness of the Servant (**no deceit was found in his mouth**). But its main point was to demonstrate that Jesus' suffering was unprovoked and undeserved. He endured this in silence. Verse 23 is not dependent on Isa 53 in word or phrase. Nonetheless, it applies the Servant Song to the example of Jesus' own reaction to suffering in two different ways.

First, negatively, Peter highlights what Jesus did not do. In the face of insults and suffering, **he did not retaliate** and **he made no threats.** Unlike the Maccabean martyrs, who called down God's vengeance and judgment upon their persecutors (2 Macc 7; 4 Macc 10), Jesus was silent in his own defense.

Second, positively, Peter outlines what Jesus did do: **he entrusted himself to him who judges justly.** The verb **entrusted** (*paredidou*) means ***handed over, delivered, committed*** (BDAG, 762). Its imperfect tense indicates a repeated past action, qualifying perhaps Jesus' entire incarnate career. In other words, when he was suffering Jesus kept on entrusting his situation to God, knowing that God would judge the situation justly.

Carver suggests that Jesus "kept entrusting Himself" to God in two ways:

> One, He recognized the "justice" of His suffering on behalf of sinners; such was necessary to bridge the gap between a holy God and sinful man. It was right for love's sake that such shame, pain, and curse be His, for in it the righteous God was righteously judging sin. To suffer in the likeness of Christ is to participate in the bridge that unites God and man! Two, Jesus was entrusting himself to God for His ultimate vindication as the Righteous One by His resurrection. In His suffering as the sinless One for sinners, Jesus committed all personal justification to His Father. (1987b, 97)

The example of Christ establishes a pattern for the Christian response to unjust suffering. Believers not only emulate the example of Christ but also participate in the kind of life Jesus lived on our behalf (see Carver 1987b, 96).

(2) Christ as Savior (2:24-25)

■ **24** The portrayal of Christ changes in v 24. In vv 22-23, Peter's reflection on Jesus' suffering draws him into a discussion of its saving effects. "Christ was not only a Model but a Mediator" (Ball 1966, 263). The transition in vv 24-25 from the second person plural (**you**) to the first person plural pronoun (**we**) is one aspect of this shift. Christ, the ethical example, gives way to Christ, the Redeemer. The language of v 24 depends heavily on Isa 53, especially v 4 ("Surely he took up our infirmities and carried our sorrows"), v 11 ("And he will bear their iniquities"), and v 12 ("For he bore the sin of many").

The phrase **he . . . bore our sins** is unique. It does not simply reflect traditional sacrificial rites. The verb **bore** (*anēnegken*) is used in the LXX for carrying a sacrifice and laying it on the altar (e.g., Gen 8:20; Lev 14:20). But there is no OT precedent for anyone bearing **sins** and laying **sins** on the altar. Some suggest that Peter depended on the image of the scapegoat (Lev 16) or some other Levitical sacrifice. But it is more likely that he used general sacrificial language to portray the significance of Christ's death.

The verb **bore** is in the aorist tense. It indicates a definite event, not a repeated action as with the imperfect tense of "entrusted" in v 23. The words **in his body** emphasize that Jesus' redemptive suffering was as a real human being. Peter reminds his suffering readers that Christ also suffered as he bore their sins. The word **tree** (*xylon, **wood***) is used in Acts (5:30; 10:39; 13:29) to refer to the (wooden) cross on which Jesus died. The word choice may allude to the curse attached to one hung on a tree (see Deut 21:22-23; Gal 3:13). The allusion heightens the significance of Christ's voluntary, undeserved death for the sins of others.

Christ died to produce new life in those who believe. Christ died for this purpose (*hina*): **so that we might die to sins and live for righteousness.** The verb *apogenomenoi*, **die,** does not occur in the LXX and is found only here in the NT. It means "to be afar off, separated, take no part in" (Büchsel 1964, 686). In classical Greek, the word meant "to die," as in "to cease to be what one was before" (Zodhiates 1992, 220). The word is used here in contrast to **live;** thus, to **die.** One purpose of Christ's death was to bring an end to the former sinful lives of believers.

In addition, Christ's death enables believers to **live for righteousness.** Here, **righteousness** (*dikaiosynēi*) "denotes the high standard of moral behavior expected of Christians" (Kelly 1969, 123). It echoes the call to holiness expressed in 1:15. Christ's victory over sin and death enables believers to share in his experience of separation from sin and a life set apart for righteousness (see Rom 6:11). This expectation is the basis for the Wesleyan understanding of sanctification.

In the last phrase of v 24, Peter quotes from Isa 53 again. This time Isa 53:5: **by his wounds you have been healed.** The word **wounds** (*mōlōpi*) refers to the welts left on the body by the stripe of a whip. The bodies of slaves undoubtedly carried wounds and bruises from undeserved beatings. The identification of their **wounds** with those of Jesus must have provided a poignant illustration of their participation in the life of Christ.

Like Isa 53:5, Peter uses physical healing as a metaphor for spiritual wholeness. The words **you have been healed** do not insinuate that conversion will automatically result in physical healing. Rather, they point to the spiritual reality that believers can be restored to health from the wounds of past sins.

■ 25 The phrase **sheep going astray** is from Isa 53:6. The past of Peter's audience was an "empty way of life" (1 Pet 1:18), a life of "ignorance" (1:14). Here it is compared to **sheep going astray.** This is a clear reference to their pagan past.

The verb **have returned** (*epestraphēte*) does not imply a relationship with Christ before they strayed away. This verb is used frequently in the NT to describe "turning" or "being converted" from sin (Acts 3:19; 9:35; 11:21; 14:15; 1 Thess 1:9). A striking contrast is created by the aorist tense of the verb **have returned** in comparison to the present tense of the verb **going astray.** "The aorist looks at the decisive action in contrast to their former habitual wandering" (Blum 1981a, 236). They were once lost and wandering without any direction in their lives. Now, they have decisively and deliberately come to where they belong.

Through conversion, believers have come **to the Shepherd and Overseer of** their **souls.** Both terms are used of God in the OT ("shepherd": Gen 48:15; Ps 23; "overseer": Job 20:29 LXX; see Wis 1:6). Here, they describe Christ (see also 5:4). The image of sheep in v 25*a* inevitably elicits the description of Christ as **Shepherd**. He feeds, protects, leads, and cares for his sheep. **Overseer** (*episkopon*), sometimes translated "bishop," refers to one who inspects and keeps watch over others. **Shepherd** and **Overseer** are closely connected here. Both terms reinforce the watchful, protective care of Christ.

Peter vividly portrays Christ:

- As Example, he is the pattern for believers.
- As Savior, he atones for their sins.
- As Shepherd and Guardian, he protects, feeds, and oversees his followers.

Such a Christ is superbly able to help them bear their righteous suffering.

FROM THE TEXT

Christlikeness and Suffering. The call to holiness and Christian discipleship is often a call to suffering. The NT does not promise a carefree life in this world. On the contrary, those who heed the call of Christ often face hardship and suffering (John 14:18; Phil 1:29; Heb 13:13; Jas 1:2).

Sentimentality is often attached to Jesus' call to his followers: "Take up [your] cross and follow me" (Mark 8:34; see Matt 10:38; Luke 14:27). But the reality of this call is a forewarning of hardship, suffering, and ultimately death. Perhaps no one captured the essence of this call more vividly than Dietrich Bonhoeffer, who wrote, "When Christ calls a man, he bids him come and die" (1959, 99).

Many believers expect the path to Christlikeness and holiness to be paved with social acceptance, prosperity, and ease. But in reality, righteousness/holiness more often follows a narrow path that encounters difficulty, rejection, and pain. It is not a path created by convenience for oneself, but one created by devotion to Christ. Suffering is not chosen because it is popular, easy, or enjoyable. It is, however, the path Jesus himself walked. The question is not whether our path following Christ will involve suffering or pain. It is whether our love and obedience to Christ is enough to keep us following him anyway.

Victory over Sin. The heart of the gospel is articulated in v 24: **He himself bore our sins in his body on the tree, so that we might die to sin and live for righteousness.** "Few statements in the NT exceed this in theological import" (Mounce 1982, 37). The Christian teaching of salvation and forgiveness of sins is founded upon this reality. Jesus did not die a tragic death on the cross. He bore our sins on the cross and died as a representative of all sinful humanity. This is the life-transforming conviction of all believers. This makes the sacrificial act of Jesus on the cross different from the countless other sacrificial and noble acts of others who died unjust deaths.

When God raised Christ from the dead, he affirmed that the power of sin had been broken once and for all. But this is only true for those who identify themselves with Christ by faith and obedience. Just as Christ died for our sins and was raised to new life through his resurrection from the dead, so believers are called to die to sin and live for righteousness. Jesus did not bear our sins on the cross only so that believers could be forgiven. His resurrection power also enables believers to rise above sin and truly live for righteousness. Victory awaits those who heed the call of Christ to holiness, which means truly following after him!

2. Instructions for Wives (3:1-6)

BEHIND THE TEXT

The purpose of Peter's instructions for families (*Haustafeln*, see the Behind the Text comments on 2:11—3:12) is quite different from Paul's similar domestic codes in Colossians and Ephesians. Peter's guidelines appear in the context of his discussion of suffering.

> The omission of an address to masters, the shortening of the address to Christian husbands, and the lengthening of the addresses to slaves and women were changes that the author of 1 Peter made to the *Haustafel* to fit his specific purpose of writing to Christians suffering in non-Christian homes and living in what were really situations of persecution. (Bauman-Martin 2004, 267)

The unique background of persecution and suffering that underlies these instructions must be kept in mind.

The instructions to wives (3:1-6) are notably longer than the corresponding instructions to husbands (3:7). This probably has a simple sociological explanation. In antiquity the conversion of married women was more problematic than the conversion of married men. It was customary for wives to adhere to the religion of their husbands.

The instructions to wives can be divided into three parts: (*a*) the basic exhortation (3:1-2), (*b*) an elaboration on true beauty (3:3-4), and (*c*) a biblical example (3:5-6).

IN THE TEXT

a. The Basic Exhortation (3:1-2)

■ **1** The writer now turns his attention to the relationship of marriage. Married women are addressed first: **Wives, in the same way be submissive to your husbands. In the same way** does not mean that wives must submit to their husbands like slaves submit to their masters. The participle translated **be submissive** connects this verse to the basic command to all believers to "submit yourselves for the Lord's sake to every authority" (lit., ***to every human creature;*** 2:13). "Wives are to express their submission 'to every human creature' by their submission to their own husbands" (Davids 1990, 115).

The admonition to wives to be submissive to their husbands is not a unique directive for women only. The command **be submissive** is the underlying theme of this entire section (2:13—3:7). Moreover, the submission of wives to their husbands was not an ideal peculiar to the Christian faith. Rather, it was a societal norm in first-century Greco-Roman society (Balch 1981, 97-99; see Achtemeier 1996, 206-7). Thus, Peter's injunction to wives to be submissive to their husbands "is not a matter of theological principle so much as it is a matter of avoiding unnecessary conflict" (Achtemeier 1996, 209).

The command to **be submissive** is not necessarily a theological principle. But the purpose of spousal submission is decidedly theological, more specifically, evangelistic. Peter enjoins Christian wives to submit to their husbands **so that, if any of them do not believe the word, they may be won over.**

The word is a reference to the gospel message about Jesus Christ (see 4:17). The phrase **do not believe** (*apeithousin*) describes something more than passive disbelief. It portrays "those who deliberately and persistently set themselves against the claims of the gospel" (Hiebert 1984c, 184): they "do not obey the word" (NRSV). This verb strongly suggests the active opposition of pagan husbands to the Christian faith. "Though women are enjoined to be subordinate to their husbands, this passage does not suggest that they are to endure abuse in silence" (Perkins 1995, 57).

The conditional phrase **if any of them do not believe** implies that some wives have Christian husbands. Peter's focus, however, is clearly on the wives of non-Christian husbands. This is clear from his hope that **they may be won over.**

The verb **may be won over** refers to conversion. Paul uses the same verb to explain his goal of winning as many people to Christ as possible (1 Cor 9:19-22). The result Peter envisions is not merely the cessation of opposition and hostility toward the Christian faith by unbelieving husbands, but their positive and wholehearted conversion.

The means by which Peter expects these husbands to be converted is **without words by the behavior of their wives. Behavior** (*anastrophēs*) plays a crucial role in 1 Peter (see 1:15; 2:12). The holy behavior (*anastrophē*) of Christian wives (including submission) may result in the conversion of their husbands.

The phrase **without words** (***a word***) does not prohibit wives from speaking about their faith to their husbands. Rather, it is a verbal play on words with the previous phrase **if any of them do not believe the word.** "Those who are impervious to the proclaimed word of the Christian gospel can and will be changed by the unspoken testimony of their own devoted wives" (Michaels 1988, 158). Where words fail, the powerful testimony of a holy life prevails.

■ **2** This verse is "redundant" (Michaels 1988, 158). It essentially repeats the thoughts expressed in the latter part of v 1. Unbelieving husbands will be won over **when they see the purity and reverence of your lives.** The participle **when they see** (*epopteusantes*) was used in 2:12 to describe the impact of the good deeds of Christians on unbelievers in general—they will be converted. In 3:2, the word portrays the husband's close, eyewitness observation of the daily conduct of his wife.

The phrase **of your lives** translates *anastrophēn,* which refers once again to the ***behavior*** of Christian wives. It is modified with the adjective ***pure*** (*hagnēn*). The pure conduct of wives is not limited to sexual chastity, although it would include it. It "denotes that purity in character and conduct that should characterize all of the Christian life" (Hiebert 1984c, 185).

The word **reverence** (*en phobōi*) can be translated ***in fear.*** Literally, v 2 can be rendered as ***when they observe your pure behavior with fear.*** The reference to ***fear*** (*phobos*) does not describe the wives' respect for, or fear of, their husbands (see v 6, where Peter counsels wives not to fear their husbands). Rather, *phobos* describes the wives' reverent attitude toward God. Thus, the motivation for submissive wives is the same as the motivation for submissive slaves (see 2:18). The foundation of their submission is their ***reverential fear*** of God.

Contemporary readers may fail to note the radical attitude toward wives (and women in general) reflected here. What is surprising is not that wives are enjoined to submit to their husbands. This was traditional during this era in Greco-Roman society. What is surprising is the way they are addressed. Peter addresses them "as independent moral agents whose decision to turn to Christ he supports and whose goal to win their husbands he encourages. This is quite a revolutionary attitude for that culture" (Davids 1990, 116). Far from undermining and undercutting the value and role of Christian women, Peter's instructions insist upon their innate value and spiritual importance.

b. An Elaboration on True Beauty (3:3-4)

Peter's attention shifts to a discussion of true beauty. A contrast is created between a woman's external adornment and her inner character. These verses do not dictate a specific dress code for women nor do they prohibit certain types of adornment. Instead, they emphasize the eternal, unfading beauty of her inward character in contrast with the transient attraction and value of external adornment.

This excursus on beauty is not irrelevant to the injunction to wives in vv 1-2. Peter realizes that the kind of beauty that will win pagan husbands to Christianity is not external. It will be the inner beauty of **a gentle and quiet spirit** (v 4).

■ **3** The Greek construction of vv 3-4 is awkward. But the meaning is clear enough: True beauty is not outward (v 3) but inward (v 4). Verse 3 describes the **outward adornment** that is not a trustworthy gauge of true beauty. Peter's negative example consists of three parallel clauses: (1) ***braiding of hair,*** (2) ***putting on of golden things,*** (3) ***wearing of clothes.***

> The incorporation of all three into his appeal suggests that Peter's interest is not so much in denouncing certain modes of dress for their own sake, as in making the more general point that outward adornment—of any kind—is not what counts in the sight of God. (Michaels 1988, 160)

Some have interpreted these words to mean that women should not braid their hair or wear golden jewelry. But this viewpoint cannot be sustained for, by the same reasoning, one would also have to prohibit women from wearing clothing. Peter's point is not to prohibit these, but to insist that they fail to show a woman's true beauty.

■ **4** The focus of v 3 is negative. But the focus of v 4 is positive: "Virtue is one garment that the Christian woman can wear with pride" (Davids 1990, 118). The phrase **inner self** is literally ***the hidden part of the human heart.*** The term

heart (*kardia*) regularly identifies the seat and center of human life. The ***heart*** represents who a person truly is at the deepest and most personal level. The ***hidden part*** (*kryptos . . . anthrōpos*) of the heart accentuates the inward sphere. For Peter, the essence of feminine beauty is determined not by outward personal adornment but in the sphere of the inward attitudes of the heart.

The attitude of the heart is further depicted as **the unfading beauty of a gentle and quiet spirit.** Literally, this is ***the imperishable adornment or quality of a gentle and quiet spirit.*** The adjective ***imperishable*** (*aphthartōi*) in 1:4 describes the inheritance reborn believers may expect. In 1:23, it characterizes the seed by which believers are reborn. Here, the imperishable quality that constitutes true beauty likewise belongs to Christian women because of their conversions.

Characteristic of this inherent and supernaturally endowed beauty is **a gentle and quiet spirit.** The term *praeōs* describes a woman "as gentle, considerate, and unassuming in [her] relations to others" (Hiebert 1984c, 188). The adjective **quiet** (*hēsychiou*) describes "a spirit that calmly bears disturbances created by others and that itself does not create trouble" (Verbrugge 2000, 235). Wesley notes, "A meek spirit gives no trouble willingly to any; a quiet spirit bears all wrongs without being troubled" (1981, n.p.). There is nothing distinctively feminine about **a gentle and quiet spirit.** These same character qualities are recommended to both men and women elsewhere in the NT (e.g., 3:16; 1 Cor 4:21; Gal 6:1-2; 1 Thess 4:11; 1 Tim 2:2).

The value of **a gentle and quiet spirit** is not that it pleases husbands of Christian wives, although this is true enough. It **is of great worth in God's sight.** The phrase **of great worth** (*polyteles*) means literally "extravagance" or "lavish expense." Secular literature used the phrase regularly in traditional denunciations of wealthy women and their adornments (Michaels 1988, 161). Peter boldly uses it here in a positive way. The irony only heightens the stark contrast between human and divine values. The world's sense of beauty requires extravagant and expensive clothing and adornment. God's sense of beauty elicits an extravagance of inward beauty, characterized as the submission of a gentle and quiet spirit.

The phrase **in God's sight** makes the difference. God views **a gentle and quiet spirit** as a lavish adornment. Such a spirit will inevitably be beautiful to others, including unbelieving husbands. But most importantly, it is **of great worth** to God. Once again, the spiritual motivation of pleasing and fearing God is Peter's major consideration.

c. A Biblical Example (3:5-6)

■**5** Peter points to wives in the OT as examples of the submissive beauty he prescribes to Christian wives. He describes these women as **holy** because they were among God's chosen people, set apart for God alone. They were distinguished from other women because they **put their hope in God.**

Hope plays a key role in this Epistle. It is the steadfast confidence and conviction that God will be true to his promises. Peter reminds Christian wives that it was this quality of submissive gentleness and quietness with which OT women made **themselves beautiful** (***adorned themselves***). The final phrase of v 5 picks up the primary theme of Peter's instructions throughout this section: **They were submissive to their own husbands.**

■**6 Sarah** was the first of the submissive OT wives Peter mentions. She **obeyed Abraham and called him her master.** The reference to Sarah's obedience is somewhat surprising. In the NT household codes (1 Pet 2:18—3:7; Col 3:18—4:1; Eph 5:22—6:9), slaves and children are commanded to be "obedient" to masters and parents, but elsewhere never wives. Wives are to be "submissive" to their husbands.

Another surprising element of Peter's example of Sarah is the phrase Sarah **called him her master** (*kyrion*). The Greek word *kyrios* is typically translated "Lord," "master," or "sir." The word *kyrios* for **master** here undoubtedly depends on Gen 18:12. There Sarah refers to Abraham as her "master" (LXX: *kyrios*). This word probably implied to Peter the concept of "obedience" as a natural corollary. Besides, the word "obedience" would be a welcome stylistic variation from the preceding repeated word "submission" (Michaels 1988, 165).

Despite the reference to obedience here, it is not the definition of submission commended in this passage. Sarah's obedience is instead an example of submission. "As Sarah is one example of the holy women mentioned in v 5, so her obedience is one example of the subordination of which the author is speaking (vv 1, 5)" (Achtemeier 1996, 215).

The second half of v 6 describes Christian wives as children of Sarah. **You are** (= ***have become***) **her daughters** (*hēs egenēthēte tekna*) is a "historical aorist" (Hiebert 1984c, 190). The aorist denotes a past action, and it undoubtedly refers back to their conversion. They proved themselves to be Sarah's daughters by their similar conduct (see John 8:39).

Verse 6 concludes with two present participles (***doing good*** and ***not fearing any fear***). Some interpreters assign these participles a conditional force: Christian wives *become* Sarah's daughters **if** they **do what is right** and **if** they fear no one. But this "would imply that the readers were believing women through their good works" (Best 1971, 127). Conversion is never portrayed in the NT as a result of good works. But it is certainly evidenced by good works.

Thus, it is better to understand these participles as having a complementary force. The present participles reflect actions that completed and demonstrated the wives' conversion. Doing good works and fearing no one are the *result* of their faith, not the *condition* of their faith.

The inclusion of the participle **and do not give way to fear** probably refers to the current situation of Peter's female readers. He "can hardly be thinking of anything else than the intimidation that might be attempted by a husband displeased with his wife's new faith" (Beare 1961, 131). Sarah's exemplary obedience is combined with the command not to be fearful. This encourages women to do what is right, despite the opposition of their pagan husbands. In this way, Peter's instructions are paradigmatic for the way all Christians should live under hostile and threatening circumstances (see 3:14)—without fear.

3. Instructions for Husbands (3:7)

■ **7** Peter's instructions to husbands are much shorter than to slaves or wives. This brevity can probably be attributed to two factors. First, the reference to "joint heirs" in v 7 (RSV) indicates that mixed marriages are not in view here. Second, societal expectations dictated that wives should adopt the religion of their husbands. The marital complications of mixed marriages were far less troublesome for Christian husbands.

Husbands are commanded to **be considerate as you live with your wives, and treat them with respect.** There are no main verbs in v 7. The main verb is probably again to be inferred from the imperative of 2:13, where Peter calls upon his readers to submit themselves to every human creature. This seems to be the intention of the opening phrase **in the same way.**

Verse 7 consists of two participial phrases coupled with two comparisons. These phrases are literally ***living together according to understanding*** and ***showing honor.*** The first way husbands must fulfill their obligation of submission (2:13) is by living with their wives with understanding. The comparison coupled with the first phrase is literally ***as a weaker vessel as the woman.*** Greco-Roman society generally considered women to be physically weaker than men (Kelly 1969, 133). The comparative adjective **weaker** suggests that Peter considered both men and women frail vessels. The implication is not that women (or wives) are weak and men (or husbands) strong.

It is possible that wives were considered **weaker** because of their role in marriage. Her voluntary submission to her husband made her "vulnerable, open to exploitation" (Foh 1979, 133). But Christian husbands must not take advantage of their wives' marital vow of submission. Rather, they should live together with understanding.

Second, Christian husbands must ***show honor*** to their wives. The comparison coupled with this second participial phrase reminds husbands that their wives are ***also co-inheritors of the grace of life.*** Christian wives are equal to their husbands in spiritual privilege and eternal importance. The superior status of men in secular society does not carry over into the Christian community. In the spiritual realm, God considers men and women equals (see Mark 12:25; Gal 3:28).

In the last phrase of v 7, Peter provides a practical reason why husbands should conduct themselves with honor toward their wives: **so that nothing will hinder your prayers.** The word translated **hinder** is a military term referring to throwing obstacles in the way. The verb **hinder** (*enkoptesthai*) is in the passive voice (***will be hindered***). It probably is a divine passive. That is, God will not hear or heed the prayers of husbands who behave inappropriately toward their wives.

C. Conclusion: Practical Instructions to the Christian Community (3:8-12)

■ **8 Finally** signals the conclusion of the section; **all of you** emphasizes that the whole church is addressed. Peter concludes his *Haustafeln* with general instructions for Christians in any situation (vv 8-9), followed by an OT citation to drive his point home (vv 10-12).

The ethical instructions in v 8 utilize five adjectives. These are as prescriptive as descriptive of the Christian community. The first and fifth adjectives describe the way one should think; the second and fourth, the way one should feel. These four depend on the central adjective calling for mutual love. This chiastic (X-shaped) structure, highlighting love, can hardly be accidental.

The first adjective calls believers to **live in harmony with one another** (*homophrones;* ***likeminded***). Believers need not share identical opinions; but they should share a common focus on the Lord (see Phil 2:2; 3:12-15). Christians live in harmony with one another because they share the mind of Christ (see Rom 15:5).

The second adjective is **sympathetic** (*sympatheis;* ***sharing common feelings***). Christians should be ready to share the feelings of others—to "rejoice with those who rejoice" and "mourn with those who mourn" (Rom 12:15).

The third adjective is ***brotherly love*** (*philadelphoi*). Its central position among the adjectives underscores that Christian love underlies all five characteristics. The call to family-like mutual love among believers is almost certainly derived from Jesus' command to "love one another" (John 13:34-35).

The fourth adjective, **compassionate** (*eusplanchnoi*) denotes the deepest of human emotions. The verbal form of this cognate family of words appears in the Synoptic Gospels describing Jesus as deeply moved emotionally (see Matt 9:36; Mark 1:41; Luke 7:13).

The fifth adjective is **humble.** It "marks the inner attitude of those who are voluntarily submissive to authority over them" (Hiebert 1984c, 199). These five characteristics are hallmarks of Christian community life.

■ 9 The discussion moves to the proper response of Christians to abusive people in a hostile world. The natural response to hostility is retaliation. The emphatic adverb *tounantion* (***on the contrary***) introduces the supernatural response Peter expects from believers: **Do not repay evil with evil or insult with insult** (see Rom 12:14, 17; 1 Cor 4:12; 1 Thess 5:15).

Instead of seeking revenge, Christians should respond by calling down God's **blessing** upon those who abuse them. **Blessing** (*eulogountes*), a present active participle, denotes the ongoing attitude and activity of believers toward those who revile them. "To 'bless' someone is to extend to that person the prospect of salvation, or the favor of God" (Michaels 1988, 178). As in 2:12, Peter presumes that the good lives and works of believers may result in the conversion of their opponents.

But here, the habitual blessing of others has a personal benefit. Christians bless others **because to this you were called so that you may inherit a blessing.** It is not that believers earn their inheritance by their works. Rather, they may jeopardize their inheritance, if they fail to conform to behavior appropriate to believers (see Rom 2:6-10; 14:10; 2 Cor 5:10; Eph 6:8; 1 Pet 4:4-5).

The phrase **to this you were called** (see 2:21) enjoins slaves to endure unjust suffering, as Jesus did. The example and teaching of Jesus undoubtedly provide the background for Peter's injunction to believers to bless those who revile them (see Matt 5:43-44; Luke 6:37-38).

■ 10-11 Peter supports his ethical exhortations with a quotation from Ps 34:12-16. These verses provide a fitting conclusion to Peter's instructions. His audience would find the psalm's theme of God's deliverance of the oppressed appropriate to their situation (Achtemeier 1996, 226).

The psalm offers four bits of advice for all who **would love life and see good days.** The terms **life** and **good days** in Ps 34 focus upon present blessings. By connecting this citation with "inherit" in v 9, Peter broadens the application to include the blessings of future salvation.

The citation parallels the ideas of the previous verses, in different words. "The themes of vv 8-9 reappear in reverse order in vv 10-11 in the quotation from Psalm 34:12-16" (Best 1971, 129). The phrase **keep his tongue from evil and his lips from deceitful speech** reflects the prohibition in v 9 against retaliating with insults. The words **he must turn from evil and do good** relates to the injunction in v 9 to repay evil with blessing. Finally, the phrase **seek peace and pursue it** echoes Peter's positive instructions in v 8.

■ **12** The closing words of the citation describe both the positive and negative sides of the divine response. On the one hand, **the eyes of the Lord are on the righteous and his ears are attentive to their prayer.** Believers should persevere in good works and righteous behavior because the Lord is watching them and hearing their prayers. But **the face of the Lord is against those who do evil.** That is, God will punish those who do evil (4:5; see Ps 34:16*b*). God can be trusted to reward and punish justly.

FROM THE TEXT

Wives and Submission to Christ. Peter instructs wives to submit to their husbands. Undergirding his instructions is the radical presupposition that women have the spiritual capacity and the personal freedom to make important individual decisions about their faith. Because wives possess freedom in Christ, Peter urges them not to abuse their freedom in Christ by feeling superior to their pagan husbands. Instead, they should become model wives of virtuous conduct and righteous submission. The motivation for submission is not fear of their husband's disapproval or retribution, but their reverential fear toward God.

Thus, the submissiveness of Christian wives is ultimately not to their husbands, but to Jesus Christ. Peter does not call for social conformity, but for a radical Christian stance that marks Jesus Christ as truly Lord. Christian wives (and all believers) should live out their faith so transparently, even in unsympathetic and threatening situations, that those who observe their righteous and virtuous conduct may be won to the faith.

Prayer and Christian Conduct. Peter mentions prayer as a normal and essential element of the Christian life. He takes for granted "that where there is true religion in right exercise, there is prayer as a matter of course" (Barnes 1962, 1417). As important as prayer is, however, it is useless unless accompanied by proper conduct. The Hebrew prophets and early Christian tradition clearly emphasize the inherent connection between worship and behavior (see Isa 1:10-17; Amos 5:21-24; Matt 5:23-24; 1 Cor 11:20-29; Jas 4:2-3).

First Peter echoes this conviction in his household codes. It is an illusion that one's relationship to God need not affect one's relationship to other people. Rather, the relationship of believers with God affects every other relationship, inside and outside of the family. But the converse is also true. Ruptured and inappropriate human relationships endanger our relationship with God (3:7).

V. SUFFERING AS BELIEVERS: 1 PETER 3:13—4:19

BEHIND THE TEXT

This section of 1 Peter is understood by some as "the main section of the letter" (Kelly 1969, 139). It deals explicitly with the problem of suffering inflicted upon believers. The suffering alluded to earlier in the letter (1:6-7; 2:12, 15, 19-21; 3:9) here becomes the central theme. Peter encourages his beleaguered readers to stand strong and steadfast in the face of suffering.

This portion of 1 Peter can be divided into five sections, each with the basic theme of suffering:

1. The blessing of suffering for righteousness (3:13-17)
2. The example and victory of Christ (3:18-22)
3. Freedom from sin (4:1-6)
4. Living for God (4:7-11)
5. Participation in Christ's suffering (4:12-19)

A. The Blessing of Suffering for Righteousness (3:13-17)

■ 13 The rhetorical question, **Who is going to harm you if you are eager to do good?** is closely related to the quotation in 3:10-12. It affirms God's blessing upon those who "seek peace" and "do good." The implied answer to the question in v 13 is "No one." This is not to suggest that true Christians will not face persecution. Rather, it assures them that, regardless of the suffering they might experience, nothing can ultimately harm them (see Rom 8:31). Augustine wrote, "If you love the good, you will suffer no loss, because whatever you may be deprived of in this world, you will never lose God, who is the true Good" (cited in Bray 2000, 103).

■ 14 The emphatic phrase **but even if** implies that people are not normally persecuted for doing good. But such suffering cannot be ruled out. Acknowledging this possibility, Peter writes, **But even if you should suffer for what is right, you are blessed.** Peter uses the optative mood of the verb, rare in the NT, to address the "sporadic reality" of suffering for his widely scattered audience (Achtemeier 1996, 231).

The suffering Peter speaks about is not a result of failures on the part of believers. It is for doing **what is right** (*dikaiosynē; "**righteousness**"* or "**upright behavior,**" BDAG, 248). Unlike Paul, who uses *dikaiosynē* to describe "justifying righteousness," the term here describes the righteous deeds that flow out of justification. Peter addresses the suffering his audience experiences precisely because they are Christians.

When one suffers for doing what is right, the result is blessing (**you are blessed;** *makarioi: "**happy,**"* BDAG, 610). This echoes Jesus' beatitude: "Blessed [*makarioi*] are those who are persecuted because of righteousness, for theirs is the kingdom of heaven" (Matt 5:10). *Makarioi* does not describe those who are merely happy, but those on whom God's blessing rests. Different words for **blessing** are used in 1 Pet 3:9 and 1:3 than in 3:14 and 4:14:

> The first (*eulogētos*), found in 1:3 with a cognate form in 3:9, focuses attention on the divine source of the blessing. The second (*makarios*), used in 3:14 and 4:14 as also in the Sermon on the Mount, concentrates on the happy result. (Polkinghorne 1969, 593)

To the promised **blessing,** Peter adds the command, **Do not fear what they fear; do not be frightened** (see Isa 8:12 LXX). Throughout 1 Peter, *phobos*, **fear,** has a positive connotation as the reverential awe God deserves (1:17; 2:17; 3:2). Here, Peter reminds Christians that the only one they should

fear is God. If they fear God alone, there is no need for terror in the face of any kind of danger.

■ **15** The negative commands of v 14 prepare the way for the positive command in v 15: **But in your hearts set apart Christ as Lord**. This citation of Isa 8:13 substitutes **Christ** for "Lord God." Typical of Peter's high Christology, he simply assumes that Christ is coequal with God.

To **set apart** (*hagiasate*) can mean to ***"sanctify,"*** *"make holy,"* or **"set aside**." Here, however, it means **"to treat as holy, *reverence"*** (BDAG, 9-10; see Hiebert 1984c, 212). Believers need not try to make Christ more holy, but "to treat him as holy, to set him apart above all human authority" (Davids 1990, 131). The aorist tense underscores the decisive action to which Peter calls believers. Christ should be set apart once and for all as Lord.

The prepositional phrase **in your hearts** identifies the center of Christians' lives. It is "where fear would reside, if it were present" (Selwyn 1947, 193). Instead of harboring fear, believers should reverence Christ, and so banish fear of all else. The phrase **in your hearts** does not imply that faith is to be a private matter, not discussed in public (see v 15). Rather, true reverence is at the center of who believers are as persons. "Genuine faith must of necessity rise from the depths of personal experience. Lip service to creed and custom fall short. Eternal issues are decided in the lonely reaches of the human heart" (Mounce 1982, 52).

Reverence of Christ is integral to setting him apart as Lord. It leads believers to **always be prepared to give an answer to everyone who asks** them **to give the reason for the hope that** they **have.** The words **answer** (*apologia*) and **reason** (*logos*) are sometimes used within formal legal settings (e.g., Acts 15:26; Phil 1:7, 16). Although probably not in view here, Michaels suggests: "Peter sees his readers as being 'on trial' every day as they live for Christ in a pagan society" (1988, 188; but see Beare 1961, 138; Knox 1953, 189). As such, they should always be ready to **give an answer**.

Christians are not required to know the answer to every theological question someone might ask regarding the Christian faith. But they should be able to provide an intelligent account of what they believe and what they have experienced. "Our faith must be a first-hand discovery, and not a second-hand story" (Barclay 1960, 273).

As Christians, you will be questioned about **the hope that you have. Hope** is one of Peter's favorite words for the Christian faith. For him the Christian life is a life of hope (see 1:3, 13, 21; 3:5). In 1 Peter, hope is virtually synonymous with faith, but with a decidedly future orientation. Even during suffering, hope is the distinguishing mark of faith that overcomes all threats.

How an answer is given is sometimes as important as *what* answer is given. The spirit of the Christian witness is as significant as its content. Peter invites his audience to answer the questions of outsiders **with gentleness and respect. Gentleness** (*prautētos*) should describe the attitude of believers toward those who question their faith. It denotes an attitude of ***"gentleness, humility, courtesy, considerateness, meekness"*** (BDAG, 861). In contrast, **respect** (*phobos*) refers to the attitude believers have toward God (see 1:17; 2:18; 3:2). Their profound reverence for him enables them to answer the challenges of unbelievers appropriately.

■ **16** Here Peter explains the reason why believers should answer unbelievers "with gentleness and respect" (v 15). In their answers, believers must keep **a clear conscience.** Modified by the adjective ***good*** (*agathē*), **conscience** refers to the "[good] attitude towards God that determines all other attitudes" (Achtemeier 1996, 236).

Believers maintain a clear conscience **so that** (*hina*) **those who speak maliciously against** their **good behavior in Christ may be ashamed of their slander** (see 2:12, 15; 3:1-2). Peter's concern is not just any **behavior** (*anastrophē*) that may cause derision. He calls for conduct, not that is considered politically correct in the general culture, but **in Christ.** In Paul's letters, **in Christ** is a favorite term of Paul, appearing more than 160 times. Outside of Paul, the phrase is found only in 1 Peter (3:16; 5:10, 14). Here the phrase **in Christ** means "to think and act within the sphere of the influence of Christ" (Achtemeier 1996, 236). In other words, the **good behavior** of believers flows out of their relationship to Christ.

As a result of the **good behavior** of believers, their slanderers will ***be put to shame*** (*kataischynthōsin*). In Jewish literature, ***shame*** is usually conceived as utter defeat and disgrace in battle or before God. Believers are promised that their trust in God will not be put to shame and that their enemies will be exposed to shame (e.g., Pss 6:10; 22:5; 25:2-3). Peter probably does not envision this vindication occurring in the present, but at the final judgment. Then the accusers of Christians will ***be put to shame,*** when they "give account to him who is ready to judge the living and the dead" (4:5; see 2:12; but see Achtemeier 1996, 102; Michaels 1967, 398). The tables will be turned; persecutors will be put to shame (see 2 Thess 1:4-10).

■ **17** This verse reiterates Peter's instruction to slaves in 2:20. **It is better, if it is God's will, to suffer for doing good than for doing evil.** The appeal to **God's will** reminds believers that suffering—even unjust suffering—does not automatically fall outside God's purposes (see 4:19). Indeed, suffering sometimes lies within the scope of God's will, seen from a final, redemptive perspective. But it is seldom immediately apparent from a human standpoint how unjust suffering can be **better.** Peter focuses on the wider perspective of God's will and purposes. Certainly, nothing can be said for suffering **for doing evil**.

FROM THE TEXT

The Synergism of Sanctification. Entire sanctification is a work of grace by which God himself purifies and sanctifies believers for greater power and service in his kingdom. Peter embraces this notion as he describes his readers as experiencing the "sanctifying work of the Spirit" (1:2). And he calls them to "be holy in all [they] do" (1:15).

But Peter also envisions the active participation of believers in this sanctifying process. He calls them not only to be set apart but also **in** their **hearts** to **set apart Christ as Lord** (3:15). It is futile to try to receive God's sanctifying fullness unless we consciously and deliberately reverence Christ as Lord at the center of our lives. Believers are passive recipients of God's sanctifying work. But they are also active participants as they deliberately submit to the sovereignty of Christ.

Christian Apologetics. Christians should be able to explain and defend their faith. This does not mean that every Christian must enroll in a course on apologetics. But it does imply that believers should give reasonable thought to their faith. "It is, in fact, one of the tragedies of the modern situation that there are so many Church members who, if they were asked what they believe, could not tell anyone, and who, if they were asked why they believe it, would be equally helpless" (Barclay 1960, 273).

Christianity is described and characterized as "faith." But it is not groundless or irrational. There is an inner logic and simplicity to the Christian faith that can be compelling to unbelievers. But this occurs only if the faith is actually articulated in a thoughtful way by believers. Peter's instructions presuppose that the faith of believers is vibrant and personal. Thoughtful articulation of the Christian faith is virtually meaningless apart from the witnesses' personal experience of the living **hope** they profess.

B. The Example and Victory of Christ (3:18-22)

BEHIND THE TEXT

This passage exhibits some of the most profound and important features of the NT doctrine of salvation. It speaks of Christ's dying for our sins (v 18), the resurrection of Christ (v 21), baptism of believers (v 21), Christ's ascension to heaven (v 22), and his exaltation at the right hand of God (v 22). These affirmations "echo those found elsewhere in the NT and other early Christian writings and there is no reason to doubt that our writer is drawing on the common forms of Christian belief" (Best 1971, 136).

At the same time, this passage contains other elements that are so obscure as to be "bizarre" (Hanson 1982, 105; see Achtemeier 1996, 240-46). Luther wrote, "A wonderful text is this, and a more obscure passage perhaps than any other in the New Testament, so that I do not know for a certainty just what Peter means" (1990, 166).

The obscurity of the passage is primarily in the description of Christ in v 19, where he is portrayed as preaching **to the spirits in prison.** This obscure passage is often combined with another in 4:16—that Christ "preached even to those who are now dead" (4:6). These passages (along with Job 38:17; Ps 68:18-22; Matt 12:38-41; Acts 2:22-32; Rom 10:7; Eph 4:7-10) are considered the biblical basis for the creedal teaching of the *descensus ad inferos*. That is, they account for the reference to Christ's descent into hell in the Apostles' Creed.

Some interpreters propose that Peter may have appealed to apocryphal traditions of Enoch as a source for his teaching here (see Goodspeed 1954, 91-92). For instance, in *1 En.* 12—16 Enoch is told to proclaim doom to the fallen angels who were disobedient during the days of Noah. Such interpreters claim that Peter's readers would naturally make the connection between *1 Enoch* and Peter's comments in v 19 (France 1977, 269-70). But would Peter's Gentile audience have been aware of *1 Enoch*? While some of the language of vv 18 and 22 reflect early Christian tradition, vv 19-21 are probably "an independent construction of the writer" (Best 1971, 136).

Among the many controversial passages in the NT, 1 Pet 3:18-20 is unique. It is virtually impossible to arrive at anything close to a "majority view" among exegetes, ancient or modern. For this reason, we cannot be dogmatic about its interpretation. We should approach it humbly with a high degree of tolerance for alternative views. Comments on 1 Pet 3:18-22—just five of the letter's 105 verses—fill nearly ten percent of Achtemeier's massive commentary on 1 Peter (1996, 239-74).

Verse 19 raises four hotly disputed questions: (1) Who are the **spirits in prison**? (2) Who **preached** to them? (3) What was **preached**? (4) When was it **preached**? Feinberg (1986, 306-9) identifies four main lines of interpretation pursued in answer to these questions.

The first sees the passage as a reference to preaching in the underworld to human beings. There are differences, however, as to whether this preaching is accomplished through Christ, Enoch, or the spirits of dead apostles.

The second main line of interpretation takes the passage as a reference to Christ preaching to fallen angels in the intermediate period between his death and resurrection. The purpose of this preaching is usually understood as the announcement of victory over or condemnation of these fallen angels.

The third approach claims that Christ did the preaching after his ascension. Most adherents of this view argue that the preaching was not limited to the underworld.

The fourth interpretive tack, the one taken in this commentary, takes the passage as a reference to Christ in his preincarnate state preaching in the days of Noah. Christ preached by the Spirit through Noah as he was building the ark. This interpretation finds contextual support within 3:18-20. It has the advantage of viewing Peter's remarks in vv 19-20 as an integral part of his discussion rather than a digression or an interpolation (Beare 1961, 144).

IN THE TEXT

■ **18** Peter holds up the example and victory of Christ to encourage his readers. The discussion of the suffering of believers (3:13-17) leads to the topic of Jesus' saving death (see 2:21). **For Christ died for sins once for all.** English translations differ as to whether the original text read **Christ died** (*apathanen*) **for sins** (also NASB) or "also suffered [*epathen*] for sins" (NRSV). Both readings have strong ancient manuscript support. But "suffered for sins" makes better sense within the context of believers' suffering. The meaning of the two readings is not significantly different. Christ's suffering included his death (see Achtemeier 1996, 247).

Once for all (*hapax*) indicates that Christ's death is efficacious for all time. *Hapax* contrasts the idea of "once" against "again and again." It emphasizes the finality of the once-for-all suffering and death of Christ.

Lest his readers misinterpret **for sins** as referring to Christ's own sins, Peter explains: **the righteous for** (*hyper*) **the unrighteous.** This emphasizes the innocence of Christ. The preposition *hyper* highlights Christ's death as *on behalf of* those who believe rather than *instead of* the death of unbelievers. The purpose of this phrase is twofold. First, it emphasizes the innocent, unjust suffering of Christ. Second, it reminds the readers that Christ's suffering and death benefits them. Namely, Christ, the righteous one, suffered for the sins of the unrighteous ones in order **to bring** those who trust in him **to God.**

The expression **to bring you to God** is unusual among biblical explanations of the purpose of Christ's atonement. "Peter is creating a new metaphor, for no other NT writer has this active picture of Jesus leading the Christian to God" (Davids 1990, 136). The expression fits well into Peter's perception of the Christian life as following Christ (2:21; 4:13). Moreover, it provides a concise description of the purpose of the once-and-for-all death of Christ. Christ died in order to bring sinners into a right and intimate relationship with God.

The last phrase declares that **he was put to death in the body but made alive by the Spirit.** Some believe Peter's primary intention is to contrast the nouns **body** (*sarki*, ***flesh***) and **spirit** (*pneumati*). Others believe he contrasts the verbs **put to death** and **made alive.** Both contrasts emphasize Christ's atoning victory for believers by his death and resurrection. Christ's victory is the foundation and cause of the salvation of believers. This is the point of the passage. Christ's suffering and death on the cross originally seemed to point to his humiliation and defeat. But the resurrection, by which he was **made alive by the Spirit,** transformed apparent defeat into victory.

By their identification with Christ through faith, believers share in Christ's victory and vindication, regardless of any unjust suffering they may have to endure (see Achtemeier 1996, 251). Peter contrasts the Lord's willingness to suffer harm and even death in this world for the sake of an eternal and spiritual gain ("life"). Peter's readers should not be surprised if they experience the same kind of harm and suffering as they identify themselves with Christ. Despite such suffering, they too, through Christ, will be **made alive by the Spirit.**

■ **19-20** In the realm of the Spirit's activity **through whom** (*en hōi;* "in which," NRSV; see Grudem 1988, 157) **also he went and preached to the spirits in prison who disobeyed long ago when God waited patiently in the days of Noah while the ark was being built.**

The word **spirits** can refer to angelic spirits (Matt 8:16; Heb 1:14) or to the spirits of dead people (Matt 27:50; Luke 23:46; John 19:30; Acts 7:59; 1 Cor 5:5). Thus, **spirits in prison** could refer to deceased humans in hell or fallen angelic spirits there. Biblical precedents can be found for both options (2 Pet 2:4; Jude 6; and Luke 16:23-24; 2 Pet 2:9). The context must determine which kind of **spirits** Peter intended. In v 20, the spirits are described as those **who disobeyed . . . in the days of Noah while the ark was being built.** "These phrases indicate that only human spirits can be intended, for nowhere in the Bible or in Jewish literature outside of the Bible are angels ever said to have disobeyed 'during the building of the ark'" (Grudem 1988, 159). But several apocryphal works blame the enigmatic "sons of God" in Gen 6:1-6, understood as fallen angels, for the human wickedness that occasioned the flood (see *1 En.* 6—15; *3 En.* 28—29; *Jub.* 5; 7).

The phrase **when God waited patiently in the days of Noah** also points to the identification of the **spirits** as human spirits. God gave people the opportunity to repent before the flood (see 2 Pet 3:3-4; Rom 2:4; Acts 17:30). And yet there is never any hint in biblical or extrabiblical sources that fallen angels are given the opportunity to repent (see Jude 6). The chance to repent is only given to sinful human beings.

If the **spirits** in v 20 refer to fallen angelic spirits, why did Peter single out those who disobeyed in the days of Noah? There are no explicit references to fallen angels in the Genesis account of the flood. But there are many other examples of "notorious sinfulness" in the Bible, not the least of which would be the sinfulness represented by Sodom and Gomorrah. These considerations make it most likely that the **spirits** were disobedient humans during the time of Noah.

The problem with this interpretation is that **spirits** is an unusual way of referring to disobedient people. "This is best explained by understanding the text to mean 'spirits who are now in prison' (i.e. at the time Peter was writing), but who were people on earth at the time of Noah, when Christ was preaching to them" (Grudem 1988, 159; see the NASB: "the spirits now in prison").

The reference to **preached** (*ekēryxen*) substantiates this interpretation. *Kēryssō* is used in the NT and LXX to refer to evangelistic preaching, calling for repentance and faith. "There is no reason to reject the normal NT meaning of 'preach,' i.e., that it relates to salvation" (Best 1971, 144).

If **spirits** refer to fallen angelic beings, why and what would Christ be preaching to them? Those who take this view usually argue that the preaching is not evangelistic. Rather it is "an announcement to the fallen angels of his triumph over them and all evil through his death and resurrection" (France 1977, 271). But this explanation is problematic.

First, for what end would Christ preach victory or condemnation to these angels? It was certainly not to effect their salvation. Scripture offers no hint that fallen angels are salvable. It was also "certainly not to inform them of something they did not know, and given the character of Christ, it is not likely that he would do so to taunt them" (Feinberg 1986, 329).

Second, why would angelic spirits of the days of Noah be singled out? If the purpose of Christ's preaching was to announce his victory or condemnation, it would seem more natural for this announcement to include all fallen angels and not only the fallen angels of Noah's time.

It makes much more sense to take the phrase **preached to the spirits in prison** as a reference to human spirits.

First, this allows the word **preached** to have its normal evangelistic connotation. By the power of the Holy Spirit Christ preached through Noah to the people of Noah's day to give them an opportunity to repent before the flood.

Second, this interpretation explains the reference to disobedience in v 20. Namely, these spirits **who disobeyed long ago . . . while the ark was being built** are now in "prison." That is, they are being punished now for their disobedience to the preaching of Christ through Noah then.

Thus, the words **he preached to the spirits in prison** mean that Christ through Noah preached a message of repentance to the people of Noah's day. These disobedient people are described as **spirits in prison** because they are now dead and imprisoned in punishment for their disobedience. "The point is that, from Peter's perspective as he writes 1 Peter 3:19, the spirits are disembodied and in prison, though they were not in that state when they heard the message" (Feinberg 1986, 330).

There are many striking and useful parallels that existed between the situation of Noah and that of Peter's audience (see Grudem 1988, 160-61).

- Like Noah and his family, they were a minority surrounded by hostile unbelievers.
- Noah was righteous in a wicked world; likewise, Peter exhorts his readers to be righteous in the midst of wicked unbelievers (3:13-14, 16-17).
- Noah witnessed boldly to those around him; similarly, Peter's readers were to witness boldly (3:15).
- Noah knew that judgment was soon to overtake the world. Peter reminds his readers that God's judgment is certainly coming, perhaps soon (4:5, 7, 17).
- Noah was finally saved with a "few" others; likewise, Peter encourages his readers' faith by reminding them that, though they are few, they, too, will finally be saved (3:22).

These parallels explain Peter's insistence that Christ preached through Noah. This interpretation fits seamlessly into Peter's argument in this section of the letter.

Peter observes that in **the ark . . . only a few people, eight in all, were saved through water.** Water was a means of salvation for Noah and his family just as the resurrection of Christ is the means of salvation to Christian believers. Note the parallel between **saved through water** (*di' hydatos*; v 20) and **saves . . . by the resurrection of Jesus Christ** (*di' anastaseōs*; v 21).

■21 The correspondence between the experience of Noah and of Christian believers is focused in the word **symbolizes** (*antitypon:* antitype, "resemblance, correspondence" [Zodhiates 1992, 196]). God saved Noah **through water** of the flood just as Christ saves believers through baptismal water (see Rom 6:1-11).

This is the only explicit reference to **baptism** in the letter. Some suggest that the word **now** in v 21 identifies the entire letter as a baptismal liturgy. They imagine that candidates for baptism were in the water at this point (e.g., Reicke 1964, 74). But it is more likely that **now** refers to the new era of God's salvation in which Peter and his readers lived. The lack of additional references to baptism makes the assumption that this Epistle reflects a baptismal sermon highly unlikely.

This is the only passage in the NT in which the idea is explicitly articulated that "baptism saves" (but see Mark 16:16). Even here, it is not intended as a maxim of salvation theology; it is merely a feature of Peter's ark-typology. He immediately qualifies the statement to eliminate any tendency his audience might have to attach magical status to the sacrament.

First, Peter explains negatively that the significance of baptism is not found in **the removal of dirt from the body,** that is, in an outward act of washing. "The outward act does not bring salvation in itself, but only as it represents a right inward attitude" (France 1977, 274). As important as baptism is, the sacramental washing cannot be equated with salvation itself.

Second, Peter explains that baptism *is* saving, not in the sense that it removes the "dirt of sin" from the body. It represents a **pledge of a good conscience before God** (compare **good conscience** here to "a pure heart" in 1 Tim 1:5). This points to "a consciousness of what God wants that will lead one to do it" (Achtemeier 1996, 270). A **good conscience** does not refer to feelings of innocence, but to genuine inward purity that results in righteous behavior.

> A "good conscience" is the product of the Spirit's purifying work in a person's heart on the basis of "obedience" to the Christian gospel, but "good conscience" by itself does not save. Only God can save, and God's willingness and power to save are visibly and audibly invoked in baptism. (Michaels 1988, 216)

God alone can save. But salvation is dependent upon a positive human response to God's saving initiative. The word **pledge** (*eperōtēma*) emphasizes this human response (see Best 1971, 148; Achtemeier 1996, 270-72). Candidates for baptism were often required to make a "pledge" of their faith before they were baptized.

Thus, a **pledge of a good conscience before God** does not mean that believers asked God for a good conscience. Rather, believers, who already claimed a **good conscience** by faith in Christ, pledged to remain loyal to God (France 1977, 275).

The last phrase of v 21 is foundational to Peter's understanding of baptism: **It saves you by the resurrection of Jesus Christ.** Baptism does not save because of its outward washing effect or because of the candidate's pledge of continued loyalty to God, but because of **the resurrection of Jesus Christ** (see Rom 6:1-11). "Not only is baptism an act of commitment by the candidate; it is also a uniting with the risen Christ giving him the power to live up to his commitment" (France 1977, 275).

■ 22 Verse 22 provides a threefold depiction of the triumph of Christ. Christ's suffering and death were vindicated through his resurrection. Peter claims that Christ **is at God's right hand,** the highest position of honor and authority imaginable. Christ's exaltation proceeded from this resurrection through two additional stages.

- First, his ascension: he **has gone into heaven** (see Mark 16:19; Luke 24:51; Acts 1:6-11), which culminates in his heavenly enthronement.
- Second, his session: Christ is enthroned **with angels, authorities and powers in submission to him.** Peter describes the submission of all things to him by appealing to Pss 8:6 and 110:1.

For Peter's suffering readers, these words must have been an encouragement to persevere. Christ's death was not the final defeat but the prelude to his ultimate vindication and exaltation over all the evil powers arrayed against the Christian community. By participating in his suffering, perhaps even to the point of death, they are assured of a share in his vindication and exaltation. "The ability of the powers to afflict them now through their persecutors is not the last word; the reign of Jesus Christ is" (Davids 1990, 147).

FROM THE TEXT

He Descended into Hell? First Peter 3:18-19 is often cited as a proof text for the creedal line about Jesus' descent into hell. But it is far from clear what was on Peter's mind when he wrote: Christ **went and preached to the spirits in prison.** The phrase "he descended into hell" does not appear in any editions of the Apostles' Creed before 390, and not again until 650 (Schaff 1977, 54).

The history of the creed's teaching concerning Christ's descent into the place of eternal punishment is spotty and late. And there are other NT texts that would seem to speak against this understanding of the line (see Luke 23:43; John 20:17). Perhaps it means no more than that Christ went to the place of the dead. The meaning of 1 Pet 3:18-19 is far too controversial and uncertain to defend this late creedal affirmation.

Despite the controversy and disagreement surrounding 3:18-22, a valuable truth is clearly contained here. Just as certainly as the flood eventually came in the days of Noah, so also final judgment will come to our world, and Christ will ultimately triumph over all evil in the universe. In this unshakeable hope believers should take heart and stand firm.

Baptism. The importance of baptism is strongly emphasized throughout the NT. But it is boldly described in 1 Pet 3:21 as the **baptism that now saves you.** Although baptism is used as the supreme analogy of the believers' experience of salvation, Peter clearly rejects any notion of baptismal regeneration. Baptism by itself has no inherent saving power. Yet baptism possesses a unique and powerful role in the establishment and preservation of salvation: **baptism now saves you . . . by the resurrection of Jesus Christ.**

In *The Book of Common Prayer,* the sacrament of baptism is described as consisting of two parts: "the outward visible sign, and the inward spiritual grace." This balance of the "outward" and "inward" elements corresponds with the divine initiative and the human response that are integral to the saving experience of baptism.

Peter maintains this balanced view of baptism. He describes the human response as the believers' **pledge** to God to maintain a **good conscience.** This consists not only of faith in Christ but also of the appropriate behavior of such a faith. But he also describes the divine initiative: baptism only saves **by the resurrection of Jesus Christ.** Without both the enabling power of Christ's resurrection and the confessional pledge of believers, baptism effects no more than **the removal of dirt from the body.** Wesley claims that the significance of baptism is "not, indeed, the bare outward sign, but the inward grace; a divine consciousness that both our persons and our actions are accepted through him who died and rose again for us" (1981, n.p.).

Through baptism, believers make public their identification and participation in the death and resurrection of Jesus Christ. At the same time, Christ identifies and participates in the lives of believers so that they are enabled to live the kind of righteous lives they promised God they would. Baptism is indeed both an outward visible sign and the inward spiritual grace that is characteristic of salvation.

C. Freedom from Sin (4:1-6)

IN THE TEXT

Peter exhorts his readers to follow Christ's example. Surprisingly, his exhortation does not focus on Christ's baptism, exaltation, or supremacy over all powers. Instead, he draws attention to Christ's suffering, picking up the theme of suffering introduced in 3:18. The contrast of "flesh" and "spirit" in 4:6 echoes 3:18 to form an *inclusio* of 3:18—4:6. This device employs the same word or phrase at the beginning and the end of a section to form a literary frame around a discrete section. Peter's language is strongly participatory. Through their participation in the bodily suffering of Christ, believers can be set free from the tyrannical reign of sin in their lives.

■ **1** **Therefore** (*oun*) introduces the practical application of Christ's example of suffering for righteousness. His audience must resist the temptation to conform to non-Christian ways to avoid suffering. Instead, with the example of Christ before them, Christians should **arm** themselves **also with the same attitude.**

The verb **arm yourselves** (*hoplisasthe*) is a military term that means "to equip" or "to arm" with the appropriate tool or weapon. "The aorist tense called for an act that demanded resolution and determination, and the middle voice reminded the recipients of their personal responsibility and interest in it" (Hiebert 1984c, 241). Believers need to prepare themselves adequately as in 1:13.

Attitude (*ennoian*, only here and Heb 4:12 in the NT) refers to the mental activity of setting one's moral "intention" or "resolve" (see Prov 1:4, etc., LXX; Zodhiates 1992, 591). Believers are not merely to have good ideas. They are summoned to resolute action that has been carefully considered and thought through in light of Christ's suffering.

Taken out of context, this sentence could imply that believers should seek suffering and martyrdom. But Peter never praises suffering in itself as inherently beneficial for believers. He commends doing what is right. And if suffering comes as a result, so be it.

Believers **arm** themselves **with the same attitude** as Christ by choosing obedience, even if it brings suffering. They are urged to recognize that it is better to do right and to suffer for it than to do wrong (3:17-18). They are to "follow in his steps" (2:21).

Believers should follow Christ's example of suffering for this reason
4:1 (*hoti*): **because he who has suffered in his body is done with sin.** It is not that personal suffering pardons one's sins. "Christ died for sins once for all" (3:18). By faith, believers identify with Christ (i.e., **arm yourselves also with the same attitude**), as Christ identified with sinners (3:18). By identifying with Christ's sufferings, suffering believers participate in his being **done with sin.** Like Christ, they are to reject the sinful ways of the world. But unlike the sinless Christ, they must first turn away from their former ways in order to live obedient and righteous lives. And they must do so, even if this means suffering for their faith (4:2-4). Their solidarity and participation with Christ's suffering enables them to participate in his victory over sin.

By following Christ even in suffering, believers demonstrate that they have definitively broken with their old lives and desire henceforth to fear and obey God. The phrase **he who has suffered in his body is done with sin** means "he who has suffered for doing right, and has still gone on obeying God in spite of the suffering involved, has made a clear break with sin" (Grudem 1988, 167).

The attitude of Christ considers obedience to God more important than either suffering or death. It "demonstrates that the one who so suffers no longer acts in a way contrary to God's will, that is, by sinning" (Achtemeier 1996, 280).

■**2** The one who has the same attitude of Christ ***no longer lives the rest of the time in the flesh for human desires, but rather for the will of God.*** The term ***no longer*** (*mēketi*) looks *backward* at the sinful lives believers formerly lived, when they followed pagan customs and practices. The phrase ***the rest of the time*** looks *forward* to the future lives of the believers. The hope of believers lies beyond their relatively brief and limited ***time*** (*chronos*) on earth (*en sarki, **in the flesh***).

When believers take on the attitude of Christ, the orientation of their lives changes dramatically. There is a sharp contrast (*alla, **but rather***) between their old lives lived ***for human desires*** and their new lives lived **for the will of God.**

■**3** Two contrasts from v 2 continue here. First, Peter contrasts "the rest" of his audience's time on earth (v 2) with the **time in the past.** Second, he contrasts "the will of God" (v 2) with **what pagans choose to do** (*to boulēma tōn ethnōn: **the counsel of the pagans***).

The word **enough** in the phrase **you have spent enough time in the past** is used ironically, as literary understatement. **Enough** is actually more than enough, "far too much" (Beare 1961, 154). Peter's readers need a definitive break from their past. They followed the ***counsel of the pagans*** far too long before their conversion. Now, for "the rest" of their time, they must live according to "the will of God." A catalog of vices is used to describe the deeds of the pagans.

Debauchery and **lust** relate specifically to sexual excess and abuse. **Debauchery** (in the plural) denotes specific acts of sexual immorality. **Lust** (*epithymiais*) literally means "desires," but with the connotation of **lust** in conjunction with **debauchery.**

The vices **drunkenness** and **carousing** are virtually synonymous in Greek. Both carry a negative connotation in religious and secular Greek writings.

Orgies (*kōmois*) are merely "feasts." But those held in honor of Greco-Roman fertility gods were usually given over to wild immorality.

The last vice, **detestable idolatry** (*athemitois eidōlolatriais*), refers to lawless acts associated with idol worship. "Lawless" cannot mean that they are "against the laws of God." All acts of idolatry are "lawless" in this sense. Rather, they were even "against civil laws." Peter refers to "particularly evil kinds of idol worship which involved or incited people to kinds of immorality even forbidden by the laws of human government" (Grudem 1988, 169). Peter's audience had participated in such sinful behaviors in the past. "Enough of that!" Their lives were now to be characterized by obedience to God.

■**4** The change in lifestyle of these believers was dramatic enough to be noticed by their neighbors. **They think it strange that you do not plunge with**

them into the same flood of dissipation. The verb **think it strange** (present tense) indicates that their refusal of "the same excesses [*anachysin*] of dissipation" (NRSV) as their neighbors was a continual source of surprise. **Dissipation** (*asōtias*) describes conduct completely devoid of saving qualities.

Peter portrays the pagan lifestyle as a headlong rush into reckless abandon. And yet, the pagans considered their behavior normal within their society. Since all civic activities were bound up with heathen religious ceremonies, "Christians were compelled to avoid what would have seemed to their fellows a wholly innocuous cooperation" (Best 1971, 154; see Achtemeier 1996, 283-85).

Naturally, the Christian refusal to participate in such "normal" activities led pagans to **heap abuse on** (*blasphēmountes:* ***"slander, revile, defame";*** BDAG, 178) them. To blaspheme God was to ***"speak irreverently/impiously/ disrespectfully of or about"*** (BDAG 2000, 178) him (see Mark 3:28-29). This term characterizes the abuse of Christians for their nonconformity as blasphemy against God.

■5 Such blasphemy will not go unpunished. Although their abusive neighbors slander them now with apparent impunity, **they will have to give account to him who is ready to judge the living and the dead.** To **give an account** (*logon apodidonai*) may be intended as an ironic contrast to the phrase "asks you to give the reason" (*logon aitein:* ***call to account***) in 3:15 (see Beare 1961, 155). Pagans persecute and abuse Christians as they "call them to account" for refusing to participate in their godless behavior. But a reversal of circumstances will occur when all will **give account** of their actions on the day of judgment. Christ will **judge the living and the dead** (see Acts 10:42; 2 Tim 4:1; Rom 14:9). All people will be accountable to him.

■6 This verse is difficult to interpret because of the phrase **the gospel was preached even to** the **dead.** The difficulties are often related to those in 3:19 (see the commentary). Several explanations have been offered (see Kelly 1969, 172-76; Achtemeier 1996, 286-91). The most probable is that it refers to now deceased Christians. Peter reassures his audience that dead believers, whether from persecution or other causes, had not forfeited the benefits of following Christ (see 1 Thess 4:13-18). The gospel was preached to **those who are now dead** while they were still living. Although they were dead, the gospel had been preached to them so they might "live in the spirit according to the will of God" (NASB).

The phrase ***judged in the flesh*** (*sarki*) ***as everyone is judged*** (*kata anthrōpous;* see NRSV) emphasizes that all people, believers and unbelievers alike, will die physically (unless Christ appears first [1 Thess 4:17]). No one leaves this world alive. But ***the gospel was preached even to the now dead*** believers in order that they might **live according to God in regard to the spirit.**

Peter assures his embattled readers that their faith is not in vain. Despite their rejection by unbelievers and the death that had overtaken some fellow believers, their faith is not futile. The same judgment that will call unbelievers to account for their blasphemy (v 5) will vindicate Christians. Believers should not despair for **now dead** Christians. God will bring them life.

FROM THE TEXT

Christlikeness. Faith in Jesus Christ will save believers from judgment and condemnation in the end. But it now enables them to turn from sin and live righteous lives. Those who are forgiven by Christ are expected to break with sin and follow Christ's example. The notion that Christians and non-Christians differ only in that Christians are forgiven is foreign to Peter and the NT.

Christlikeness is not merely a slogan for Peter. It is a reality he expected to begin when they came to faith in Christ. It is to express itself in the minds, hearts, and behavior of Christians. True believers not only confess faith in Jesus Christ but also emulate his holiness (1:15), "follow in his steps" (2:21), set Christ apart as Lord in their hearts (3:15), suffer for his name (3:17), and arm themselves with Christ's attitude (4:1).

Judgment. Peter strongly affirms several central teachings of theological importance here. First, all people will be held accountable on the last day for the way they have lived (4:5). Second, Christ/God will judge every creature, living or dead (4:5). Third, believers have nothing to fear from death (4:6), for death has been swallowed up in victory (see Isa 25:8; 1 Cor 15:54). Believers will die along with unbelievers until Christ returns. But they will be made alive by God through the Spirit (4:6). Peter's letter distinguishes itself as a sourcebook of historic Christian theology.

D. Living for God (4:7-11)

BEHIND THE TEXT

The doxology at the end of v 11 led some earlier scholars to suggest that 1 Peter was a composite letter. They proposed that it consisted of two earlier writings (1:1—4:11 and 4:12—5:14) secondarily combined by a later editor. This theory has been largely abandoned today. There is evidence that some letters do conclude with a doxology (e.g., Rom 16:25-27; 2 Pet 3:18; Jude 25). But this is not always the case. Doxologies regularly appear within the body of letters when there is a reference to God or Christ (e.g., Rom 1:25; 9:5; 11:36; Gal 1:5; Eph 3:21; 1 Tim 1:17; Rev 1:6). Such is the case here in 1 Pet 4:11.

In addition, 4:7-11 is strongly linked with the rest of the letter. For instance, v 7 sounds a clear note of the impending end. The expectation of an imminent end of all things underlies the rest of the Epistle, almost to the extent that it becomes a thematic refrain (see 4:13, 17-18; 5:1, 4, 6, 10). Thus, 4:11 does not mark the conclusion of some earlier letter, as some critical scholars contend. It functions as a doxological interlude within the letter's thematic focus upon the imminent end of history.

Verses 7-11 conclude the central part of the letter. They shift the focus from how the Christian community is to behave in relation to society at large to the inner life of the community. Thus, they function as a transition to the closing paragraphs of the letter (Achtemeier 1996, 293).

IN THE TEXT

■ **7** Peter reminds his readers that they live in the end times. That Christ stands "ready to judge" (v 5) implies that the end is near. But v 7 articulates this explicitly: **the end of all things is near** (see BDAG, 270; see Matt 3:2; Mark 1:15; Rom 13:12; Phil 4:5; Heb 10:25; Jas 5:8; Rev 1:3). The expectation of Christ's imminent return is common in the NT (Rom 13:12; Phil 4:5; 1 Thess 4:15; Heb 10:25; Jas 5:8; Rev 1:3; 22:10).

Peter does not speculate on the times, conditions, or signs of the end. However, the perfect tense of the verb **is near** indicates that a continuity exists between the present times and the last decisive intervention of God through Jesus Christ. The final drama is already underway, and the last act is fast approaching.

That **the end . . . is near** is no cause for panic. The proximity of the end means that "there is time for action, but no time to waste" (Michaels 1988, 245). Thus, Peter exhorts his readers to behave appropriately.

Since the end is near, **therefore** believers must **be clear minded and self-controlled.** The verbs **be clear minded** and **be . . . self-controlled** are aorist imperatives. Urgent, decisive action is called for. "The two verbs together suggest a disciplined life, with all the faculties under control and the energies unimpaired by any kind of excess" (Beare 1961, 158).

The purpose (*eis*) of this discipline is ***for your prayers.*** It is not simply **so that you can pray,** but so that you can pray more effectively and appropriately. Peter's emphasis on mutual love in the following verse insinuates that prayer is the primary means of growth in the believers' fellowship with God. It also enables believers to love one another.

■ **8** The disciplined life that enables believers to pray effectively also leads them to ***remain constant in your love for one another.*** The initial phrase **above all** (see "all" in v 7) does not minimize the importance of prayer. Rather, it highlights "the characteristically Christian emphasis on the primacy of love" (Beare 1961, 158). Does the repeated emphasis on mutual love (see 1:22) indicate that the believers' love for one another was being tested by the trials they were facing? This is certainly possible.

Regardless, Peter calls them to a ***constant*** and fervent **love.** "Agape love" can be commanded because *agapē* is not primarily an emotion but a decision of the will that leads to action. Love and its corresponding actions will be the dominant theme of the remaining verses of this section.

Christians must love one another **because love covers over a multitude of sins.** This quotation from Prov 10:12 (see Jas 5:20) has two plausible interpretations: (1) God forgives the sins of those who love others. (2) Those who love overlook the sins and wrongs of others. The second option is preferable (see Achtemeier 1996, 295-96).

This saying does not concern our sins against God but our failures in relation to each other. When a community of Christians loves one another, the wrongs and offenses that inevitably happen in human relations are overlooked and forgotten. Peter's point is not *theological,* that God overlooks our sins when we love others. It is *social;* we overlook the sins of those we love.

■ 9 There are no verbs in this verse. It consists of only an adjectival phrase: **hospitality to one another without grumbling.** With this, Peter provides a practical expression of the kind of mutual love that should characterize believers.

Hospitality was highly valued in the early church. It expressed the fellowship of believers in one another's homes. And it supported the missionary travels of apostles, preachers, and teachers (Heb 13:1-2; 3 John 5-8).

Believers should extend hospitality **without grumbling.** *Gongysmou* is "the sound made when murmuring or muttering in a low and indistinct voice with the idea of complaint" (Zodhiates 1992, 379). Such **grumbling** would undermine the value of the hospitality. Peter expected cheerful and ungrudging hospitality as a concrete expression of Christian love.

■ 10 Peter makes two important affirmations about the Christian community. First, ***each believer has received a spiritual gift.*** A **gift** (*charisma,* from "grace" [*charis*]) is "a non-material" endowment, "bestowed through God's generosity on individual Christians" (BDAG, 1081). Not a natural talent or ability, it is a God-given capacity for service received by believers at conversion (see Rom 12:6; 1 Cor 12:4, 9, 28, 30-31).

Second, the purpose of gifts is **to serve others** (see 1 Cor 12:7-11). Spiritual gifts are for use in the life of the church. They are not given for one's own personal enjoyment.

Faithfully administering is literally ***good stewards*** (*kaloi oikonomoi*). An *oikonomos* was a **"manager of a household or estate"** (BDAG, 698; see Luke

16:1, 3). In the household of faith Christians are to manage God's spiritual gifts for the purpose of serving one another. The diversity of spiritual gifts is explicitly acknowledged in the phrase ***the manifold graces of God*** (*poikilēs charitos theou*)—**grace in its various forms.**

■ 11 Two general examples are given as to how God's gifts should be used. Peter does not enumerate the spiritual gifts as Paul does (nine gifts in 1 Cor 12:7-11; seven gifts in Rom 12:6-8). Yet the two basic categories of "speaking" and "actions" naturally include all the gifts mentioned by Paul.

First, the gift of speaking is addressed: **If anyone speaks, he should do it as one speaking the very words of God.** The scope of **speaking** is not limited to church officials or leaders, but includes all believers. **Speaks** (*lalei*) often designates public activities like preaching and teaching. But it includes a wide array of other verbal activities such as singing and sharing words of praise and testimony in the community gatherings or in ministering to the sick and in private conversations.

Whatever the situation, a believer should speak **as one speaking the very words of God.** The **words of God** elsewhere in the NT refer to the Jewish Scriptures (Rom 3:2) or to the "living words" that Moses received from God to give to the people of Israel (Acts 7:38). The adverb **as** (*hōs*) clarifies that speakers cannot claim that their words are actually God's own **words.** Rather, believers speak "with the seriousness of purpose which one would use if one were speaking God's words" (Grudem 1988, 176).

The speech of Christians must communicate "the character of God's words" and their "divine intention," not their own (Achtemeier 1996, 299). To pass off our own ideas and purposes as the **words of God** is to abuse them. The line between authority and presumption, especially for teachers and preachers, is thin. Believers must be careful to ensure that their words convey the true intentions of God, not their own.

Second, **if anyone serves, he should do it with the strength that God provides.** *Diakonei* refers to all forms of Christian service other than speech (v 10). This service to others is not accomplished in one's own strength. To do so would lead to weariness or pride. We are to serve with **the strength that God provides.** Everything worthwhile accomplished among God's people has its source in God.

The purpose of Peter's instructions is ultimately theocentric. Christians love and serve one another ***so that in all things God may be glorified through Jesus Christ.*** It is not that Jesus Christ glorifies God. Rather, he makes it possible for Christians to glorify God by what they do and say.

Mention of the glorification of God prompts Peter to offer a doxology in praise to God. Although **to him** grammatically might refer either to Jesus

Christ or God, the focus here is upon God (note the triple repetition of *theos*). **Glory** (*doxa*) is so common to NT doxologies that the name "doxology" is derived from it. *Doxa* describes the radiant splendor and majesty characteristic of deity.

Power (*kratos*) and **glory** are combined in only one other NT doxology (Rev 1:6). But **power** is combined with other qualities in several others (1 Tim 6:16; Jude 25; Rev 5:13). **Power** emphasizes "the irresistible might which ensures God's triumph over every evil force" (Kelly 1969, 182).

Peter attributes this **glory and . . . power** to God **for ever and ever.** The word **amen** is found at the end of most doxologies. It translates a Hebrew term that means "certainty, truthfulness, and faithfulness" (Dearman 1985, 29). It is used in both the NT and the Septuagint as a congregational liturgical response affirming what has been said or prayed (see Achtemeier 1996, 300). It means "So be it" or "May it be so."

E. Participation in Christ's Suffering (4:12-19)

BEHIND THE TEXT

Peter reinforces and intensifies the theme of suffering believers begun in 3:13. No longer is it addressed in general, as potential or possible. Now suffering is approached in specific terms as probable and actual.

Some interpreters take this shift as an indication that 4:12 marks the beginning of a different Epistle, editorially appended to the foregoing. But this change may well be due to the diverse experiences of Peter's readers in their different provinces of Asia Minor. The references to suffering are more specific here. But the same theme of sharing in Christ's suffering unifies the letter.

IN THE TEXT

■ **12** For the second time in this Epistle, the readers are addressed as ***beloved*** (see 2:11). Peter reminds his suffering **friends** that they are bound together in a fellowship characterized by love (*agapētoi*).

Peter exhorts: ***Do not be surprised at the fiery ordeal which comes upon you . . . as though something strange were happening to you.*** The verb *xenizesthe* (**be surprised**) in 4:4 appeared in Peter's observation that pagans **think it strange** (*xenizontai*) that Christians do not participate in their sinful lifestyle. The wordplay is probably intentional. Although unbelievers are "surprised" by the circumspect behavior of believers, believers should not be "surprised" that unbelievers expose them to rejection and persecution.

Fiery ordeal (*pyrōsei*) is used figuratively to describe graphically the **painful** severity of the readers' **trial**. The noun *pyrōsei* describes the purification of gold and silver by fire. Thus, Peter implies that these trials may have a positive purifying effect. The prepositional phrase *pros peirasmon* identifies the ***fiery ordeal*** as having the purpose of putting them ***to the test.***

The same images of fire and testing were alluded to in 1:6-7. There Peter explains that God uses such trials to prove the faith of believers. Peter urges his audience not to **be surprised** by their trials. Such tests provide them the opportunity to demonstrate the authenticity of their faith. The present tense verbs "presuppose an enduring situation rather than an unexpected crisis" (Kelly 1969, 185).

■ **13** ***Instead*** of being surprised, believers should ***rejoice*** (*alla . . . charēte*). Peter explains why (*katho:* ***inasmuch as***): ***you share in the sufferings of Christ.*** **Share** (*koinōneite*) is the verbal derivative of the noun *koinōnia* ("fellowship"). It has the connotation of having something in common with another. Peter perceives the Christian life as a participation in the experiences of Christ for the purpose of salvation. Communion with Christ involves a partnership with him in his death and resurrection (Rom 6:5). It is symbolized in baptism (1 Pet 3:21).

But union with Christ invariably means that believers participate in the whole pattern of Christ's life. This includes sharing in his suffering for righteousness (1 Pet 2:20-21; 3:17-18; Rom 8:17; Phil 3:10; Col 1:24; 2 Tim 3:12; 1 John 2:6). The salvation of believers is closely tied to their identity with Christ. Thus, the more they suffer for Christ, the more they should **rejoice. Rejoice** in the present tense means they should ***keep on rejoicing*** to the same extent that they ***continue to share*** (present tense) **in the sufferings of Christ.**

Peter's audience's present share in Christ's suffering allows them to experience joy already. But this present joy fades in comparison with the future ***rejoicing with exceeding joy*** they will experience when Christ's **glory is revealed** (see also 1:7, 13). Peter refers to the second coming of Christ as a time of **glory** and exaltation. Believers may presently face persecution for their faith in Christ. But they will participate in the **glory** and the ***exceeding joyfulness*** of Christ on the day of his return.

■ **14** Peter reiterates the principle of Christian suffering, now identified in terms of verbal abuse. **If you are insulted because of the name of Christ, you are blessed** (see 3:14). This recalls the words of Jesus (see Matt 5:11; Luke 6:22). Suffering itself is not inherently beneficial. The "blessing" of insult is grounded in its cause; namely, **because of the name of Christ.**

The verb **insulted** (*oneidizesthe*) in the Bible describes the ridicule and verbal abuse heaped on God and those who follow him (Pss 42:10; 69:9; Isa 37:17; Matt 27:44; Rom 15:3; Heb 11:26). Here, it seems to specify the nature of the ***fiery ordeals*** as verbal abuse. But the possibility of physical abuse cannot be eliminated. The present tense of the verb suggests that Peter's audience were victims of a continual onslaught of slander, reproach, and defamation. This was their actual situation, not just a possibility: the conditional **if** should be translated ***when.***

Although they are being abused, believers are **blessed** because **the Spirit of glory and of God rests on** them. **Spirit** (*pneuma*) is certainly the Holy Spirit—**the Spirit . . . of God.** The **Spirit** as **the Spirit of glory** may allude to the Shekinah glory of God, which rested on the tabernacle (Selwyn 1947, 222). The main point, however, is that **the Spirit** bestows his **glory** on believers. The future "glory" (v 13) invades their present experience of the sanctifying Spirit.

The phrase "On their part he is evil spoken of, but on your part he is glorified" found in the KJV is absent in the earliest and most reliable manuscripts. They probably "were added as an explanatory gloss" (Metzger 1994, 625).

The Spirit . . . rests on you echoes the messianic prophecy regarding the branch of Jesse: "The Spirit of the LORD will rest on him" (Isa 11:2). This promise is extended to all who carry the name of the Messiah and are willing to suffer for his sake. Christians insulted because of Christ share in his messianic blessing—the Spirit's glorious presence.

■ **15** Only suffering for the sake of Christ is blessed. In order to erase any misunderstanding, Peter writes, ***But let none of you suffer as a murderer or a thief or a wrongdoer or as a meddler.*** This list of prohibited behaviors is certainly not exhaustive.

The list is divided into two parts by the double repetition of the adverb **as** (*hōs*). The first mentions **murderer, thief,** and **wrongdoer.** These represent behaviors the readers would immediately accept as extreme. **Murderer** and **thief** often appear in NT vice lists (Matt 19:18; Rom 2:21; 13:9; Jas 2:11; Rev 21:8). A **wrongdoer** (*kakopoios*) was "one who does evil" (Grundmann 1965, 485; see 2:12, 14, and 3:17). Unlike **murderer** and **thief, wrongdoer** is a general term comprehending all forms of evil conduct.

The second part of Peter's list has only one word: **meddler** (*allotriepiskopos*). It is a compound noun combining the adjective *allotrios* ("belonging to another") with the noun *episkopos* ("overseer"). Etymologically, the word refers to an overseer in the sense of a steward or manager of another's possession and affairs. The word occurs only here in the NT and is not found in earlier Greek writings. Thus, its meaning can only be deduced from the context of 1 Peter, which provides few specific clues.

Beyer (1964a, 621-22) identifies four possible interpretations: (1) one who covets others' possessions; (2) one who is an unfaithful guardian of goods entrusted to him or her; (3) one who meddles in things that do not concern him or her; and (4) one who is a political agitator—a revolutionary, spy, or informer.

The third is probably the correct interpretation. The first half of Peter's list identifies criminal extremes, of which believers would never be guilty. The second half prohibits an activity they might actually have engaged in: needless meddling in another's business.

> We can only speculate what kind of meddling the writer has in mind (excessive zeal for making converts? causing discord in family or commercial life? over-eager denunciation of pagan habits? prying curiosity?), but he plainly regards it as disreputable. (Kelly 1969, 189)

■ **16** There is no blessing or glory in suffering for wrongful behavior. But the situation is completely different **if you suffer as a Christian.** The word **Christian** (*Christianos*) is used only two other times in the NT (Acts 11:26; 26:28). "According to Acts 11:26, *Christianos* was first used for Christians in Syrian Antioch." The NT references suggest that the term was applied to Christians by outsiders in ridicule (Verbrugge 2000, 610). Peter explicitly connects *Christianos* to suffering. But he instructs his readers that they should **not be ashamed** to suffer for their loyalty to Christ.

The reaction of believers to suffering for Christ is important to Peter. Negatively, they were not to be surprised by suffering (4:12). And they must **not be ashamed.** It is unclear whether his readers were facing social ridicule and isolation for identifying with Christ or formal legal prosecution. Regardless, Peter warned them against a sense of false shame.

On the positive side, Peter instructs them to **praise God that you bear that name.** He probably refers to being called a **Christian,** not simply being associated with "Christ." They were to "glorify" (NRSV, *doxazetō*) God for their connection with Christ and everything his name represented. If believers suffered for being **Christian,** it was nothing to be ashamed of, even if it brought suffering. This suffering was an opportunity to glorify God.

■ **17** Further (*hoti*), the suffering of believers is placed within the larger framework of the Last Judgment. The reality of the end times has invaded the present. It is manifested in the purification of God's people. ***For it is time for judgment to begin at the house of God.***

House of God (*oikos tou theou*) is "a fixed term for the sanctuary in the LXX" (Michel 1967, 120). Throughout this letter Peter picks up OT terminology and applies it to the Christian community. **House of God** again portrays believers as the temple or sanctuary of God (see 2:5, 9).

The judgment scene of Ezek 9 echoes in the background of v 17 (Johnson 1986, 291-93). But the concepts of v 17 are from Mal 3:1-5 and 4:1. Here, the pattern is established for "the escalation of eschatological judgment as it moves out from the house of God to those outside the covenant" (Johnson 1986, 292). Malachi pictures God's judgment as a fire, which begins in God's temple as a refiner's fire that will purify his people (Mal 3:1-5). But this same fire will consume evildoers (Mal 4:1).

In the same way, Peter envisions the suffering of believers as representing the onset of God's judgment on all people. Both believers and unbelievers will face a judgment of fire. For unbelievers (= **those who do not obey the gospel of God**), this judgment of fire means eternal destruction. But for believers, experienced in their current suffering, the judgment will purify them (1:7; 4:12).

> If the purifying fire of God's eschatological visitation, which we—his living temple—presently experience by the Spirit, entails for those united to Christ such anguish as Peter's readers are undergoing, what shall the consummation of that purifying divine presence mean for those who have rejected God's good news—if not a conflagration of utter destruction? (Johnson 1986, 292)

Verse 17 reinforces the heightened sense of eschatological expectation underlying the entire letter (see 1:5, 13; 2:12; 4:7). Peter warns his readers against denying their faith to alleviate their suffering. Their present suffering might be harsh. But a denial of their faith will only guarantee suffering that is far worse in the final judgment. Believers must remain steadfast, even in the midst of the refining fire of suffering. If judgment has already begun within the **house of God,** the final destruction of unbelievers will certainly follow shortly.

■ **18** As an illustration, Peter quotes a passage from Prov 11:31: **If it is hard for the righteous to be saved, what will become of the ungodly and the sinner?** Jesus often spoke of the difficulty of salvation (e.g., Luke 13:24). But this is not the point of this quotation. It is, instead, the impending and certain doom of unbelievers. If the fire of God's purifying holiness is so intense that the righteous feel the pain of its discipline, then the **sinner** and **ungodly** person will certainly experience God's fiery judgment as a destructive inferno.

Peter's interest in vv 17-18 is not to offer a graphic portrayal of the impending destruction of unbelievers. Rather, his purpose is to encourage believers to remain faithful in their trials and persecution. Their present suffering cannot compare to the utter destruction awaiting unbelievers.

■ **19** The conjunction **so then** (*hōste*) signals a conclusion to the foregoing paragraph. The idea of suffering **according to God's will** is also reflected in 2:15 and 3:17. It is not that suffering in itself is beneficial or that God desires his followers to suffer. Rather, Peter was convinced that suffering was an inevitable result of following God's ways instead of the ways of secular society.

Peter shifts from a direct second person address (**you**) in vv 12-16, to the first person plural (**us**) in v 17, to the third person in vv 18 and 19. When suffering for their faith, believers were to **commit themselves to their faithful Creator.** To **commit** (*paratithesthōsan*) **themselves** meant assigning their lives to a trusted person for safekeeping (see Acts 14:23; 1 Tim 1:18; 2 Tim 1:12-14). The present tense of the verb emphasizes the necessity of continually entrusting themselves to God's care. Jesus entrusted himself to God in his suffering (1 Pet 2:23; see Luke 23:46). Just so, believers were to expect God's protection because of their union with him.

This is the only passage in the NT in which God is explicitly identified as **Creator.** But creation is always viewed as his work in the NT (e.g., Acts 4:24; Rom 1:25; Col 1:16; Rev 4:11). Perhaps the title **Creator** was selected "because it involves power which is able, and love which is willing, to guard His creatures" (Bigg 1905, 182). As **faithful Creator,** God can be trusted to care for his own work by preserving those who trust him for their care.

The concluding phrase of v 19, *en agathopoiiai,* can be translated "while doing good" or "by doing good." The latter suggests that the believers entrust their lives to God precisely by doing good. The former implies that believers should trust God to protect them from danger as they continue to do good things. The latter idea seems more likely. Christians were to keep doing good,
4:19 regardless of the consequences.

Doing good is to be a characteristic feature of the Christian life (2:12, 15, 20; 3:6, 11-12, 13, 17). Suffering for good deeds is not a sign that God has abandoned them or is displeased with them. On the contrary, their suffering is a result of activity that pleases God. As such, it is part of God's will and plan. Consequently, believers are to entrust themselves to God and continue to do good. Peter assures them that God the Creator is with them and will be faithful to them.

FROM THE TEXT

End Times and Suffering. Peter wrote confidently that the end times were imminent. The soon approaching last day was the occasion for encouraging and strengthening believers to be faithful and persevere. With the end in sight, believers were called to clear mindedness, self-control, and prayer (4:7). Even their suffering was placed within the eschatological context of the imminent end. Peter was sure that their suffering was a refining precursor of the judgment that was to come upon all humanity (4:17-18).

First, believers must remain faithful in their identification with Christ, even if this means suffering.

Second, the fiery trials believers face are intended as purifying refinement. Despite the pain, the severity of their suffering is no comparison to the fire of judgment awaiting unbelievers.

Third, there is an implicit urgency to reach out to unbelievers with the saving message of the gospel. The haunting question of v 17—**what will the outcome be for those who do not obey the gospel of God?**—signals the impending doom of unbelievers. But it implicitly urges believers to bear witness to their faith by doing good and remaining faithful during trial. Faithfulness in suffering is a compelling witness (2:12; 3:2).

Encouragement for Sufferers. First Peter offers this encouragement to sufferers (Bartlett 1998, 313): First, suffering provides the test by which believers' faith and convictions are strengthened. It can serve as a refining fire to cleanse and beautify the lives and commitments of believers.

Second, through suffering believers have the opportunity to participate in Jesus' story. Believers share not only in Christ's passion but also in his glory. This will be their permanent reward at the last day. But this glory begins already in the purified lives of those who participate fully in the death and resurrection of Jesus.

Third, faithful people are invited to suffer ***in accordance with God's will*** (4:19). God apparently does not assign every believer to the path of suffering. But when suffering comes, it provides the opportunity for believers to live according to God's will, in trust and doing good. Just as suffering came to Christ uninvited, it also comes to many believers in a variety of forms, including illness, persecution, abandonment, or pain. Such suffering should lead not to despair, but to hope and comfort.

VI. LIFE IN THE CHURCH: I PETER 5:1-11

BEHIND THE TEXT

Chapter 5 begins a new section similar in format to the domestic codes of 2:13—3:7. The household tables dealt with the relationship of believers with *outsiders* (unbelieving slave masters and husbands). But 5:1-6 deals with relationships with *insiders* (others in the church).

Beginning with ch 4 the text alternates between internal and external concerns:

- 4:1-6 deals with the verbal abuse of unbelievers against the believers.
- 4:7-11 addresses the internal concern of mutual love and service within the community.
- 4:12-19 pertains to suffering caused for believers by external forces.
- 5:1-11 addresses the mutual respect and humility that believers must have for one another.

The NT instructs Christian leaders on how to aid the organization and proper functioning of the church body (e.g., 1 Tim 3:1-13; Titus 1:5-9; Acts 20:28-31). But the instructions in 1 Pet 5 are given to help the church survive the crisis of persecution that threatens it.

This section has the following subsections:

1. An appeal to the elders (5:1-4)
2. Instructions to all members (5:5-9)
3. A word of encouragement in the midst of suffering (5:10-11)

A. An Appeal to the Elders (5:1-4)

IN THE TEXT

■ **1** Peter turns his attention to the mutual relationship of believers within the church. ***Therefore*** (*oun*, untranslated by NIV and NRSV; but see NASB) indicates that the following instructions are given explicitly within the context of suffering the Christian community faced (Kelly 1969, 196).

The term **elders** can refer to elderly people in general (see 5:5) or to senior church leaders. Acts reports that Paul assigned *presbyteroi* in the churches he established (Acts 14:23). In the NT the title generally referred to church officials (e.g., Acts 11:30; 14:23; Phil 1:1; 1 Tim 5:17-19; Titus 1:5; 2 John 1; 3 John 1). The specifics of church organization at this time are unknown. But 5:1 seems to indicate that these **elders** were the officials who acted as pastoral leaders of Christian congregations. Peter does not command them, but **appeals** (*parakalō*) to them.

Peter identifies himself as (1) **a fellow elder,** (2) **a witness of Christ's sufferings**, and (3) **one who also will share in the glory to be revealed.** Apart from 1:1, this is the only self-designation of the author in this letter.

The first term, **fellow elder** (*sympresbyteros*), is found nowhere else in the NT (but see Rom 16:3, 7; Phil 2:25; Col 1:7). Peter undoubtedly used the term to underscore his empathy, rather than his authority, with the church leaders in their task. Nonetheless,

> We should not be deceived by this modest stance as if the author were presenting himself as their equal. He has already identified his authority as apostolic (1:1); and so the use of "fellow presbyter" is a polite stratagem of benevolence, somewhat as when a modern bishop of a diocese addresses his "fellow priests." (Brown, Donfried, and Reumann 1973, 152)

Second, the author identifies himself as **a witness of Christ's sufferings. Witness** (*martyr*) seems to indicate that Peter was an eyewitness of the passion of Jesus. But it can also denote one who proclaims what he has seen (e.g., John

1:19; Rom 3:21; 2 Cor 1:12; Rev 2:13) or one who has suffered for testifying to Christ (see Acts 22:20; Rev 2:13; 17:6).

Since **fellow elder** and **witness of Christ's sufferings** are connected by a single definite article (*ho*), it is most likely that Peter is identifying himself with the situation of his readers rather than with any event in the life of Jesus (see Achtemeier 1996, 323-24). In other words, **witness of Christ's sufferings** identifies Peter as one who had suffered for his testimony for Christ.

Third, Peter designates himself as **one who also will share in the glory to be revealed.** This phrase picks up the idea of 4:13, where believers are urged to rejoice in their sufferings with Christ so that they might be overjoyed "when his glory is revealed." Peter does not distinguish his position or experience as anything different from his audience. Rather, he exhorts the elders on the basis of their shared experiences. Like them, he is a **fellow elder,** a fellow **witness** to Christ who has suffered for the faith, and an expectant participant in the soon-to-be-revealed **glory** of Christ when he appears.

■ **2-3** After identifying himself with the leaders, Peter appeals to them to **be shepherds of God's flock that is under** their **care.** The imperative, **be shepherds** (*poimanate*), in the aorist tense conveys a sense of urgency. The OT frequently portrays God as the Shepherd of his people (e.g., Pss 23:1; 80:1; Isa 40:11; Ezek 34:22; Zech 10:3 LXX).

By referring to the Christian community as **God's flock,** Peter reminds the elders that their "sheep" do not belong to them or to Peter. They belong to God alone (see John 10:11-18, 26-27; 21:15-17).

Serving as overseers (*episkopountes*) is omitted by some ancient manuscripts. But it was almost certainly original, since "the three main manuscripts omitting it are all from one geographical area, while those including it are diverse in location" (Grudem 1988, 187). "Shepherd" and "overseer" appear together in 2:25, indicating that the tasks were conceived as intimately related.

Verses 2 and 3 continue with three *mē . . . alla* ("not . . . but . . .") constructions. These contrast three negative depictions of the shepherd's task with three positive descriptions.

First, Peter calls the elders to tend God's flock **not because you must, but because you are willing.** Typically, elders did not volunteer to serve. They were selected by others (see Acts 14:23; Titus 1:5). Nonetheless, they are enjoined to accept this task willingly instead of thinking of it as work that is being forced on them. This first antithesis speaks to the elder's attitude in the performance of his office.

As God wants you to be indicates that God does not want anyone to serve the church grudgingly or under constraint. Instead, elders should serve God willingly, deliberately, intentionally, and gladly.

Second, elders should shepherd God's flock **not greedy for money** (*aischrokerdōs*). This term "implies not only greed, but greed that satisfies itself through fraud" (Michaels 1988, 284-85). Peter prohibits not only fraud, but the motivation that would cause one to serve "only for the money." Elders were typically compensated for their service to the church. But their compensation was not to become the elder's primary concern. Rather, elders were to be **eager to serve** (*prothymōs*), not concerned for personal gain.

Third, elders should serve **not *as*** (*hōs*) **lording it over those entrusted to you, but being examples to the flock.** The focus shifts here from inward motivation to outward behavior. The verb **lording it over** (*katakyrieuontes;* see Mark 10:42; 2 Cor 1:24) negatively characterized Gentile rulers who "exercise their rule to their own advantage and contrary to the interests and well-being of the people" (Verbrugge 2000, 325). Elders were not to abuse their authority for personal benefit or gain. They were to be **examples to the flock.**

Leadership by example is a common NT emphasis (see Matt 10:24-25; Mark 10:42-45; Luke 6:40; John 13:15; 15:20; 1 Cor 11:1; Phil 3:17; 2 Thess 3:9). "In fact, one could well argue that, following the pattern of the ancient world and especially of Judaism, teaching and leading was for the NT basically a matter of example rather than of lecture or command" (Davids 1990, 181).

The theme of "leading by example" fits well the imagery of sheep developed in this passage. In the ancient world, the most effective shepherd was not the one who drove or threatened his flock, but the one who walked in front, calling them to follow.

Peter urged his fellow elders not to use their authority for self-aggrandizement or personal acclaim. Instead, they were to set an example that their flock would be willing and able to follow.

■ **4** Those leaders who fulfill their duty faithfully will be rewarded when Christ returns. The phrase **when the Chief Shepherd appears** identifies the timing of their reward with the second coming (see 1:5, 7, 13; 4:13; 5:1). In striking contrast to his first appearance, Christ's return would not be as an innocent lamb (1:19), but as the victorious **Chief Shepherd,** who would reward his followers.

Chief Shepherd (*archipoimenos*) is found only here in the NT. Jesus was already described as **Shepherd** in 2:25. Now that elders are introduced as shepherds, it is only natural that Jesus would be their master shepherd. Calvin writes, "The word *chief* here does not only mean the principal, but him whose power all others ought to submit to, as they do not represent him except according to his command and authority" (1948, 146-47). Peter and the fellow elders were charged to feed and care for God's flock ("Feed my sheep"; see John 21:15-17). But Christ himself is the **Chief Shepherd.**

Their earthly compensation may not have been much. But Peter reminded the elders that when Christ appeared, **you will receive the crown of glory that will never fade away. Crown** (*stephanos*) was a common image in the first century. Although often associated with royalty, it was also connected with victory in athletic contests and with rewards for service to the state. The genitive **of glory** is appositional: it explains the nature of the crown. Namely, the crown consists of the divine **glory** that will embrace all believers at the time of Christ's return.

Other crowns were woven together from the perishable leaves of ivy or olive. But the elders' crown was to be *amarantinon,* "made of the flower amaranth." The amaranth flower was used to symbolize immortality because its flower never withered and it revived when moistened with water (Robertson 1933, 132).

When Christ appears, he will reward his faithful "undershepherds" by sharing his own unfading and brilliant glory with them. "Peter does not appoint any temporal reward for bishops. As though he would say: Your office is so great that it never can be rewarded here, but ye shall receive an eternal crown, which shall follow it, if ye truly tend the sheep of Christ" (Luther 1990, 209).

B. Instructions to All Members (5:5-9)

■ **5** Beginning with ***likewise*** (*homoiōs,* **in the same way**), Peter turns his attention to the rest of the community. Some interpreters find a subordinate office of ministry in the term **young men** (*neōteroi*). But it probably is used generically to address the rest of his audience (Michaels 1988, 289). Thus, **young men** is not an indication of their age or gender. It is a contrasting description of the rest of the community as distinguished from the **elders** (Reicke 1964, 130).

The congregation is called to ***be submissive to the elders.*** There are no specific instructions concerning the congregation's submissiveness to their elders. The focus is not upon their subordination, but on the importance of being attentive to the guidance of the elders. "Even though elders/shepherds are not to be overbearing in the use of their authority, other members of the congregation may not therefore ignore what they say" (Achtemeier 1996, 332).

This general principle is to underlie all relationships within the church: **All of you, clothe yourselves with humility toward one another.** This sentence gathers into one command the instructions given both to elders and the rest of the congregation. Earlier, believers were urged to treat each other with love (4:8), hospitality (4:9), and service (4:10). Here they are commanded to **clothe** themselves **with humility** (*tapeinophrosynēn;* see Phil 2:3-4). Believers are to treat each other with mutual respect, regardless of their office, task, or function.

Peter reinforces his teaching with an OT quotation: **"God opposes the proud but gives grace to the humble"** (Prov 3:34). This reversal-of-fortunes passage was popular in the early church (see Jas 4:6; *1 Clem*. 30:2; Ign. *Eph* 5:3). Calvin writes:

> We are to imagine that God has two hands; the one, which like a hammer beats down and breaks in pieces those who raise up themselves; and the other, which raises up the humble who willingly let down themselves, and is like a firm prop to sustain them. (1948, 148)

Whether interacting with hostile and haughty members of the secular community or fellow members of the Christian community, believers are to adopt an attitude of humility. They could confidently trust God to vindicate those who were humble.

■ **6 Therefore** connects the imperative of v 6 with the quotation of v 5. Since God opposes the proud but gives grace to the humble, Peter's audience should **humble** themselves **under God's mighty hand.** Peter had already mentioned that suffering was part of God's will (3:17). It was not strange or unusual for believers to experience suffering (4:12). Suffering could serve God's refining purification of their lives (4:17-19). Thus, the duty of believers was not to resist suffering by lashing out at their persecutors or at God. Rather, they were to humble themselves under the mighty hand of God. That is, they were to ***accept*** their ***humble status.***

> The point is not that Christians have a choice of whether they humble themselves; that happens to them simply because they are Christians. The point is rather that the Christians are to acknowledge that such status conforms to God's will and to accept it for that reason, since it is the path God wishes Christians to take. (Achtemeier 1996, 338)

The phrase **under God's mighty hand** supports this viewpoint. **God's mighty hand** is frequently used in the OT for God's deliverance (e.g., Exod 3:19; 6:1; Deut 9:26) and discipline (see Job 30:21; Ps 32:4; Ezek 20:34). Peter's readers were to accept their present humble status, with its accompanying ridicule and persecution, as part of God's ultimate plan and purpose for their lives.

Believers should humble themselves under God's powerful hand so **that he may lift** them **up in due time** (*en kairōi*). In the NT, *kairos* "acquires eschatological overtones, meaning 'the time of crisis,' 'the last time,' 'the time of the End'" (Kelly 1969, 208). Peter's readers were to turn their attention from their present suffering in order to focus upon their future exaltation. They were to experience this when Christ appeared. Only then would God **lift** them **up** (*hypsōsēi*).

That humiliation leads to exaltation is a common theme in the OT (see 1 Sam 2:7-8; Ezek 17:24). Peter may have recalled the teaching of Jesus: "Everyone who exalts himself will be humbled, and he who humbles himself will be exalted" (Luke 14:11; 18:14). God's purpose is not to humiliate his followers, but to exalt them through their humble obedience to his will.

■ **7** Verses 6 and 7 form one sentence in Greek. Peter explains how believers were to humble themselves appropriately. It is by ***casting all*** their ***anxieties on him*** (echoing the language of Ps 55:22). ***Casting*** (*epiripsantes*) is an aorist participle that modifies the action of the imperative verb **humble yourselves** in v 6. *Epiripsantes* means **"to propel something from one place to another"** or **"to transfer one's concerns"** (BDAG, 378). Believers can only submit themselves completely to God when they **cast** their anxieties on him. The call to submit to persecution and suffering must have been difficult for Peter's audience to hear. But he urges them to **cast** these cares and anxieties upon God.

Peter assures believers who cast their cares on God that ***God cares*** for them. This encapsulates the message Peter wants his beleaguered readers to hear. The awe-inspiring truth that ***God cares for*** them empowers believers to live the kind of selfless, loving, humble, and holy lives Peter envisions for them throughout this letter. All Peter's instructions are founded upon the basic conviction that God ***cares*** for them, and that his "mighty hand" is intimately involved in their every experience, even their suffering. Consistent with the teachings of Jesus (Matt 6:25-34), anxiety is out of place.

■ **8** Worry is denounced, but watchfulness is demanded: **be self-controlled** (*nēpsate*) **and alert.** Both imperatives are in the aorist tense, indicating the need for decisive and immediate attention. Here, as in 1:13 and 4:7, self-control calls for sober level-headedness. This would prepare them for the challenges they face.

To be **alert** (*grēgorēsate*) calls for spiritual watchfulness—staying awake and vigilant against unexpected attacks (Oepke 1964, 338). Watchfulness in the face of present danger calls for resistance against their **enemy the devil;** he **prowls around like a roaring lion looking for someone to devour.**

Elsewhere in 1 Peter, the adversaries of believers are described in generic plural terms—the disobedient (2:7-8; 4:17), the pagans (2:12), or the foolish (2:15). But in v 8 their adversary is personified as a single opponent described as their **enemy the devil.** The term **enemy** (*antidikos*) is used only here in the NT to describe the devil. Literally, it refers to an opponent in a court of law (Prov 18:17). But it came to describe enemies in general (Esth 8:11). Here it does not refer to those who drag believers into court for trial, but to the one who opposed the plan of God and caused Christians to suffer.

The word **devil** (*diabolos*) translates the Hebrew "Satan" (*hasatan*), who deliberately slanders and accuses God and his followers (1 Chr 21:1; Job 1—2; Zech 3:1-10). In the NT the **devil** is the Tempter, the rebellious prince of evil, and the opponent and perverter of God's purposes. Peter calls his readers to watch out for the devil, because he **prowls around like a roaring lion looking for someone to devour.**

The devil is compared to a **roaring lion** (see Ps 22:13). The danger of the devil is graphically depicted by his incessant activity as "prowling around" (see Job 1:7) to **devour** someone. **Devour** (*katapiein*) is literally "to drink down" or "gulp down." It denotes the utter destruction the devil deviously seeks to inflict on careless believers.

In 1 Peter, the danger the **devil** represented was not so much physical death as spiritual death. Satan threatens to **devour** believers who turn away from their faith under the pressure of persecution. Physical death can be remedied by spiritual life (see 4:6). But spiritual death is eternal (see Matt 10:28). This explains Peter's careful summons to sober alertness.

■ **9** Christians are to respond to satanic opposition and danger, not with panic or desertion, but with firm resistance. Peter urges them to **resist him, standing firm in the faith.** They are not to "oppose their persecutors." But they are to remain "steadfast under persecution so that they do not become victims of the lion through apostasy" (Best 1971, 174). Peter assumes that Christian resistance to the devil's attacks would be successful.

The word **resist** (*antistēte*) is also used in James, where believers are promised that if they "resist the devil, . . . he will flee from" them (4:7). The believers' resistance is portrayed as an active, determined opposition that will result in successful victory over Satan.

Resistance entails **standing firm in the faith** or being "steadfast in your faith" (NRSV). **Standing firm** (*stereoi*) is an adjective describing something "firm, hard, solid, and compact, like a rock" (Hiebert 1984c, 297). In their inner attitude and resolve, believers are to stand rock-solid in their resistance to Satan.

Faith (*pistei*) depicts the arena in which spiritual battles occur. Like the other references to **faith** in 1:5, 7, 9, and 21, *pistis* does not refer to formal doctrines or beliefs, but to personal commitment and trust in God.

Believers should stand firm in their faith **because you know that your brothers throughout the world are undergoing the same kind of sufferings. Brothers** translates a feminine singular noun, *tēi . . . adelphotēti*, meaning "the brotherhood" (Zodhiates 1992, 80). **Throughout the world** sets the suffering of Peter's readers in a wider context than their local difficulties. Their experience was shared throughout the worldwide Christian family that also experienced and enduring similar suffering. "Isolation in persecution intensifies the agony; assurance that others are enduring it in the same cause consoles" (Best 1971, 175).

C. A Word of Encouragement in the Midst of Suffering (5:10-11)

■ **10-11** Believers have nothing to fear because they are supported by nothing less than **the God of all grace** (see 1:13; 4:10; 5:5). God is the ultimate source and giver of grace (5:5, 12). This final word of encouragement emphasizes the sufficiency of God's **grace** for every occasion (4:10).

God is not only infinite in grace but also the One **who called you to his eternal glory in Christ.** The idea that believers are **called** is a repeated theme (1:15; 2:9, 21). Their calling and salvation are grounded solely in their identification with the crucified and risen Christ (e.g., 1:3, 21; 2:21; 3:18). Like him their lives will include both suffering and glory.

Though rejected and unwanted by the world, God has invited Christians **in Christ** (see 3:16) to share in his **eternal glory.** This is placed in direct contrast to the phrase **after you have suffered a little while.** Throughout the letter Peter contrasts the temporary and short-lived suffering his readers are presently facing with the eternal glory they will experience when Christ returns (1:4, 6; 4:13; 5:1, 4).

The reality of their suffering is not downplayed. Indeed, it is present and real. But Christians are to take courage from the reminder of the glorious and eternal inheritance to which they have been called. Regardless of the pain and suffering they faced in the present, it would be worth it all in the future. Then they will participate in the everlasting glory and triumph of Christ's return.

The verbs at the end of v 10 depict four powerful images of what God will do for the Christians. God **will himself restore you and make you strong, firm and steadfast.** These future indicative verbs offer a divine promise. This is not simply Peter's intercessory wish or desire for them (Achtemeier 1996, 345-46).

Each verb emphasizes a special nuance of strength. **Restore** (*katartisei*) means ***"to put in order"*** or **"to cause to be in a condition to function well"** (BDAG, 526). **Make . . . strong** (*stērixei*) means "strengthen one so he can stand fast in persecution" (Blum 1981a, 253). ***Make you firm*** (*sthenōsei*) promises additional power to resist the attacks of Satan. ***Make you steadfast*** (*themeliōsei*) refers to strengthening as establishing or ***"to lay a foundation"*** (BDAG, 449).

Each term emphasizes a special nuance of strength. But all four verbs are "roughly synonymous." They bolster Peter's depiction of believers in v 9 as **standing firm in the faith** (Michaels 1988, 303). Peter's point is that, since God called them, he will also empower them to stand firm. The verbs testify to God's care for his followers. All they need—whether restoration, support, strength, or a steadfast foundation—God will provide.

Along with the promises of v 10, the brief doxology in v 11 "forms an appropriate conclusion to the entire paranesis of the letter" (Achtemeier 1996, 347). Peter praises God as having **the power for ever and ever.** As in 4:11, **power** (*kratos*) connotes strength and mastery. It is fitting that Peter emphasizes the **power** of God in this conclusion. "The one who has planned and promised is also the one to whom belongs the power to fulfill" (Davids 1990, 196). God's power assures that his plan and purpose will be accomplished in the lives of those who follow him.

FROM THE TEXT

Christian Leaders. The vocation of pastor has always been challenging. Even in Peter's day, the office of elder was vulnerable to abuse and worldly temptation, as Peter's negative prohibitions in 5:2-3 illustrate. "In exhorting pastors to their duty, he points out especially three vices which are found to prevail much, even sloth, desire of gain, and lust of power" (Calvin 1948, 142). But for each vice, Peter provides a positive remedy. It is a spirit of willingness, service, and exemplary behavior.

Much attention is given to the failings of church leaders. And, indeed, their failure is an awful blight upon the bride of Christ. But for every conspicuous failure of church leaders, there are countless ministers, elders, bishops, and pastors who willingly, sacrificially, and faithfully serve God's flock. It can only be hoped that the eyes of laypeople will not be blinded to the selfless and godly service of the many faithful leaders by the glaring failures of the few selfish and faithless ones.

God Cares. Casting all one's cares upon God is a habit that believers of every age must develop. Peter knows that Christians can be sidetracked from their devotion and commitment by the anxieties and concerns of daily life. "To be overwhelmed with anxiety is to be concerned with self rather than with Him" (Beare 1961, 178).

God knows what his people are facing. He knows our concerns. He is actively involved in the events of our lives. And, most importantly, **he cares**. The release of anxiety and worry is not a natural or easy step. But it is essential. This is why Peter calls believers deliberately and decisively to **cast** their anxieties upon God. The surrender of life's worries and anxieties into the mighty hand of God is one of the genuine marks of true faith.

Resisting Satan. Believers are part of a battle between good and evil. **The devil prowls around like a . . . lion** searching for prey. His spiritual assault calls for Christians to be alert and watchful. But his powers of deceit are no match for the mighty hand of God. Believers are to **resist** the devil. Peter promises the empowering strength of God to those who do. This will enable them to **stand firm** against the devil's attacks. Satan's power need not be a source of panic or despair for Christians, for **the God of all grace** is on their side. As Hilary of Arles vividly explains, "There is a world of difference between God and the devil. If you resist God, he will destroy you, but if you resist the devil, you will destroy him" (Bray 2000, 125).

VII. FINAL GREETINGS AND BENEDICTION: 1 PETER 5:12-14

BEHIND THE TEXT

Ancient letters often concluded with personal greetings and a short benediction or blessing from the author (see 1 Cor 16:21; Gal 6:11; Col 4:18; 2 Thess 3:17; Phlm 19). In these last verses Peter commends Silas along with the message of the letter (v 12), passes along some personal greetings (vv 13-14*a*), and concludes with a benediction of peace (v 14*b*).

IN THE TEXT

■ **12** **Silas** is a shortened Greek variant of the Latin name "Silvanus." Both names are used interchangeably in the NT (Robertson 1934, 172-73). Although **Silas** was a common name, most scholars believe his description as **a faithful brother** identifies him as the man who became Paul's traveling companion (see Acts 15:22—18:5). Paul identifies him as the co-sender of both his Thessalonian letters. We cannot prove that the Silas of 1 Peter is the Silas of Acts and Paul's letters. But most scholars agree: "there is no reason for disputing the identity" (Selwyn 1947, 9-10; but see Achtemeier 1996, 350-51).

Peter acknowledges that he wrote this letter **with the help of Silas.** The phrase **with the help of Silas** (*dia Silouanou:* "through Silas") can be interpreted in three different ways: (1) Silas was to deliver the letter; (2) Silas was the amanuensis to whom Peter dictated the letter; or (3) Silas composed the letter under Peter's general instructions.

The connection between **I have written to you** and ***through Silas*** probably identifies Silas as a participant in the writing process, not merely a letter bearer. But scholars debate how much Silas participated in the composition of the letter. The range of opinions runs the gamut. Kelly (1969, 215) argues that Silas is the actual author of the letter. Lohse (1991, 134) contends that the mention of Silas is only a fabrication of "an anonymous author" to gain acceptance. Lacking additional evidence, this debate will undoubtedly continue unresolved.

Surprisingly, Peter claims to have written **briefly** (*di' oligōn:* "in a few [words]"). One hundred five verses seem hardly to qualify as "brief." The author of Hebrews makes the same claim of brevity (13:22). This reference is probably "a formal statement of politeness, for most letters were supposed to be brief" (Davids 1990, 199). But 1 Peter is brief compared to the importance of its message.

The letter was written with the purpose of **encouraging you and tes-**
5:12 **tifying that this is the true grace of God. Encouraging** (*parakalōn*) takes the form of "exhorting" (see 2:11; 5:1). The hortatory tone is evident throughout the letter. **Testifying** (*epimartyrōn*) involves "confirming the testimony" (Beare 1961, 183).

The letter alternates sections witnessing to the content of the Christian faith with sections exhorting its readers to the appropriate response to the faith. Thus, the phrase **encouraging you and testifying** is a very fitting summary of the entire letter.

Peter affirms that **this** message of salvation—both present and future, which his letter conveys—**is the true grace of God.** Despite his audience's doubts and suffering, Peter affirms the truth and the reality of the grace of God they had received. Finally, he exhorts them one last time to **stand fast in it.**

At the risk of oversimplification, the message of the letter may be summarized in this final injunction: **stand fast.** Now is not the time to back away from the **true grace of God** they had received. As they resist the attacks of the devil represented by their current suffering (5:8-9), they must **stand fast** until death or until Christ returns. Peter's admonition to **stand fast** echoes the words of Eph 6:13—"after you have done everything, . . . stand."

■ 13 The personal greetings of the letter are found in the sentence, **She who is in Babylon, chosen together with you, sends you her greetings.** Some suggest **she** is a reference to Peter's wife. But if **she** refers to Peter's wife, it is difficult to explain why he would refer to her cryptically as **she who is in Babylon** instead of mentioning her by name.

It is more likely that **she** refers to the church. In Greek "church" (*ekklēsia,* added to the text in a few ancient manuscripts) is a feminine noun. Thus, it was grammatically appropriate to refer to the church with a feminine designation (see 2 John 1, 13; Eph 5:22-33; Rev 19:7; 21:2; 22:17).

Babylon has been interpreted both figuratively and literally by various scholars (see Introduction). Some argue for the literal understanding of **Babylon** as a specific location in Egypt or in Mesopotamia. But most scholars believe it figuratively depicts Rome. Rome was often identified with Babylon in both Christian (Rev 14:8; 17:5, 18; 18:2) and Jewish tradition (*Sib. Or.* 5:143, 159; *2 Bar.* 11:1; 67:7).

"Babylon is the place of exile (Ps 137; Isa 43:14 in context with 5-6) and it is a wicked and haughty city (Isa 13; Jer 50—51; Dan 5:17-31). In Revelation it is also the place of persecution (Rev 17:5-6)" (Davids 1990, 202). All these meanings would be appropriate for 1 Peter.

By referring to Rome as **Babylon,** Peter is not trying to disguise his location. He is merely continuing his imagery of the church as the new people of God (see 1:1; 2:9-10).

Chosen together with you echoes the description of Peter's audience as "God's elect" (1:1). He affirms the elect status of the church **in Babylon** (Rome) as part of the brotherhood "throughout the world," mentioned in 5:9. As believers who were **chosen together with you,** this church shared in their divine election. But the modifier **in Babylon** implies a share also in their suffering and their status as "resident aliens" as well. **Babylon** is a reminder that "it is not just the Christians in Asia Minor who are aliens and exiles. Babylon was the place of Judah's exile, and in Babylon as in Asia Minor, Christians are still outsiders, exiles, until Christ returns in glory" (Bartlett 1998, 318).

The church in Rome from where Peter wrote **sends you her greetings, and so does my son Mark.** Early church tradition has traced virtually every known feature of Peter's life, and there is no other indication that he had a son named Mark. Thus, **Mark** probably refers to John Mark, the presumed author of the second Gospel, closely associated with Peter during the later years of his life. The description of Mark as **my son** was probably intended as a spiritual designation, not one of physical lineage (see 1 Tim 1:2, 18).

■ 14 Peter encourages his readers to **greet one another with a kiss of love** (*philōmati agapēs;* compare *philōmati hagiōi,* "a holy kiss" in Rom 16:16; 1 Cor

16:20; 2 Cor 13:12; 1 Thess 5:26). Justin Martyr assigned "the kiss . . . a regular place in the Eucharistic liturgy" by the middle of the second century (Best 1971, 179-80).

Love is a persistent theme of this letter (see 1:22; 2:11, 17; 4:8, 12). Thus, it is not surprising that the liturgical kiss is described as **a kiss of love** (rather than "a holy kiss"). This reinforces the emphasis upon brotherly love. A kiss on the cheek was a common Oriental greeting and farewell among friends (see Luke 7:45), as common as shaking hands in the West. Peter calls to his readers: **Greet one another with a kiss of love.** The kiss gave genuine expression to their common bond of love in Christ.

The letter concludes with a simple benediction: **Peace to all of you who are in Christ.** With the word **peace** (*eirēnē*), Peter probably has in mind the wider range of meaning represented by the Hebrew word *shalom* (see 1:2, "grace and peace"). *Shalom* conveys a sense of well-being and salvation. In the midst of the outward turmoil of persecution and suffering, the blessing of **peace** would be a peculiarly appropriate wish for Peter's readers.

The source and foundation of **peace** is explicitly recognized as **in Christ.** As the one who "suffered for you, leaving you an example" (2:21), Christ perfectly models how believers should respond to situations of suffering. Moreover, he guarantees **peace** to those who identify themselves completely with him—not only in his suffering, but also in his ultimate vindication and victory.

2 PETER

INTRODUCTION

Second Peter is arguably the most neglected book in the NT. Although its opening verse claims it was written by the apostle Simon Peter, there are more doubts expressed about the authenticity of 2 Peter than any other NT writing. The unpopularity of this book is intensified by its primarily argumentative and negative outlook. The original readers of the letter were threatened by the immoral lifestyle and errant doctrine of false teachers. Consequently, its author attacks and rebukes these opponents extensively and mercilessly. Accustomed to turning to Scripture for nurture or inspiration, many readers are put off by the aggressive onslaught of 2 Peter's criticism of false doctrine and its teachers.

Nonetheless, 2 Peter offers a message today's believers should not be so quick to ignore. Believers can learn from the ancient message of 2 Peter to be on guard against postmodern forms of ethical relativism and theological pluralism. This letter reminds Christians that the only solid foundation for truth is found in the Scriptures and the apostolic tradition. It warns believers of the risk of being carried away by lofty-sounding arguments or a lifestyle of selfish convenience. Sometimes believers need to be reminded of the dangers of false teaching and the condemning lies of its proponents as well as the truth of God's plan of salvation through Jesus Christ. Second Peter is the passionate broadcast of these important reminders.

A. Authorship

Second Peter begins with the assertion that it was written by **Simon Peter, a servant and apostle of Jesus Christ** (1:1). The author claims to have been an eyewitness of Jesus' transfiguration (1:16-18). He refers to Paul as his **dear brother** (3:15) in such a way that he "appears to put his own authority on the same level as that of the apostle to the Gentiles" (Martin 1978, 383). As a result, this letter has traditionally been identified as the second Petrine Epistle with the Apostle Peter as its author.

The Petrine authorship of 2 Peter, however, has been widely rejected by modern scholars. Kelly writes, "Scarcely anyone nowadays doubts that 2 Peter is pseudonymous" (1969, 235). Thus, most contemporary scholars believe 2 Peter was written at a later date by an unknown author writing what he believed Peter would have said under the circumstances.

The arguments against Petrine authorship are numerous and varied. But for each objection, counterarguments have been posed in rebuttal. The scope of the present commentary prohibits an extensive discussion of the complex arguments and counterarguments for and against Petrine authorship. But we will give attention to many of them in the course of our interpretation of the text of 2 Peter. The following is an overview of the discussion (see Blum 1981b, 258-60).

Arguments Against Petrine Authorship	Counterarguments
1. The letter was not widely known or recognized by the early church.	1. Lack of popularity could be due to the letter's brevity. Lack of circulation could be attributed to an original audience in a sparsely populated or remote area.
2. The letter's style is very different from 1 Peter.	2. Evaluation of stylistic differences is highly subjective. Differences could be explained by different amanuenses (secretaries) writing the letters.
3. Peter's name was used in connection with some gnostic literature.	3. The early church eventually recognized and accepted 2 Peter despite the existence of gnostic writings in his name. This argues in favor of genuine Petrine authorship.

4. Second Peter seems to be dependent upon the letter of Jude.	4. It is impossible to demonstrate almost any literary argument.
5. The language and concepts are too Hellenistic for a Galilean fisherman.	5. We know too little about the influence of Hellenism upon Peter to be sure. An amanuensis could explain Hellenistic influence.
6. The problem of the delay of Christ's return is a second-century issue.	6. Various NT texts demonstrate that this was already a concern in the first century (see Matt 25:1-13; John 21:20-23; Acts 1:6-11; 2 Thess 2:1-4; Heb 9:28).
7. The Pauline letters referred to in 3:15-16 were not collected or considered Scripture until the second century.	7. This reference to Paul's letters does not necessarily include all of Paul's letters. It may refer only to those known to the author.
8. The letter sounds like "early Catholicism" rather than the first generation of Christians.	8. That a concern for orthodoxy and tradition is a sign of "early Catholicism" is subjective and arbitrary.
9. If Peter wrote it, why was there so much doubt about it and reluctance to accept it by the early church?	9. This would be perfectly normal if Peter wrote to Christians in a remote area, preventing early circulation of the letter. The circulation of pseudonymous works in Peter's name may have caused the hesitancy.

The arguments concerning the authorship of 2 Peter are complex and problematic. Gilmour observes that "those defending the traditional view and those positing some form of non-Petrine production often use similar arguments to prove their case" (2001, 291). The result is an impasse. "The arguments for and against have been repeated time and again but the fact remains that there is simply not enough evidence to achieve a consensus" (Gilmour 2001, 308).

Pseudonymous Writings

Many scholars simply presume that the practice of falsely ascribing a literary work to a well-known teacher or leader ("pseudepigraphy") was broadly es-

tablished and accepted by early Christians. Scores of such works survive; others known to have existed are no longer extant.

But there is also considerable evidence that early church leaders emphatically condemned pseudonymous works. When an Asian presbyter admitted composing a document titled *Acts of Paul* in Paul's name, both he and his work were condemned. Tertullian (A.D. 160-230) declared that the author was not "fit to hold office in a Christian church," although he "claimed to have done it from the highest motive, for love of Paul" (Guthrie 1970, 679).

In A.D. 190, Bishop Serapion of Antioch wrote of the pseudonymous *Gospel of Peter:* "We receive both Peter and the other Apostles of Christ; but as experienced men we reject the writings falsely ascribed with their names, since we know that we did not receive such from our fathers" (cited by Guthrie 1970, 679). But his assessment was on theological, not literary or historical grounds.

Thus, "deliberate pseudepigraphy was not . . . an established and acceptable convention." The "overwhelming majority" of the surviving pseudonymous writings are tendentious, mostly gnostic, "and many were clearly written to propagate such views." They are quite different in content from the canonical works (Walls 1979, 638-39).

Wilder's recent study on the early church response to pseudonymity concludes:

> First, the second-century church did not readily accept pseudonymity; they greeted the fictive use of an apostle's name with disdain. Second, the rejection of certain apostolic pseudepigrapha by the early church favors the view that to add pseudonymously to an existing body of literature, i.e. the genuine writings of the apostles, was a violation of their written work. Third, both the authenticity of writings and their content were decisive criteria for the early church when recognizing books as normative. (Wilder 2004, 256)

For further reading on the early church's reluctance to accept pseudonymous writings, see:

Guthrie, Donald. 1965. The Development of the Idea of Canonical Pseudepigrapha in New Testament Criticism. Pages 14-39 in *The Authorship and Integrity of the New Testament.* Edited by Kurt Aland. London: SPCK.

Wilder, Terry L. 2004. *Pseudonymity, the New Testament, and Deception.* Lanham, Md.: University Press of America.

For a standard discussion of the contrasting view see:

Aland, Kurt. 1965. The Problem of Anonymity and Pseudonymity in Christian Literature of the First Two Centuries. Pages 1-13 in *The Authorship and Integrity of the New Testament.* Edited by Kurt Aland. London: SPCK.

Given the early church's reluctance to accept pseudonymous writings, we cannot presume that 2 Peter was written under an assumed name. The early church ultimately concluded that Peter was its author. But its perceived apostolic teaching, not its authorship, made it authoritative and led to its canonical status. Decisions about authorship are a historical judgment, not a value judgment. Credible, confessing Christians defend both sides in the debate. There is no right or wrong side, just different sides, with different consequences.

Ultimately, one's personal presuppositions draw the final straw and place its small but decisive weight upon the evenly balanced scale of decision. I have serious misgivings about the Petrine authorship of 2 Peter. That it was virtually unknown during the first two hundred years of church history is baffling. And its close parallels with the shorter letter of Jude suggest literary dependency.

But 2 Peter displays no gnostic or doctrinally distinctive views that require it to be seen as necessarily a product of the second century. Despite doubts, the early church ultimately accepted 2 Peter as canonical and acknowledged its Petrine origin. Likewise, despite my reservations, I cautiously affirm the Apostle Peter as the author of 2 Peter.

B. The Relationship Between 2 Peter and Jude

The similarities between 2 Peter and Jude are striking. Both are written against essentially the same false teaching. And the words and descriptions denouncing the heresy are clearly similar. Some of the more striking parallels include:

Jude		*2 Peter*
4	the false teachers' "condemnation" from the past	2:3
4	[they] "deny" the "Sovereign and Lord"	2:1
6	angels confined for judgment—"gloomy" (2 Peter) and "darkness" (Jude, translating the same Greek word, *zophos*)	2:4
7	Sodom and Gomorrah as examples of judgment of gross evil	2:6
8	[they] "reject [Jude]/despise [2 Peter] authority"	2:10
9	angels do not bring "slanderous accusation[s]"	2:11
12	[the false teachers are] "blemishes"	2:13
12	Jude: "clouds without rain, blown along by the wind" Peter: "springs without water and mists driven by a storm"	2:17

18	“scoffers” following “their own evil [Peter]/ungodly [Jude] desires”	3:3

(Moo 1996, 16)

The parallels are not lengthy; but they are remarkable. Many involve words and expressions not used elsewhere in the NT, occurring in the same order in both letters.

Most interpreters agree that such parallels necessitate some kind of literary or oral dependence. Three possibilities have been suggested: (1) Peter borrowed from Jude; (2) Jude borrowed from Peter; (3) both borrowed from a common source no longer in existence.

Traditional scholars believed Jude borrowed material from 2 Peter. They presumed “that the Apostle Peter would hardly have borrowed from a lesser figure, Jude, whereas the converse was quite plausible” (Neyrey 1993, 120). Recent scholars, however, believe 2 Peter borrowed from Jude for a variety of reasons:

First, the similarities in Jude appear in a compact and succinct form in one brief chapter. But the similarities in 2 Peter are spread over three chapters. It seems more probable that 2 Peter borrowed randomly from Jude than that Jude condensed his material from 2 Peter.

Second, 2 Peter discusses the delay of Christ’s return, but Jude does not. The concern over the delay arose later in church history. Thus, Jude’s omission may indicate an earlier date.

Third, 2 Peter places the OT historical examples in chronological order. Jude’s noncanonical examples (the archangel Michael and the prophet Enoch) are omitted in 2 Peter. Both changes may be explained as editorial corrections by 2 Peter (see van Houwelingen 1993, 18).

On closer inspection, these arguments prove to be largely subjective. First, there is no reason why Jude could not have condensed the material of 2 Peter. “In addition to originality, brevity can also point to a later work of summarization” (van Houwelingen 1993, 18). Second, the lack of discussion of the second coming in Jude may indicate only that it was not an issue for his readers. Arguments from silence are not compelling, nor do they indicate an earlier date. Third, Jude could have added extrabiblical examples to his letter because he considered them relevant and meaningful for his audience.

In summary, the evidence is not compelling enough to make it a working hypothesis (Moo 1996, 18). All three theories are plausible, but the evidence for literary interdependence between Jude and 2 Peter is too ambiguous to be certain. “The problem, like so many other purely literary problems of NT criticism, must be left unresolved” (Guthrie 1970, 925). This commentary notes parallels between 2 Peter and Jude but makes no assumption as to their interdependence.

C. Audience

Some scholars assume 2 Peter was written to the same audience as 1 Peter. Evidence for this conclusion is found in the comment: "this is now my second letter to you" (3:1). If this refers to 1 Peter, the letter is addressed to Christians in "Pontus, Galatia, Cappadocia, Asia and Bithynia" (1 Pet 1:1).

The reference to a previous letter might not be to 1 Peter but to an otherwise unknown letter. If it refers to 1 Peter, why does he make "virtually no use of the content of that first letter" (Hillyer 1992, 10)? The two letters have little shared subject matter, beyond the description of both letters as "reminders to stimulate you to wholesome thinking" (3:1).

First Peter evidences little familiarity with its widely-scattered audience. But the author of 2 Peter seems to know his audience well. He may even have completed a preaching mission among them (1:16). The reference to a second letter need not imply that 1 Peter was the first. I presume that the audiences of 1 and 2 Peter are probably different.

In this letter Peter probably has a predominantly Gentile audience in mind. It is addressed "to those who . . . have received a faith as precious as ours" (1:1). This seems to compare the readers' faith to that of *Jewish* Christians. Moreover, the letter's readers are said to have escaped the "corruption in the world caused by evil desires" (1:4). This "fits Christians from a Gentile background better than Jewish Christians" (Moo 1996, 25).

Peter assumes his readers are familiar with Paul (3:15). This may indicate an audience somewhere in Asia Minor, where Paul spent much of his time evangelizing. Second Peter was accepted first in Asia Minor. This lends credibility to the likelihood of an Anatolian audience. But this is far from certain. There is simply not enough evidence to determine the destination.

D. Place and Date

The letter's place of origin is also unknown. Many favor Rome, since Peter is known to have been there. But the letter offers no information as to Peter's situation or location at the time of writing. Since Peter traveled widely, the letter could have been written from anywhere in the Mediterranean world.

The date depends on one's conclusion concerning authorship. The letter has been dated as early as A.D. 60 and as late as A.D. 160. The reference to Paul and "all his letters" (3:16) requires a date after a number of Pauline letters were written and circulated. This sets the earliest possible date for 2 Peter at around A.D. 60. It is a mistake to interpret "all his letters" as a reference to "a fixed collection of Paulines already recognized as canonical" (Green 1987, 41). This would require a date as late as A.D. 160. But this is unnecessary. All Paul's letters refers simply to "all the letters known to the writer" (Mayor 1978, 165).

If Peter was not the author, then 2 Peter was probably composed sometime between A.D. 80 and 120. If Peter wrote it, it was probably written between A.D. 64 and 68, shortly before his death (see 1:13-14). Sensing his martyrdom approaching (John 21:18-19), Peter wrote this last letter of advice and warning before his death.

E. Genre and Unity of the Letter

The unity of 2 Peter has been challenged by various scholars (see van Houwelingen 1993, 26-27). Some take the polemical digression against false teachers in ch 2 and its close association with Jude as an indication that ch 2 was composed separately from the other two chapters. Other scholars contend that 3:1 marks the beginning of a separate letter. Thus, chs 1 and 2 represent the previous letter to which 3:1 refers.

Despite these objections, most scholars recognize the cohesive unity of 2 Peter. The letter displays a remarkable structural unity. The first chapter establishes the true teaching of the Christian faith, especially as it relates to Christ and moral behavior. Chapter 2 describes the depravity of the false teachers, who deny the true teaching of the Christian faith. Chapter 3 explains the Christian teaching about the end times, especially the promised return of Christ and the ethical behavior expected of those who would be prepared for his coming. The seamless transition from one topic to the next suggests the inherent unity of the letter.

Bauckham argues that 2 Peter "belongs to two literary genres, the letter and the testament" (1983, 131). The epistolary genre is especially evident at the beginning: the typical elements of salutation (1:1), greeting (1:2), and occasion (1:12-15) are visible. Moreover, the author identifies his writing as a "letter" in 3:1. Thus, 2 Peter follows the literary patterns of an ancient letter.

But 2 Peter also "uses the literary conventions of a testament, that is, a farewell discourse in which a departing hero tells the future and gives advice on proper behavior in the present and future" (Harrington 2003, 229; see, e.g., Deuteronomy; Josh 23—24; *T. 12 Patr.*; and John 14—17). In testamentary style, Peter anticipates his death (1:12-15), presses his readers to remember his teaching and example (1:12-15; 3:1-2), makes predictions about the future (2:1-4; 3:3), and issues moral exhortations his readers are to follow (1:5-7; 3:11-18). Thus, 2 Peter follows the genre conventions of both an ancient letter and a testament.

F. Purpose of the Letter

Second Peter was written to remind its readers of the true tenets of the Christian faith and to warn believers against the deceptions of false teachers. Its specific occasion was Peter's recognition that his death was approaching (1:13-14). Also, his readers were facing the grave danger posed by false teachers (2:1-3).

Peter reminds his readers that faith in Jesus Christ is not based upon myths or clever stories (1:16). Rather, its foundation is laid in the sure revelation of God and the testimony of eyewitnesses and apostles (1:16-21). Peter urges believers to continue to grow in their saving knowledge of Christ. Christians can be confident of their salvation as they persistently pursue Christian moral virtues in ever increasing measure (1:5-10).

Peter also warns his readers of false teachers (2:1-22) who deny the second coming of Christ (3:3-4) and live immoral and greedy lives (2:1-3, 13-16). As Christians await the sure return of Christ, they must remain alert to error in preparation for his return by living holy and godly lives (3:11-18).

G. The Identity of the False Teachers

Many attempts have been made to identify Peter's opponents. From Peter's arguments against them, they were probably libertines who promised a freedom that, in practice, amounted to nothing more than moral license for sexual depravity (2:19). They considered themselves Christians (2:20-21). But practically, they denied the lordship of Christ (2:1). Peter calls them "false teachers" (2:1) whose greedy and immoral lifestyle brings the Christian faith into disrepute (2:2-3).

It is difficult to ascertain the precise nature of the false doctrine Peter opposed. The false teachers reject the second coming (3:4) as based upon "cleverly invented stories" of the apostles (1:16). They also reject their accountability to a final day of judgment (2:3, 9-10). The targets of the false teachers are recent or unestablished converts (2:18).

The deceptive appeal of the false teachers seems to rest upon their: (1) use of lofty and impressive rhetoric (2:18); (2) appeal to the lustful desires of sinful humanity (2:18); and (3) misinterpretation and distortion of Paul's teachings to justify their perversion of the Christian lifestyle (3:16). Peter claims they are self-deceived (2:12-14) and destined to ultimate destruction and condemnation (2:3, 9-10).

Traditionally, the false teachers have been identified as gnostics. They were often associated with the sexual immorality denounced in the letter. Moreover, gnostics claim that salvation is acquired through revealed knowledge (*gnōsis*). Peter emphasizes saving knowledge (*epignōsis*) in contrast to the alleged knowledge (*gnōsis*) of his opponents.

But the traditional identification of the false teachers has been convincingly rejected. "There is no evidence of cosmological dualism (spirit versus matter), which is often taken as a defining feature of Gnosticism" (Harrington 2003, 235). Moreover, Peter uses both terms for knowledge (*epignōsis* and *gnōsis*) without any indication of a biased preference for either. Bauckham notes, "Careful study shows that . . . 'knowledge' in 2 Peter (*epignōsis* and *gnōsis*) is free of polemical overtones and cannot have been a catchword of the opponents" (1983, 157).

Neyrey suggests the false teachers may have espoused a doctrine similar to that of the Epicureans (1993, 122-28; 1980, 407-31). They embraced the complete transcendence of God. That is, God was unconcerned with humanity, much less morality. Epicureans did not believe God worked in the world according to some divine plan. The world appeared by chance and humans were free to live as they pleased. They expected no judgment, denying an afterlife with rewards or punishments. Epicureans were infamous even among pagans "as immoral people whose 'theology' encouraged wickedness and vice" (Neyrey 1993, 123).

Epicurean thought could have influenced the false teachers of 2 Peter. But that is as far as the evidence goes. The false teachers were undoubtedly influenced by a number of popular pagan ideas and beliefs current in their time. Epicureanism could have been one of these influences. But there is not enough evidence to identify the false teachers as exclusively Epicurean.

Not every false teaching can be neatly identified and categorized under a convenient label. There is simply not enough historical information about the audience, their location, or the false teachers to identify them conclusively.

H. Themes of the Letter

Day of Judgment. Several striking themes surface in 2 Peter. The letter strongly affirms Christ's return accompanied by the day of judgment. God's perspective on time is different from the human perspective. While Christ's return may appear to be tardy and overdue from a human viewpoint, it is not so for God (3:8). The apparent delay in Christ's return is due to the patience of God. This allows more time for believers to pursue holiness and for the ungodly to repent (3:9, 15). But Christ will certainly return at an unexpected time; and the world will be subjected to judgment (3:9-10). At that time the ungodly will be condemned and destroyed (2:1, 3*b*, 9-10*a*, 12; 3:7, 16). But believers will be warmly welcomed into the eternal kingdom (1:11), where they will dwell in a new heaven and a new earth (3:13).

The final judgment will resemble God's acts of judgment recorded in the OT. God did not spare the fallen angels whom he sent to hell (2:4). He did not spare the world in the time of Noah (2:5). He did not spare Sodom and Gomorrah (2:6). Therefore, believers should know he will not spare the ungodly at the day of judgment (2:9). But God rescued righteous Noah and Lot from destruction. So he can be trusted to save the righteous on the last day (2:5-9).

Second Peter is the only NT writing that explicitly describes the judgment of God as accompanied by the destruction of the world by fire (3:7, 12). The creation of the world took place by the power of God's word. Likewise, the power of God's word destroyed the world with water during the days of Noah. In the same way, the word of God will effect divine judgment and destruction on the world by fire at the last day (3:5-7). "This same Word of God will also create the new heavens and the new earth, where only righteousness can dwell (3:11-13)" (Watson 1998b, 330). Peter connects the second coming with the day of judgment. God is the Judge of the last day (3:5-10), but this day corresponds with the day of Christ's return (3:4).

Scripture and Apostolic Tradition. Second Peter strongly asserts that orthodox Christian doctrine is based on the dual foundation of Scripture and apostolic tradition (1:16-21; 3:2). The false teaching is based on empty, lofty-sounding arguments that appeal to the lustful desires of sinful humanity (2:18). In contrast, Peter urges his readers to recall the words of the holy prophets (Scripture) and the teachings of Jesus (tradition) and the apostles who pass it on (3:2). With his repeated appeal, Peter establishes Scripture and apostolic tradition as the litmus test for orthodox Christian teaching.

Divine Inspiration. One of the NT's greatest statements about divine inspiration is contained in this letter. The holy Scriptures are not the result of the prophets' own interpretation. Rather, Scripture is divinely inspired because the prophets spoke the words of God as they were "carried along by the Holy Spirit" (1:21). Likewise, the apostles' testimony is inspired inasmuch as they were eyewitnesses of Christ's majesty (1:16) and they heard the voice of God concerning Christ (1:17-18).

Surprisingly, Peter considers an unspecified collection of Paul's letters as inspired Scripture (3:16). Just as the OT prophets were moved by the Holy Spirit, Paul wrote his letters "with the wisdom that God gave him" (3:15). This precedent facilitated the later church's establishment of a Christian canon that was deemed both authoritative and inspired and was placed on an equal footing with the OT Scriptures.

The Evidence of a Holy Lifestyle. A final theme is the emphasis on the believers' holy lifestyle as an inherent reflection of their faith in Christ. The false teachers' denial of Christ's return and judgment led them into immoral sensuality and greed. In contrast, Peter emphasizes that saving knowledge of Christ leads believers into truth and righteousness, which enable them to "escape the corruption . . . caused by evil desires" (1:4). Everything needed for salvation and a moral life of virtue is grounded in the knowledge of Christ (1:3-4). "Christians must make every effort to grow in righteousness in order to confirm Christ's call and election (1:3, 11; 3:18)" (Watson 1998b, 330).

Moral effort includes pursuing and nurturing the ethical virtues, which prevent believers from becoming ineffective and unproductive (1:5-8). Peter calls his readers to live holy and godly lives as they anticipate the return of Christ. When he comes believers should be at peace with Christ. This is possible only as they emulate Christ in their daily behavior (3:14).

According to 2 Peter, bad teaching results in bad behavior. Likewise, incorrect behavior reflects an incorrect faith. "Immoral behavior is an affront to Christ's status as Lord and Savior. It amounts to denying his authority and maligning the way of truth (2:1-2)" (Watson 1998b, 331). Thus, one of the pervasive themes of 2 Peter is that true saving knowledge of Jesus Christ as Lord and Savior will motivate believers to make every effort to live virtuous and holy lives.

COMMENTARY

I. GREETING: 2 PETER 1:1-2

BEHIND THE TEXT

The Apostle Peter is commonly known by three names in the NT: **Simon, Peter,** and Cephas. **Simon** is his Jewish birth name (John 21:15). At Caesarea Philippi Jesus gave **Simon** the name **Peter** (Aramaic: *Cephas*) when he made the confession that Jesus is Messiah (Matt 16:13-16; Mark 8:27-30; Luke 9:18-20; see John 1:42). **Peter** (or Cephas) is derived from the word for "rock" (Greek: *petros;* Aramaic: *kephas*).

The manuscripts are equally divided in their spelling of **Simon**. Some contain the Greek spelling *Simōn* while others use the more uncommon Hebrew spelling *Symeōn*. *Symeōn* is probably the original. *Simōn* was probably intended as a correction by copyists for clarification (Metzger 1994, 629). Some believe the name *Symeōn* reflects a weak attempt by a pseudonymous writer to lend authenticity to 2 Peter (Kelly 1969, 296). But it is difficult to understand why a writer would assume the less common name. Peter himself would probably spell his name *Symeōn,* since this Semitic spelling "would have been the form natural to him from birth" (Moo 1996, 33).

IN THE TEXT

■ **1** Second Peter begins with the three customary elements of all ancient letters: (1) writer's name, (2) name of the audience, and (3) introductory greeting.

The writer is identified as **Simon Peter.** Since Greek was so prevalent, many people used one name from their native language and a second name in Greek. Thus, **Simon** (*Symeōn*) is the Jewish name and **Peter** (*Petros*) is the Greek name.

The author describes himself as **a servant and apostle of Jesus Christ** (see 1 Pet 1:1). Peter was *sent out* (*apostolos: **one who is sent out***) by **Jesus Christ** to preach the good news (see John 21:15-19; Matt 28:16-20). **Of . . . Jesus Christ** emphasizes the origin and nature of Peter's authority. Peter does not claim personal or inherent authority; his authority is derived from **Jesus Christ.**

A **servant** (*doulos: **slave***) depicts a bondservant "who is in a permanent relation of servitude to another, his will being altogether consumed in the will of the other" (Zodhiates 1992, 483). By juxtaposing **servant** and **apostle,** he paradoxically emphasizes both his dependence on Christ and his authority as his ambassador (van Houwelingen 1993, 28).

The letter is addressed ***to those who have received a faith of equal privilege as ours through the righteousness of our God and Savior Jesus Christ.*** This description makes three important points:

First, Peter emphasizes his readers' ***equal privilege*** with the apostles before God. ***Equal privilege*** (*isotimon*) can refer to ***equal value*** (NIV: **a faith as precious as ours**) or ***equal privilege*** (NASB: "a faith of the same kind as ours"). *Isotimon* in secular Greek denoted "the same status and rank in civil life" (Stählin 1965, 349). Thus, ***equal privilege*** is the more likely meaning. By virtue of their **faith,** all believers are equal in status before God.

The comparison **as ours** (*hēmin*) has been taken in three ways: (1) The writer assures Jewish readers that their faith is equal to that of the apostles (Stählin 1965, 349, n. 32). (2) Peter assures a Gentile audience that their faith places them on equal footing with Jewish Christians (Mayor 1978, 81). (3) If the letter is pseudonymous, the author places the faith of later believers on a par with first-century Christians (Kelly 1969, 297). Assuming Petrine authorship, the second option is preferable (see Acts 10:34). Gentile Christians are not second-class believers. Their privileges are the same as those of Jews.

Second, Peter's description of his audience as those who have **received a faith** emphasizes the divine/human cooperation of salvation. **Faith** (*pistis*) here carries the typical meaning of ***the act of believing,*** not "a body of doctrine" (Green 1987, 68). **Faith** stresses a Christian's deliberate act of putting trust in Christ. But **received** recognizes faith as a gift of God. Salvation depends on a personal decision to believe. But the ability to believe is a gift from God, **received** through Jesus Christ. This God-given capacity to believe is what Wesley called prevenient or "preventing grace" (1979b, 509, 512). Thus, Peter underscores a divine-human synergism in salvation. We must choose to exercise our God-given capacity to believe to be saved. Significantly, Peter acknowledges that his readers have received this privileged salvation.

The third point Peter clarifies in his description of the audience is this: Faith is received **through the righteousness of our God and Savior Jesus Christ**. Unlike Paul's usage, **righteousness** here "regularly means justice or fair dealing" (Hillyer 1992, 158). This characteristic of God, his **righteousness,** is the source of salvation. Thus, Peter associates *dikaiosynē* with its ethical connotations (2:5, 7-8, 21; 3:13)—***justice*** or ***fairness.*** Because God is fair, he has justly given Peter's audience a faith that grants them equality with all Christians. "Each Christian receives from the gracious righteousness of God, which acts impartially towards all, an equal faith which makes all equally righteous before God" (Stählin 1965, 349).

The phrase **our God and Savior Jesus Christ** is christologically significant. The omission of the Greek article ("the") before **Savior** identifies Jesus as **God** here. This is comparable to the similarly constructed phrase **our Lord and Savior Jesus Christ** in 1:11; 3:18; see 2:20 and 3:2. In this phrase, both **Lord** and **Savior** identify Jesus Christ. Robertson notes, "The grammar demands that one person be meant" (1933, 147; but see Neyrey 1993, 147-48). This is one of the few verses in the NT in which Jesus is explicitly called **God** (see John 1:1; 20:28; Heb 1:8-9).

Savior (*sōtēros*) is relatively rare in the NT, appearing only sixteen times as a christological title. But it is a favorite designation by Peter, who uses the term five times (1:1, 11; 2:20; 3:2, 18). As **Savior,** Jesus rescues humanity from their sins and keeps them safe (= salvation).

■ **2** The first part of the greeting—**grace and peace be yours in abundance**—is identical to the greeting in 1 Pet 1:2. **Grace** (*charis*) and **peace** (*eirēnē*) appear in the greetings of all the Pauline letters. This greeting combines the usual Greek epistolary greeting (*chairein:* ***greetings***) with the customary Hebrew greeting (*shalom*, in Greek *eirēnē:* ***peace***). "In the Christian context these terms refer to what God has made possible through Jesus' death and resurrection: divine favor ('grace') and 'peace' with God and with other persons" (Harrington 2003, 240). The passive verb *plēthyntheiē,* ***may they be in abundance,*** expresses the desire that Peter's audience might experience these divine gifts in ever increasing measure.

The means by which **grace and peace** are increased in the lives of believers is **through the knowledge of God and of Jesus our Lord. Knowledge** (*epignōsei*) is a significant term in 2 Peter (1:2, 3, 8; 2:20). "Conversion to the Christian faith can be described almost technically as coming to a knowledge (*epignōsis*) of the truth" (Schmitz 1976, 405). The ***true knowledge*** **of God and of Jesus our Lord** excels the false knowledge (*gnōsis*) of his opponents, who continue in immoral behavior (2:17-21). His opponents claim "knowledge" (*gnōsis*), but his audience possesses "true knowledge" (*epignōsis*). ***True knowledge*** of Christ produces **grace and peace** in abundance in believers. It will also lead to godliness and holiness (1:3-8).

In his greeting Peter foreshadows one of the primary concerns of this letter: "Those who have experienced this enlightening *epignōsis* [should] go on in Christian growth so as to be able to withstand false teachers and avoid apostasy" (Picirelli 1975, 93). True knowledge (*epignōsis*) is centered in Christ; it transforms belief and behavior.

FROM THE TEXT

Equality of Believers. Peter strongly affirms the equality of all Christians. There are no second-class believers. All ***have received a faith of equal privilege as ours.*** God shows no favoritism based on race, gender, age, or seniority. His plan of salvation through Jesus Christ embraces all. Peter denies spiritual elitism based on faith or maturity. Even the capacity to believe is a gift of Christ. There are no superior levels of faith among Christians.

Jesus as God. Peter's identification of Jesus as **our God and Savior** provides a part of the biblical basis for the orthodox doctrine of the Trinity. To insist that Jesus is God is not to replace God. Nor does it deny monotheism by adding another God named Jesus alongside the Father. Rather, it recognizes Jesus, along with the Father, as truly God. Subsequent centuries of theologians would struggle to define the precise relationship between the First and Second Persons of the Godhead. But their conclusions are grounded upon convictions derived from early believers like Peter that Jesus embodies God (see also Col 2:9).

Knowledge and Faith. It is possible to overemphasize either the cognitive or emotive aspects of Christianity. The cognitive side approaches Christian faith as a system of facts, doctrines, and codes to be memorized and believed. The emotive side pursues the Christian faith as a source of personal fulfillment through an intimate relationship with Jesus Christ.

Peter recognizes that **grace and peace** is the result of a faith that touches both the heart and the head. "In our day we are rightfully warned about the danger of a sterile faith, of a 'head' knowledge that never touches the heart. But we need equally to be careful of a 'heart' knowledge that never touches the head" (Moo 1996, 39). Intellectual faith without a personal relationship with Jesus Christ is ineffective. Likewise, a personal relationship with Christ without any theological knowledge is inadequate. Peter urges believers to pursue a relational knowledge of God in Jesus Christ that connects both head and heart. As believers comply in knowledge and experience, **grace and peace** overflow with abundance.

II. TRUE KNOWLEDGE OF THE CHRISTIAN FAITH: 2 PETER 1:3-21

BEHIND THE TEXT

In vv 3-21 Peter establishes the source, nature, and foundation of true knowledge. In order to oppose false teachers, we must have a correct understanding of true knowledge. In this section, Peter first identifies the source of knowledge as divine power for godliness (1:3-4). Second, he describes the virtuous nature of true knowledge (1:5-11) as exemplified in the moral behavior of believers. Third, he identifies the foundation of knowledge as based upon the testimony of eyewitnesses and Scripture (1:12-21).

IN THE TEXT

A. Divine Power for Godliness (1:3-4)

■**3** The NIV and NRSV omit the Greek particle *hōs* (***as***) that begins v 3. They apparently take it as merely marking the beginning of a new paragraph articulating the kind of lives to which God calls believers. Some translations translate *hōs* as an indication that vv 3-4 are meant to continue v 2 (KJV: "according as"; NASB: "seeing that"). But as Bauckham observes, "The connection with v 2 is largely stylistic, whereas the connection with vv 5-7 is fundamental to the flow of argument" (1983, 173). Thus, v 3 marks the beginning of the first main section of the letter.

Peter's assertion that **divine power has given us everything we need for life and godliness** reflects **his** abundance. The pronoun could refer to God or Jesus. The reference to **divine power** would normally point to God. But the proximity of "Jesus our Lord" (v 2) makes it probable that **his** refers to Jesus (see also 1:16).

Greek literature frequently referred to **divine power** (*theia dynamis*). But it is found only here in the NT. The conviction that God's power is active in Christ is expressed frequently in the NT (e.g., Matt 24:30; Mark 5:30; Luke 4:14; Rom 1:4; 1 Cor 5:4; Heb 1:3).

Christ's divine power **has given us everything we need for life and godliness.** The perfect tense of the verb **has given** describes a completed action with an ongoing effect. Through the gift of the Spirit, Christ's divine power, received at conversion, continues to provide all believers with all that is required to live godly lives (see Blum 1981b, 268).

Everything we need covers every circumstance of a believer's life. But the focus of this **divine power** is **life and godliness** for the believer. **Godliness** (*eusebeian:* ***good worship***) denotes respect for God's will resulting in "a life which is morally good" (Foerster 1971b, 184). Thus, **life and godliness** refers to ***a godly life.*** Peter strongly criticizes the false teachers' claim to possess special knowledge of Christ, despite their immoral lives (2:2, 14, 18-19). True knowledge enables believers to live holy lives, reflecting God.

The divine power that enables believers to live godly lives comes **through our knowledge of him.** This **knowledge** (*epignōseōs*) refers to the fundamental knowledge of Christ gained in conversion. In conversion Christ gives "everything necessary for a God-fearing life" (Bauckham 1983, 178). **Him who called us** might refer to Christ's call of the apostles, rather than the call of all believers (Bigg 1905, 253). But it is more likely that Peter intended the calling of all, since he challenges all believers to **make** their **calling and election sure** (1:10).

Christ invites believers by virtue of **his own glory and goodness. Glory** (*doxa*) in the NT often describes the "manifestation of the Divine character" (Mayor 1978, 85). In 1:17 Peter will declare that Christ received honor and glory at his transfiguration. But here, Christ partakes of the same glory that characterizes God.

Goodness (*aretē*) has many possible meanings, including "eminence, merit, virtue, or self-declaration" (Bauernfeind 1964a, 460-61). Together, **glory and goodness** are "virtually synonymous." They denote "the manifestation of divine power" (Bauckham 1983, 179). Christ's **glory and goodness** calls believers to salvation. And his **divine power** gives them everything needed for godly living.

Christ's **glory and goodness** "refers to the incarnate life, ministry and resurrection of Christ as a manifestation of divine power by means of which he called men and women to be Christians" (Bauckham 1983, 179). Christ's all-encompassing sufficiency for believers is poignantly portrayed in this verse.

■ **4** By means of his glory and goodness (= **through these**), Christ **has given us his very great and precious promises.** The exact nature of the **promises** is unspecified. But in 3:13, God's promise is identified as "a new heaven and a new earth, the home of righteousness." Thus, **promises** here probably refer to the OT expectation of a new era of messianic salvation and blessing.

God's promises enable believers to **participate in the divine nature.** The aspiration to be godlike appears frequently in Greek philosophical and religious thought. Greek dualism divides existence between the immortal spiritual/divine world and the mortal physical/material world. Dualistic thought pictures salvation "in ontological terms as escaping from one kind of reality (the perishable being of the ordinary world) in order to participate in another kind of reality (the imperishable being of God)" (Wolters 1990, 29). In its gnostic expression, dualism insists that the body is inherently evil whereas the spirit is inherently good.

Despite linguistic similarities, Peter's understanding of salvation is neither dualistic nor gnostic. He does not imagine that believers partake of the essence of God in order to escape from the body and become gods. Instead, through Christ, believers share in the holiness of God. And thus they are conformed to the image of Christ.

Peter's understanding of divine participation is fundamentally different from the Greek conception, although the language is similar. In Greek thought, participation in the divine nature is either "innate" or "attained by effort" (Mayor 1978, 87). Peter describes participation in the divine nature as a gift of Christ.

Participation in the divine nature has practical and moral implications. Christ's promises enable believers to participate in the divine nature ***after having escaped the corruption in the world caused by evil desires***. The aorist participle ***having escaped*** indicates that believers escape from corruption *before* they may share in the divine nature. The sequence is more logical than chronological. In another sense, participation in the divine nature is the *means* by which believers escape the corruption in the world.

Some interpreters maintain that **escape the corruption in the world** describes only a future, heavenly prospect, not a present, earthly experience (Calvin 1948, 371). This view is based on the mistaken assumption that humanity is unable to avoid sin, not on the biblical text. Second Peter rejects the claims of false teachers that divine grace frees them from moral obligations. These frauds intended "to go on sinning. But the gift of the divine nature" enables believers "to counter the fascination of evil desires which lead one to sin" (Hillyer 1992, 161-62).

The corruption in the world is **caused by evil desires.** The emphasis on "godliness" (v 3) in contrast to **evil desires** makes it clear that escaping corruption does not await a future existence in heaven. It refers to the renunciation of sin by believers in the present. Hillary of Arles wrote, "Just as God stepped out of his nature to become a partaker of our humanity, so we are called to step out of our nature to become partakers of his divinity" (cited in Bray 2000, 133). Christ participated in our humanity during his earthly ministry so that we might participate in his divinity here and now. Believers renounce sin and share in the righteousness and holiness of God (= **the divine nature**) on earth.

Participation in the divine nature is not the goal of the Christian life; it is the starting point. Through Christ's "divine power" and "glory and goodness" (v 3), believers are empowered to **escape the corruption in the world caused by evil desires.** Christ enables them to participate in his holiness and righteousness in this life.

> Peter maintains that corruption and mortality are not due to matter, but to sin. You do not escape them by cult initiation now and the immortality of the soul after death, but by God implanting a new nature, Christ's own, within you, which will produce holiness of life now, and will flower into the fullness of knowing him after this life is over. (Green 1987, 74)

The pseudo-knowledge of the false teachers led to a life of continuous immorality. By contrast, true knowledge of Christ imbues believers with the divine power they need for lives of godliness and holiness.

Further Reading on Participation in the Divine Nature

Christensen, Michael J., and Jeffrey A. Wittung, eds. 2007. *Partakers of the Divine Nature: The History and Development of Deification in the Christian Traditions.* Grand Rapids: Baker Academic. (Esp. 81-92, 219-29.)

Finlan, Stephen, and Vladimir Kharlamov, eds. 2006. *Theosis: Deification in Christian Theology.* Eugene, Oreg.: Wipf and Stock.

McCormick, K. Steve. 1991. Theosis in Chrysostom and Wesley: An Eastern Paradigm on Faith and Love. *WesTJ* 26:38-103.

B. The Virtuous Nature of True Knowledge (1:5-11)

BEHIND THE TEXT

Believers are enjoined to pursue a list of virtues. Such catalogs of virtue "were no new creations, but based on Jewish and pagan series" (Deissmann 1978, 315; compare Gal 5:22-23; 2 Cor 6:6-7; Eph 6:14-17; Phil 4:8; Col 3:12-14; 1 Tim 3:2-3; 6:11; Titus 1:7-8; Jas 3:17; 2 Pet 1:5-8). Second Peter employs more Greek moral terms for its virtues than other NT lists (esp., **goodness** [*aretē*], **self-control** [*enkrateia*], **godliness** [*eusebeia*], and **brotherly kindness** [*philadelphia*]; Harrington 2003, 248). Yet every NT virtue list borrows to a greater or lesser extent from Greek ethical terminology. "Since Gentile converts were already familiar with it, missionaries were saved an immense amount of labor" (Easton 1932, 10).

Peter's list "contains two different strands of virtues, some of which are specifically Christian (faith, hope, love) and some more properly Greco-Roman (self-control, piety, kinship affection)" (Neyrey 1993, 154). Significantly, Peter's list begins with **faith** and ends in **love.** The virtues "begin with the fundamental requirement of Christianity and . . . culminate in its highest achievement" (Easton 1932, 11). This renders Peter's catalog thoroughly Christian, despite its Greek moral terminology.

Peter's list utilizes the literary device known as sorites (= *gradatio* or *climax*). Sorites is "a set of statements which proceed, step by step, through the force of logic or reliance upon a succession of indisputable facts, to a climactic conclusion, each statement picking up the last key word (or key phrase) of the preceding one" (Fischel 1973, 119). This does not assign greater value to each succeeding virtue; all are equally important. The most significant aspect of the sorites in 2 Peter is the foundational virtue (**faith**) and the climactic virtue (**love**). "All of the specifically Christian virtues are joined with more popular ones to suggest a completeness of moral response" (Neyrey 1993, 155).

IN THE TEXT

■ **5 For this very reason** gathers up everything said in vv 3-4. In light of all these divine gifts and promises, believers must **make every effort to add to** their **faith.** Believers are not passive recipients of salvation. On the contrary, they must actively pursue holiness.

Effort (*spoudē: **earnestness, diligence, zeal***) is a favorite word of Peter (1:10, 15; 3:14). It "denotes quick movement or haste in the interest of a person or cause. But it also commonly denotes earnestness or zeal in performance" (Hiebert 1984d, 44). Believers share a part in their salvation and spiritual maturity. "We are to bring into this relationship, alongside what God has done, every ounce of determination we can muster" (Rogers and Rogers 1998, 581).

Peter's list of virtues illustrates how Christian faith is to be worked out in behavior. The list is a sequence of ethical characteristics. Each new virtue is based on and springs from the previous virtue. There seems to be no discernable logical or spiritual significance to the sequence. "Only two virtues have a clearly intelligible place in the list: *pistis* ('faith') in first place, and *agapē* ('love') in last place" (Bauckham 1983, 185). The other virtues are presented at random.

The foundational virtue is **faith** (*pistis*), thc basis of the Christian life. It is the initial step of accepting God's love and calling in Christ. "Saving knowledge" (*epignōsis;* 1:3) of Christ is received by **faith. Faith** is the foundation upon which all the other virtues are based.

Believers are commanded to **add** the other virtues to their faith. **Add** (*epichorēgēsate*) is a vivid metaphor used for the "action of citizens in ancient Athens who provided the chorus in the drama festivals with their necessary equipment" (Leaney 1967, 107). These citizens generously sponsored the performance. The name for these contributors (*chorēgi*) became the basis for the verb (*epichorēgein*) to denote generous and costly cooperation.

> Believers, Peter is saying, must be lavish in the time and effort they put into developing their Christian lives—not being satisfied with getting by on the minimum, but striving like the *chorēgi* of old to achieve the finest and most attractive production. (Hillyer 1992, 164)

■ **5-7** Believers are called to add seven virtues to faith: **goodness, knowledge, self-control, perseverance, godliness, brotherly kindness,** and **love.** Each virtue adds another piece of the puzzle to Peter's portrayal of Christian life.

Goodness (*aretēn: **moral excellence***) is a classic term from Greek ethics. In v 3 it describes the **goodness** of Christ. It probably refers to the submission of Christ to live, die, and be resurrected to save believers. **Goodness** involves doing what is right even when it is difficult.

Knowledge (*gnōsin*) does not refer to the saving knowledge (*epignōsis*) that makes a person a Christian (1:2, 3). Instead, *gnōsis* depicts "the wisdom and discernment which the Christian needs for a virtuous life and which is progressively acquired" (Bauckham 1983, 186). Saving knowledge (*epignōsis*) is an immediate gift of God to those who repent of their sin and place their faith in Christ for salvation. In contrast, **knowledge** (*gnōsis*) within this catalog of virtues depicts the knowledge of Christ that is gradually acquired throughout the Christian walk.

Self-control (*enkrateian*) was a popular term in Greek moral codes. It depicts the Greek ideal of being able to exercise restraint against excessive indulgence in physical desires. Believers must exercise **self-control** to "resist the false teachers who indulge their lusts, become corrupt, and entice others to do the same" (Watson 1998b, 337).

Perseverance (*hypomonēn*), like **faith** and **love,** is found in other NT catalogs of virtue (Rom 5:3-4; 1 Tim 6:11; 2 Tim 3:10; Titus 2:2; Rev 2:19). It refers to "courageous and steadfast endurance in the face of suffering or evil" (Bauckham 1983, 186). To show **perseverance** is to trust in God and to hope for the fulfillment of his promises.

Godliness (*eusebeian*) describes a respectful attitude toward God, acknowledging his authority, and obeying his will. It carried the general meaning of "religion" in popular pagan usage. "Perhaps Peter uses it here in deliberate contrast to the false teachers, who were far from proper in their behavior to God and their fellow men" (Green 1987, 79).

Brotherly kindness (*philadelphian:* ***brotherly love***) is affection for other Christians as brothers and sisters in Christ (see 1 Pet 1:22-23). The importance (and difficulty) of practicing *philadelphia* is probably the reason why **brotherly kindness** is emphasized so strongly in the NT (e.g., Rom 12:10; 1 Thess 4:9; Heb 13:1; 1 John 5:1; see 1 John 4:20).

The last virtue is **love** (*agapēn*). It is difficult to distinguish the meaning of **love** (*agapē*) from **brotherly kindness** (*philadelphia*). The difference is not so much a variation in meaning as it is a variation in degree. "*Agapē*, then, is not a completely different love, but embraces 'love of the brethren' as one sphere of Christian love in its fullest scope—that Spirit-given act of the will by which we treat other people with active benevolence" (Moo 1996, 47).

The bookend virtues of **faith** and **love** are supremely important in the list. The other six virtues are not specifically Christian, but common in secular Greek moral codes. Their distinctly Christian flavor depends on their placement between the quintessential Christian virtues. **Faith** is the essential foundation of the Christian life. And **love** is the goal and the glue of every other virtue (see Green 1987, 80).

■ **8** True knowledge of Christ produces these moral and virtuous qualities in believers. At issue is not whether believers have these virtues, but to the extent to which they will allow them to develop and be exhibited in their lives. Thus, Peter calls his readers to cultivate these virtues **in increasing measure.**

The positive result of pursuing these virtues is that **they will keep you from being ineffective and unproductive.** The words **ineffective** and **unproductive** are virtually synonymous here. To be **ineffective** (*argous*) is to be ***without work, idle.*** To be **unproductive** (*akarpous*) is to be ***without fruit, unproductive***. **Ineffective** persons "avoid labor for which they should assume responsibility." Unfruitful persons are "barren of moral and spiritual activities" (Barnett 1957, 178). Without the active cooperation of believers, all the virtuous qualities given by Christ in conversion stagnate and come to nothing. When Christians cultivate these virtues, they avoid becoming **ineffective** and **unproductive.**

In your knowledge (*epignōsin*) **of our Lord Jesus Christ** is probably directed against the false teachers. They boast of their special knowledge of Christ, but their lives are devoid of any moral virtues (2:2-3, 13-14, 18-19). In contrast, believers have everything they need for life and godliness through their saving knowledge of Christ. If they will cultivate the virtues, this **knowledge** (*epignōsis*) will remain effective and fruitful.

■ **9** Those who neglect the virtues are **nearsighted and blind.** The actual Greek word order is reversed—***blind and nearsighted.*** How can one who is **blind** be **nearsighted**? The explanation for this odd combination is probably found in the form and meaning of **nearsighted** (*myōpazōn*).

Myōpazōn means not only nearsighted, but ***blinking or shutting one's eyes.*** Christians who do not practice the virtues are **blind** precisely because they have willfully closed their eyes to the light. "Spiritual blindness descends upon the eyes which deliberately look away from the graces of character to which the Christian is called" (Green 1987, 82). This is the accusation Peter levels against the false teachers in 2:17 when he declares that "blackest darkness is reserved for them."

Such a person **has forgotten that he has been cleansed from his past sins.** Fruitless Christians have **forgotten** what Christ has done for them. **Forgotten** (*lēthēn labōn:* ***has received forgetfulness***) stresses deliberate forgetfulness. This is not due to a momentary lapse in memory, but a deliberate effort to put something out of their minds.

Such a person has forgotten **that he has been cleansed from his past sins.** Many interpreters take "the cleansing" (NRSV) as an allusion to baptism. This is possible, but certainly not necessary. It probably refers to conversion as the forgiveness and cleansing from sins (see Heb 1:3; 1 John 3:3). When converts make no effort to grow in their faith, they have effectively turned their backs on Christ (2:21). They have forgotten his empowerment to live godly lives received in conversion.

■ **10-11** **Therefore** draws together all of vv 3-9. The imperative **be . . . eager** (*spoudasate:* ***be zealous, make an effort***) repeats the basic exhortation in v 5—**make every effort** (*spoudē*). The focus of this effort and zeal is **to make your calling and election sure.**

Calling (*klēsin*) and **election** (*eklogēn*) are closely related. They affirm that Christ has **called** believers to himself (1:3). Although **calling** is logically subsequent to **election,** there is no distinction between them here. The two words together "emphasize the single concept Peter has in mind: God's, or Christ's, effective drawing of the sinner to himself for salvation" (Moo 1996, 49).

Peter's command to **make your calling and election sure** seems paradoxical. While election depends on God alone, salvation is contingent upon humanity's response and acceptance. Peter emphasizes both sides of the paradox. Both election and free will are equally relevant and true. God calls and draws people to salvation through Christ. But believers must receive and obey his call to participate in salvation. Believers make their election **sure** (*bebaian*) by obeying Christ and deliberately growing in grace.

For if you do these things reiterates the importance of our role in salvation. **These things** refers to the exercise and progressive cultivation of the Christian virtues (1:5-7). If believers rigorously confirm their calling with an appropriate lifestyle, Peter assures them of two things, negatively and positively:

First, negatively: **you will never fall** (*ptaisēte:* ***stumble, fall***). **Fall** may be used "figuratively, meaning to fall into sin" (Zodhiates 1992, 1251; see Jas 2:10; 3:2). But here it is not asserted that believers will never sin (e.g., Moffatt 1928, 183). It probably means "to fall" in the sense of what a blind or shortsighted person might do (1:9). They will not fall into the disaster of a life of sin and a failure to reach final salvation (see Jude 24). Believers who persist in their journey will not fail to reach their final destination—**the eternal kingdom.**

Second, positively: **you will receive a rich welcome into the eternal kingdom of our Lord and Savior Jesus Christ.** Peter uses a vivid play on words in this passage. In v 5 *epichorēgeō* describes the effort believers should exert "to add" Christian virtues to their faith. In v 11, the same verb describes the lavish effort God exerts to include them in Christ's kingdom. "If we generously put ourselves out in obedience to God and give him what we have, he will generously put himself out for us, so to speak, and lavishly equip us for life in the everlasting kingdom" (Green 1987, 84).

Peter paints a splendid picture of the glorious reward (**rich welcome:** "entry . . . will be richly provided," NRSV) believers can expect from God. Thus, "final salvation is not man's achievement but the gift of God's lavish generosity" (Bauckham 1983, 193).

Two observations about the **kingdom** should be noted. First, it is an **eternal kingdom** (only here in the NT; but see Luke 1:33). **Eternal kingdom** is not a reference to heaven, but "to the cosmic reign of God in righteousness in the new heaven and new earth (3:13)" (Bauckham 1983, 192).

Second, the **kingdom** belongs to **our Lord and Savior Jesus Christ** (see Matt 16:28; John 18:36; Ps 2:6). It is entered only by virtue of one's relationship with him (see Mark 10:17, 21, 24, 26). **Lord and Savior** is a favorite description of Jesus in this letter (1:1, 11; 2:20; 3:2, 18). It underscores that to enter into Christ's kingdom, Christ must be one's **Savior.**

FROM THE TEXT

Christ's All-Sufficiency. Peter pictures Christ as available to believers (1:3) and all-sufficient to their needs. Christ's **glory and goodness** call us. The redemptive **knowledge** of Christ saves us. Christ's **divine power** enables us to live godly lives. Believers need no other patron or advocate on their behalf. In him we find our calling, our salvation, and the enabling power to live righteous and holy lives.

Participation in the Divine Nature. Christ has made it possible for believers to **participate in the divine nature** (1:4). This is not the Greek philosophical understanding of salvation—escape from bodily existence and to be unified with the divine essence inherently residing within one's being. Peter insists that salvation is not an innate human or divine quality waiting to be discovered. It is an extraordinary gift of Christ, who **has given us everything we need** for salvation (1:3).

Nonetheless, Peter recognizes a sense in which salvation allows believers to participate in the divine nature. The corporate solidarity of Christ and believers is the foundation for many early Christian concepts of salvation. For instance, Paul perceives believers as sharing or participating in Christ's destiny. This includes both his death and his resurrection. Believers participate in Jesus' vindication by God (e.g., Rom 5:15; 1 Cor 10:16; Gal 2:20; see Powers 2001, 231-34). Similarly, John reports Jesus urging his followers to "remain in me, and I will remain in you" (John 15:4). Jesus prays for the unity of believers with God and himself: "Father, just as you are in me and I am in you . . . may they also be in us" (John 17:21). Like Paul and John, Peter perceives believers as so united with Christ that they can be said to **participate in the divine nature.**

Through their union with Christ, believers share in God's own holy life, separated from the corrupt world around them. **For this very reason** (1:5) Peter calls believers to progress in holiness and godliness. Salvation is not simply Christ's work *in* us; it is also his work *through* us, demonstrated by a life of holiness. Holiness is conformity to the image and person of Christ in one's disposition and behavior.

As participants in the divine nature, believers do not vie for equality with God. They declare with Paul, "I have been crucified with Christ and I no longer live, but Christ lives in me" (Gal 2:20). This attitude and the accompanying virtuous behavior are the essence of the divine nature in which all believers may participate.

Divine Initiative and Human Response. There is a synergism between the divine initiative in salvation and the human response. Peter strongly affirms God's gracious gift of salvation through Christ. God calls and elects through Christ; his **divine power has given** believers **everything** they **need for life and godliness.** At the same time, Peter equally stresses human responsibility in salvation. He calls believers to **make every effort to add to** their **faith** and to **make** their **calling and election sure** by practicing and cultivating a virtuous life.

Is salvation dependent upon God's gracious election or upon humanity's obedient faith and good works? The NT answers this question with a consistent and resounding, "Yes!" That is to say, *both elements* are essential to salvation (see Phil 2:12-13; Jas 2:17).

Peter makes a significant contribution to this discussion. Harrington writes:

> The initiative is with God, and the divine calling makes it possible to become "partakers in the divine nature" (1:4). Yet this great dignity demands by way of response religious and moral seriousness (the practice of and growth in the virtues) on the part of those who have been called and gifted by God. (2003, 250)

Logically, God's gracious initiative precedes and enables the human response (Wesley 1979b, 508-9). But God's initiative demands a positive human response for salvation to occur. Wesley explains it in this way, "First, God works; therefore you *can* work. Secondly, God works, therefore you *must* work" (1979b, 511).

God's grace and election do not eliminate the need for human response. Those who fail diligently to pursue and exhibit godly behavior are **nearsighted and blind** (v 9). They are doomed to stumble and **fall** in their journey into Christ's eternal kingdom. Those who are called and elect demonstrate it by responding appropriately to God's grace. They will practice and cultivate moral virtues through Christ's power. God, in turn, will provide them with a lavish and **rich welcome** into Christ's **eternal kingdom.**

C. The Foundation of Knowledge (1:12-21)

BEHIND THE TEXT

Some point to the language of 1:12-15 as evidence that 2 Peter conforms to the genre of a farewell speech or testament. This genre has several notable features apparent in 2 Peter (Moo 1996, 64). The speaker:

a. knows he is about to die (see 2 Pet 1:12-15)

b. gathers around him his children or disciples (see 1:12-15; 3:1-2)

c. impresses on his audience the need to remember his teaching and example (see 1:12-15; 3:1-2)

d. makes predictions of the future (see 2:1-4; 3:3)

e. gives moral exhortations (throughout 2 Peter)

The assumption that 2 Peter is a farewell testament is problematic for several reasons. Nearly all ancient testaments were pseudonymous (but see Deuteronomy and John 14—17). They were typically written in the name of a great hero of the faith after that hero's death. While some argue that 2 Peter is pseudonymous, this is debatable. Furthermore, testaments were almost always presented as a farewell speech of the hero to his people. Second Peter otherwise resembles an ancient letter. But there are elements of the letter that were almost certainly influenced by the testament genre. But this does not preclude the probability that it was an authentic letter by the Apostle Peter.

The transfiguration of Christ is alluded to in 1:17-18 (see Matt 17:1-13; Mark 9:2-13; Luke 9:28-36). Some scholars believe this allusion is artificially imposed. This allegedly exposes the letter as a forgery. Curiously, Peter's description of the transfiguration does not match the vocabulary of the Gospel accounts, which one would expect a forgery to do. Scholars debate the source of the aberrant wording in this passage. Such differences could be explained as a result of Peter's personal memory of the event. After all, according to the Gospels, he was present on the mountain when the transfiguration occurred.

In 1:12-21, Peter establishes a twofold foundation for true, saving knowledge through Jesus Christ. The first is the apostolic witness (1:12-18). It is represented by Peter's eyewitness experience of Jesus' honor and glory in his earthly ministry. The second foundation is found in the inspired words of Scripture (1:19-21).

IN THE TEXT

1. Eyewitnesses (1:12-18)

■ **12** The purpose of 2 Peter was to **remind** its readers (see also 3:1-2) of the apostolic teaching upon which the Christian faith is based. **So** (*dio: there-*

fore, for this reason) demonstrates that Peter's comments are based upon the foundational teaching of the true, saving knowledge set forth in 1:3-11. This reminder is all the more important for believers faced with the challenge of false teaching.

The grammar of **I will always remind you** (*mellēsō aei hymas hypomimnēiskein*) is difficult. It could be translated as ***I am always going to be reminding you*** or ***I will take care to remind you.*** The former option is preferable, since it indicates that the letter was intended to be "a *permanent* reminder of his teaching, not only to be read on one specific occasion, but to be available at all times" (Bauckham 1983, 195).

Peter will remind them of his teachings, **even though you know** (*eidotas*) **them and are firmly established** (*estērigmenous*) **in the truth you now have.** The complimentary language reflects conventional courtesy. "Given the emotional tone and the intensity of the polemic in the rest of the letter, it seems that in the writer's mind this assurance about the readers was probably more wishful thinking than reality" (Harrington 2003, 251). Peter recognizes the need for believers to be reminded of the foundational principles of the faith. Even beyond the challenge of false teaching, they, and we, need to be reminded of what we already know.

■ **13-14** It was **right** (*dikaion*) for Peter to remind them of these things because his time was limited. He intended to keep reminding them of the apostolic teachings, he says, **as long as I live in the tent of this body.**

The reference to the body as a **tent** (*skēnōmati*) was a common metaphor in Greek and early Christian writings (see 2 Cor 5:1, 4). "It conveys the image of the body as a temporary dwelling-place for the soul, folded up and abandoned when the soul leaves it at death" (Bauckham 1983, 198).

Peter believed his death was impending: **I know that I will soon put it aside.** The adjective **soon** (*tachinē*) can also mean ***sudden.*** Some interpreters assert that Peter is alluding to the sudden, violent nature of his death, not its nearness (Green 1987, 89). But the context and urgency of his words make it more probable that he is referring to the imminence rather than the nature of his death.

As our Lord Jesus Christ has made clear (*edēlōsen*) **to me** seems to allude to some kind of prophecy or revelation Peter had received. The verb *dēloō* is often used "of the communication of cultic mysteries . . . and of divine revelation given in dreams or other ways" (Bultmann 1964b, 61). Peter may refer to an undocumented prophecy from Christ (Mayor 1978, 102). But more likely he had in mind the prediction of his death in John 21:18-19.

John 21 does not explain how Peter would know his death was coming **soon.** But the adverb *kathōs* connecting Peter's reference to his death to a revelation of Jesus indicates correspondence (***just as***) rather than cause (***because***). Thus, "the general sense of the passage must be: 'I know that I am going to die soon—and this corresponds to Christ's prophecy'" (Bauckham 1983, 199). As Peter contemplated recent events, he apparently recognized that his death must be near. Nero's opposition to the Christian faith and persecution of its leaders and Peter's advancing age conformed to Christ's prophecy in John 21.

■ **15** In view of his impending death—**after my departure,** Peter assured his readers that **I will make every effort to see that . . . you will always be able to remember these things. Departure** (*exodon*) is "a dignified euphemism for death" (Kelly 1969, 314). Luke uses *exodos* to describe Jesus' death in his transfiguration narrative (Luke 9:31). Since Peter speaks of the transfiguration in the following verses (2 Pet 1:16-18), he may allude to the Lukan text. But the widespread common usage of this term for death makes any dependence upon Luke unnecessary and unlikely.

Peter uses the future tense to describe the effort he **will make** to ensure his readers constantly remember his teachings. Scholars debate whether the reminder refers to the current letter, a different letter, or a future letter. Some propose he had the Gospel of Mark in mind, since early tradition connects Mark's Gospel to Peter. Others maintain he refers to a future visit intended to reinforce his teaching. All such suggestions are purely speculative. It is likely that Peter refers to the current letter.

It seems peculiar for Peter to refer to the current letter in the future tense, however. But this view has the advantage of connecting the future tense of v 15 with the future of v 12. This ties the whole paragraph together. Through this letter, Peter hoped to provide a permanent reminder of his apostolic teaching.

■ **16** Peter's language changes from using the pronoun "I" in vv 12-15 to **we** in vv 16-21. **We** must refer to Peter and the other apostles, since he was not the only one to witness the transfiguration (vv 17-18). By using **we,** Peter contrasts the teaching of the false teachers with the witness and preaching of all the apostles.

The message believers must remember pertains to **the power and coming** (*parousia*) **of our Lord Jesus Christ.** *Parousia* is the technical term used for the second coming of Christ (e.g., Matt 24:3, 27; 1 Cor 15:23; 1 Thess 2:19; 3:13; 4:15; 5:23). The phrase **power and coming** is probably a hendiadys (a figure of speech joining two nouns by "and" instead of using a noun and a modifier), here emphasizing Christ's ***powerful coming.***

Peter denies that the teaching of Christ's return is based on **cleverly invented stories.** This may have been one of the accusations of the false teachers. **Cleverly invented** (*sesophismenois*) and **stories** (*mythois*) were pejorative terms in ancient Greek (Bauckham 1983, 213-14). **Stories** (*mythoi: **myths, fables***) was a term of "frivolous mockery . . . rejection and criticism" in secular writings. The word was used with "complete repudiation" by the NT writers (Stählin 1967, 779, 781). Peter probably referred to **cleverly invented stories** for two reasons:

> The writer's intention is probably both to rebut the charges leveled by the false teachers against the Church's expectation of the Parousia and also at the same time to imply that their doctrines are, by contrast, indeed fables, mere human speculations and inventions. (Cranfield 1960, 180)

The verb **told** (*egnōrisamen*) is significant. *Gnōrizō* (*"make known, reveal"*; BDAG, 203) is frequently used in the NT for imparting revelation (e.g., Luke 2:15; John 15:15; Rom 16:26; Eph 6:19; Col 1:27). Here it is used of the apostles' preaching of the gospel, which included the expectation of the second coming.

Peter and the other apostles **were eyewitnesses of his majesty. Eyewitnesses** (*epoptai: **spectators, observers***) is found only here in the NT. As a technical term in Greek mystery religions, it denoted those initiated into the cult (Michaelis 1967, 373-74). If Peter has this nuance in mind, the term emphasizes that his opponents were outside the circle of initiates to which Peter and the other apostles belong. But if Peter has only the general sense of **eyewitness** in mind, the word "is used here to enhance the splendor of the vision, and the honor done the disciples, at the Transfiguration" (Strachan 1979, 130).

Peter and the apostles were eyewitnesses of Christ's **majesty** (*megaleiotētos*). This was used most commonly of divine grandeur and majesty. Here it refers specifically to the "supernatural quality of Jesus, unveiled at the Transfiguration, which is seen as a trustworthy anticipation of His Second Coming in might and glory" (Kelly 1969, 318).

■ **17-18** These verses describe the glorious event Peter claims to have witnessed. The references to "majesty" (v 16), the **voice** that came **from heaven** (vv 17, 18), and **the sacred mountain** (v 18) indicate that Peter refers to the transfiguration (Matt 17:1-9; Mark 9:2-10; Luke 9:28-36).

Peter asserts that Jesus **received honor and glory from God the Father. Honor and glory** may be another example of hendiadys. If so, he refers to the ***exalted majestic glory*** Jesus received from God. If the terms have individual significance, **honor** would refer to Christ's exalted status and **glory** to Christ's splendid appearance (Moo 1996, 72).

God is identified as **the Father** to underscore Jesus' divine sonship affirmed by the heavenly voice. Jesus **received honor and glory from God.** Thus, Peter's theology does not reflect Greek notions of divine men, whose innate divine nature struggled to surface and escape the confines of the human body. Rather, the transfiguration both reveals and affirms Jesus' divine glory.

Jesus received this glory **when the voice came to him from the Majestic Glory.** The Gospels record only three instances when a heavenly **voice** was audibly heard during Jesus' earthly ministry: at his baptism (Matt 3:17; Mark 1:11; Luke 3:22), at the transfiguration, and during the week of Jesus' Passion (John 12:27-30).

Peter describes the voice as coming **from the Majestic Glory,** that is, from God. This is an example of the Jewish custom of avoiding the name of God out of respect.

The voice of God declares, ***This is my Son, my Beloved; with him I am well pleased.*** The Greek version of these words in 2 Peter is different from any of the versions in the Gospels. But it is most similar to the wording in Matthew. Second Peter omits the final command, **Listen to him!** This is found in all three Gospel accounts of the transfiguration. If 2 Peter is the creation of a late pseudonymous author, he might have been expected to reproduce the wording from one of the Gospel accounts.

The grammatical structure and word order (*ho huios mou ho agapētos mou houtos estin*) suggest the translation "This is my Son, my Beloved" (NAB, NRSV) instead of "This is my beloved Son" (KJV, NASB). Thus, the voice confers three important titles upon Jesus at the transfiguration.

1:17-18 First, the voice identifies Jesus as **my Son.** This reflects the language God used to address the messianic King as his own Son in Ps 2:7.

Second, Jesus is called ***my Beloved.*** This title is derived from either Gen 22:2, 12, 16 or Isa 42:1. In both passages, "the special love of God the Father for his Son involves a special calling in God's purpose" (Bauckham 1983, 220). The title emphasizes "the uniqueness of the relationship of Father and Son" (Schrenk 1964a, 741).

Third, Jesus is described as the one ***with him*** God is ***well pleased*** (*eudokēsa*). This title is drawn from the first Suffering Servant song in Isa 42:1. Of all the terms for election, *eudokēsa* "brings out most strongly the emotional side of the love of Him who elects" (Schrenk 1964a, 740). The term carries the special sense of God's good pleasure in electing and conferring his glory on Jesus.

Peter affirms that **we ourselves heard this voice that came from heaven.** He was not only an "eyewitness" but also an "ear witness" of the transfiguration (Moo 1996, 73). Whereas the voice emanated **from the Majestic Glory** in v 17, in v 18 it is **from heaven.** Both expressions are an example of circumlocution, the Jewish custom of respectfully avoiding the pronunciation of the name of God.

The writer emphatically states that **we ourselves heard** (*hēmeis hēkousamen*) **this voice . . . when we were with him on the sacred mountain.** Some interpreters identify the emphatic **we ourselves heard** as a "forced" attempt by a forger trying to identify himself as Peter. Some regard **sacred mountain** as a reflection of a later generation of Christians, which considered sites of events during Jesus' ministry "taken up into and sanctified in the religious consciousness of the Church" (Strachan 1979, 131).

But **sacred mountain** (*hagiōi orei:* ***holy mountain***) does not require a late date. It would have been natural to describe the mount as holy (i.e., ***set apart***) because of what happened there. Moreover, it is subjective to identify allusions to events in Peter's life as evidence of an imitator. Nothing about this description of the transfiguration inherently discounts it as an authentic description of the event by Peter himself.

The original basis for knowledge of the second coming is the eyewitness accounts of Peter and the other apostles, illustrated by the transfiguration of Jesus. "The primary use of the story here is to base the claim about divine judgment on the highest authority, God's word as witnessed by the apostle" (Perkins 1995, 175).

But why does Peter call upon the transfiguration as the defining event upon which true knowledge of the second coming can be established? One would expect him to appeal to a resurrection or ascension story to guarantee the certainty of the future coming Christ (e.g., Acts 1:9-11). Some scholars account for this unexpected basis by explaining the transfiguration as "a 1:17-18
resurrection appearance . . . transferred to the life of Jesus" (Carlston 1961, 233). But this theory has been resoundingly refuted (Stein 1976, 79-96). "The Transfiguration experience had an intimate relationship to the Parousia of Jesus from the start" (Moo 1996, 74).

The transfiguration must have had a profound impact upon the apostles. For Peter, what counted most "were the majesty of Jesus, the voice from heaven, and Peter's role as an eyewitness" (Harrington 2003, 259). As in the Gospels, the transfiguration is interpreted in 2 Peter as the anticipation of the future appearance of the glorious Son of Man coming in his kingdom. It ideally served to reinforce the truth of the gospel as proclaimed by the apostolic witnesses, including Peter himself.

2. Inspired Words of Scripture (1:19-21)

Peter's second foundation for true knowledge and the second coming of Christ is found in the inspired Scriptures. The two topics might seem distant and unrelated. But they were closely connected within the teaching of Peter's opponents. The false teachers' general misunderstanding of true knowledge led to their specific misunderstanding and denial of the second coming. They claimed that the apostolic message about true knowledge in general, and about the second coming specifically, were based upon **cleverly invented stories** (v 16).

Peter objects to this accusation, first, by reminding his audience that he and other apostles witnessed the revelation of Christ's glory at the transfiguration (vv 16-18). Second, he objects by emphasizing the reliability of revelation as revealed in the inspired Scriptures (vv 19-21). "The reliability of revelation is the idea that links verses 16-18 and verses 19-21" (Moo 1996, 75).

■ **19** In addition to eyewitness accounts, Peter asserts that ***we have the prophetic word made more certain.*** The phrase ***the prophetic word*** has been interpreted as referring to OT messianic prophecies, to OT and NT prophecies, or to the transfiguration itself as a prophecy of the Parousia. But "all known occurrences of the phrase refer to OT Scripture" (Bauckham 1983, 224). Thus, it is best understood as a reference to OT Scripture in general. The pronoun **we** includes all Peter's readers, not simply the apostles. This is evident in his next statement: **you will do well to pay attention to it.**

Made more certain (*bebaioteron:* **more certain**; **made** is added by the NIV) can be interpreted in two ways. It can mean that the OT Scriptures are more reliable than apostolic testimony, or that OT prophecies are made more certain by the eyewitness accounts of apostles. Both views are possible; but the latter option seems more probable.

The eyewitness accounts of the apostles are identified as the first foundation of true knowledge and the certainty of Christ's second coming in vv 16-18. It would make no sense for Peter immediately to undermine this by stating that the apostolic witness is less reliable than the prophetic scriptures themselves.

Peter's "testimony about the Transfiguration gives to the prophetic word an even greater certainty than it had before" (Moo 1996, 76). There is greater certainty because the events witnessed by apostles confirm the fulfillment of the OT prophecies. Thus, "Peter indicates that the OT prophets spoke of the same things he did and that their words are made more certain because the Transfiguration is a foreview of their fulfillment" (Blum 1981b, 274).

Since Scripture is reliable, believers should **pay attention to it.** The comparison of God's Word to a **light** in a **dark place** (*auchmerōi topōi*) was a well-known metaphor (Ps 119:105), although the word **dark** (*auchmēros*) appears only here in the NT. It refers to "a condition of dirt and filth produced through neglect. The light of the lamp exposes the condition" (Hiebert 1984e, 161). The world and the human mind were **dark** because of ignorance of God's prophetic word. The Scriptures provide a divine ray of **light** that exposes and illuminates the darkness **until the day dawns and the morning star rises in your hearts.**

Day is an abbreviation of the OT idea of "the day of the Lord." It refers to the future time when God will decisively intervene in human history to save his people and judge his enemies. God fulfilled his promises concerning this **day** through the death and resurrection of Christ. But the "day of the Lord" still awaits its final consummation in the second coming of Christ (e.g., Rom 13:11-12; Phil 2:9-11; 1 Thess 4:14-17; 5:1-8).

Morning star (*phōsphoros:* ***light bringer***) probably refers to Christ himself, since Scripture uses **star** as a messianic reference (Num 24:17; Rev 22:16). "This clause must be a pictorial description of the way in which, at His Coming, Christ will dissipate the doubt and uncertainty by which their hearts are meanwhile beclouded and will fill them with a marvelous illumination" (Kelly 1969, 323).

Some scholars do not consider the **morning star** that **rises in your hearts** to be a reference to the second coming. They contend that it refers to the individual experience of enlightenment by believers in this life (Delling 1964, 953). Peter's point, however, is that the partial light of prophecy will become superfluous when the full light of God's revelation becomes apparent at Christ's return. The NT consistently describes faith as an activity of the hearts of believers (see Rom 10:9; 1 Pet 3:15). It is only natural that Christians should receive and perceive this final revelation at the last day **in** their **hearts.**

■ **20** Peter tells his readers there is one primary point (*touto prōton:* ***this first thing***) they **must understand.** Unfortunately, the point is vague. The phrase in question is *idias epilyseōs*. There is a question about the correct understanding of *epilyseōs*, **interpretation,** as ***untying*** or ***unraveling.*** But the crucial issue is the translation of the word *idias*. Within the passage the phrase can be translated in either of two ways.

The NASB and NRSV translate this passage: "no prophecy of Scripture is a matter of one's own interpretation." The NIV translates it: **no prophecy of Scripture came about by the prophet's own interpretation.** The word *idias* may be interpreted as **the prophet's own.**

The first translation (NASB, NRSV) understands the verse as dealing with the issue of *interpretation* (so Kelly 1969, 323-24). The second translation (NIV) understands the verse as dealing with the issue of *inspiration* (so Bauckham 1983, 231). The arguments for both translations are formidable (see Moo 1996, 777-78, and Bauckham 1983, 228-31).

If the NASB and NRSV are correct, Peter's point is about the correct *interpretation* of Scripture. Private individuals cannot interpret Scripture any way they want. There is just one true interpretation of Scripture (Mayor 1978, 196-98); namely, that which was divinely intended by the Holy Spirit. The true guide for this interpretation is the church, not self-appointed individuals

(Bigg 1905, 269-70). This view anticipates the argument of 2:1-3, where false teachers are condemned for secretly introducing destructive heresies. These were probably based on their own interpretation of the Scriptures and the Christian faith.

If the NIV is correct, Peter's point is about the *inspiration* and *authentication* of Scripture. Scripture is not derived from prophets but from God himself. This view connects vv 20-21 to v 19. Believers should pay close attention to the prophetic word (v 19) because they know that it does not originate from human beings (v 20), but from God (v 21).

The NIV probably best reflects Peter's intention. In Hellenistic Jewish and early Christian discussions, *idios* (in *idias epilyseōs*) "seems to have been virtually a technical term" (Bauckham 1983, 229) denying the human origin of prophecy. Peter probably intended to discuss the origin rather than the interpretation of Scripture. The prophetic word is certain (v 19) because prophets did not make up what they wrote (v 20).

■ **21** Whereas v 20 addresses the reliability of Scripture, v 21 explains the origin of Scripture. This is the nearest to an explanation of the inspiration of Scripture found in the Bible. **For prophecy never had its origin in the will of man, but men spoke from God as they were carried along by the Holy Spirit.**

Peter's vivid wordplay cannot be rendered well into English. The phrases **never had its origin** (*ou . . . ēnechthē*) and **were carried along** (*pheromenoi*) are derived from the same Greek verb (*pherein: **to bear or carry***). Prophecy was never ***carried*** (*pherein*) by human preferences, but prophets **spoke from God** as they were **carried** (*pherein*) . . . **by the Holy Spirit.** Peter used this same verb to describe the divine voice ***carried*** (*pherein*) from heaven at the transfiguration (1:17-18). What the apostles "heard from heaven at the Transfiguration and the words that the prophets spoke came from the same place: God himself" (Moo 1996, 79).

With the phrase, **men spoke from God as they were carried along by the Holy Spirit,** Peter carefully establishes the paradoxical truth of the divine-human interplay in inspiration. The false teachers claimed that prophecy was of merely human origin. Peter confirms human participation in the writing of Scripture, but emphatically insists that these human words were **from God,** who inspired the writers through the work of the Holy Spirit.

The verb **carried along** was used to describe a ship driven by the wind (Acts 27:15, 17). "The prophets raised their sails, so to speak (they were obedient and receptive), and the Holy Spirit filled them and carried their craft along in the direction he wished" (Green 1987, 102). It remains a mystery precisely how this happens. But Peter affirms that as the prophets spoke by the direction and guidance of the Holy Spirit, God spoke.

FROM THE TEXT

Reminders Needed. First, Peter urgently desired to **remind** his readers of the apostolic teachings about the Christian faith. They already knew and were **firmly established in the truth** (1:12). Even knowledgeable and firmly established believers need to be reminded of the basic tenets of the gospel. We never outgrow the necessity of being reminded of the essence of the faith. This is the function of the teaching and preaching office of the church and daily devotional reading of Scripture.

Second, firmly established believers who know the truth can still be vulnerable to false teaching. Even the strongest believers can stumble and fall if they do not continue to grow spiritually. Believers at all maturity levels need to be reminded regularly of the truth. We need to be encouraged in our faith, lest our faith be weakened and undermined. Perhaps this is what Hebrews meant in urging, "Let us not give up meeting together, as some are in the habit of doing, but let us encourage one another" (Heb 10:25). As members of the body of Christ, we encourage and remind one another of the truth of the gospel. If we isolate ourselves from the body, we become easy prey to the false teachings of the enemy of our faith.

Scriptural Inspiration. The proper understanding of the inspiration of Scripture is that humans spoke for God under the inspiration of the Holy Spirit. Popular understanding of the inspiration of Scripture seems to gravitate toward two extremes. The one so emphasizes the divine origin of inspiration (that *God* inspired the Bible) that human involvement is virtually eliminated. The other emphasizes the human origin of inspiration (that *men* wrote the Bible) so that divine involvement is practically eliminated.

Peter articulates a mediating position: **men** spoke from **God.** Prophets genuinely chose their words, deliberately and consciously according to their own vocabulary, style, and social situation. But the words they chose were the words that God wanted them to use to communicate his message to humankind. Exactly how they were able to speak their own words as the words of God is not explained. Peter simply asserts that this happened **as they are carried along by the Holy Spirit** (1:21). We will never fully understand how divine inspiration occurs. But no doctrine of Scripture can neglect either the human participation or the divine inspiration in the origin of Scripture.

Cornerstones of the Christian Faith. Peter establishes two important cornerstones for the truth of the Christian faith:

- First, his own personal experience as an eyewitness of the ministry of Christ (1:16-18)
- Second, the reliability of the inspired word of Scripture (1:19-21)

Peter recognizes that his own personal experience corresponds perfectly with the promises and prophecies of Scripture. Thus, he declares that **we have the word of the prophets made more certain** (1:19). Importantly, the Word of God is not meant only to be read and believed. Scripture is meant to be experienced personally by believers. God is not only faithful in the pages of Scripture but also faithful in the pages of our personal life. The truth of God's Word is confirmed in the personal experience of believers as the Holy Spirit, the Living Christ, intimately applies Scripture in transforming ways. Peter's eyewitness experience of Jesus' transfiguration confirmed the Scriptures, making them all the more reliable and certain for him.

Likewise, each believer is an *eyewitness* of the truth of Scripture and the faithful reliability of God to his promises. Salvation is not just a promise from Scripture, but a relationship to be experienced through Christ as mediated by the Holy Spirit. We are never more certain of the truth of the Bible than when it is experienced and lived out in our lives.

Further Reading on Scripture

Bassett, Paul M. 1978. The Fundamentalist Leavening of the Holiness Movement, 1914-1940. The Church of the Nazarene: A Case Study. *WesTJ* 13:65-85.

Callen, Barry L., and Richard P. Thompson, eds. 2004. *Reading the Bible in Wesleyan Ways: Some Constructive Proposals.* Kansas City: Beacon Hill Press of Kansas City.

Lodahl, Michael. 2004. *All Things Necessary to Our Salvation: The Hermeneutical and Theological Implications of the Article on Holy Scripture in the Manual of the Church of the Nazarene.* San Diego: Point Loma Press.

Peterson, Eugene H. 2006. *Eat This Book: A Conversation in the Art of Spiritual Reading.* Grand Rapids: Eerdmans.

III. FALSE TEACHERS AND THEIR TEACHING: 2 PETER 2:1-22

BEHIND THE TEXT

The close parallelism between Jude and 2 Peter is especially visible in the description of the false teachers and their teaching in ch 2. Similarities include the following:

1. The false teachers advocate immorality and are themselves immoral (2 Pet 2:2, 13-14, 19; Jude 4, 8).
2. They make boastful and extravagant claims (2 Pet 2:18; Jude 16).
3. They are greedy for gain (2 Pet 2:14; Jude 16).
4. They blaspheme angelic beings (2 Pet 2:10-12; Jude 8-10).
5. They are doomed to destruction (2 Pet 2:1, 3, 9, 12; Jude 11, 13). (Barker, Lane, and Michaels 1969, 355-56)

The similarities include the use of unusual words, striking metaphors, and similar OT illustrations like Sodom and Gomorrah and the prophet Balaam.

Because of these parallels, many scholars suggest that one letter is dependent upon the other. Usually, 2 Peter is thought to be dependent upon Jude. Despite the parallelism, there is little verbal agreement between the letters. As a result, there is insufficient evidence to draw any firm conclusions about the literary dependence between the letters (see Introduction).

Chapter 2 focuses on the false teachers and their teaching. In the first section, the false teachers are described (2:1-3). The second looks at the fate of the ungodly and the rescue of the righteous (2:4-10*a*). Third, Peter condemns the character and conduct of the false teachers (2:10*b*-22).

A. False Teachers Described (2:1-3)

BEHIND THE TEXT

One characteristic of 2 Peter is its seamless transitions from one topic to the next. In 1:16—2:3, Bauckham (1983, 236) observes the following chiastic (X-shaped or envelope) structure:

A. Apostles (1:16-18)
  B. OT prophets (1:19-21)
  B'. OT false prophets (2:1*a*)
A'. False teachers (2:1*b*-3)

The case for chiasm is strengthened by the repetition of fabricated "stories" in 1:16 and 2:3. Peter compares and contrasts the apostles with false teachers. The former are falsely accused of using **cleverly invented stories** (1:16); the latter actually use **stories they have made up** (2:3). Peter's organization positions him to attack false teaching while defending the true faith.

IN THE TEXT

■ **1** Peter reminds his readers that **there were also false prophets among the people** during OT times. Legitimate prophets were inspired (1:21). The **false prophets,** who claimed to speak for God, actually only advanced their own ideas and thoughts.

Peter predicted that just as there were false prophets in OT times, **there will be false teachers among you.** False prophets in the OT shared three characteristics: (1) they did not speak with divine authority; (2) they denied the prophecies of future judgment by the true prophets; (3) they were condemned to punishment by God (Bauckham 1983, 238). Peter applies these characteristics to the false teachers of his day: (1) unlike the apostles, the **false teachers** do not speak with divine authority; (2) like the false prophets of old, they scorn the idea of a judgment to come (3:3-10); (3) like the false prophets, they will also be condemned by God (2:13, 20).

Peter's opponents are called **false teachers** instead of **false prophets.** The terms could be interchangeable (Bigg 1905, 271). But they are probably not called **false prophets** because they did not specifically claim prophetic inspiration for their teaching. Nonetheless, as **false teachers** they bring **swift destruction on themselves.** This is because they **secretly introduce destructive heresies, even denying the sovereign Lord who bought them.**

Many interpreters note the future tense in these verses: **there will be false teachers among you** (emphasis added). Some interpret the future tense as verification of the pseudonymous nature of the letter. For instance, Bauckham writes, "The future tense is used, of course, because although the author is referring to a reality of his own time, he is writing in the person of Peter, and so, as was appropriate in a testament, he represents Peter as prophesying the advent of false teachers after his death" (1983, 239). But this is not a required conclusion.

In fact, Peter oscillates between the present and future tenses. In 2:1 and 3:3, the arrival of false teachers is spoken of as future; but in 2:11, 17, 20, and 3:5 the false teachers are portrayed as already present. "The combination of future and present is intended to stress the correspondence between prophecy and event" (Green 1987, 104, n. 1). Peter emphasizes that there always have been and always will be false teachers among the people of God, just as the OT prophets and Jesus himself foretold (e.g., Deut 12:2-6; Matt 24:24). Rather than a mark of a pseudonymous author, the future tense is more likely a literary technique. By reminding his audience of these predictions, Peter helps them prepare for the appearance of false teaching among them (Moo 1996, 92).

False teachers **will secretly introduce** (*pareisaxousin:* ***bring in alongside***) **destructive heresies.** The verb **secretly introduce** always carries the connotation of something underhanded or clandestine. The false teachers do not openly oppose the apostles; they work behind the scenes in covert and devious ways.

The expression **destructive heresies** may be misleading, even though it is a literal translation. **Heresies** did not become a technical term for unorthodox teaching until the beginning of the second century (Ignatius, *Trallians*, vi). Literally, *hairesis* refers to "a private, unauthorized school or party" (Verbrugge 2000, 21). Thus, "destructive opinions" (NRSV) may be a better translation. Nonetheless, these "opinions" are **destructive.** This underscores Peter's point that those who teach and follow this path will bring destruction and condemnation upon themselves.

The false teachers are **even denying the sovereign Lord** (*despotēs*) **who bought them.** The term *despotēs* is applied to God or Christ four other times in the NT (Luke 2:29; Acts 4:24; Jude 4; Rev 6:10). The term "typically refers either to the head of the household, who has absolute rights over his family and slaves (2 Tim 2:21; Titus 2:9; 1 Pet 2:18) or to a ruler with sovereign power, such as the Roman emperors" (Neyrey 1993, 191). Jesus, as the Master **who bought them,** is the figurative head of the household and his slaves.

New Testament writers sometimes speak of Christ purchasing the freedom of his followers at the price of his blood (1 Cor 6:20; 7:23; 1 Pet 1:18-19; Rev 5:9; 14:3-4). Here Peter does not clarify how Christ bought **them** (i.e., his followers) nor what price was paid or to whom. He undoubtedly alludes to Christ's death on the cross and his subsequent resurrection. This is the source of the deliverance and salvation of sinners. Christ's atoning death and resurrection includes both liberty and obligation for believers. "Christianity is, indeed, a religion of liberty; but it also demands loving bondservice to Jesus the Redeemer" (Green 1987, 106). The false teachers either forgot or never knew this.

The false teachers are accused of **denying** the Lord. But how are they **denying** him? There are two possibilities: (1) through their skeptical denial of the second coming, or (2) by teaching and practicing immorality. The latter is more probable, since it fits the context better. The false teachers implicitly **deny** the Lord through "their shameful ways" (2:2).

As a result, they bring **swift destruction on themselves.** The reference to **destruction** in 2 Peter is a metaphor for the day of judgment (see also 2:3; 3:7, 16). There is tragic irony here. The false teachers proclaimed freedom from destruction (2:19); they scoffed at the second coming (3:3); and they gave themselves to immoral and "shameful ways" (2:2). But they will face certain and **swift destruction** for their immoral way of life on the day of Christ's return, which they so vigorously denied.

■ **2-3** Peter identifies the motive, method, effect, and end result of the false teachers in vv 2-3 (Hillyer 1992, 183-84). Their *motive* is **greed** (v 3). In the NT, **greed** "is always used in a bad sense and depicts an insatiable craving and grasping for more of that to which one does not have a just right" (Hiebert 1984a, 262). Christian teachers have the right to financial support (1 Cor 9:1-14; Gal 6:6; 1 Tim 5:17-18), but should not be motivated by financial gain (1 Pet 5:2). Unlike true teachers, false teachers are motivated by **greed**.

The *method* of false teachers is to **exploit** people **with stories they have made up** (v 3). Peter turns the accusations of the false teachers back onto themselves. They accused the apostles of using "cleverly invented stories" (1:16) supporting the second coming. But, in fact, the false teachers are the ones who have concocted fanciful **stories.** These were motivated to **exploit** (*emporeusontai:* ***make money out of*** or ***cash in on***) their deluded followers.

Delling (1968, 272) suggests that **exploit** is used as part of a wordplay. The false teachers had been "bought" (2:1) through Christ's unselfish act of love on the cross. But they greedily try to ***cash in on*** other believers through their fabricated **stories.** Unlike the sovereign Lord they claim to follow, their *motive* and *method* are utterly and despicably mercenary.

The *effect* of the false teachers is disastrous. **Many will follow** the **shameful ways** of the false teachers. Unfortunately, there will always be people who are attracted to new and different teachings. This is especially true if those teachings tiptoe around the requirements of a moral lifestyle and the accountability of believers to a holy and righteous God. But believers should not confuse popularity with reality. Because of the popular but immoral instruction of the false teachers, **the way of truth** will be brought **into disrepute.**

The expression **way of truth** does not appear elsewhere in the NT. But the disciples of Jesus "followed him on the way" (Mark 10:52 NRSV) and the Christian movement itself came to be known as "the Way" (Acts 9:2; 19:9, 23; 22:4; 24:14, 22; see John 14:6). Paul described the Christian way of life with the metaphor of "walking" (Rom 6:4; 13:13; 14:15; Gal 5:16; Phil 3:17; 1 Thess 2:12), which "implies that disciples walk in a certain way" (Neyrey 1993, 192).

Peter is fond of the imagery of **the way.** The Christian faith is **the way of truth** (2:2), "the straight way" (2:15), and "the way of righteousness" (2:21). And he denounces false teaching as "the way of Balaam" (2:15) that leads to **shameful ways** (2:2).

Thus, by **way of truth** he seems to mean a morally pure life characterized by virtue (see 1:4-7). The immoral and **shameful ways** of the false teachers demonstrate that they are "denying the Sovereign Lord who bought them" (2:1). As a result, the Christian faith is brought **into disrepute** (*blasphēmēthēsetai:* ***will be blasphemed***).

The *end result* of false teaching is **condemnation** and **destruction** (v 3). The **condemnation** of the false teachers **has long been hanging over them** (*ouk argei:* ***is not idle***), **and their destruction has not been sleeping.** Anticipating 3:9, Neyrey observes that Peter's words here already reject "the opponents' slur on delayed judgment ('judgment is idle; destruction naps')" (1980, 415).

The condemnation of false teachers is inevitable. Their certain doom is heightened by the threefold repetition of **destruction** (*apōleia*) in these three verses. Those who lead others to **destruction** with **destructive heresies** are doomed to **destruction** themselves.

FROM THE TEXT

Eternal Security? Peter describes the false teachers as **denying the sovereign Lord who bought them** (2:1). The Reformed doctrine of the perseverance of the saints (= eternal security) is often based upon the idea of a limited atonement. That is, its advocates believe that the saving effects of Christ's death and resurrection are *limited* to only those individuals God predestined to be saved through Christ's death. They suppose that Christ "bought" certain individuals through his death on the cross; and these are eternally secure. A popular form of this doctrine in everyday language is "once saved, always saved."

Peter's words in 2:1 contradict this teaching. Peter describes the false teachers as **denying the sovereign Lord who bought them.** Christ died for the false teachers. He **bought** them through his death. But they denied him and are headed for destruction. Wesley notes that the Lord bought them "with his own blood. Yet these very men perish everlastingly. Therefore Christ bought even them that perish" (1981, n.p.). This passage "remains one of the strongest in support of unlimited atonement" (Chang 1985, 61).

Orthodoxy vs. Orthopraxis. True Christianity is not merely a matter of embracing correct doctrine. Believers also need to adopt a morally disciplined way of life. The truth of the beliefs Christians accept is made known and exemplified in the way they live their daily lives. Although it may not always be immediately apparent, people notice the way believers live. Throughout history, there have been countless testimonies about how a believer's life—an act of kindness, a word of compassionate concern, an unexpected expression of sacrificial love—has influenced another to place his or her faith and trust in Christ.

Conversely, "the truth can also be maligned by the way we choose to live and can become a source of ridicule for those who have yet to accept the way of truth" (Watson 1998b, 346). All believers must pose the heart-searching question: Does the example of my life lead people closer to Christ or push them away? How many people have rejected the Christian faith because of the behavior of unfaithful Christians? The path to destruction is marked not only by examples of false teaching but also by misleading examples of a false Christian lifestyle.

B. The Fate of the Ungodly and the Rescue of the Righteous (2:4-10*a*)

BEHIND THE TEXT

Peter provides three examples of God's judgment upon the ungodly (vv 4-6). The warning of condemnation and destruction (v 3*b*) segues perfectly into the three illustrations of God's judgment (vv 4-6). In fact, the transition is so smooth that some suggest the new paragraph begins with v 3*b* (see Bauckham 1983, 245; Neyrey 1993, 196). However, since vv 4-10*a* are a single sentence in Greek, it is more appropriate to attach v 3 to the previous section.

But v 3 is truly transitional: it concludes the description of the false teachers in vv 1-3 and it introduces the discussion of their fate (along with the fate of the righteous) in vv 4-10*a*.

The two examples of fallen angels and Sodom and Gomorrah (vv 4-6) are also found in Jude 5-7. However, Peter uses the example of the flood instead of Jude's example of the Exodus from Egypt. Also, unlike Jude's list, Peter places his examples in chronological order.

Some interpreters assert that these similarities betray a dependence of 2 Peter upon Jude. But the differences should not be overlooked. Bauckham notes, "There are strong indications that in vv 4-9 2 Peter is independently drawing on a paraenetic tradition similar to that which lies behind Jude 5-7" (1983, 246). There are undeniable similarities in the content of 2 Pet 2:4-6 and Jude 5-7. But these similarities may indicate a shared common source rather than literary interdependence.

Verses 4-10*a* seem to have the following organization:

IF:

v 4: **God did not spare angels** (negative example)
v 5: God did not **spare the ancient world** (negative example)
v 5: God **protected Noah** (positive example)
v 6: God **condemned the cities of Sodom and Gomorrah** (negative example)
vv 7-8: God **rescued Lot** (positive example)

THEN:

v 9*a:* God **knows how to rescue godly men** (positive conclusion)
vv 9*b*-10*a:* God knows how **to hold the unrighteous for judgment** (negative conclusion)

The lengthy examples in the first part of the sentence (vv 4-8) make the certainty of judgment and deliverance in the second part of the sentence (v 9) all the more forceful and emphatic.

IN THE TEXT

I. Three Examples of Judgment and Deliverance (2:4-8)

Peter bases his certainty of divine retribution and divine reward on God's consistent action in the past. Each example reinforces Peter's insistence in v 3*b* that the Judge of sin is neither idle nor asleep.

■ **4** The first example of God's retribution on **angels when they sinned** does not immediately bring to mind any OT occurrence. "Nowhere does the Old Testament cite an unambiguous reference to God's judgment on angels" (Moo 1996, 101). Most interpreters presume that Peter takes for granted the interpretation of Gen 6:1-4 prevailing in his time. He alludes to the story in which the "sons of God" (= "angels") lusted after and married human women (Gen 6:1-4). This sin precipitated the flood.

The history of interpretation of Gen 6:1-4 is documented in noncanonical literature of the so-called intertestamental period. Apocryphal writers speculated that heavenly Watchers (= angels) sinned and were subsequently punished by God in the flood. The most developed form of this story is found in *1 Enoch*. In *1 Enoch* (10:4-12) these angels are cast into hell and confined in chains of deepest darkness until the time of the judgment. Peter's description of the punishment of the angels in 2:4 parallels that described in *1 Enoch*. It seems probable that he was influenced by this Jewish tradition about God's punishment of fallen angels.

Peter proclaims that God punished the angels and **sent them to hell, putting them into gloomy dungeons to be held for judgment. Hell** here is *Tartarus*. In classical mythology Tartarus was "the subterranean abyss in which rebellious gods and other such beings, like the Titans, were punished" (Rogers and Rogers 1998, 585). The word was appropriated by Hellenistic Judaism as a synonym for hell (see Job 40:20; 41:24; Prov 30:16). In *1 Enoch, Tartarus* is the awful abode of the fallen angels until their final judgment and destruction (20:2).

To translate *Tartarus* as **hell** in 2 Peter is misleading. Like *1 Enoch*, Peter uses *Tartarus* to refer to a preliminary place of punishment, where angels are **held for judgment.** In contrast to the typical perception of **hell** as a place of final and endless punishment, Peter uses *Tartarus* to mean a place of temporary punishment and confinement. He expected fallen angels to remain in this place of temporary punishment until their final destruction and punishment at the day of judgment.

Instead of **gloomy dungeons,** some versions, translating a different manuscript reading, describe God as confining the fallen angels to "chains of darkness" (KJV, NAB, NRSV). They read *seirais* ("chains") instead of *sirois* ("caves or pits"). The parallel in Jude 6 uses "chains." A scribe familiar with Jude probably changed the lesser known word "caves" for the better known "chains" in 2 Pet 2:4.

Peter's purpose was to remind his readers that God **did not spare** the angels when they sinned. If exalted angels were not spared from punishment for disobeying God, then the punishment and condemnation of rebellious humans was all the more certain and inescapable.

■ **5** The second example is the story of the flood in Noah's day (see also 1 Pet 3:20; 2 Pet 3:5-6). God did not spare the angels, and he also **did not spare the ancient world when he brought the flood on its ungodly people.** The **ungodly** (*asebōn*) "had no time whatever for God" (Green 1987, 110). Peter does not describe their sins. But their designation as **ungodly** implies their rebellion and opposition to everything associated with God.

The first example of the fallen angels does not contain a contrasting positive example. But the second and third negative examples "are also balanced off with the positive examples of Noah and Lot (which are not in Jude)" (Harrington 2003, 266). In contrast to the **ungodly** who were not spared, God **protected Noah, a preacher of righteousness, and seven others.**

Noah is depicted as **a preacher of righteousness.** The OT never mentions Noah preaching. The idea was probably derived from Jewish tradition, which mentions Noah preaching (e.g., Josephus, *Ant.* 1.74; *Sib. Or.* 1.128-29, 148-98). It could also refer to Noah's righteous lifestyle as metaphorically condemning sin and proclaimed righteousness to his ungodly contemporaries (Gen 6:9). Calvin embraced both possibilities by explaining that Noah could be called **a preacher of righteousness** "because he labored to restore a degenerated world to a sound mind, and this not only by his teaching and godly exhortations, but also by his anxious toil in building the ark for the term of a hundred and twenty years" (1948, 398).

Righteousness is used to describe Noah's preaching in order to heighten the contrast between Noah and the **ungodly people** among whom he lived. Unlike the **ungodly people,** who were not spared by the flood, God **protected** (*ephylaxen:* ***watched, guarded, protected;*** BDAG, 1068) Noah.

The numerical reference to Noah **and seven others** probably serves the same function as in 1 Pet 3:20. It underscores the small number of righteous individuals who were protected by God. "The false teachers may be attracting quite a following, and some of Peter's readers may be discouraged about that. They need to remember that the godly are often few but that God is always faithful to preserve them" (Moo 1996, 104). In this second example, then, Peter alludes to Noah and the flood to reinforce the certainty of God's judgment of those who live disobedient and ungodly lives while he rescues his righteous followers.

■ **6** The third example is the condemnation of the cities of Sodom and Gomorrah (Gen 19). The examples move from destruction by water to destruction by fire (see 1 Pet 3:6-7; Luke 17:26-29). God condemned Sodom and Gomorrah **by burning them to ashes.**

Jude also refers to the destruction of Sodom and Gomorrah, but it goes on to specify the sins of the people (v 7). Peter merely notes that the citizens of these cities were **ungodly.** Another difference between Jude and 2 Peter is the omission in Jude of the positive example of God's deliverance of Lot (2 Pet 2:7-8). The similarities and differences between Jude and 2 Peter point to a common literary tradition behind the two letters rather than a direct dependence of one writing upon the other.

God destroyed Sodom and Gomorrah by raining down burning sulfur on them (Gen 19:24), **by burning them to ashes** (*tephrōsas*). The two accounts are not contradictory. Genesis describes the *means* of their destruction; Peter describes its *result*. The image of the smoldering ashes of Sodom and Gomorrah was used by Jewish writers before Peter (e.g., Philo, *Mos.* 2.56; Josephus, *J.W.* 4.483; *4 Ezra* 2:9; Wis 10:7). Peter uses the well-known Hellenistic Jewish image of burning ashes to describe the destructive result of God's condemnation of these two infamous cities.

God made Sodom and Gomorrah **an example** (*hypodeigma*) **of what is going to happen to the ungodly.** A *hypodeigma* is an "example, model, or even pattern" (Schlier 1964, 32-33). "There is an inevitable pattern of events: sin, unconfessed and unforsaken, will lead to judgment and destruction" (Hillyer 1992, 189). What happened to Sodom and Gomorrah is sure to happen to the ungodly false teachers of his time, despite their denial and scorn of coming judgment.

■ **7-8** Although God destroyed these two wicked cities, **he rescued Lot.** The verb for **rescued** (*ryomai*) originally meant ***to draw or to drag along the ground.*** Eventually, the word came to convey the idea of drawing or snatching from danger, so that it was used to mean ***to rescue or deliver.*** It was used "more with the meaning of drawing to oneself than merely rescuing from someone or something" (Zodhiates 1992, 1265). God drew Lot to himself and **rescued** him.

Lot is described three times in these verses as **a righteous man** (*dikaios*). This is surprising. The OT never describes Lot as righteous. Its description of Lot is not very complimentary. "He appears simply as a man of the world (Gen 13:10-14; 19:16) who had strayed a long way from the God of his fathers. Though hospitable (19:1), he was weak (19:6), morally depraved (19:8) and drunken (19:33, 35)" (Green 1987, 112). According to Gen 19:16, Lot was so reluctant to leave sinful Sodom that he had to be dragged out of the city. This may have influenced Peter's use of *ryomai* (***rescue by dragging from danger***) to describe Lot's deliverance. The description of Lot as **righteous** may be derived from Jewish tradition (see Philo, *Mos.* 2.58; Wis 10:6; 19:17). Or perhaps it served as a contrast to the **lawless deeds** and **filthy lives** of the sinful in Sodom.

Far from perfect, Lot never lost his basic orientation to the Lord. Despite Lot's shortcomings, Peter described him as **distressed by the filthy lives of lawless men** (v 7) and **tormented in his righteous soul by the lawless deeds he saw and heard** (v 8). "Lot's moral sensitivity made his life among the Sodomites unbearable, just as the life of faithful Christians among the false teachers and those influenced by them will become unbearable" (Harrington 2003, 267-68). But God can be trusted to rescue the righteous, just as he rescued Lot.

2. The Conclusion: The Certainty of Deliverance and Judgment (2:9-10*a*)

■ **9** Since the OT repeatedly demonstrates that God can be trusted to save the righteous and to punish the wicked, **then the Lord knows how to rescue godly men from trials and to hold the unrighteous for the day of judgment, while continuing their punishment.** The verb **rescue** (*ryesthai*) is the same one that described Lot's deliverance from the destruction of Sodom. Their destruction is the example and pattern of "what is going to happen to the ungodly" (v 6). Likewise, the **rescue** of Lot is the pattern of what is going to happen to the righteous. Peter's affirmation of the deliverance of the righteous is a striking departure from the writing of Jude, which discusses only the punishment of the wicked.

God will rescue the righteous **from trials** (*peirasmou: **temptations***). "The idea here is primarily of those surroundings that try a man's fidelity and integrity, and not of the inward inducement to sin, arising from the desires" (Strachan 1979, 136). God knows how to rescue godly people from testing, affliction, and even temptations that arise from daily exposure to unbelievers. Just as God rescued Noah and Lot, he can be trusted to save other righteous people from the trials and constraints caused by their sinful surroundings.

The examples also demonstrate that God knows how **to hold the unrighteous for the day of judgment, while continuing their punishment.** The participle **continuing their punishment** (*kolazomenous*) has been interpreted in two ways. It can refer to preliminary punishment of the wicked before the final judgment (see 2:4). Or it can refer to punishment at the day of judgment. It is more likely that Peter meant the day of judgment. His main point is the impending fate and doom of the false teachers. Their destruction and condemnation are certain, although they were not yet apparent.

■ **10*a*** The certainty of punishment and destruction ***is especially true of those who go after flesh in a passionate longing for defilement and despise authority.*** In the context of the references to Sodom and Gomorrah (vv 6-8), ***go after flesh*** (*sarkos*) ***in a passionate longing for defilement*** might be an allusion to the sin of the men of Sodom (Gen 19:1-11). This phrase most likely refers to depraved sexual sin in general.

They also **despise authority** (*kyriotētos: **lordship***). **Authority** may refer to: (1) some kind of angelic hierarchy (Eph 1:21; Col 1:16); (2) the authority of the church; (3) the lordship of Christ, whom the false teachers despise and deny (2:1); or (4) all authority in general. The false teachers denied the Lord by their refusal to follow his moral instructions. This made them parade examples of the rejection of authority.

But Peter referred to the "slander [of] celestial beings" (2:10*b*) and implied that they mocked the teaching of the apostles (1:16). This seems to indicate that their disdain for authority was more general in nature than simply a rejection of the Lord's authority. The false teachers' disdain for **authority** is probably best understood in a general sense. It refers to their universal disregard and contempt of all authority, except their own self-seeking desire.

FROM THE TEXT

A Modern Predicament? "Peter faced a curiously modern predicament" (Green 1987, 115). There were people in the church who lived sexually immoral lives and tried to justify it. Mocking the teachings of the church and the example and authority of Christ, they rejected the idea that God would judge them for following their passionate desires (v 10). What was worse, the infection of their immoral behavior was spreading. The situation Peter faced could have been taken from the front pages of today's newspapers.

As in Peter's time, today's society flaunts sexual promiscuity, homosexual behavior, and blatantly disregards a virtuous and moral lifestyle. Many people scoff at the idea of personal accountability or a day of judgment for their conduct. Often their hollow excuse is that God (if he exists) would not deny the fulfillment of their pleasure or desires, regardless of how depraved or self-obsessed they might be. Peter reminded believers that people could not do this and get away with it in God's world. God's judgment of sin and sinners is certain.

The Promise of Judgment and Deliverance. Peter reminded his readers of God's retribution on the fallen angels and the wicked people of Noah and Lot's days. The pattern of God's destructive judgment on wickedness and sin is firmly established in the pages of Scripture. The certainty of judgment there is like a dark cloud that hovers incessantly (although sometimes imperceptibly) above every human who ever lived. The justice of God may be delayed, but it cannot be avoided.

But alongside this dark pattern of judgment is a bright and promising pattern of divine deliverance of the righteous. The silver lining of that dark cloud is the promise of God's grace. As with Noah and Lot, God will rescue those who seek and follow him.

The Surprising Example of Lot. The surprising description of Lot as a **righteous man** is a subtle comfort. The OT does not portray Lot as a sterling example of a righteous man. In fact, Genesis amply documents the shortcomings of Lot. But God rescued Lot! Although he was surrounded by moral decay and depravity, Lot never lost sight of the Lord. Peter presumes that Lot was **distressed** and **tormented** by the sinfulness around him. Despite the perverse attraction his sinful culture exerted on him (Gen 19:16), Lot rejected Sodom, and God **rescued** him.

Peter might have used Abraham as his example of God's deliverance of a righteous man, spared while Sodom and Gomorrah were destroyed (Gen 18). Instead, he uses the example of the weak and often-tempted Lot. Perhaps Peter selected Lot because his readers could identify with him. Believers seldom feel they measure up to the standard of faith and righteousness exemplified by Abraham. It is much easier to identify with Lot—distressed, tormented, and tempted by the sin surrounding him. Lot's story is a story of God's indescribable grace. If God could rescue Lot, he can be trusted to rescue us as well.

C. The Character and Behavior of the False Teachers (2:10*b*-22)

BEHIND THE TEXT

The second part of v 10 marks the beginning of a new sentence. It begins Peter's descriptive denunciation of the false teachers.

These verses consist of a string of loosely structured denunciations of the false teachers. The language and images parallel Jude 8-13 and 16. The negative characterization of the false teachers progresses as follows: (1) their arrogance (vv 10*b*-12), (2) their blatant immorality (vv 13-14), (3) their greed (vv 15-16), (4) their hollow and deceptive teachings (vv 17-19), and (5) their revolting apostasy (vv 20-22).

IN THE TEXT

1. Their Arrogance (2:10*b*-12)

■ **10*b*-11** The false teachers are **bold and arrogant.** The words are similar in meaning. As **bold,** they practice a "reckless daring that defies God and man." As **arrogant,** they obstinately please themselves at all costs (Green 1987, 116). Used together, Peter portrays the false teachers as audacious and completely self-absorbed.

The translation and meaning of vv 10*b*-11 are obscure. Literally, this can be translated: ***Bold and arrogant, they do not fear the glorious ones while blaspheming them, whereas angels, although they are greater in strength and power, do not bring slanderous judgments against them before the Lord.***

The words ***glorious ones*** (*doxas*) and ***against them*** (*kat' autōn*) are problematic. *Doxas* (***glorious ones***) must refer to angelic beings. Otherwise v 11 makes no sense. But are they *evil* or *good* angelic beings?

Depending on one's answer, these verses can be interpreted in two different ways: (1) Peter accuses the false teachers of insulting and blaspheming the evil fallen angels, something even good angels do not do. Or, (2) Peter accuses them of insulting and blaspheming good angels. Angels do not slander false teachers before the Lord (Bauckham 1983, 261). Both interpretations make acceptable sense of the passage.

The parallel passage in Jude 8-9 tips the scale in favor of the first interpretation. Jude accuses false teachers of slandering celestial beings. Jude adds, "But even the archangel Michael, when he was disputing with the devil about the body of Moses, did not dare to bring a slanderous accusation against him, but said, 'The Lord rebuke you!'" (v 9). "If the angels who did not sin withhold accusation against those who did, then there is no place for man (who is inferior in strength and power) to revile and insult the fallen angels" (Mounce 1982, 131). Peter denounces the arrogant false teachers who rush in with blasphemous judgments where even angels fear to tread.

What were the false teachers doing? Peter considered their behavior arrogant, ignorant, and foolhardy. But the obscurity of his language makes more specific conclusions speculative at best. Two suggestions merit mention. Moo
2:10*b*-12 thinks their blasphemy consisted in "a general denial of the existence of [angelic] beings" (1996, 123). This fits their materialistic orientation (2:3) and their skepticism about the second coming and judgment (1:16; 3:3-5).

The second suggestion connects their blasphemy of angels to their arrogant immorality.

> When they were rebuked for their immoral behavior and warned of the danger of falling into the power of the devil and sharing his condemnation, they laughed at the idea, denying that the devil could have any power over them and speaking of the powers of evil in skeptical, mocking terms. (Bauckham 1983, 262)

■ **12** The false teachers **blaspheme in matters they do not understand** (*agnoousin*). *Agnoousin* is the verbal negation of *gnōsis* (***knowledge***). Peter is taking a jab at the arrogant, self-proclaimed "knowledge" of the false teachers. They claim special knowledge about various spiritual matters—God, Jesus, the angels, the Christian life, the second coming, humankind. But they are actually completely ignorant of these matters (see Harrington 2003, 272).

In their ignorance, they can be compared to **brute** (*aloga*) **beasts.** Like **beasts,** they are irrational, *aloga* (***illogical***). They are merely **creatures of instinct** (*physika*). *Physika* is used "in contrast to participation in the divine nature" in 1:4, "humans in their natural state" (Verbrugge 2000, 596). True believers participate in the divine nature through their saving knowledge (*epignōsis*) of Christ (1:3-4). But false teachers arrogantly demonstrate their folly by thinking like mere **creatures of instinct.**

Are they compared to **brute beasts** because of their irrational ignorance of spiritual realities? Or, is the comparison referring to their animal-like, sexually immoral behavior? Peter may have had both comparisons in mind (Moo 1996, 124).

The comparison of false teachers and brute beasts reconnects with the theme of certain destruction (see 2:1-3). Irrational animals are **born only to be caught and destroyed.** Similarly, false teachers ***like beasts will also be destroyed.*** They will suffer a destruction that is similar (in its suddenness and violence or in its finality) to the slaughter of animals by hunters (Bauckham 1983, 264).

2. Their Blatant Immorality (2:13-14)

■ **13** Peter describes the destruction of the false teachers as just retribution: **They will be paid back with harm for the harm they have done**—a wordplay in Greek as well as in English. The false teachers have harmed others through their false teaching and immorality. Accordingly, they will be ***rewarded*** with **harm.** This provides a perfect transition from the destruction of false teachers (v 12) to the description of their harmful immoral behavior (vv 13-14).

Peter attacks the immorality of his opponents. Their shamelessness is illustrated by **their idea of pleasure** as carousing **in broad daylight. *Carousing*** (*tryphēn: **self-indulgence, debauchery***) is often associated with drunkenness and other forms of sensuality (Bauckham 1983, 265).

Public carousing was **their idea of pleasure** (*hēdonēn*). The Greeks included hedonism "among their four 'deadly sins,' sometimes contrasting it with reason (see 'unreasoning animals' in v. 12)" (Moo 1996, 125). That their immoral activity takes place **in broad daylight** instead of concealed by darkness accentuates Peter's portrayal of his opponents as both shameful and shameless.

Their reprehensible behavior had become **blots** (*spiloi*) **and blemishes** (*mōmoi*) upon the fabric of the believers' fellowship. Peter will provide a direct contrast to these defiling influences upon the church in 3:14. There Greek *a*-negative forms of these terms urge his readers to be "spotless" (*aspiloi*) and "blameless" (*amōmētoi*) as they prepare for the return of Christ.

The false teachers were evidently participants in the activities of the church. They indulge **in their *deceitful* pleasures while they feast with you. Feast** almost certainly refers to the "love feast" (*agapē* meal; Jude 12) usually held in conjunction with the Lord's Supper. The abuse of the community meal was well-documented by Paul in 1 Cor 11:17-34.

Peter uses a striking wordplay. He does not describe the celebrations of his readers as "love feasts" (*agapais*). Rather, because of the participation of the self-indulgent false teachers, they had become "deceit feasts" (*apatais*). Instead of celebrating love (*agapē*) at the Lord's Supper, they celebrated deceit and lust (*apatē*).

■ **14** Peter poignantly describes the behavior of the false teachers: **With eyes full of adultery, they never stop sinning** (= ***They have eyes full of an adulteress***). "Their eyes are always looking for a woman with whom to commit adultery" (Bauckham 1983, 266). The false teachers **never stop sinning.** As they gather with believers to celebrate Holy Communion, they lustfully ogle the women as potential sexual partners. Kelly observes, "The errorists have so lost moral self-control that they cannot look at a woman without imagining or wishing themselves in bed with her" (1969, 342).

Likewise, **they seduce** (*deleazontes*) **the unstable.** *Deleazontes* ("to lure by the use of bait"; BDAG, 217) uses the imagery of hunting and fishing. They used bait to lure fish to the hook or to entice animals into their trap. The word could describe any kind of moral temptation (Jas 1:14).

The victims of their schemes were **the unstable,** in contrast to those "firmly established in the truth" (1:12). The **unstable** probably refers to recent converts (see 2:18) still unable to discern the destructive threat of the false teachers' immoral behavior.

Furthermore, **they are experts in greed.** ***Trained*** (*gegymnasmenēn*) is the term from which the English word "gymnasium" is derived. The word "is drawn from the realm of athletics; it suggests that long, hard, and disciplined struggle to become proficient in a sport" (Moo 1996, 126). In contrast to the **unstable** inexperience of the recent converts they were targeting, the false teachers were **experts** in deceptive schemes and selfish **greed.**

The transition from sexual depravity in v 14*a* to **greed** in v 14*b* appears rather abrupt. But **greed** (*pleonexia*) has a broader scope than mere love of money. It is the desire for more of anything—sexual pleasure, power, food, etc. (see Eph 4:19). In vv 15-16, Peter addresses the wicked greed of his opponents. As **experts in greed,** they undoubtedly loved money. But within the present context, **greed** probably conveys the broader meaning of ***lust for more.*** This would include the gratification of sexual lusts as well as greed for more money. In this way, **greed** provides a fitting transition from the discussion of his opponents' immoral sexual behavior to their mercenary love of money, which he will denounce in vv 15-16.

Peter calls his opponents **an accursed brood** (*kataras tekna: **children of a curse***). "Children of . . ." is a "Hebraism" for identifying one's character (Bauckham 1983, 267). For example, Isaiah condemned the wicked as "children of destruction" (57:4). That is, they were characterized by and doomed for destruction. As ***children of a curse,*** the false teachers were under God's curse, dooming them to eternal condemnation.

3. Their Greed (2:15-16)

■ **15** The false teachers were cursed because **they have left the straight way and wandered off.** In 2:2, Peter described the "way of truth." In the ancient world, a philosophy was "a way" of life. Obedience to God was the right or straight way (see 1 Sam 12:23; Hos 14:9). The false teachers have **left** (*kataleipontes: **abandoned***) **the straight way and wandered off.**

Wandered off (*eplanēthēsan*) is the passive form of a word that means ***led astray*** or ***deceived*** (BDAG, 821). In the NT, ***going astray*** is not considered accidental or harmless, but deliberate and culpable. "To be a Christian is to have left behind the time of straying" (Braun 1968, 243). People who abandon the straight path of obedience to God are lost. The false teachers were lost because they **wandered off to follow the way of Balaam son of Beor.**

The Story of Balaam

In Num 22—24, Balak, the King of Moab hired the prophet Balaam to curse the Israelites. When Balaam went to meet Balak, God sent an angel to block his path. Balaam was blind to the angel's presence, but his donkey saw the angel and refused to follow the path. After Balaam hit the donkey, the Lord opened the mouth of the donkey to rebuke Balaam and his blindness. When Balaam's eyes were opened, the angel rebuked him for following a way that was "recklessness" (Num 22:32). Jewish tradition expanded upon the story of Balaam, depicting him as a notorious liar, a proponent of sexual immorality, and a classic example of one driven by greed and avarice (Neyrey 1993, 211).

The analogy of Balaam served Peter's purpose in several significant ways. First, Balaam vividly illustrates the motivation of greed that drives the false teachers. Balaam is described as one **who loved the wages of wickedness.** Second, Num 31:16 attributes the sexual immorality of the Israelites in Baal-Peor (in Num 25) to the evil influence of Balaam. Balaam represents a striking prototype of the immoral false teachers. Third, the description of Balaam's behavior as following a way that was "recklessness" (Num 22:32) presents a vivid contrast to the **straight way** of truth the false teachers left behind. These censorious characterizations of Balaam strongly denounce the behavior and the motivation of the false teachers.

■ **16** The utter folly of Balaam is emphasized by the fact that **he was rebuked for his wrongdoing by a donkey.** In Numbers, it was the angel who rebuked Balaam rather than the donkey. The donkey simply complained against Balaam's unjust beatings. But Peter follows Jewish tradition in attributing the rebuke to the donkey (Bauckham 1983, 268).

Peter's description of his opponents as **brute beasts** (2:12) may have prompted him to cite the story of Balaam. The irony of the story is profound: Balaam, the prophet of God, is supposedly able to *see* God's will and to *speak* about the purpose and judgment of God. But he was unable to see an angel standing right in front of him. And his speechless donkey not only sees the angel but also pronounces a prophetic rebuke of Balaam.

> Balaam's judgment was swayed by his greed so that he actually thought he could succeed in his plan of opposing God's will. Similarly the false teachers, who deny the reality of God's judgment, foolishly imagine they can sin with impunity. But in Balaam's case even his donkey knew better! (Bauckham 1983, 270)

4. Their Hollow and Deceptive Teaching (2:17-19)

A noticeable shift in emphasis begins in v 17. In 2:10-16, Peter criticizes the false teachers' *character.* They are arrogant, shamelessly immoral, and greedy. But in 2:17-22, he directs his attention to the *teaching* of his opponents

2:16-17 and its destructive impact.

■ **17** The opening words **these men** (*houtoi*) are used repeatedly in Jude to mark a transition. Peter does not use this phrase (2:12, 17) as frequently as Jude, nor does he use it as a transition marker.

Two metaphors describe the unfulfilling and unsatisfying false teachers. First, they are **springs without water.** In the arid Middle East, springs of water are highly valued. "A water-rich spring or well of water is an ancient image of wisdom (Prov 13:14; 18:14; Sirach 24:23-31)" (van Houwelingen 1988, 192). A spring gives life and, in many cases, even saves life. Peter compares the teaching of his opponents to a **spring**—a promising source of water and wisdom—which turns out to be empty and useless.

Second, they are **mists driven by a storm. Mists** (*homichlai*) is a rare word, used only here in the NT and seldom in other Greek literature. In one of its rare occurrences, Aristotle (*Meteor.* 1.346b) "tells us that the *homichlē* is the haze which heralds dry weather, but is so easily dispersed by a sharp gust of wind" (Green 1987, 126). This metaphor identifies false teachers as unstable and without substance. Taken together, these two metaphors emphasize the "disappointing emptiness" (Fuhrman 1967, 332) of the false teachers and their teaching.

The last phrase picks up the theme of judgment: **Blackest darkness is reserved for them. Darkness** is often depicted as the judgment of the wicked (Matt 8:12; 22:13; 25:30; 2 Pet 2:4; Jude 6, 13). Calvin envisions a correspondence of the false teachers' punishment with their crime. He writes:

> By naming the mist or the blackness of darkness, he alludes to the clouds which obscure the air; as though he had said, that for the momentary darkness which they now spread, there is prepared for them a much thicker darkness which is to continue for ever. (Calvin 1948, 407)

■ **18** The false teachers are like waterless springs and unstable weather because **they mouth empty, boastful words.** Peter's language is full of sarcastic derision. **They mouth** (*phthengomenoi*) is the same verbal root used to describe the speech of Balaam's donkey. The donkey "mouthed" better insight and doctrine than the false teachers.

Boastful (*hyperonka:* ***unnaturally swollen***) depicts the speech of these men as high-sounding and haughty. But their lofty verbosity is **empty** (*mataiotētos*). Their words sound impressive, but they are deceptive, ultimately worthless, frustrating, and futile, because they can never attain their goal (Moo 1996, 142).

These men attract the attention and imagination of gullible hearers **by appealing to the lustful desires of sinful human nature. Lustful** (*aselgeiais:* ***licentiousness***) denotes an exorbitant excess in lifestyle. It is used ten times in the NT, "mostly in vice lists, where it is often linked with other sexual sins" (Verbrugge 2000, 76). Peter uses the word earlier to describe the "shameful ways" (2:2) of the false teachers and the "filthy" lifestyle of the people of Sodom and Gomorrah (2:7). Here it describes the excessively **lustful desires** of the ***flesh*** (*sarkos*) to which the false teachers appeal in order to win adherents. Thus, the false teachers employ two deceptive means to attract followers: they mouth grandiose words and they appeal to the **lustful desires** of the flesh. "Grandiose sophistry is the hook, filthy lust is the bait" (Bigg 1905, 285).

With impressive rhetoric, the false teachers appealed to base desires to **entice people who are just escaping from those who live in error.** The verb **entice** (*deleazousin*) describes the way they "seduce the unstable" (2:14). They set out bait to lure easy victims into their trap. The **people who are just escaping** describes new converts, still "unstable" (2:14) in their understanding of the faith.

Error (*planēi*) regularly describes pagans and their errant way of life (see Rom 1:27; Titus 3:3). Recent converts from paganism were an easy target for the impressive-sounding but worthless teaching of Peter's opponents. Peter passionately condemns the false teachers for their habit of preying on weak and unstable recent converts.

■ **19** With lofty words appealing to base lusts, the false teachers made the lying **promise** of **freedom.** Peter does not specify what their promise of **freedom** entailed. But he notes the irony: they promise freedom **while they themselves are slaves of depravity** (*phthoras*). *Phthora* can denote ***moral*** or ***physical corruption***—depravity or mortality.

Thus, the content of the **promise** of **freedom** can be narrowed down to two main possibilities. They promised their followers freedom: (1) from eschatological judgment (see 1:16-21; 3:3-12) or (2) from any external moral constraint (see 2:2, 10, 13-16, 18). Both are possible, but the latter is more probable (see v 20; Moo 1996, 144). Although they proclaim personal freedom from the restraints of sexual morality, their immoral lifestyle demonstrates their own slavery to depravity.

The verse concludes with a proverb: **for a man is a slave to whatever has mastered him** (see John 8:34; Rom 6:16). Peter's proverb is derived from the practice of enslaving enemies captured in battle. Puffed-up claims of freedom were rendered meaningless by the paralyzing immorality that controlled the lifestyle of the false teachers.

5. Their Revolting Apostasy (2:20-22)

■ **20** It is unclear whether **they** refers to the false teachers or to their naive followers here (see v 18). Since the closest antecedent is the false teachers in v 19, most scholars believe correctly **they** refers to the false teachers.

Peter describes the former condition of the false teachers: ***For*** **if** (*ei gar*) **they have escaped the corruption of the world by knowing our Lord and Savior Jesus Christ.** Peter presumes that the false teachers were once orthodox believers. The phrases **escaped the corruption of the world** (1:4) and **knowing** (*epignōsis*) Christ (1:3) earlier in the letter positively describe the experience of true believers. Peter does not question the reality of the prior conversion of his opponents. He candidly describes them with the same language he used earlier to describe true believers.

Despite their prior conversion, the false teachers had fallen away. Although they had once escaped from the **corruption of the world,** they are now again **entangled in it and overcome. Entangled** probably renews the fishing metaphor used to describe the false teachers' devious methods in 2:14 and 18. If this is true, the false teachers' predicament is tragically ironic. Namely, they have become **entangled** in the very nets they had set out for their unwitting prey.

Overcome (*ēttōntai*) is the same verb as "mastered" (*ēttētai*) used in the proverb in v 19. Not only do the false teachers dabble with dangerous teaching and practices, but they have been **overcome** and "mastered" by their own fallacious thinking and behavior.

The teachers had once experienced true salvation through Jesus Christ. But they allowed themselves once again to become entangled and overcome by sin. As a result, **they are worse off at the end than they were at the beginning.** This conclusion is reminiscent of the vivid words of Jesus about the evicted evil spirit who repossessed his former house (Matt 12:43-45). "A servant who willfully disobeys his master is far more culpable than one who disobeys through ignorance" (Green 1987, 130). For those who have knowingly and deliberately rejected the truth, God's judgment will be more severe.

■**21** Peter considered ignorance of the truth preferable to outright rejection of it. He employs "way" language again (see 2:2, 15). **The way of righteousness** is common in the Bible (Job 24:13; Prov 21:16, 21; Matt 21:32). Here **righteousness** (*dikaiosynēs*) refers to ***right behavior.*** Peter undoubtedly had the immoral behavior of the libertines in mind.

Verse 21 reinforces the evidence that the false teachers were once Christian converts (v 20). **Known** (*epegnōkenai*) is a verbal cognate of **knowledge** (*epignōsis*), used in this letter to describe believers (1:2, 3, 8; see 2:20). Peter does not say false teachers *claimed* to know the way of righteousness; rather, they had **known** it.

Moreover, Peter asserts that **the sacred command . . . was passed on to them. The sacred command** (*hagias entolēs:* "holy commandment," NRSV) "is here used in the same way as 'the way of righteousness,' as a description of Christianity considered as a body of ethical teaching" (Bauckham 1983, 278). 2:20-22

Peter does not have one particular command in mind here. He uses **command** in the singular to summarize the totality of Christian teaching with special emphasis upon its ethical demands. The verb **was passed on** (*paradotheisēs*) "is an important NT term for the transmission of the Christian faith" (Blum 1981b, 282-83; see 1 Cor 15:3).

There can be no doubt the false teachers had been genuinely converted. They had **known** the true Christian way of life. The correct teachings of the Christian faith had been faithfully **passed on** to them. Nonetheless, they decided to **turn their backs** (*hypostrepsai: **turn away and go back***) on their Christian faith.

Peter does not specify the worsened condition that results from the false teachers' denial and rejection of the faith they once possessed. He implies that their fate and condemnation as apostates will be all the more horrific.

■**22** Two proverbs illustrate the revolting nature of the false teachers' apostasy. They are **true** of them, or they have ***happened*** (*symbebēken*) in their case. One proverb is derived from Scripture and the other from the secular world. Both pigs and dogs were considered by Jews to be unclean. The proverbs are closely related to each other and probably make the same point.

The first proverb—**A dog returns to its vomit**—is derived from Proverbs: "As a dog returns to its vomit, so a fool repeats his folly" (26:11). This proverb fits the discussion of the apostasy of the false teachers perfectly. They have turned their backs on the Christian faith in order to return to immorality and sin. The proverb illustrates how "they are worse off at the end than they were at the beginning" (2:20). "What satisfaction can a dog find in vomit if before that he could not even digest that food when it was fresh? The very thought is disgusting and is a picture of irrational reflex action" (Dunham 1983, 50).

The second proverb—**A sow that is washed goes back to her wallowing in mud**—is derived from a well-known Greek saying. Like the proverb, it provides a vivid image of a disgusting return to filth and decay.

These proverbs provide a fitting conclusion to the disparagement of the false teachers. Peter has already alluded to animals in his negative depiction of his opponents (2:12, 16). Now he revives the animal analogy by referring to two animals Jews considered filthy and disgusting. Having been once washed clean by faith in Jesus Christ, the false teachers have reverted to the immorality of the pagan world. In this way, they are like a dog that vomits indigestible food. But then they go back and eat it again. Or they are like a clean pig that cannot resist the urge to go back and wallow in the mud again. In each case, the result is revolting and disgusting.

FROM THE TEXT

Peter's Uncivil Discourse. Peter's criticism of the false teachers is extremely harsh and negative. Viewed in light of Jesus' command to "love your enemies" (Matt 5:44), Peter's disparagement of false teachers might even appear unchristian. But his character assassination should be read from its ancient context.

First, it was common practice in the first century to portray one's enemies in the worst possible light. It was socially acceptable to associate one's opponents with a variety of negative images to undermine their influence and diminish their appeal. Peter's attacks conform to the expectations of his time.

Obviously, the social customs of the twenty-first century are very different from those of Peter's time. Believers must speak out against false and dangerous teaching. But we must do so within the social parameters of our culture and time. The kind of negative portrayals Peter applies to his opponents would be considered inappropriate and unacceptable by most people today. Sadly, a possible exception is found in the mud-slinging and perverting "spin" of modern politicians. Thus, the language and style of Peter's denunciation of his opponents should not be propagated as the normative response of believers to their opponents. Peter's denunciation does not justify arbitrary and vengeful tirades against every form of opposition.

Second, despite Peter's shocking language, one must not forget the insidious threat the false teachers represented to the Christian faith. It is bad enough that they opposed the teaching of the apostles while they shamelessly taught and practiced an immoral lifestyle. But they also targeted the most vulnerable Christians: recent converts and young believers who were still unstable in their faith. In his harsh attack, Peter used a socially accepted method of his time to oppose this serious challenge to the survival of the faith.

Although the methods will undoubtedly vary, today's believers must also oppose false teaching and challenges to the faith (see 1 Pet 3:15-16). Contemporary Christianity faces the problem that relativism has eroded the conviction that falsehood should be opposed. Even more threatening is the treacherous doubt created by relativism that falsehood even exists. It is frightening to think that our objection to Peter's flagrantly negative language might not be so much against his language as it is an objection to the fact that Peter even dared to call the false teachers wrong!

Heresy and Immorality. Peter berated the false teachers for their behavior as much as for their teaching. This is not to say that wrong teaching is less serious than wrong behavior. Rather, it emphasizes the fact that what people truly believe will ultimately affect the way they behave. This observation is immediately apparent in the example of the false teachers. The false teachers do not believe in the second coming or the day of judgment that Christ's return will inaugurate. As a result, they engage in sexually immoral behavior and mock the idea of accountability for their actions. Likewise, belief and behavior are interconnected for believers. In ch 1, Peter proclaims that genuine faith in Christ ("true knowledge") will result in a virtuous life (1:3-9).

Stewards of Tradition. Peter's letter reminds Christians of their responsibility to be faithful stewards of Christian tradition and teaching. The grandiose-sounding doctrine of the false teachers was denigrated because it was empty. It was all show and no substance, like a waterless spring or an evaporating mist. Believers must be sure to establish their teaching on the solid rock of Scripture. Fine-sounding arguments or lofty words can never be substituted for the rich substance of the faith as taught in Scripture. The fruit of our teaching will become evident in the lifestyle and behavior of our hearers.

Christian Perseverance. The innate connection between belief and behavior is also evident in Peter's undeniable assertions that Christians can apostatize from the faith. Salvation is not only dependent upon a profession of faith but also must be lived out in righteous and virtuous behavior. If salvation were merely a matter of a profession of faith, the false teachers would not be subject to condemnation. They certainly continued to claim salvation through Christ. However, their immoral behavior betrayed their lack of genuine faith and true salvation.

Good works and righteous behavior are the inevitable fruit of salvation. Believers are urged to pursue the virtues diligently in order to prevent their "knowledge of Christ" (i.e., salvation) from becoming ineffective or unproductive (1:8). The false teachers selfishly despised authority while they pursued greed, exploited others, and cultivated vices instead of the virtues. Consequently, they lost the salvation they had once experienced.

The same danger of apostasy exists for every believer who falls prey to the erroneous idea that people can be saved while they continue to engage in sinful behavior. All believers can slip and fall into sin. True believers do not try to justify or accommodate sin in their lives. Rather, they confess their sin to God, seek Christ's forgiveness, and pray for the Spirit's power to avoid and defeat sin.

IV. THE PROMISE OF CHRIST'S COMING: 2 PETER 3:1-16

BEHIND THE TEXT

Chapter 3 marks another transition. After denouncing the false teachers in ch 2, Peter returns to his main purpose of warning and encouraging his readers.

After 3:2, the parallels with Jude end. Like Jude, 2 Peter marks the transition from attack to encouragement with the phrase **Dear friends.** Both letters call their readers to remember the apostles' words and issue a warning against scoffers or mockers. Following these points of similarity, the letters move in different directions toward their respective conclusions.

Second Peter 3:1-16 contains four distinct but closely related discussions:

1. The prediction of scoffers (3:1-7)
2. The delay of Christ's coming (3:8-9)
3. The certainty of Christ's coming (3:10)
4. Concluding exhortations (3:11-16)

A. The Prediction of Scoffers (3:1-7)

BEHIND THE TEXT

The argument moves through three stages. First, Peter urges his readers to remember what they learned from Scripture and from apostolic teaching (vv 1-2). Second, he warns of scoffers who will mock their teaching (vv 3-4). Third, he rebukes the scoffers for ignoring the truth (vv 5-7). The paragraph is framed with the idea of "remembering" (Moo 1996, 161).

1. Remember the Truth (3:1-2)

■ **1** Attention now shifts to the readers as **Dear friends** (*agapētoi: **beloved ones***). This term of endearment is used four times in this last chapter (vv 1, 8, 14, 17). Peter has not forgotten the false teachers and their errant doctrine. But his main attention and concern are now focused on fellow believers.

Peter identifies his work in progress as **my second letter to you.** Scholars are divided as to the identity of the first. Most consider this a reference to 1 Peter. But there are problems with this assumption. First, Peter claims that both letters are intended **to stimulate you to wholesome thinking.** This description does not fit the content of 1 Peter well. Second, Peter seems intimately familiar with his audience's situation in 2 Peter. But his personal knowledge of his audience's situation in 1 Peter appears rather limited.

Many scholars who believe **my second letter** alludes to 1 Peter argue that 2 Peter was written pseudonymously. This reference allegedly reveals the forger's attempt to lend authority and credibility to his falsely ascribed writing.

Some argue that **second letter** points to a lost earlier letter of Peter. It is plausible that Peter wrote more letters than the two Epistles bearing his name in the NT. If so, some of these letters have been lost. We know that Paul wrote three letters that apparently no longer survive: a previous letter (1 Cor 5:9), a sorrowful letter (2 Cor 7:8), and a letter to the Laodiceans (Col 4:16).

If 2 Peter was written by the apostle, **second letter** probably alludes to a lost and otherwise unknown first letter to the same readers. All conclusions about the previous letter must remain speculative.

Second Peter was written as a reminder **to stimulate you to wholesome thinking. Wholesome** conveys the idea of "unmixed, ***pure,* without hidden motives**" (BDAG, 282). With the threat of false doctrine and immoral lifestyle lurking in the background, Peter wants to ensure that his readers' understanding will not be distorted or led astray.

■ **2** Peter elaborates on the "reminders" mentioned in v 1. First, he urges his readers **to recall the words spoken in the past by the holy prophets.** He may have had a specific OT passage in mind. Several prophets mention scoffers who mock the delayed judgment of God (e.g., Amos 9:10; Jer 5:12-24; Ezek 12:22). But **holy prophets** probably makes a general reference to the entire OT.

Second, Peter urges his audience to recall **the command given by our Lord and Savior through** their **apostles.** The grammar of this phrase is awkward, but **command** is associated with both the Lord Jesus and the apostles. "The commandment is primarily Christ's, but also in a secondary sense the apostles' because they were the people who preached it to the readers" (Bauckham 1983, 287).

In 1:16-19 Peter asserts that the Holy Spirit enabled apostles and prophets to bear witness to "the power and coming of our Lord Jesus Christ" (1:16). The false teachers deny both that Christ is powerful (ch 2) and that he is coming again (ch 3) (Green 1987, 135). In the midst of conflicting claims and conclusions, Peter appeals to the Christian authority for determining right doctrine and behavior: the words of the **holy prophets** and the teaching of the **Lord and Savior** transmitted through the **apostles.** In affirming this foundation for "wholesome thinking" (v 1), Peter "stresses the link between the prophets who foreshadowed Christian truth, Christ who exemplified it, and the apostles who gave an authoritative interpretation of it" (Green 1987, 135).

What is the **command** mentioned as coming from the Lord through the
apostles? In the NT, "the word always refers to some kind of demand or requirement" (Moo 1996, 164). As in 2:21, the singular **command** probably 3:2
does not refer to one particular commandment, but "to the substance of the
Christian faith proclaimed by the apostles" (Harrington 2003, 282-83). In
both passages *entolē* brings a strong moral nuance to the Christian faith. Peter is not thinking of a list of moral "dos and don'ts." He wants his readers to
pursue and conform to the image of Christ. Here, the underlying message of 2
Peter is similar to the message of 1 Peter to "be holy in all you do . . . because
I am holy" (1 Pet 1:15-16).

The language of v 2 serves as evidence for the non-Petrine authorship of 2 Peter. For instance, Kelly claims,

> The expression **your apostles** could not of course have been penned by the historical Peter; it inadvertently betrays that the writer belongs to an age when the apostles have been elevated to a venerated group who mediate Christ's teaching authoritatively to the whole Church. (1969, 354)

But **your apostles** could merely distinguish *those* apostles who had preached to and founded these churches from the rest of the apostles (Bauckham 1983, 287). Nothing about **your apostles** inherently necessitates a late date for this letter or disqualifies Peter as its author. They are *their* apostles in the sense that Peter's readers had first heard and accepted the gospel through them. Peter urges his audience to recall the moral demands of the gospel they had heard and received from these original preachers.

2. Warning About Scoffers (3:3-4)

■ **3** Believers must **understand** (see 1:20) **that in the last days scoffers will come, scoffing and following their own evil desires.** Although these scoffers were already present when Peter wrote, he used the future tense to identify his as **the last days.** The future tense, **scoffers will come,** could indicate that a pseudonymous author was quoting a prophecy of the Apostle Peter (Bauckham 1983, 288). But Peter himself could also have referred to a prediction of Jesus (Matt 24:10-11; see Matt 7:15; 24:5, 24; Mark 13:22). Believers were not to be surprised by the appearance of scoffers and false teachers. Indeed, their appearance was to be expected.

The future tense **will come** and the phrase **in the last days** might seem to refer to a time in the distant future. But the discussion of the scoffers indicates that these predictions are already being fulfilled in the false teaching in the churches. Throughout the NT, believers understand themselves to be living **in the last days.** The advent of Jesus opened the final chapter of human history, although it has not yet been completed.

In the last days "is a fascinating description of the Christian era, and preserves the tension between what is already realized in Christ and what lies ahead" (Green 1987, 137). Thus, believers should not be surprised or puzzled by false teachers threatening the church. They should **understand** that their appearance marks the necessary birth pains preceding the messianic age and the second coming of Christ. Ironically, the "adversaries who denied the parousia were themselves a proof of its imminence" (Fornberg 1977, 61).

Scoffers "is a derogatory term for someone who despises and ignores religion and morality" (Watson 1998b, 355). They are depicted as **scoffing and following their own evil desires** (*epithymiais*)**.** Often in this letter *epithymiai* is used to describe the ungodly orientation of sinful and sexually immoral people (1:4; 2:8, 10). The present scoffers follow **their own . . . desires** and direction instead of God's. "Cynicism and self-indulgence regularly go together" (Green 1987, 138). The scoffing words and immoral deeds of the false teachers indicate that their coming was evidence of the arrival of the last days.

■ **4** "Scoffers" typically are people who mock the faith in general. But here it refers to a group of professed believers (2:18-22) who mocked the specific belief that Christ would return. Their mocking consisted of the question, **Where is this "coming" he promised?** ("Where is the promise of his coming?" NRSV).

In the LXX, *pou estin* (**where is**) is the standard rhetorical form the enemies of God's people cynically use to taunt his people: "Where is your/their

God?" (Pss 42:3, 10; 79:10; Joel 2:17; Mic 7:10). The question of the false teachers is not an innocent request for information. It is a cynical and mocking challenge to the teaching of Christ's return.

The basis of the scoffers' challenge is their assumption that the return of Christ is long overdue. They interpret his delay to be an indication that he is not coming at all.

In addition to the unfulfilled expectation of the second coming, the false teachers point to the unchanging world. From their perspective both factors are evidence that the second coming and judgment day will never occur. Peter portrays them as saying, **Ever since our fathers died, everything goes on as it has since the beginning of creation.**

Some scholars assume that **our fathers** refers to the first generation of Christians. According to these scholars (e.g., Bauckham 1983, 291), the false teachers were saying, "The return of Christ was promised to take place before the death of the fathers. The fathers have died and *still* nothing happens." This interpretation is often considered incontrovertible evidence of pseudonymity. A second generation author assumed Peter's name and penned this letter after Peter's death and the death of other first generation Christian **fathers.**

It is certainly possible that **our fathers** refers to first generation Christians. But it is equally possible that **our fathers** refers to the OT patriarchs as in every other occurrence of the phrase in the NT (e.g., Acts 3:13; 7:12; Rom 9:5; 11:28; 15:8). This second understanding of **our fathers** fits Peter's argument well. He has mentioned several times already that the doctrine of eschatological judgment is rooted in the OT (1:16-19; 3:2).

It is noteworthy that the opponents did not say that everything continued as it had *since the coming of Christ.* Instead, they say that everything continues as it has **since the beginning of creation.** This phrase makes the OT background of **our fathers** even more probable. Green writes, "The mockers were twisting the Old Testament Scriptures; it is, appropriately, out of the Old Testament that Peter confounds them" (1987, 140).

Thus, the reference to the death of **our fathers** does not provide incontrovertible evidence for the non-Petrine authorship of 2 Peter. The apostle himself could plausibly have penned these words in response to the false teachers' argument against the Christian belief in Christ's return and final judgment.

3. The Scoffers Have Forgotten the Truth (3:5-7)

BEHIND THE TEXT

Second Peter 3:4-10 reveals a chiastic (X-shaped or envelope) structure. The scoffers deny the return of Christ because it is long overdue and because the world appears to be unchanging. In typical chiastic fashion, Peter answers these objections in reverse order. The structure may be presented as follows:

A. The *Parousia* of Christ is overdue (v 4*a*)

B. The world is unchanging (v 4*b*)

B'. Denial of an unchanging world (vv 5-7)

A'. Denial of an overdue *Parousia* (vv 8-10)

■ **5-6** Peter refutes the idea that the world has not changed "since the beginning of creation" (v 4). Peter and his readers *remember* the words spoken by the prophets (v 2). Unlike them, the false teachers ***willfully ignore*** (*lanthanei . . . thelontas*) the lesson of the great flood in Noah's day. *Lanthanei* means **"succeed in avoiding attention or awareness"** (BDAG, 586). Coupled with *thelontas* (= ***wish, will, take pleasure in;*** BDAG, 448), this expression underscores the deliberate willfulness of the false teachers to ignore the teaching of the OT. Their error is not due to simple, honest oversight. Their error lies in their deliberate and blatant refusal to recognize the lessons of Scripture.

The Scriptures teach that the world came into being at a certain point in time (v 5). And it was destroyed by God at a certain point in time (v 6).

Although Peter's meaning is easy enough to comprehend, the language he uses is more difficult to understand. Some of the difficulty arises because of his attempted wordplay on **water** (*hydōr*). In v 5, he refers to the role of water in the
3:5-7 creation of the world (see Gen 1:1, 6-10): **by God's word the heavens existed and the earth was formed out of water and by water.** In v 6 Peter infers that the same **waters** were used to destroy the world (see Gen 6—8): **By these waters also the world of that time was deluged and destroyed.** This wordplay seems to say that the world was created by water and destroyed by the same water.

It seems unlikely that Peter considered water the basic building material of creation. He does not say the **heavens** and **earth** were *created* **out of water and by water.** He asserts that they **existed** (*ēsan*) out of water and by water. The story of creation explains the emphasis upon **water** (Gen 1:2-10). The earth is described as a watery chaos (1:2) and the land appears out of the water (1:6-10). Thus, the expression **out of water** (*ex hydatos*) is clear. Likewise, the earth was **deluged and destroyed** by water in the time of Noah.

The false teachers' contention that all things have remained the same since the beginning of creation is false. They ***willfully ignore*** the evidence of Scripture. Since their premise of an unchanging world is false, their conclusion that Christ will not return in judgment must also be false.

■ **7** Peter affirms that **the present heavens and earth are reserved for fire.** It was "by God's word" (v 5) that the world of Noah's day was destroyed; **by the same word** the world will be destroyed again.

The heavens and earth **are reserved for fire**. **Reserved** means ***to store up*** or ***to save up.*** It is usually used in a positive sense to gather a treasure. Here it refers to God stocking up a judgment of fire.

This is the only passage in the NT (along with 3:10) that seems to teach that the world will be destroyed by **fire.** This image is probably derived from OT portrayals of the Day of the Lord (Ps 97:3; Isa 66:15-16; Dan 7:9-10; Mic 1:4; Mal 4:1). In such apocalyptic texts the image of **fire** is often not intended literally; rather, "it means purification and the destruction of evil when God comes to judge the world" (Green 1987, 144).

Peter explicitly connects **fire** with judgment by clarifying that the world is **being kept for the day of judgment.** The occasion of the fiery judgment will be the **day of judgment. Being kept** (*tēroumenoi*) is borrowed from the military world. It summons the image of watchful guarding of a prisoner by a prison warden. It emphasizes the certainty that the **day of judgment** will take place, despite the denial of the scoffers.

The purpose of the fire will be the judgment and **destruction of ungodly men.** The association of **fire** with the **destruction of ungodly men** implies that **fire** relates more to the judgment of sinners than to the destruction of the world (Green 1987, 144). Peter's anticipation of "a new heaven and a new earth" (3:13) probably foresees a time when the created order will no longer be subject to the effects of ungodliness and sin (see Rom 8:18-22; 1 Cor 15:24-28). While a fiery destruction of the entire universe cannot be completely ruled out, all that Peter actually says "is that the heavens and earth are kept in store for fire in anticipation of the judgment of ungodly men" (Green 1987, 144).

FROM THE TEXT

Scoffers and Mockers. The foundation of Christian doctrine and behavior is Scripture and the teaching of the apostles. Peter's opponents were not the last people to try to deny Scripture and reinterpret the gospel to fit their own agenda and unrighteous behavior. Every era of history has been challenged by similar individuals. The method of these individuals often follows the path of mockery and lofty-sounding arguments.

In modern times scoffers produce arguments about a closed universe governed by laws of cause and effect. They assert that the laws of nature eliminate the possibility of miracles or divine intervention. But the laws of nature are God's laws, and the predictability of cause and effect is attributable to God's faithfulness (Col 1:16-17).

Creation. Peter's insistence that the creation of the world was the result of **God's word** is significant. Scientists and scholars may debate how the world came to be. But the biblical record is clear: Our world found its true origin as God spoke it into existence. Regardless of how scientific theories about origins, intelligent design, and evolution dominate the discussion, believers stand firm upon the conviction that everything that exists is a result of the creative word of God.

The End Times. Discussions about the end times have fascinated people since before the time of Jesus Christ. Peter asserts that **the present heavens and earth are reserved for fire** (3:7). Many debate whether these words expect a literal destruction of the world through fire or figurative judgment and punishment of the ungodly. With the ongoing threat of nuclear or biological annihilation, few people today espouse the belief in an unchanging or eternal world. But many deny God by asserting the future of earth will be determined by fate or chance.

Believers are reminded that God is in control. He remains actively involved in the events of our lives and the history of the world. Thus, even while human sinfulness hurtles the world toward a conflagration of punishment and destruction, believers retain the steadfast confidence that God is in control.

B. The Delay of Christ's Coming (3:8-9)

IN THE TEXT

3:8 ■**8** The idea of *remembering* (3:1) remains dominant in these verses as Peter responds to the scoffers' objection about the delay of Christ's return. Earlier, he rebuked the false teachers for ***willfully ignoring*** the lessons of Scripture (3:5). Using the same verb, he exhorts his readers ***not*** to ***ignore this one thing.***

Believers should not ignore that **with the Lord a day is like a thousand years, and a thousand years are like a day** (Ps 90:4). Psalm 90:4 contrasts the eternity of God with the brevity of human life. But Peter uses this verse to contrast the eternity of God with the impatience of human speculations (Green 1987, 146). God does not experience time as humans do. An eternity in the eyes of humans is a brief moment in the eyes of God. When humans ignore the divine perspective like the false teachers have done, they grow impatient and doubtful about God's promises.

This verse (along with Rev 20:1-6) was used to support a second-century doctrine called chiliasm. Chiliasm teaches that the Day of the Lord will result in a thousand year period of Christ's reign over the earth (e.g., Justin, *Dialogue* 81; *Epistle of Barnabas* 15.4; Irenaeus, *Against Heresies* 5.23.2; 5.28.3). Today this teaching is called premillennialism.

But this is not Peter's point. Peter does not say God's day *equals* a thousand years, but that God's day is **like** (*hōs*) a thousand years. Thus, believers should not grow impatient or short on faith when the promises of God are delayed. "God is under no compulsion to carry out his promise according to man's understanding of time" (Mounce 1982, 141).

■ **9** God has a purpose in his delay of Christ's return. Peter assures his readers that **the Lord is not slow in keeping his promise, as some understand slowness.** Peter often refers to Jesus as **Lord** (1:2, 8, 11, 14, 16; 2:1, 20). But **the Lord** is most naturally understood here as referring to God as in v 8.

Slow "carries the pejorative nuance of 'slack'" (Kelly 1969, 362). Peter does not deny the delay of Christ's return. Instead, he denies that this delay (from a human perspective) is an indication of God's weakness or disinterest in human affairs.

As some understand slowness probably refers to the false teachers. They undoubtedly interpreted the delay as a denial of Christ's return. Peter insists that delay does not mean nonfulfillment. Christ's return may be **slow,** but it does not mean that God has ***slacked off*** (*bradynei*) from his promise. He may be late, but he is not too late.

The delay in Christ's return is because **he is patient with you, not wanting anyone to perish, but everyone to come to repentance.** Patience (*makrothymei*) and mercy are often connected in Scripture (Exod 34:6; Num 14:18; Ps 86:15; Jonah 4:2; Rom 2:4; 9:22; 1 Pet 3:20). Peter claims in no uncertain terms that God wants **everyone to come to repentance** (see also John 3:16; Rom 2:4; 11:32; 1 Tim 2:4). This does not mean that every person will repent (v 7). But it reveals the heart and desire of God to make salvation possible to everyone who will repent.

This passage challenges the Reformed teaching of predestination, whereby God preordained all people to salvation or condemnation before the beginning of time. Some try to preserve the notion of predestination by limiting the range of the phrase **with you** to the elect (Moo 1996, 188). But this neglects the last clause of the verse, where Peter declares God wants **everyone to come to repentance. Everyone** (*pas*) means literally ***all.*** There is no grammatical or contextual indication that **everyone** is limited to a select group of people (i.e., those of **you**). Rather, **everyone** indicates God has made **repentance** and salvation possible for every person.

True knowledge of Christ brings one to **repentance.** Whenever **repentance** (*metanoia*) is used in the NT, it conveys a ***"turning about"*** (BDAG, 640) or ***change of direction.*** It denotes a reversal of direction in the life and behavior of believers. God's desire is for **everyone to come to repentance.** The immoral character and behavior of the false teachers were clear indications they had not repented. Ironically, they interpreted the delay of Christ's return as an indication of God's weakness or disinterest in human affairs. In reality,

Christ's delay is a signal of God's patience and mercy. Even the false teachers were given the added opportunity to come to repentance.

C. The Certainty of Christ's Coming (3:10)

■ **10** Peter moves from argument to affirmation. Christ's return may be later than expected, but he will certainly return. His readers are reminded that **the day of the Lord will come like a thief.** The verb *hēxei,* **will come,** is placed emphatically at the beginning of the sentence, underscoring the certainty of Christ's return.

A **thief** analogy is often used to denote an unexpected arrival (Matt 24:43-44; Luke 12:39-40; 1 Thess 5:2; Rev 3:3; 16:15). "The image supports the common NT perspective that since the precise time of the day of the Lord remains uncertain one should always be on guard in one's behavior" (Harrington 2003, 289). Peter uses the simile of a **thief** to warn his readers of the danger of being lulled into sleep or inattentiveness by the delay of Christ's return or by the false teaching of the scoffers. "The simile is quite effective in conveying both the unexpectedness of the parousia and the threat of judgment it brings to those who impose on the impatience of God by delaying their repentance" (Watson 1998b, 357).

Peter describes three cosmic events that will accompany Christ's return:

The heavens will disappear with a roar; the elements will be destroyed by fire, and the earth and everything in it will be laid bare. The impact of Christ's coming moves in descending order from **the heavens** to **the elements** to **the earth.** The Day of the Lord will have a cataclysmic impact on all creation.

It is difficult to understand and translate this section of the letter. The first problem has to do with the meaning of **elements** (*stoicheia*). *Stoicheia* can be interpreted in either of two ways.

First, it could refer to the elements—fire, water, air, and earth—that most Greeks believed to be the basic building blocks of the physical universe. If this is the meaning of *stoicheia,* Peter asserts that the basic **elements** of creation will be subjected to God's judgmental fire.

Second, *stoicheia* could refer to the heavenly bodies: the sun, moon, stars, and planets. The advantage of this interpretation is that it picks up OT language of the destruction of the heavenly bodies in the end times (e.g., Isa 34:4).

Nevertheless, the first option is probably preferable. In v 12, Peter says the heavens will be consumed by fire, and the "elements" (*stoicheia*) will melt in its heat. In this passage *stoicheia* includes the earth, not simply the heavenly bodies. In the day of judgment the elements of the earth will be overcome by fire.

The second problem is caused by several textual variants of the last verb. Depending upon the Greek variant, the phrase could be translated as **the earth and everything in it will be laid bare** (*heurethēsetai*) ("disclosed," NRSV); "the earth and its works *will be burned up"* (*katakaēsetai*) (NASB, see KJV); or "the earth with everything in it *will vanish"* (*aphanisthēsontai*) (GNT).

The reading with the strongest manuscript evidence is the first: **the earth and everything in it will be laid bare.** The problem is that this reading does not make much sense. This difficulty probably caused some early scribes to change the final verb to create the textual variants (Metzger 1994, 636).

Will be laid bare (*heurethēsetai*) means literally ***will be found*** or ***will be manifest.*** In this sense the last phrase probably means "the earth and 'all its works' will be manifest, disclosed in their fullness to God, at the time of judgment" (Moo 1996, 191). Peter describes the intense, penetrating judgment accompanying Christ's return. All earth and creation will be **laid bare** and exposed to the critical judgment of God in terms of their motive, purpose, and existence (see Heb 4:12-13). Peter asserts that this judgment will not be limited to humanity only. Rather, the entire **earth and everything in it** will be exposed to God's judgmental scrutiny at the last day.

Calvin on 1 Peter 3:10

Calvin argues that Peter's graphic depiction of the end times in v 10 is intended primarily as a springboard into the exhortations of vv 11-13. Furthermore, 3:10
he cautions interpreters not to look too closely at this verse as the foundation of a timetable or road map for the events of the end times. He writes:

> What afterwards follows, respecting the burning of heaven and earth, requires no long explanation, if indeed we duly consider what is intended. For it was not his purpose to speak refinedly of fire and storm, and other things, but only that he might introduce an exhortation, which he immediately adds, even that we ought to strive after newness of life. . . . Mischievous, then, are those interpreters who consume much labor on refined speculations, since the Apostle applies his doctrine to godly exhortations.
>
> Heaven and earth, he says, shall pass away for our sakes; is it meet, then, for us to be engrossed with the things of earth, and not, on the contrary, to attend to a holy and godly life? (Calvin 1948, 420)

FROM THE TEXT

God's Timing. God's timetable does not correspond to our human timetable. Believers tend to despair of God's promises when they do not occur as quickly as expected. Noting the danger of impatience, Watson writes, "We may not scoff verbally, but our prayer life, church attendance, and overall life-style may begin to suffer as we despair of God's promises" (1998b, 358). God's timing is not ours.

Peter reminds believers of God's patience and faithfulness to fulfill his promises. God's work may appear slow from our impatient, finite perspective. But as believers recall the faithful record of God's actions in their past, we discover that his timing is always perfect.

God's Plan of Salvation. Peter declares that **the Lord . . . is patient with you, not wanting anyone to perish, but everyone to come to repentance** (3:9). God wants all people to be saved. But this does not guarantee that all people actually will be saved. Through Christ God has made it possible for all people to repent and be saved. But some will exercise their God-given freedom to exclude God and reject his offer of salvation.

God sovereignly decided to create humanity in his image with the freedom to accept or reject his offer of love and salvation. Unless God denies this freedom to choose, some people will be saved and some will perish (3:7). But those who reject God's salvation do not perish because God wills it. Peter reminds his readers, God does not want **anyone to perish, but everyone to come to repentance.**

D. Concluding Exhortations (3:11-16)

BEHIND THE TEXT

Many NT letters conclude with a reminder of the coming of Christ and the kind of behavior believers should display in anticipation of his return (see Rom 13:11-14; 1 Cor 15:58; Gal 6:15; Eph 5:10-18; Phil 4:4-9; Col 4:2-6; 1 Tim 6:13-15*a*; 2 Tim 4:1-5; 1 Pet 5:1-10). Likewise, the conclusion of 2 Peter includes moral and ethical injunctions to believers. In contrast to his opponents, Peter urges his readers to anticipate the certainty of Christ's return while they live holy and godly lives. As is common to other hortatory sections of the NT, there is little evidence of any logical or sequential order to the structure of the exhortations.

■ **11** Peter sums up the teaching of the preceding verses with the phrase, ***since everything is to be dissolved in this way. All these things*** (*toutōn . . . pantōn*) refers to the subjects enumerated in v 10: "the heavens, . . . the elements, . . . and the earth." ***Is to be dissolved*** (*luomenōn:* ***unloosed*** or **destroyed** [NIV, NASB]) is present tense. Thus, the opening phrase of v 11 could be translated as ***since everything is disintegrating in this way.*** The present tense is probably meant to emphasize the certainty of imminent (yet future) judgment and destruction. The false teachers contend that the world is unchanging and that judgment is merely a myth. But "the seeds of the destruction which will overtake them at the last day are already at work within them" (Mayor 1978, 161). The Day of the Lord with its destructive judgment is perceived as imminent.

With the impending dissolution and judgment of the world in view, **what kind of people ought you to be?** Peter answers immediately: **You ought to live holy and godly lives.** The certainty of the timing of the imminent arrival of the Day of the Lord was not to unsettle them. It was not to be a cause for moral abandonment, as it was for the false teachers. Nor were believers to live in moral resignation or fear. The inevitability of judgment should spur believers to righteous living.

Believers should **live holy lives. Holy** means ***pure, blameless*** as well as ***set apart*** for God. Believers should reflect God's character of holiness in their lives. Likewise, they should **live godly lives** (*eusebeiais*), reflecting the God they had come to know in Christ. The language is similar to that of 1 Peter, where believers are urged to conduct themselves with a life of holiness and righteousness (1:15-16, 22; 2:1-2, 12, 15; 3:1-2, 16). In both letters, Peter asserts that a standard of holiness must permeate every area of believers' lives. Anything less than **holy and godly** conduct marks a deficiency in the believers' preparation for the Lord's coming. Peter's language ensures that holiness of heart and life is not only possible but also expected of true believers.

■ **12** Believers should live holy and godly lives **as they look forward to the day of God and speed its coming.** Despite the graphic language of destructive judgment associated with this day (vv 7, 10, 11), the **day of God** should not elicit anxiety or fear for believers. Rather, they should **look forward** to its arrival.

Looking forward is a key theme of this section. This verb is repeated three times in vv 12-14. "The attitude of expectancy suggested by the word 'look forward' is often mentioned in Scripture as particularly appropriate for God's people (see, e.g., Hab 2:3-4; Matt 11:3; Luke 7:19-20)" (Moo 1996, 197). God has a plan toward which all creation is progressing. The hope that results from looking forward is the foundation for the holy lifestyle to which believers are called (1 Pet 1:13-16).

As believers live in holiness and godliness, they **speed its coming. Speed** (*speudontas*) always carries a sense of ***hastening*** in the NT (Luke 2:16; 19:5, 6; Acts 20:16; 22:18). "Clearly this idea of hastening the End is the corollary of the explanation (v 9) that God defers the Parousia because he desires Christians to repent" (Bauckham 1983, 325). From the human standpoint, repentance and holy living may work together to hasten the return of Christ.

The idea of hastening the coming of Christ may seem strange, but it was firmly entrenched in Jewish thinking. Several rabbis maintained the Messiah would come only if the people of Israel would repent and perfectly keep the law (see Bauckham 1983, 325). In Acts, Peter urged the people to "repent, then, and turn to God, so that your sins may be wiped out, that times of refreshing may come from the Lord, and that he may send the Christ, who has been appointed for you—even Jesus" (3:19-20). Is the only thing delaying the return of Christ the failure of believers to live holy and godly lives?

Peter reminds his readers the Day of the Lord **will bring about the *dissolution* of the heavens by fire, and the elements will melt in the heat.** The verb **will melt in the heat** (*kausoumena*) is found only here in the NT. But it is used in the LXX to describe the melting of the mountains at the eschatological coming of God (Mic 1:4; Isa 34:4). Peter draws upon these OT portrayals for his depiction of the end times. As in v 10, **elements** (*stoicheia*) probably refers to the basic materials of the earth (including the earth itself). Despite the graphic language of destruction, the dominant image of this consuming **fire** is that of purifying judgment.

■ **13** The Day of the Lord will not only bring judgment. Peter asserts that **in keeping with his promise we are looking forward to a new heaven and a new earth.** This hope is based upon Isa 65:17 and 66:22. These are the only OT passages in which the idea of a new heaven and earth are expressed. John picks up this imagery in Rev 21:1.

The prospect of **a new heaven and a new earth** widens the believers' understanding of the scope of God's redemptive plan through Jesus Christ. Early Christians "believed that God was going to do for the whole cosmos what he had done for Jesus at Easter" (Wright 2008, 93). Despite the vivid language of fire and destruction, Peter held fast to the hope of a new beginning through the resurrection of Jesus Christ. Not only sin-burdened humanity, but all creation longs for the transformation initiated and made possible through Christ's resurrection. As Wright observes, "What creation needs is neither abandonment nor evolution but rather redemption and renewal; and this is both promised and guaranteed by the resurrection of Jesus from the dead. This is what the whole world's waiting for" (2008, 107).

The new heaven and earth are characterized as **the home of righteousness. Home** (*katoikei*) is a verb that describes "a certain, fixed and durable dwelling" (Zodhiates 1992, 851). It is contrasted with *paroikos*, which Peter used to describe believers as "strangers" in the present world (1 Pet 2:11; see 1:17). Although believers presently live as "aliens and strangers" (1 Pet 2:11), they eagerly look forward to the day when this world will pass away, and they will live in **the home of righteousness.**

It is this new heaven and earth "where righteousness is at home" (NRSV) that provides the background for Peter's exhortation to "live holy and godly lives" (v 11). One's vision of the future is always a determining factor of behavior in the present (see Barclay 1960, 409-10). Peter urged his readers to live holy and godly lives that were fit for a future **home of righteousness.**

■ **14** The phrase **since you are looking forward to this** encompasses Peter's teaching of both the dissolution and re-creation of the world. This is the third time Peter uses the verb **looking forward** (*prosdokōntes*) in vv 12-14. Such expectancy for the future should make us receptive to instructions and exhortations concerning the present.

Peter calls his readers to **make every effort to be found spotless, blameless and at peace with him.** As in 1:5, Peter urges his readers to **make every effort** (*spoudasate*) to live pure and holy lives before God. **To be found** (*heurethēnai*) carries a judicial overtone (see also v 10). It depicts the scene of a court of law where the judge declares whether he has "found" the defendants innocent or guilty (Moo 1996, 207). Peter urges believers to commit themselves to a life of holy living now so that at Christ's return they will **be found spotless** and **blameless.**

Spotless and **blameless** are essentially synonyms depicting moral purity (Bauckham 1983, 327). Peter uses these same terms to depict Christ as "a lamb without blemish or defect" (1 Pet 1:19). In essence, he urges his readers to conform to the spotless, blameless pattern of the life of Christ himself. He wants them to be Christlike.

The contrast with the lifestyle and behavior of the false teachers is vivid. In 2:13, Peter uses the same words (without the *a*-negative) to identify the false teachers as mere "blots and blemishes" (*spiloi kai mōmoi*) in the sight of God. In contrast, believers are to be **spotless** and **blameless** (*aspiloi kai amōmētoi*), exemplifying a lifestyle that is the opposite of the false teachers.

At peace with him (*en eirēnēi*) is an added quality at the end of the verse. *Eirēnē* could refer to the believers' sense of tranquillity and assurance in the face of Christ's return. But more likely **peace** refers to reconciliation with God (see Rom 5:1-2). "In their pursuit of holiness they have put out of their lives all those things that would evoke Christ's condemnation" (Hiebert 1984b, 332). Peter insists that the link between faith and conduct must be maintained.

■ **15a** After summoning his readers to live with Christlike purity, Peter urges them to **bear in mind that our Lord's patience means salvation.** The false teachers understood the delay of Christ's coming as a sign of God's "slowness" (v 9). By contrast, believers should regard the delay as evidence of God's saving purposes toward humankind. Since it is a sign of God's **patience** (*makrothymian;* from the same root word as "patient" in v 9), the delay of Christ's return should be taken advantage of by Christians for pursuing **salvation.**

It is unclear whether Peter sees the delay of Christ's return as an opportunity for believers to secure their own salvation or to evangelize unbelievers.

He probably has both elements in mind. "While God is waiting, He is both giving time for the unbeliever to be saved, and for the believer to be working out his salvation (see Phil 2:12, 13) in terms of progress in sanctification" (Wheaton 1970, 1258).

■ **15*b*-16** The delay of Christ's return is a sign of God's patience **just as our dear brother Paul also wrote you with the wisdom that God gave him.** The words **just as** indicate that Peter perceives his own teaching to be in full agreement with Paul. Some attempt to identify a specific Pauline letter Peter may have in mind, but any conclusions are purely speculative. The point made in vv 14-15 "is very general—Christians need to live holy lives in light of the coming of Christ—and Paul touches on this subject in virtually every letter he wrote" (Moo 1996, 210). Thus, what **Paul also wrote you** could refer to any one, or even all, of Paul's letters.

Paul wrote ***according to the wisdom given him.*** Most scholars agree that ***given*** (*dotheisan*) should be interpreted as a divine passive, with God as the implied agent of the action. Thus, Peter emphasizes that Paul's wisdom in his letters is not due to an innate ability or intelligence on Paul's part, but it is divinely imparted. God gave Paul the wisdom to understand and explain the gospel to believers.

Peter and Paul

3:15*a*-16 Paul writes about a confrontation with Peter in Gal 2. In light of this confrontation, some argue that the affectionate description of Paul as **our dear brother Paul** excludes the possibility that Peter could have written this letter. But there is no biblical evidence of an ongoing disagreement or conflict between these two leading apostles. Indeed, the simplicity of Peter's designation of Paul as **our dear brother** "is in full accord with the warm, familiar relations between leaders in the early church (see Acts 15:7, 25; 1 Cor 4:17; Eph 6:21; Col 4:7)" (Hiebert 1984b, 333).

Moreover, this simple description of Paul aligns itself better with other writings of the first century than with the writings of the second century. In the second century, Paul is routinely described with more exalted terms (e.g., Clement of Rome: "the blessed Apostle Paul"; Ignatius: "Paul, the holy, the martyred, the deservedly happy"; Polycarp: "the blessed and glorified Paul"; see Hiebert 1984b, 333). Thus, it would be perfectly natural for Peter to call Paul his **dear brother.** The designation fits well with early Christian usage.

Paul **writes the same way in all his letters, speaking in them of these matters.** The reference to **all his letters** indicates Peter's familiarity with at least several of Paul's writings. The claim of some interpreters that **all his letters** must refer to the entire collection of Pauline letters is unfounded. This would deny Petrine authorship. It would have been impossible for Peter to be familiar with *all* of Paul's canonical letters. This phrase simply means "'all the letters known to the writer'" (Mayor 1978, 165).

Peter observes that Paul's letters **contain some things that are hard to understand. Hard to understand** (*dysnoēta*) "is a rare word, with a nuance of ambiguity about it" (Green 1987, 159). The word describes something difficult to grasp, either because the statement is ambiguous or because it is capable of being misinterpreted. Peter clarifies that **ignorant and unstable people distort** the things they read. The problem does not lie so much in the obscurity of Paul as in the ignorant perspective of those who **distort** his writings (Bauckham 1983, 331).

Paul had to deal with people who distorted his teachings in order to justify their own immoral or selfish behavior (e.g., Rom 3:8; 1 Cor 6:12-20; 10:23-24; Gal 1:6-9; 5:11-13). Likewise, Peter speaks of **ignorant and unstable people** who **distort** the writings of Paul. **Ignorant** and **unstable** are found only here in the NT. The words do not describe two different groups, but one group having both characteristics. The **ignorant** (*amatheis*) lack training more than they lack knowledge. The **unstable** (*astēriktoi*) are "those whose habits are not fully trained and established" (Strachan 1979, 147). Thus, they were untrained and unrestrained in their interpretation of Paul's writings. **Ignorant and unstable people** must be another negative assessment of the false teachers. The false teachers probably distorted portions of Paul's writings to justify and legitimize their false teaching and immoral behavior.

In addition to Paul's letters, these people distort **the other Scriptures.** With this phrase, Peter unapologetically classifies the Pauline letters as authoritative Scripture. This phrase is understood by some as proof that Peter could not have written this letter. They object that such a high view of Paul's letters could not have emerged as early as the mid-60s A.D.

Peter's estimate of Paul's letters as comparable and equal to **the other Scriptures** is surprising. But the formation of authoritative writings was an arbitrary process for which there was no predetermined timetable. By the end of the second century, Paul's letters "had attained fully scriptural status over a very wide area" (Gamble 1992, 854). One can only speculate as to how early this perception was authentically verbalized.

Those who **distort the Scriptures** do so **to their own destruction. Distort** (*streblousin: **twist or wrench***) describes the stretching of a victim on the rack during torture. This does not describe someone who accidently misunderstands or honestly misinterprets a passage of Scripture. Rather, Peter has in mind the willful distortion of Scripture. These people take a passage of Scripture and, like a victim on the rack, force it to say what they want it to say. The punishment for such abuse is condemnation leading to **destruction** (*apōleia,* see 2:9; 3:7).

FROM THE TEXT

The Call to Holiness. Peter urges believers **to live holy and godly lives** (3:11). Holiness is not a special hobby for a few extremely devout believers. Rather, Peter calls *all believers* to a lifestyle of holiness as the only appropriate way for Christians to prepare for the coming of the Lord. Believers anticipate a new heaven and earth that will be **the home of righteousness** (v 13). Consequently, they must **make every effort** (v 14) to live holy lives that are fit to dwell in this new world. Peter described what **holy and godly lives** (v 11) look like in 1:5-7, where he urged his readers to seek and practice the moral virtues. If believers want to live in the glorious **home of righteousness,** their faith must demonstrate itself in a holy lifestyle. This is foundational to the biblical call to holiness of heart and life.

Anticipation and Preparation. Anticipation and preparation are closely connected. Since the false teachers denied the return of Christ, they had no anticipation of his coming. Consequently, they sensed no need for preparation. Instead, they opted to indulge the immoral desires of their physical bodies with selfish and lustful behavior. For them, the Day of the Lord would come **like a thief** (3:10), exacting its destruction unexpectedly and disastrously.

3:11-16 By contrast, true believers anticipate the day of Christ's return. Consequently, they prepare themselves by making every effort **to live holy and godly lives** (v 11). In this way, they will be found pure and blameless like Christ himself at the day of his return. For them Christ's return will not bring condemnation or fear, but confirmation and reward. For this reason, believers eagerly **look forward** (v 12) to the day of Christ's coming with the echo of John's *maranatha* prayer on their lips: "Come, Lord Jesus" (Rev 22:20).

Interpretation of Scripture. Anyone can accidently misinterpret and misunderstand a passage of Scripture. But this threat is greater for those who do not actively pursue a holy and godly lifestyle. Sin blinds us to the truth. As with the false teachers, sin tempts us to change the truth of Scripture to match our behavior instead of submitting our behavior to the truth. For this reason, believers must always be on guard against convenient interpretations of Scripture. One indispensable benefit of regular corporate worship is the opportunity it offers to examine one's understanding of the Bible within a Christian context. Without the corrective influence of corporate worship, believers become vulnerable to their own subjectivity if not sin's subtle delusions.

V. CONCLUSION AND DOXOLOGY: 2 PETER 3:17-18

IN THE TEXT

A. Conclusion (3:17-18*a*)

■ **17** Peter addresses his readers one final time as ***you*** **dear friends** (*hymeis . . . agapētoi*, ***you . . . beloved***). "It is because of his love that he has spoken so plainly; that same love now prompts a final charge" (Green 1987, 162). **Therefore** (*oun*) marks these words as the conclusion to the letter. Peter "concludes his letter with a double exhortation which succinctly gathers the themes treated in chapters 2 and 1 respectively" (Kelly 1969, 374). Thus, the negative exhortation to **be on your guard so that you may not be carried away . . . and fall** reflects the warnings about false teachers in ch 2. Conversely, the positive exhortation to "grow in the grace and knowledge" (v 18) reiterates a key theme from ch 1.

Since you already know this (*proginōskontes*) means literally ***knowing beforehand.*** Having read the letter, Peter's audience is now forewarned and forearmed. Thus, Peter exhorts them: **be on your guard.** The present tense of this imperative suggests a constant state of watchfulness. The danger they face is the risk of being **carried away by the error of lawless men.** The words **error** (*planēi*) and **lawless men** (*athesmōn*) describe the false teachers (see also 3:7, 18). Peter warns his readers not to become **carried away** (*synapachthentes*) by the false teachers and their behavior. The implication is that "if they keep too close company with such people they will be led away from Christ" (Green 1987, 162).

The danger of being **carried away** is the risk they might **fall from your secure position. Fall** (*ekpesēte*) "denotes an act of falling away from or out of a higher to a lower position or condition" (Hiebert 1984b, 337). The believers' **secure position** (*stērigmou*) is a stark contrast to the **unstable** (*astēriktoi*) position of those who **distort** Scripture (v 16). Believers must guard against behavioral and doctrinal errors of the false teachers. Otherwise, their *stable* position in Christ may become *unstable* through the deceptive and subtle influence of these wicked people.

Believers enjoy a **secure position** of salvation through faith in Christ. Christians can have confidence in their salvation. But Peter also warns believers about falling off this foundation. "Confidence in our status with Christ should never lead to a presumption on God's grace that leads us to toy with the danger of false teachers or that negates the serious striving after holiness" (Moo 1996, 213). For this reason, Peter urges his readers to constantly **be on . . . guard** against evil influences that might cause them to fall.

■ **18*a*** One way to avoid falling is to maintain a constant guard against the deceptive error of lawless people. A second way to avoid falling is to **grow in the grace and knowledge of our Lord and Savior Jesus Christ.**

An effective safeguard against falling is for believers to be on their guard *and* to **grow** (*auxanete*) in their faith. **Grow** is present tense, indicating continual growth in faith. Salvation is an ongoing, never-ending process of growth. As long as believers continue to grow, there is no danger of falling. But when they think they have grown enough, they are vulnerable to being carried away by false teaching.

Peter enjoins his readers to grow in **grace and knowledge. Grace** (*charis*) denotes the free and unmerited favor of God toward sinful humanity. The phrase **of our Lord and Savior Jesus Christ** makes it explicit that God's grace is revealed most visibly through Jesus Christ. Growth in grace takes place as believers submit themselves in character and in life fully to the revealed will and purposes of God.

Along with growth in grace, believers must grow in **knowledge** (*gnōsis*). Peter uses *epignōsis* to describe the ***saving knowledge*** of God and Christ (1:2, 3, 8; 2:20). "*Epignōsis* designates the fundamental Christian knowledge received in conversion, whereas *gnōsis* is knowledge which can be acquired and developed in the course of Christian life" (Bauckham 1983, 338). Thus, when Peter urges his readers to **grow in the . . . knowledge** (*gnōsis*) of Jesus Christ, he calls them to grow in their knowledge *about* Christ.

Believers need knowledge *of* Christ (*epignōsis*), gained only through a personal, saving relationship with him. But they also need knowledge *about* Christ (*gnōsis*); that is, a theological understanding of who and what he was and is, and what he has done and does. This knowledge is gained supremely through studying Scripture. When confronted by false teaching, believers need to be armed with true **knowledge** about Jesus Christ. As they continue to **grow** in this **knowledge,** they will be better equipped to withstand the threat of false teaching that may challenge their faith.

Both **grace** and **knowledge** are associated with **our Lord and Savior Jesus Christ.** This full confessional title is found four times in this letter (1:11; 2:20; 3:2, 18). It is a fitting summary of Peter's high Christology. It focuses the readers' attention on the primacy of Jesus Christ, both theologically and ethically, which is essentially the point of contention between Peter and the false teachers.

B. Doxology (3:18*b*)

BEHIND THE TEXT

Most NT Epistles conclude with personal greetings and a final blessing of grace upon the readers. In contrast, 2 Peter ends with a doxology, an ascription of glory (*doxa*) to Christ. The appearance of a doxology at the end of a letter is rather unusual in the NT, occurring only here and in three other letters (Rom 16:25-27; Phil 4:20; Jude 24-25).

Peter's doxology is also unique because it is directed toward Christ instead of God. Every doxology in the NT is directed toward God except three: 2 Tim 4:18; Rev 1:5-6; and 2 Pet 3:18. Some argue that 2 Peter's Christ doxology indicates a second-century origin. But the doxologies in Revelation and 2 Timothy demonstrate that, although rare, doxologies to Christ were possible in the first century.

IN THE TEXT

■ **18*b*** Peter concludes his letter with a simple exclamation of glory to Christ: **To him be glory both now and forever! Glory** (*doxa*) refers to the radiant splendor and majesty characteristic of deity. The doxology to Christ is unusual, but not so surprising in light of the rest of the letter. "The false teachers detracted from Christ's glory *now*, by a wicked life, and from His glory *then*, by denying the parousia" (Green 1987, 164). Peter addresses both concerns within the letter. In this final word of glory, then, he ascribes all glory to Christ **both now and forever.**

The way **forever** is articulated is unusual. In most doxologies, **forever** is expressed with the phrase *eis tous aiōnas* (= ***into the ages***). However, Peter expresses **forever** here with the phrase *eis hēmeran aiōnos* (= ***unto the day of eternity***).

Throughout ch 3, Peter has directed his readers' attention to the day when Christ will return and God's judgment and promises will be fulfilled (3:7, 10, 12). In this last phrase of his letter, he proclaims that **glory** should be ascribed to Jesus Christ **both now** and until the day of Christ's return—a ***day of eternity*** that will last **forever.** Throughout the letter, Peter has rebuked the false teaching that Christ will never return. It is only fitting that he finishes with a confident exclamation of glory and praise to Christ and the glorious unending day when Christ will indeed return.

FROM THE TEXT

The last verses of Peter's letter can be summarized with the command-
3:17-18 ing motto: Wait, watch, and work.

Wait. Ever since the ascension of Jesus and the promise of his second coming (Acts 1:11), believers have been waiting for Christ's return. As the delay in Christ's return extended, false teachers—both present and past—have denied and mocked the notion of his return. Peter boldly calls Christians to *wait.* The delay in Christ's return is not due to any deficiency on God's part. Rather, the delay is due to God's patience and desire to see more people brought to salvation (3:9, 15).

Watch. While they wait, however, Christians need to *watch.* Peter strongly urges believers to **be on your guard** (3:17). The time of waiting, regardless of how long it might extend, should not be a period of inattentiveness or carelessness. First Peter 5:8 warned readers to be alert because "the devil prowls around like a roaring lion looking for someone to devour." Likewise, in this second letter, Peter commands his readers to be watchful lest they be **carried away by the** deceitful **error of lawless men** who would ultimately cause them to fall.

As the delay in Christ's return approaches the end of its second millennium, the danger of inattentiveness has grown even more threatening. Jesus' warning to "watch and pray so that you will not fall into temptation" (Matt

26:41) has never been more relevant than it is for believers today. Peter reiterates the same commanding warning.

Work. As they watch, Christians are also called to *work*. Believers should not only remain alert but also **grow** more **in the grace and knowledge of . . . Christ** (3:18). It takes effort and persistent *work* in order to **grow**, and Peter calls believers to do it. One way to grow is by pursuing the moral virtues described in 1:5-7. Peter urges believers to pursue and possess the virtues "in increasing measure" so that they can remain effective and productive (1:8). There is never an appropriate time for believers to stop in their growth or to fall back on the imagined laurels of their **secure position** (3:17) of salvation.

Christians must continue to grow in their relationship with the Lord (*epignōsis*) and in their knowledge of the Lord (*gnōsis*) until the very end. Additionally, Peter declares that Christ's delay is a sign of God's patience so that more people can come to **salvation** (v 15). Believers are called not only to work out their own salvation but also to extend the promise of salvation to others along the way.

Thus, believers are called to wait, to watch, and to work. Peter's commanding challenge to wait, watch, and work is still the most effective means for believers to be assured of effectiveness, productivity, and security within the walk of faith.

JUDE

INTRODUCTION

Jude is one of the shortest letters in the Bible. Sandwiched between the letters of John and the Revelation, Jude is arguably the least well-known writing of the Christian Scriptures. Its obscurity is further enhanced by its title Jude, a name found nowhere else in the NT. Jude's message is essentially negative. He targets a group of false teachers who have deceptively infiltrated the church. All these factors ensure that Jude will probably never top anyone's list of favorite biblical books.

Nonetheless, the message of Jude is a relevant and needed warning against false teaching and pseudo-Christianity. Jude sounds an alarm against a form of Christianity that tries to separate Christian belief from Christian behavior. The chords of Jude's message seem out of tune in the cacophony of today's popular clamor for tolerance and moral relativity. But its message is as necessary as ever.

A. Authorship

The author identifies himself as "Jude (*Ioudas:* ***Judas***), a servant of Jesus Christ and a brother of James" (v 1). ***Judas*** is a common name, occurring forty-four times in the NT. Likewise, "servant of Jesus Christ" often designates followers of Jesus. On the basis of this information, the author could have been any follower of Jesus who happened to be named Jude. But he also calls himself "a brother of James" (v 1).

> This could only be the one great well-known James, the brother of the Lord (James 1:1; Gal 1:19; 2:9; 1 Cor 15:7). Jude is mentioned among the brothers of Jesus: in Mark 6:3 he is mentioned in the third place; in Matthew 13:55 he is in the fourth place. Concerning this Jude, however, we know nothing further. (Kümmel 1975, 427)

Along with James, Joseph, and Simon, Jude was a half-brother of Jesus. It is peculiar that Jude identifies himself as a brother of James instead of a brother of Jesus. Scholars, as early as Clement of Alexandria in the early third century, claim that humility may have prevented Jude from mentioning his familial relationship with Jesus.

There is strong evidence Jude was accepted early as authoritative by the church. "It finds a place in the second-century Muratorian Canon; Tertullian recognized it as an authoritative Christian document, so did Clement of Alexandria, who wrote a commentary on it" (Green 1987, 48). Origen and Eusebius note some doubts about Jude, but these doubts were isolated to the Syrian church in the East. Jerome explains the reservations concerning Jude: "Because he appealed to the apocryphal book of Enoch as an authority it is rejected by some" (cited by Green 1987, 48). Despite isolated objections, the external attestation for the acceptance of Jude is early and widespread.

In more recent years, some scholars argue that Jude is the pseudonymous work of an unknown Jewish Christian. Three main arguments have been presented.

First, the content of the letter requires a late date because it reflects "early Catholicism" and combats Gnosticism of the postapostolic era (Watson 1998a, 474). "Early Catholicism" is a term coined sometime around the turn of the twentieth century. Early Catholicism can be distinguished by three main features: (1) the fading of Parousia hope, (2) increasing institutionalization, and (3) the crystallization of the faith into set forms (Dunn 1977, 344).

Jude is often offered as a representative example of early Catholicism. But Bauckham argues convincingly that "none of these three features is evident in Jude" (1983, 8). The assumption that Jude combats an established form of Gnosticism has been strongly challenged by various scholars (see Guthrie

1970, 911; Bauckham 1983, 12-13). Thus, both objections—Jude's reflection of "early Catholicism" and its connection to Gnosticism—are unfounded.

Second, some argue Jude is pseudonymous because he "excludes himself from the apostles, whom he presents as belonging to a previous generation (v 17)" (Watson 1998a, 474). Watson notes that Jude excludes himself only from the apostles who founded the churches he addresses, and not from the apostolic era (1998a, 474). The fulfillment of the apostolic prophecy of scoffers in the church (v 17) does not require a long time. Nothing in v 17 requires a postapostolic interpretation.

Third, the author's proficiency in Greek disqualifies Jude as the letter's source. This conclusion is based on a doubtful assumption concerning Greek competence in first-century Palestine. Blum writes, "Greek was the lingua franca of the Mediterranean world, and the presence of the Decapolis to the east and to the south of the Sea of Galilee provided ample opportunity for Greek influence on nearby Nazareth" (1981c, 382).

There are no compelling reasons to refute the traditional view that the author of this letter was Jude, the brother of James and Jesus. Barclay concludes from the evidence that the letter "is attached to his name, and there could be no reason for so attaching it unless he did in fact write it" (1960, 202-3).

B. Audience

Jude addresses his readers in general terms, describing them as "called . . . loved . . . and kept" by God the Father and Jesus Christ (v 1). Despite this inclusive description, Jude was not writing a general warning against heresy to all Christian believers. Rather, he had a specific group of Christians in mind. These believers were facing the threat of immoral false teachers who had infiltrated their fellowship (vv 3-5, 17-18, 20). Jude apparently did not found this church himself. He mentions nothing of his ministry among them, referring only to what they had received from other apostles (v 17). But he was familiar with the readers and their situation.

Jude's readers were probably Jewish Christians. Jude quotes and alludes to Jewish documents and traditions without explanation (vv 9, 14-15). Only a Jewish audience could be expected to be familiar with such material.

The audience was probably Jewish Christian. But the immoral character and lifestyle of the false teachers suggests that these teachers were probably Gentiles. We can only speculate as to the specific location of Jude's audience. They would have lived in a predominantly Gentile context where strong Jewish teaching was largely lacking. Scholars have suggested Palestine, Egypt, Syria, and Asia Minor as possible locations of Jude's audience (Bauckham 1983, 16).

Paul's reference to the "Lord's brothers" in 1 Cor 9:5 "suggests that Jude may well have traveled extensively in the eastern Mediterranean world" (Moo 1996, 28). If true, Jude's readers could have been located virtually anywhere within the Roman Empire. The most that can be ascertained about Jude's readers is they were Jewish Christians in a predominantly Gentile society.

C. Place and Date

The place from which Jude writes his letter is unknown. Jude may have composed his letter while in the land of Israel or from any other location he may have traveled. It is simply impossible to know.

The date of the letter is inevitably connected to its authorship. If the letter was written pseudonymously, it could have been composed as late as the beginning of the second century. I assume the letter was written by Jude the brother of Jesus and James. Thus, the letter was probably written between A.D. 40 (to allow time for the false teaching to develop and infiltrate the readers' church) and A.D. 80 (when even a younger brother of Jesus would have been about 70).

The literary relationship between Jude and 2 Peter is relevant in dating both letters. Much of Jude parallels 2 Pet 2. (See the Introduction to 2 Peter.) The issue of the letters' interdependence is widely debated. Their similarities suggest they were composed about the same time. If 2 Peter is Petrine, it was probably written in the mid-60s. Jude was probably written no later than A.D. 70.

D. Genre and Literary Style of the Letter

The genre characteristics of a letter are especially visible in the opening and closing of Jude. Verses 1-2 contain a customary epistolary opening; vv 3-4 correspond to the typical introductions of ancient letters, identifying the principal occasion of the letter (Neyrey 1993, 26). Following these typical epistolary elements, however, the body of the letter (vv 5-23) has the basic rhetorical pattern of a sermon. The letter concludes with a doxology in vv 24-25. Thus, Jude might be described as an epistolary sermon (see Bauckham 1983, 3).

The literary style of Jude is unique. It contains Semitisms as well as standard Greek idioms and poetic phrases (Neyrey 1993, 27). The most unique characteristic of Jude is its fondness for triple expressions. The occurrence of triplets is prolific. For example, the addressees in v 1 are "called . . . loved . . . kept." Other triplets appear in the benediction (v 2), the identification of the opponents (v 4), and so forth (see Neyrey 1993, 28). Triplets are a common feature in Hebrew and Christian Scriptures (Neyrey 1993, 29). In Jude they provide a regular rhythm throughout the letter. They produce a compelling sense of urgency to its message.

E. Purpose of the Letter

Jude contains a series of warnings concerning a group of deceivers who have slipped into the church. Jude's intention to write a treatise about salvation to his readers (v 3) was altered by the threat the intruders presented. So he wrote a strong denunciation of the false teachers instead. Jude urges his audience "to contend for the faith that was once for all entrusted to the saints" (v 3). The majority of the letter consists of a condemnatory portrayal of the pseudo-Christians who were threatening the church through their immoral lifestyle and false teaching.

F. The Identity of the Opponents

The letter of Jude is a polemical attack on false teachers threatening the fellowship of the readers' church. It is difficult to pin down the identity of the intruders more precisely. Jude assumes his readers are already familiar with their actions and teachings. Thus, his task "is not to provide an objective and even-handed description (like a professor), but rather to warn his readers about the moral and spiritual dangers that the intruders represent (like a preacher)" (Harrington 2003, 180). Consequently, scholars can only speculate about Jude's opponents by reading between the lines of his passionate condemnation of them.

The opponents seem to be a group of itinerant charismatics who have infiltrated the church. They claim to be believers, but their lifestyle and teaching reveal their true identity as "godless men, who change the grace of our God into a license for immorality" (v 4). They effectively "deny Jesus Christ" as their "Sovereign and Lord" (v 4). Most of Jude's polemic focuses on the intruders' lawless character, especially blatant immorality, which "pollute their own bodies" (v 8).

Jude compares their behavior to the "sexual immorality and perversion" of the people of Sodom and Gomorrah (v 7). Instead of living godly lives, they "follow their own evil desires" (v 16). They reject all moral authority, including the law of Moses (vv 8-10) and the instructions of Jesus himself (vv 4, 8). They justify their behavior by appealing to "charismatic inspiration, manifested in prophetic visions (v 8)" (Bauckham 1983, 11). With audacity, they "slander celestial beings" (v 8) and assert their own superiority to angels.

Jude's opponents were not merely members of the church but also posed as teachers (vv 11-13). Jude describes them as "blemishes" on the church's fellowship meals (v 12). They made empty promises (vv 12-13), meant only to gain a following (v 16). Since they were dependent on the church's hospitality and financial support, Jude accuses them of being motivated by greed. They preached a convenient and popular message in order to reap the financial benefits of their approval (vv 12, 16). These "grumblers and faultfinders" (v 16) caused division among believers (v 19). Their behavior and teaching made it clear: they "do not have the Spirit" (v 19).

Some scholars identify the intruders as gnostics (e.g., Blum 1981c, 385) or proto-gnostics (Rowston 1975, 555-57), because of their moral autonomy and disrespect toward angels. But the letter offers no evidence of "the cosmological dualism of true Gnosticism" (Bauckham 1983, 12).

The data is insufficient to identify Jude's opponents with any known heretical movement in the first or second century. Nevertheless, the characteristics of the intruders are paralleled in other early Christian congregations. It appears that itinerant charismatics were often a source of trouble in the churches (Matt 7:15; 2 Cor 10—11; 1 John 4:1; 2 John 10). Hospitality and financial support were easily abused and exploited by itinerant evangelists (Rom 16:18; 1 Tim 6:5; Titus 1:11; *Did.* 11—15).

Some early Christian troublemakers claimed an elite spiritual status due to their alleged heightened experience and possession of the Spirit (1 Cor 1—4; 12—14; 15). Some asserted spiritual authority on the basis of private visionary experiences (2 Cor 12:1-3; Col 2:18; Rev 2:24). The antinomianism of Jude's opponents "resembles the attitude of the Corinthians (1 Cor 5:1-6; 6:12-20; 10:23) and the prophetic teaching of 'Jezebel' and her followers (Rev 2:14, 20-22)" (Bauckham 1983, 12). Some churches had to deal with "highly liberated" individuals who considered themselves freed from and above the teaching of the OT Law (Gal 5:18). Some charismatics considered themselves superior to the angels (1 Cor 6:3), thought by some Jews to be mere mediators of the Mosaic law (Gal 3:19; Acts 7:53).

Thus, Jude's opponents bear a striking resemblance to other problem groups that surfaced in the early Christian movement. Many such challenges faced the church in various areas of its expansion. As the Christian church advanced through Greco-Roman society, some believers misunderstood the Christian message of salvation and freedom. Others tried deliberately to change the message through blatant false teaching. In either case, Jude perceives them as perverting the authentic gospel by their actions and teachings. He stringently warns his readers against their incipient and encroaching danger.

Jude's opponents are probably not representatives of a specific heretical movement. Rather, they represented a typical kind of misunderstanding and false teaching that accompanied the explosive spread of the Christian message.

G. Themes of the Letter

1. Christian Faith and Practice

One underlying theme of Jude's letter is an emphasis upon the content of the Christian faith. The majority of the letter is a polemic against false teaching. But Jude never clarifies specifically what constitutes correct teaching. Rather, he "assumes that there is a 'faith' committed to the Church, a truth by which it stands or falls and which is not to be tampered with" (Beasley-Murray 1965, 74).

Thus, one major theme of Jude is the Christian faith. Jude calls his readers to adhere to the proclamation of the gospel, that is, "the Faith," as it was received from the apostles (vv 3, 5, 17). Paul and other early believers spoke of faith in a subjective sense ("I believe *in* . . ."). By contrast, Jude speaks of faith in an objective sense ("I believe *that* . . ."). Thus, he emphasizes the *content* of faith instead of the *act* of believing.

Despite Jude's emphasis on the Christian faith, his concern is not doctrinal issues, but the moral implications of errant doctrine. His opponents' rejection of moral constraints led to blatant and shameless immorality. Indeed, the false teaching of the intruders had become a "license for immorality" (v 4). For Jude, correct beliefs lead to correct behavior. Likewise, false beliefs lead to improper behavior. Although Jude does not identify the content of his opponents' heresy, their immoral and improper behavior was proof enough of their false doctrine and teaching. What people believe matters. Although it might not be immediately apparent, the fruit of bad faith often turns out to be rotten and deplorable.

2. Living in the End Times

Another theme of Jude is the understanding that believers are already living in the last days. The presence of scoffing opponents indicated that the end time was imminent (vv 17-19). Just as God acted in the past to condemn sinners, he will surely judge sinners at the last day (vv 5-13). In contrast, faithful Christians will be received with mercy, and they will be rewarded with eternal life (vv 2, 21, 24).

Heightened eschatological expectation assigned believers a double duty. First, they must remain faithful themselves as they "contend for the faith" (vv 3, 20-21). Second, they must try to save others from the fire of judgment by extracting them from the false teachers (vv 22-23).

3. Christology

Jude affirms the lordship of Jesus Christ repeatedly and powerfully (vv 4, 14, 17, 21, 25). Christ not only preserves believers in their salvation (v 1), but salvation is possible only through him (v 25). As "Sovereign" (v 4) and "Lord" (vv 4, 14, 17, 21, 25), Christ demands obedience. Ultimate salvation requires the lifelong obedience of Christians to him (v 21).

Those who live immoral lives, effectively denying the lordship of Jesus Christ (v 4), will ultimately and certainly be judged and condemned (vv 5-13). Throughout the letter, salvation is inextricably linked to Christ the Savior. Salvation is possible through the *keeping power* of God and his Son Jesus Christ (vv 1 and 24). The evidence of salvation is demonstrated in the moral behavior and obedience to Christ of true believers. By the enabling mercy of Jesus Christ, they build themselves up in the faith, pray in the Holy Spirit, and keep themselves in God's love (vv 20-21).

COMMENTARY

I. GREETING: JUDE 1-2

BEHIND THE TEXT

The writer identifies himself as ***Judas,* a servant of Jesus Christ and a brother of James.** The name Judah in Hebrew was ***Judas*** (*Ioudas*) in Greek. English Bibles usually render the name as "'Jude,' mainly to distinguish him from Judas Iscariot, the disciple who 'handed over' Jesus" (Harrington 2003, 185).

Besides Judas Iscariot, four individuals bear the name "Judas" in the NT: (1) Judas son of James, one of the twelve disciples (Luke 6:16; Acts 1:13); (2) Judas the Galilean, an infamous revolutionary (Acts 5:37); (3) Judas Barsabbas, a prophet in the early church (Acts 15:22, 27, 32); and (4) Judas the brother of Jesus (Matt 13:55; Mark 6:3). The only Judas in the NT identified as having a brother named James is the brother of Jesus. Thus, the author probably intended indirectly to identify himself as the brother of Jesus.

IN THE TEXT

■ 1 Like most ancient letters, Jude begins with the author's name, the audience, and a greeting.

The author identifies himself by name (**Jude**), by status (**a servant of Jesus Christ**), and by relationship (**a brother of James;** Hillyer 1992, 231). **Jude** (*Ioudas*) is transliterated elsewhere in the NT as "Judas." Judas was a popular Jewish name. Judah was one of the sons of Jacob (e.g., Gen 29:35), the tribe that gave its name to the entire people of Israel in NT times: Jews are Judeans. The name became prominent after the Maccabean Revolt (167-164 B.C.), led by Judas Maccabeus.

Jude almost certainly refers to the brother of Jesus. The Gospels identify four brothers of Jesus by name: James, Joseph, Judas, and Simon (Mark 6:3; Matt 13:55). Little is known about Jude or the other brothers of Jesus. Like his other brothers, though, Jude was not a follower of Jesus during his earthly ministry (Mark 3:21, 31-35). The resurrected Jesus appeared to James (1 Cor 15:7). Did he also appear to Jude and the other brothers at the same time? Was Jesus' resurrection the impetus for Jude's coming faith? His self-designation as **a servant of Jesus Christ** clearly identifies Jude as a devoted follower of Christ.

Jude makes two claims about himself. First, he is **a servant** (*doulos*) **of Jesus Christ.** A *doulos* was not "a servant who is free to change his master but a slave who is the property of his master" (Cranfield 1960, 152). Peter and Paul similarly describe themselves as servants of Jesus Christ (Rom 1:1; Phil 1:1; 2 Pet 1:1). Surprisingly, neither James nor Jude make any reference to their blood relationship with Jesus in their letters. Both describe their relationship to Jesus as merely that of **a servant.**

In addition to subservience to Christ, the phrase **servant of Jesus Christ** identifies authority within the Christian faith. "Everywhere the emphasis of the phrase is . . . not merely a confession of the saving act of Jesus, but also a description of the specific office of the men who use it" (Rengstorf 1964b, 276). Jude uses this title "to establish his right to address Christians with an authoritative word from the Lord" (Moo 1996, 222). As a **servant of Jesus Christ,** Jude does not claim personal authority based upon his family relationship with Jesus. Instead, he writes humbly from an authority derived from Christ, as Jesus' bondservant, not as his brother.

Second, Jude claims that he is **a brother of James.** It was customary in NT times to be identified through one's father (e.g., Mark 3:17; John 21:15). It was extremely rare to be identified through one's brother. Remarkably, no additional modifier is added to the common name **James** (Jacob in Hebrew) to specify his identity. "There is no parallel in the NT, and the expression only makes sense if **James** is a prominent person whose identity will be immediately recognized" (Kelly 1969, 242).

Several men named "James" appear in the NT: (1) the son of Zebedee, one of Jesus' disciples (Matt 10:2); (2) the son of Alphaeus, another disciple (Matt 10:3); (3) the younger son of Mary (not Mary the mother of Jesus; Mark 15:40); (4) the father of the apostle Judas (not Iscariot; Luke 6:16; Acts 1:13); (5) the brother of Jesus (Mark 6:3). Only the last **James** was so prominent as to require no further identification. This James led the Jerusalem church for many years (Acts 12:17; 15:13; 21:18). Paul identifies him as one of the "pillars" of the faith (Gal 2:9). Moreover, the only brothers named James and Judas in the NT were the brothers of Jesus. Thus, it is virtually certain that **James** refers to Jesus' brother.

It seems unexpected that Jude would identify himself as **a brother of James** instead of a brother of Jesus. Notably, the book of James does not use the title to identify its author either (Jas 1:1). Paul identifies him as Jesus' brother (Gal 1:19; see 1 Cor 9:5). Most scholars explain this omission as a mark of humility. "Jude's physical relationship to Jesus did not bring him any spiritual benefit" (Moo 1996, 222). Jude may have avoided mentioning his family relationship because it was irrelevant to the nature and purpose of his letter.

Jude writes **to those who have been called.** Kelly (1969, 243) observes that ***the called*** is "to all intents and purposes synonymous with 'a Christian'" (see Rom 1:6, 7; 8:28; 1 Cor 1:2, 24). These are those who "belong to the new people of God" (Bauckham 1983, 26). Jude's audience was clearly Christian.

In addition to **called,** Jude's audience is identified as **loved by** (*en:* ***in***) **God the Father.** The unusual phrase ***loved <u>in</u> God*** identifies love as the product of a relationship with God. Since Christians are ***in*** fellowship with God, they are loved ***in*** God the Father.

Believers are also **kept by Jesus Christ.** Jude reminds his readers of the continuous *keeping power* of Jesus Christ, who holds his followers fast. False teachers were challenging and threatening the faith of true believers (vv 4-16). Jude's reminder that they were **kept by Jesus Christ** must have been reassuring.

Later, Jude will urge his readers to "keep yourselves in God's love" (v 21). There are two sides to Christian perseverance. Through Christ, God faithfully keeps his followers. But it was the followers' task to ***keep themselves*** in the love of God. Believers face many challenges and trials as they follow Christ. Jude reminds them of God's promise to watch over them at every moment, protecting them in and through Jesus Christ.

Jude is fond of triple expressions (Perkins 1995, 146). No fewer than twenty triplets appear in the letter (Charles 1991, 106-24; see Introduction). The first is in v 1, where believers are described as **called, loved,** and **kept.** Jude may have borrowed these descriptions from the Servant Songs of Isaiah, where Israel is called (Isa 41:9; 42:6), loved (Isa 42:1; 43:4), and kept (Isa 42:6; 49:8; Bauckham 1983, 25). Jude's repeated triplets fixed his "message in the mind of the audience" (Perkins 1995, 146). As **called, loved,** and **kept,** Jude's audience enjoyed the favor, status, and assurance of followers of Jesus Christ.

■ **2** Jude's triplets are evident also in his greeting: ***May mercy, peace, and love be given you in abundance.*** He prays that all three qualities may be given his audience **in abundance** (*plēthyntheiē:* "filled to capacity"; Hillyer 1992, 235).

Mercy and **peace** were part of typical Jewish blessings (see the priestly blessing of Num 6:22-26). **Mercy** (*eleos*) denotes God's kindness toward his covenant people and **peace** (*eirēnē*), the resulting well-being (Bauckham 1983, 27). **Mercy** is rarely found in NT blessings (1 Tim 1:2; 2 Tim 1:2; 2 John 3). Usually, **grace** appears in its place. But "the meaning is much the same: God's unmerited favor bestowed on sinners for their salvation" (Moo 1996, 224). The prayer-wish of **love** (*agapē*) reinforces the Christian character of the blessing. God's **love** is a repeated theme in the letter (vv 1, 2, 21).

All three terms indicate what God does for believers. "Mercy is his compassion, peace is his gift of quiet confidence in the work of Jesus, and love is his generosity in granting us his favors and meeting our needs" (Blum 1981c, 387). These virtues are neither attained nor sustained through self-effort. They are God's gifts.

The terms **mercy** and **love** are repeated in the closing exhortation. Jude urges his readers to "keep yourselves in God's *love* as you wait for the *mercy* of our Lord Jesus Christ" (v 21, emphasis added). Believers cannot earn God's **mercy, peace and love.** But they must cooperate with God's grace in their lives. Verses 22-23 imply that they should extend this same **mercy, peace and love** to others.

FROM THE TEXT

Exemplary Humility. Jude foregoes any acclaim that might come with the recognition of his personal relationship with Jesus as his brother. Instead, he humbly identifies himself as **a servant of Jesus Christ.** As a servant, Jude claims no authority or special privileges of his own. Rather, he submits to the authority of Christ.

The Gospels indicate that Jude and his brothers did not accept the servant ministry of Jesus (Matt 12:46-50; Mark 3:21, 31-35; Luke 8:19-21). Despite their intimate familiarity with Jesus, they did not accept him until after his resurrection. Jude and at least one of his brothers—James—finally understood their brother's mission and purpose. They followed him in faith and obedience.

Jude's humble designation of himself as a **servant** demonstrates that he eventually grasped the significance of Jesus' servant ministry. He finally got it. In our own society, name-dropping and similar status-seeking strategies are prevalent, even in the church. Jude reminds us of the only essential qualification of a genuine Christian leader: the overwhelming recognition that one is **a servant of Jesus Christ.**

Christian Assurance. Jude assured his first readers (and all who have read the letter since) that they are **kept by Jesus Christ** (v 1). Unfortunately, some believers presumptuously misunderstand this assurance. Convincing themselves that since they are **kept by Jesus Christ,** they imagine that salvation is theirs regardless of how they live. As a result, they engage in activities and habits that bring shame to the name and cause of Christ. Ironically, there are other Christians who are unable or unwilling to trust Christ to keep them in his care. Ignoring Jude's assurance, they travel the Christian path with great fear of God's displeasure.

Believers may be assured that God's faithfulness will sustain their faith. They are not irrevocably saved by a one-time profession of faith. Believers play a crucial role in the maintenance of their salvation. They must **keep** themselves **in God's love** (v 21). Faith in Christ is not only a profession to be made but also a life to be lived. Believers are not alone in this process. All the resources of God are available to them through Christ. Christ ***keeps*** them secure as they continue to follow and emulate him. In temptation, discouragement, and difficulty, believers have God's **mercy, peace and love** through the *keeping power* of Christ's firm grasp.

II. PURPOSE AND OCCASION OF THE LETTER: JUDE 3-4

BEHIND THE TEXT

Most ancient letters include a brief thanksgiving after the opening greeting of the letter. Jude skips the thanksgiving and proceeds immediately to the purpose (v 3) and occasion (v 4) of the letter.

Jude draws a strong contrast between believers and the ungodly infiltrators. This is often marked by two repeated phrases. Jude's Christian readers are called **dear friends** (*agapētoi:* ***beloved;*** vv 3, 17, 20). He refers to the ungodly as **these men** (*houtoi;* vv 8, 10, 12, 16, 19). These phrases serve as a helpful rhetorical device for distinguishing the protagonists from the antagonists. They also create an "us versus them" mentality among Jude's readers. This exclusive mentality would likely strengthen the believers' ability to protect themselves against the temptations of the **godless** intruders and their sinful behavior.

The contents of the letter are foreshadowed in the opening verses. First, Jude exhorts his readers to contend for the faith handed down to them (v 3). Second, he explains they must fight for the faith: because godless people have infiltrated the Christian community. These godless individuals threaten to pervert the moral teachings of the Christian faith (v 4). After describing and condemning the ungodly (vv 5-19), Jude exhorts his readers to build themselves up in the faith (vv 20-23).

Thus, a chiastic (X-shaped or envelope) structure unifies the letter (vv 3-23):

A. Exhortation to contend for the faith (v 3)

B. Threat of godless people (v 4)

B'. Condemnation of godless people (vv 5-19)

A'. Exhortation to keep the faith (vv 20-23)

IN THE TEXT

A. Purpose: Contend for the Faith (v 3)

■3 Jude calls his readers **dear friends** (*agapētoi:* ***loved ones, beloved***). Jude
uses a derivative of *agapē* (**love**) in each of the first three verses of this letter.
He "does not merely talk about love; he displays it, both in the repeated af-
3 fectionate address of **dear friends** and also in the serious warning and stern
rebuke he administers throughout the Epistle" (Green 1987, 170).

Apparently, Jude had intended **to write to** his readers **about the salvation we share** (*hē koinēs hēmōn sotēria:* ***our common salvation***). Some maintain Jude emphasizes the commonality of Jewish (like Jude) and Gentile Christians (like his audience). But there are no clear indications that his audience was Gentile. If his audience was predominantly Jewish, **the salvation we share** underscores the salvation all Christians enjoy in common.

But the positive and joyous letter he intended to write was not to be. The intrusion of godless people forced Jude to write a strong letter of warning and condemnation against the godless infiltrators.

Jude **felt** he **had to write and urge** his readers **to contend for the faith that was once for all entrusted to the saints.** Jude does not use an imperative in this verse. But the present participle **urge** (*parakalōn:* "appealing," NASB) has the effect of a command. Jude calls his audience to **contend for the faith.**

Contend (*epagōnizesthai*) is a compound verb borrowed from the realm of athletics. The verb urges the readers to "agonize," as in "an athletic contest." They are "to 'fight, struggle, strive'" (Earle 1984, 115) against their opponents. They are not only to passively resist the false teaching but also to actively and energetically fight for the Christian faith. Since **contend** is in the present tense, they are to *continue* to fight until they win.

Faith is typically used in the NT to denote the act of believing. Believers are those who place their faith in Christ. Jude uses **faith** differently, to refer to the content of what is believed, not the act of believing. Thus, **faith** refers to a body of teachings about God, Christ, and the Christian lifestyle. Jude's concern for **faith** is focused upon the ethical implications of the gospel. For Jude, the fight for the Christian faith is a battle not only for doctrinal orthodoxy but also for the moral lifestyle consistent with the faith.

The teachings of the Christian faith were **once for all entrusted to the saints. Saints** (*hagiois:* ***holy ones***) often refers to Christian believers (e.g., Acts 9:13, 32; Rom 1:7; 2 Cor 1:1; Heb 6:10; Rev 5:8). Here it refers to "those who have been called" (Jude 1), Jude's **dear friends** (v 3). **Saints** have been set apart for God himself. It does not refer to Christian leaders, but to all people of God.

The faith was **entrusted to the saints. Entrusted** (*paradotheisēi:* ***delivered, handed on***) is a technical term for passing along of authorized tradition (see 1 Cor 11:2; 15:1-3; 2 Thess 3:6; 2 Pet 2:21). Since false teaching threatened the church, Jude reminds and assures his audience that the message of salvation passed down to them is genuine and **once for all.**

> The faith was "once for all" entrusted to believers because its content cannot change. God's action in Christ is once for all (Rom 6:10; Heb 9:12, 26-28; 10:10; 1 Pet 3:18) and need not (and in fact cannot) be presented in any other fashion (like that of the false teachers). (Watson 1998a, 485)

The Christian faith was endangered by the godless people within the community. Jude's purpose was to engage his readers in the struggle on behalf of the Christian faith.

B. Occasion: Threat of Godless People (v 4)

■ **4** Believers must contend for the faith because **certain men . . . have secretly slipped in among you. Certain men** has a "contemptuous ring" to it (Kelly 1969, 248). Jude assumes his readers know who they are, so he does not bother to name them.

Jude's contempt for these anonymous troublemakers was heightened by their method of operation. They did not openly identify themselves and their errant teaching. Instead, they **secretly slipped in** (*pareisedysan:* ***infiltrated***) **among** Jude's friends. The verb, found only here in the NT, "tends to carry the connotation of secrecy or stealth" (Bauckham 1983, 35). The word was

> used of the clever pleading of a lawyer, gradually insinuating his version of the evidence into the minds of judge and jury. It describes the action of a spy stealthily getting into the country, or of someone sneaking in by a side door. (Hillyer 1992, 238)

Among you indicates the false teachers slipped into the church. These intruders hide their true nature and purpose. These **certain men** are the "wolves in sheep's clothing" Jesus had warned his disciples about (Matt 7:15). Jude does not identify these unnamed frauds specifically. But he provides a vivid fourfold description of them:

First, their **condemnation was written about long ago** (i.e., ***long ago written beforehand***). Scholars debate the identity of these writings. Suggestions include apostolic writings like 2 Peter, apocryphal writings like *1 Enoch*, or even "heavenly writings" (see Bauckham 1983, 35-36). Jude probably is referring to the writings and examples he will mention in the balance of the letter. The judgment **written about long ago** includes citations from the OT (vv 5-8, 11), Jewish traditions (vv 9, 14-16), and the teaching of the apostles (vv 17-18). The condemnation of the intruders was long established in these various writings.

Second, Jude describes his opponents as **godless men** (*asebeis*). *Asebeia* describes "complete contempt for God and His will" (Foerster 1971a, 188). The word is broad enough to embrace a wide array of sins. It was typically used to describe irreverence in an ethical sense—"not theoretical atheism, but
4 practical godlessness" (Bauckham 1983, 38). For Jude, **godless** best described these lawless and immoral intruders (see vv 4, 15, and 18).

Third, these godless men **change the grace of our God into a license for immorality. Grace** describes God's free gift through Jesus Christ as the forgiveness and liberation of believers from the power of sin and the condemnation of the Law. Apparently, the intruders misrepresented God's grace to mean they were free to engage in all kinds of sexual depravity. **Immorality** in 2 Peter describes lustful behavior (2:18). The word typically refers to "sexual excess" (Bauernfeind 1964b, 490).

Fourth, Jude depicts **certain men** as those who **deny Jesus Christ our only Sovereign and Lord.** Grammatically, this phrase could refer to God and Christ individually: "the only Lord God, and our Lord Jesus Christ" (KJV). **Sovereign** is typically reserved for God alone. It is used to describe Christ only in 2 Pet 2:1. But a single Greek article (*ton* = ***the***) connects **Sovereign** with **our Lord Jesus Christ** (so also NASB). Thus, Jude describes Jesus using language typically reserved for God alone.

The false teachers **deny** Christ. They may have denied certain doctrinal teachings about Christ. But the reference to Jesus as **our only Sovereign and Lord** calls "attention to Jesus' right to demand obedience from his followers"

(Moo 1996, 231). Jude probably referred to the teachers' ethical denial of the moral teachings of Christ, implicit in their shameful behavior. In the Mediterranean world, a slave's disobedience brought "shame to the slave and dishonor to the master" (Watson 1998a, 485). Since they identified themselves as Christians, their behavior shamed the church and dishonored Christ, whom they claimed as **Lord.**

FROM THE TEXT

Internal Threat. The greatest challenges threatening the Christian faith arise from *inside* the community of faith. Jude was adamant against the intruders because they **secretly slipped in among** (v 4) the church. Like the legendary Trojan horse, the false teachers had infiltrated the church. Their false teaching and aberrant behavior heaped destruction upon other unsuspecting believers. In response, Jude calls believers to **contend for the faith that was once for all entrusted to the saints** (v 3).

Through the centuries, the Christian faith has been passed on from believer to believer in an unbroken chain stretching back to Jesus himself. "Each individual Christian has the dual responsibility of maintaining that truth unadulterated and of carefully handing it on to others" (Hillyer 1992, 238). The survival of the Christian faith depends upon faithfulness to both responsibilities. The church is most vulnerable when it is attacked from the *inside.*

Faith and Obedience. Jude contains a scathing rebuke of those who claim to follow Jesus Christ, but whose lifestyle denies his moral teachings and example. Believers must not pervert God's grace into an excuse to live sinful lives that do not glorify him. As the **only Sovereign and Lord,** Christ demands obedience. This calls for doctrinal understanding, but also a holy lifestyle. Jude reminds Christians it is possible to *explicitly affirm* the lordship of Jesus Christ while we *implicitly deny* him through immoral and un-Christlike behavior. The result of such behavior is condemnation.

Spiritual Warfare. Believers must **contend for the faith** (v 3). This calls for more than self-defensive measures. Jude calls for the church to take the offensive against those who pervert the Christian faith. He appeals to Christians to contend for the faith both positively and aggressively. Believers should not only articulate their doctrinal convictions but also commit themselves to a lifestyle that corresponds to what their faith proclaims. Jude expects believers to pursue the Christian life with the same dedication and passion as an athlete who trains to win a sporting event.

> Contending involves building up the church in the faith (v 20) and proclaiming the faith to those who are no longer contending for it in order to rescue them from judgment (vv 22-23). Contending for the faith occurs

in private and public prayer, in Bible study, in worship, and in outreach of any kind. (Watson 1998a, 486)

III. DESCRIPTION AND CONDEMNATION OF THE UNGODLY: JUDE 5-19

BEHIND THE TEXT

Jude now turns his attention to the ungodly intruders who threaten the Christian community. His denunciation of the ungodly may appear arbitrary and unrestrained. But his approach fits the Jewish exegetical pattern of midrashic (Ellis 1978, 221-36). Jude provides five citations (vv 5-7, 9, 11, 14-15, 18), each followed by a commentary (vv 8, 10, 12-13, 16, 19). This technique proves that the intruders' "condemnation was written about long ago" (v 3). The citations are not all from the OT. Jude draws from sources familiar to his readers, including two apocryphal quotations (vv 9 and 14-15) and an apostolic prophecy (v 18). These citations develop a powerful prophecy-fulfillment theme, underscoring the inevitable condemnation of the false teachers.

The interwoven nature of the midrashic technique makes it difficult to provide a consistent outline of Jude's reasoning. This difficulty is illustrated by the vastly different outlines that have been suggested for Jude. I will discuss Jude's description and condemnation of the ungodly under three main subheadings:

1. Three examples of punishment (vv 5-7)
2. Description of the ungodly (vv 8-13)
3. Prophecies against the ungodly (vv 14-19)

IN THE TEXT

A. Three Examples of Punishment (vv 5-7)

Jude's examples seem to be from the OT, but his reference to angels is obscure (v 6). Little explanation is provided for these examples except that they **serve as an example of those who suffer the punishment of eternal fire** (v 7). They establish the reality and certainty of divine destruction and punishment of those who disobey God's will.

I. Exodus (v 5)

■5 Jude's readers ***know all these things once and for all.*** (The NRSV reading here, "the Lord, who once for all saved," translates a secondary manuscript
5 variant.) Jude reminds his well informed readers what the Scriptures say
about ungodly intruders. This "disclosure formula" functions as a transition to
the body of the letter (Neyrey 1993, 58; see 2 Pet 1:12).

Once and for all recalls the command to believers to "contend for the faith that was once and for all entrusted to the saints" in v 3. Jude is not providing new information. Rather, he reminds his readers of ***all*** they already know ***once and for all.*** He alludes to the essentials of the faith they received at their conversion (Bauckham 1983, 48). This does not imply that Jude's readers knew the detailed content of these verses already. But they were already familiar with the traditions and scriptures Jude was about to bring more fully to their attention.

The first example is the exodus, when **the Lord delivered his people out of Egypt.** The exodus was the defining moment of Israel's birth and existence. For Jews, the exodus was the preeminent example of God's grace and saving intervention. God **delivered** (*sōsas:* ***saved***) Israel from slavery in the land of Egypt.

Despite this defining moment of salvation history, the Lord **later destroyed those who did not believe.** The word **later** (*to deuteron:* ***the second time***) is probably intended to distinguish between God's first saving intervention at the exodus and his subsequent act judging their disbelief. Those "the Lord had saved were not thereby immune from subsequent judgment" (Bauckham 1983, 50). The same holy God, who had graciously rescued them, later destroyed the disobedient.

Jude's message is clear: God's forgiveness/salvation does not mean he will not punish the forgiven/saved if they fall away through unbelief. His example suggests that the opponents were once orthodox Christians who turned away from their faith. "This warning applies most obviously to the Christian intruders, but it has relevance for Jude's readers also" (Harrington 2003, 196). Despite past actions of grace and deliverance, God will punish disbelief and disobedience at the day of judgment.

2. Evil Angels (v 6)

■ **6** The second example is obscure. Jude refers to **the angels who did not keep their positions of authority but abandoned their own home.** Some interpreters suggest this example alludes to the fall of the angels that occurred when Satan rebelled against God (a highly debatable interpretation of Isa 14:12-14). More likely Jude had the prevailing Jewish interpretation of Gen 6:1-4 in mind. In this enigmatic passage, the narrator describes how "the sons of God" came down to earth to marry and bear children with "the daughters of men" (Gen 6:2).

Jewish tradition identified the sons of God as fallen angels who had illicit intercourse with human women. The sin of these angels explains the sexual immorality that reigned in the days before the great flood. One early interpretation of this story appears in the apocryphal *1 En.* 6—16. There "some angels plot and rebel against God and his good angels, and descend to earth where they introduce all kinds of sinful behavior among humans" (Harrington 2003, 196). Since Jude clearly quotes from *1 Enoch* in vv 14-15, it seems probable that he has *1 Enoch* in mind here as well.

The angels possessed **positions of authority** (*archēn:* ***rule***)—"a position of heavenly power or sphere of dominion, which the angels exercised over the world in the service of God" (Bauckham 1983, 52). Despite their former status, the angels turned away and **abandoned their own home** by rebelling against God.

As punishment for their disobedience and rebellion, the fallen angels are **kept in darkness, bound with everlasting chains for judgment on the great Day** (see *1 En.* 10:4-6). **Darkness** was a common image for divine punishment in the ancient world (see 2 Pet 2:4; Jude 13). **The great Day** refers to the future time when God will intervene at the end of history to save his people and punish his enemies. Although their ultimate condemnation will not take place until the last day, the evil angels are already being punished in **darkness** and in **everlasting chains.**

Jude's description of the evil angels contains an unmistakable touch of irony. Although these angels did not **keep** (*tērēsantas*) their positions of authority, but disobeyed and abandoned their rightful home, God **has kept** (*tetērēken*) them chained in darkness awaiting final destruction. "Here we find a negative counterpart to the situation of the righteous, whom God 'keeps' (v 2) and who are therefore to 'keep' themselves in God's love" (Moo 1996, 242). Even though the intruders masquerade as true believers, they, like the evil angels, will ultimately receive the punishment they deserve.

3. Sodom and Gomorrah (v 7)

■ **7** The example of **Sodom and Gomorrah** is undoubtedly the most famous story of divine judgment in the Bible (see Luke 17:28-29; 2 Pet 2:6-8). The destruction of **Sodom and Gomorrah** included **the surrounding towns** (see Deut 29:23), thus underscoring the contaminating threat of immorality.

God punished these cities because they **gave themselves up to sexual immorality and perversion.** The phrase **in a similar way** (*hōs*) connects the sin of the fallen angels with the sin of Sodom and Gomorrah. Some argue that **sexual immorality and perversion** points specifically to homosexual intercourse. But the phrase could refer to unnatural sexual relations between angels and humans.

In Gen 19, the Sodomites were punished because they wanted to have sexual intercourse with the good angels, who were guests in Lot's home. Thus, "just as the angels fell because of their lust for women, so the Sodomites fell because of their lust for angels" (Green 1987, 180).

This interpretation is supported by the phrase translated **perversion** (*apelthousai opisō sarkos heteras: **going after different flesh;*** NASB: "strange flesh"). Thus, here, **perversion** refers to the unnatural act of humans lusting after angels (see Bauckham 1983, 54).

This interpretation is not without its problems: First, it is improbable that ***flesh*** (*sarx*) would be applied to angelic spirits. Second, there is no indication that the men of Sodom knew the "messengers" were angels, rather than the men they appeared to be. Genesis 19 presents the sin of Sodom as depraved sexual sin—***going after other flesh***—not the unnatural desire for intercourse with angels. Jude probably associates God's judgment on Sodom and Gomorrah with the sexual immorality of the cities in general.

Sodom and Gomorrah **serve as an example of those who suffer the punishment of eternal fire.** These cities "are set before the eyes of the world as a sample of divine retribution" (Lee 1962, 167). The Gospels frequently use

eternal fire to describe the torments of hell reserved for the punishment of the wicked (e.g., Matt 5:22; 13:40; Mark 9:43-47). Ancient writers considered the desolate area around the Dead Sea a continuous reminder of God's destructive judgment on sin (see Philo, *Mos.* 2.56). The "still burning site of the cities [was] a warning picture of the eternal fires of hell" (Bauckham 1983, 55).

Jude specifically identifies Sodom and Gomorrah as the **example** of God's punishment. But each of the examples in vv 5-7 could represent the kind of punishment those who rebel against God can expect. Ungodly and rebellious behavior will not go unpunished.

FROM THE TEXT

Punishment for the Ungodly. The three examples in vv 5-7 provide a poignant reminder that the ungodly will eventually be punished. Reminders of punishment are usually unpopular, but they are necessary for people who tend to scoff at the notion of personal accountability. There have always been people who scoff (v 18) at the idea of divine judgment. Jude sounds an important reminder: Although God's judgment may not be immediate or apparent, it will surely come. The assumption that a loving God could never punish sinful humanity is nothing more than a delusion. Just as sin and disobedience were punished in the past, they will be punished at the future day of judgment.

Persistent Obedience. Even though God delivered the people of Israel out of the land of Egypt, he later destroyed those who did not believe. Membership in the people of God depends upon continued obedience and adherence to the faith. It is possible for believers who were saved from sin by God in an Exodus-like experience later to be condemned by God because of disobedience and unbelief. Believers must continue to live in faith and obedience in order to be saved. The angels who refused to *keep* their position of honor in heaven are now being *kept* for punishment and judgment by God (v 6). Likewise, Christians should not assume they will be *kept* by Christ for eternal reward when they refuse to *keep* his commands.

B. Description of the Ungodly (vv 8-13)

BEHIND THE TEXT

Jude describes the ungodliness of the intruders. He employs the midrashic pattern of example and application. Jude cites several negative examples of judgment, wickedness, and immorality from various sources, and then applies them to the opponents. The purpose of this section is to portray the depravity and certain destruction of the pseudo-believers who have infiltrated the Christian community. Jude describes his opponents as ignorant, immoral slanderers (vv 8-10), and he affirms they are doomed for condemnation (vv 11-13).

IN THE TEXT

I. Ignorant, Immoral Slanderers (vv 8-10)

■ **8 In the very same way** (*homoiōs mentoi*) indicates that the three examples of punishment listed in vv 5-7 can be directly applied to the intruders who have disrupted the Christian community. Jude focuses first upon their sin. **In the very same way** means these men commit, not the same sins, but the same kinds of sins as the disobedient Israelites, the fallen angels, and the people of Sodom and Gomorrah.

Specifically, Jude says **these dreamers** (*houtoi enypniazomenoi:* ***these men in their dreaming***) **pollute their own bodies, reject authority, and slander celestial beings.** Jude repeatedly uses the demonstrative pronoun *houtoi*, **these men**, to refer to his opponents (vv 10, 12, 16, 19), the intruders who "secretly slipped in" among the believers (v 4). **Dreamers** in the OT identifies the deluded dreams of false prophets (Deut 13:1, 3, 5; Isa 56:10; Jer 23:25-32; 29:8-9). It is "probably a reference to the visions by which these men may have sought to justify their teachings and actions" (Cranfield 1960, 160).

Dreaming relates to the action of the three following verbs (Bauckham 1983, 55). Thus, it is on the basis of their delusional ***dreaming*** that they **pollute their own bodies, reject authority and slander celestial beings.** Under the guise of alleged divine revelation, the false teachers shamelessly commit and justify their ungodly deeds. In this verse of application, Jude compares the sinful behavior of his three negative examples (vv 5-7) with the behavior of **these dreamers.**

First, like the fallen angels and the people of Sodom and Gomorrah, the intruders **pollute their own bodies** (*sarka miainousin:* ***contaminate/defile the flesh***). *First Enoch* uses the same verb (*miainein*) to describe the sin of the fallen angels (= "Watchers") as "defiling themselves with women" (*1 En.* 7:1; 9:8; 10:11; 12:4; etc.). Thus, the intruders **pollute their own bodies** with sexual impurity.

Second, like the fallen angels, the false teachers ***reject the authority of the Lord*** (*kyriotēta:* ***lordship***). *Kyriotēta* can refer to the rule of human authorities (Luther 1990, 293), the authority of a certain class of angels (Col 1:16; Eph 1:21), or the lordship of God or Christ. Jude uses the related term *kyrios* ("Lord") in vv 4 and 5.

The rejection of ***lordship*** here probably parallels the accusation that the false teachers "deny Jesus Christ our only Sovereign and Lord" (v 4). Since

these men masqueraded as believers, their rejection of **authority** was probably not doctrinal. They probably did not overtly teach some christological heresy (but see Kelly 1969, 262). Their method of rejecting **authority** was undoubtedly practical. Their immoral behavior implicitly rejected the divine authority of the Lord who judges and punishes sin.

Third, like the people of Sodom and Gomorrah who lusted after the heavenly messengers, the false teachers **slander celestial beings** (*doxas blasphēmousin:* ***they blaspheme the glorious ones***). The ***glorious ones*** refer to angels (see 2 Pet 2:10). Jude's example of the archangel Michael in v 9 suggests that their **slander** probably took the form of arrogantly underestimating the power and influence of fallen angels. The archangel Michael refused even to slander the devil. His example functions as a contrast to the audacious behavior of the intruders. Jude seems to imply that they slander Satan and fallen angels.

The passage is admittedly obscure. But the slander of **celestial beings** probably means that the false teachers were denigrating the angelic powers of evil. Not even the archangel Michael was so arrogantly disrespectful (v 9).

The intruders in the church of Jude's dear friends perpetrated the same kinds of sins as the rebellious Israelites, the fallen angels, and the people of Sodom and Gomorrah. Disregarding God's punishment of wickedness, **these dreamers** exhibit the same sinfulness God has consistently punished in the past (see Watson 1998a, 489).

■ 9 The archangel Michael provides a brief contrast to the arrogant behavior of the slanderous false teachers. The **archangel Michael** is mentioned in the Bible (Dan 10:13, 21; 12:1; Rev 12:7). But there is no biblical record of a confrontation between **Michael** and the **devil** over the **body of Moses.**

Apparently, Jude drew this illustration from an apocryphal writing titled *The Assumption of Moses* (or *Testament of Moses;* Bauckham 1983, 65-76), as the early Christian writers Clement, Origen, and Didymus claimed. Jewish tradition reports that the archangel Michael was sent by God to bury the body of Moses. But the devil disputed Michael's right to provide him an honorable burial. Satan argued that Moses' body belonged to him because he was the lord of "matter" and because Moses was a murderer (Exod 2:12).

Despite the devil's provocation, Michael was not disrespectful to the devil. Jude writes that he **did not dare to bring a slanderous accusation against him.** Instead, he left the matter in God's hands, rebuking him with the words of Zechariah, **The Lord rebuke you!** (Zech 3:2).

Two conclusions can be drawn from this illustration of the conflict between Michael and the devil. First, Jude assumed his readers were familiar with this apocryphal tradition. This points strongly toward a predominantly Jewish audience.

> One of the strange things about Jude is that he so often makes his quotations, not from Scripture, but from the apocryphal books. Such quotations seem very strange to us; but these books were very popular and widely used at the time when Jude was writing, and to Jude's readers the quotations would be very effective. (Barclay 1960, 220)

Jude probably selected this story about Michael because his readers were familiar with it.

Second, despite the questions about the background, source, and authority of Jude's apocryphal illustration, its point is clear. Jude uses this analogy to condemn the slanderous behavior of the false teachers. Michael refrained from uttering disrespectful words against Satan, despite his own status and Satan's provocation. By contrast, the human intruders arrogantly slander, revile, and blaspheme angelic beings. If the greatest of the good angels refused to speak evil of the worst of the evil angels, surely no human being may speak evil of any angel.

■ **10** Unlike Michael, **these men speak abusively against whatever they do not understand.** Verses 9-10 are closely connected to the last phrase of v 8, where the intruders are accused of "slandering celestial beings." In each verse Jude uses a derivative of *blasphēmia* (***blaspheme, slander, insult***).

In v 8 the opponents are accused of "slandering" (*blasphēmousin*) angels. In v 9 they are contrasted with Michael who refused to bring "a slanderous accusation" (*blasphēmias*) against the devil. And in v 10 Jude asserts that they **speak abusively against** (*blasphēmousin*) **whatever they do not understand.** These "dreamers" claim prophetic insight and wisdom. But their behavior demonstrates complete ignorance of spiritual matters in general, and in particular the role of angels in the divine scheme of things.

Far from being spiritually enlightened, the only thing **they do understand** is derived from pure **instinct, like unreasoning animals.** Jude's comparison of the false teachers to **unreasoning animals** is probably due to their sexual excesses (see 2 Pet 2:12). Instead of following God's reasonable moral laws, they behave on a level of **instinct, like unreasoning animals.** They have no moral sense of right or wrong. "The intruders are said to act like 'animals without reason' (*aloga zōa*) because they allow themselves to be led by instinct or nature (*physikōs*) alone" (Harrington 2003, 199).

Jude points out **these are the very things that destroy them.** The false teachers reject divine punishment for their immoral behavior. Instead, they justify their immorality by appealing to visionary revelation. But God's judgment and destruction will strike the immoral intruders as it did the disobedient Israelites, the angels who rebelled, and the sinful people of Sodom and Gomorrah.

2. Doomed for Destruction (vv 11-13)

BEHIND THE TEXT

Jude turns his attention to the inevitable condemnation and destruction of his opponents. His charges here are not substantially different from those enumerated previously. However, the specific portrayal of the intruders is somewhat altered. "Whereas in vv 5-10 he portrayed the false teachers simply as sinners, in vv 11-13 he portrays them as false *teachers* who lead other people into sin" (Bauckham 1983, 79). Jude never specifically identifies the intruders as teachers. But the implications of their portrayal in vv 11-13 justify this conclusion.

Jude cites three despicable individuals from the OT, renowned for leading others into destruction (v 11). Then he describes the false teachers with an additional series of vivid metaphors that underscore their ultimate doom and destruction (vv 12-13).

IN THE TEXT

■ **11** The verse begins with the exclamation, **Woe to them!** In the Synoptic Gospels Jesus' frequent cries of **Woe** (e.g., Matt 11:21; 18:7; 23:13; Mark 14:21; Luke 6:24-26; 11:42) announce the coming doom of certain people. As in Isa 3:11, **Woe** "was used especially by the prophets in the OT to announce the pain and distress people would experience as a result of God's judgment on them" (Moo 1996, 256). Similarly, Jude pronounces **Woe** upon the intruders, anticipating the divine destruction awaiting them.

In quick succession, Jude recalls three OT examples of individuals who disobeyed God and were severely punished: **Cain, Balaam,** and **Korah.** Jewish tradition attributes more sins to Cain, Balaam, and Korah than does the OT. In Jewish tradition, all three men became "representative leaders in wickedness with followers in their reprobate ways" (Boobyer 1958, 46). More importantly for Jude's purposes, Jewish tradition gave prominent attention to the destruction God visited on them and their followers because of their sins.

First, **Cain**—the immoral intruders **have taken the way of Cain. Cain** is well-known as the first murderer, who killed his brother Abel out of envy (Gen 4:1-16). In Jewish tradition, Cain served as the classic example of an ungodly skeptic. Jewish rabbis taught that Cain corrupted humanity and "became a great leader of men into wicked courses" (Josephus, *Ant.* 1.2.2; Whiston 1957, 35). By accusing the intruders of following **the way of Cain,** Jude insinuates that they led other people into sinful immorality.

Second, **Balaam**—the immoral infiltrators **have rushed for profit into Balaam's error** (see 2 Pet 2:15-16). The greed of Balaam is firmly established in Num 22—24. Balaam was hired by Israel's enemy, King Balak of Moab, to curse Israel. Although he was ultimately unable to curse Israel, he became infamous for his willingness to try to do so for profit. Balaam was also blamed for leading the people of Israel into immorality and idolatry at Baal-peor (Num 31:16). By this analogy, Jude accused his opponents of rushing for **profit into Balaam's error** by deceiving their fellow Christians. The word **profit** implies that they were reaping financial benefits from their victims.

Third, **Korah**—Jude characterizes his opponents as like those who **have been destroyed in Korah's rebellion. Korah** is known for leading 250 prominent Israelites to rebel against the leadership of Moses and Aaron (Num 16:1-35). In response, God caused the earth to open up and swallow Korah and his followers, their families, and all their possessions. The image of Korah's destruction would have been vivid for Jude's readers. Korah led others into rebellion and destruction. Jude may also imply that "the intruders are rejecting legitimate authority within the church" (Harrington 2003, 199). Both elements—leading others into destruction and rebellion against legitimate authority within the church—are instrumental to Jude's denunciation of the false teachers.

These snapshots from the OT describe three leading characteristics of
11-13 the false teachers (Green 1987, 188). Like **Cain,** they are devoid of love and filled with immoral wickedness. Like **Balaam,** they were greedy for profit and willing to teach others that sin does not matter. Like **Korah,** they were disrespectful of the purposes of God and insubordinate to church leaders. Each character is portrayed in Jewish tradition as leading others into sin or rebellion. For Jude, the climactic verdict on the immoral false teachers is that they will also be **destroyed.**

■ **12-13** In midrashic style, Jude moves from example to application. Jude ascribes the same kind of wickedness and destruction to the false teachers as was illustrated by his three infamous examples. Six vivid portrayals of the false teachers are given:

(1) They are **blemishes at your love feasts.** *Agapē* (**love**) was the early church's favorite term for Christian love. Believers began to apply the word *agapē* to their joyful fellowship meals. At these **love feasts** (*agapais*), believers would share a meal and celebrate the Eucharist (Holy Communion) together as a body of believers.

The vulnerability of **love feasts** to greed, disorder, and drunkenness is well-documented by Paul (1 Cor 11:17-34). Peter insinuates that immorality had occurred at some of these feasts (2 Pet 2:13-14).

The intruders must have been responsible for promoting similar abuses because Jude calls them **blemishes** (*spilades*) at these love feasts. The usual meaning of *spilas* was "a rocky hazard hidden by waves, a (hidden) reef" (BDAG, 938). The false teachers were a dangerous ***hidden reef*** at the fellowship meals. "Close contact with them will result in shipwreck" (Bauckham 1983, 85). The metaphorical image of danger conveyed by *spilas* (***hidden reef***) is powerful.

The intruders participate in the feasts **without the slightest qualm** (*aphobōs: **without fear/reverence***). *Aphobōs* discloses the arrogance of the intruders. But the real danger of their shameless behavior is the misleading impression that a person can remain a Christian while practicing an immoral lifestyle.

(2) They are **shepherds who feed only themselves** (*heautous poimainontes: **shepherding themselves***). Some interpreters connect this description to the **love feasts.** Kelly maintains that this expression highlights the opponents' selfish behavior at the communal feasts. Like the selfish believers in Corinth (1 Cor 11:21), they eat in gluttony and drink in excess (1969, 271).

Shepherding in the NT usually alludes to pastoral leadership. Thus, Jude may imply that the intruders "claim to be leaders in the church, but instead of tending the flock they only look after themselves" (Bauckham 1983, 87; see Ezek 34:2). With only their own interests in mind, the false teachers gather followers only to lead them astray.

The last four metaphors are drawn from the natural world. Moo speculates that they are derived "from each of the four regions of the earth, according to the ancients: the air (clouds), the earth (trees), the sea (waves), and the heavens (planets)" (1996, 259). It is uncertain that this was Jude's intention.

(3) They are **clouds without rain, blown along by the wind.** Like **clouds without rain,** the opponents make empty promises (see Prov 25:14). They are also unstable (**blown along by the wind**). "Like clouds that produce no rain and serve only to block the sun, the opponents . . . are good for nothing" (Harrington 2003, 200).

(4) They are **autumn trees, without fruit and uprooted—twice dead. Autumn trees, without fruit** reiterates the theme of empty promises. At the end of the season, trees are expected to bear the fruit of the season. Similarly, the false teachers promise fruit but yield none.

The phrase **uprooted—twice dead** is problematic. **Uprooted** fits the analogy of trees quite nicely. But it is difficult to apply the literal meaning **twice dead** to the metaphor of trees. The phrase must describe the false teachers more directly. Two suggestions are possible:

First, **twice dead** could indicate they have returned to their preconversion condition of spiritual death. "They are called *twice dead* and *uprooted* because they had once been 'dead in transgressions and sins' (Eph 2:1) and were now dead again, in the sense that they were cut off from their life-giving root, Jesus Christ" (Green 1987, 190-91).

Second, **twice dead** could refer to their eschatological judgment at the last day. "Second death" is used in Revelation to describe the fate of the wicked at the Last Judgment (Rev 2:11; 20:6, 14; 21:8; Bauckham 1983, 88).

Both suggestions make sense within Jude's denunciatory portrayal of the false teachers. Considering the eschatological context of Jude's letter (vv 6, 14-15, 18, 21, 24), the second suggestion is perhaps the better option. But the choice is difficult.

(5) They are **wild waves of the sea, foaming up their shame.** This portrayal is probably derived from Isa 57:20: "The wicked are like the tossing sea, which cannot rest, whose waves cast up mire and mud." Like restless waves of the sea, the false teachers leave filthy scum and debris in their wake. **Shame** is actually plural, ***shames.*** Jude may be thinking of the ***shameful sins*** of the intruders.

This metaphor makes a different point than the previous images. Whereas the **clouds** and **trees** produced nothing, the **wild waves** actually produce something, but something awful. "Instead of edifying other Christians, [the intruder] soils them like the dirt thrown up by a stormy sea" (Bauckham 1983, 89).

12-13 (6) They are **wandering stars, for whom blackest darkness has been reserved forever. Wandering stars** (*asteres planētai*) could refer to meteors, comets, or falling stars. But it probably refers to the planets, whose irregular movements were not understood by the ancients. In Jewish tradition planets and falling stars were thought to be controlled by disobedient angels (*1 En.* 18:13-16; 21:3-6). Since Jude quotes from *1 Enoch* in the following verse, he probably has disobedient angels in mind when he compares the false teachers to **wandering stars.** Because of their ever-changing movement within their orbits, planets cannot be used by travelers for navigation. Likewise, the false teachers were unstable and unsafe for spiritual navigation.

For the false teachers and the fallen angels, **blackest darkness has been reserved forever. Darkness** is described as the fate of the evil angels in Jude 6. This reinforces the idea that Jude's imagery here is borrowed from *1 Enoch,* where the planets and falling stars were thought to be controlled by disobedient angels (Bauckham 1983, 89). Jude's point is that the false teachers are off course in their lives, and they will be punished by God.

Each subdivision of this section (vv 5-19) ends with a note of judgment and punishment. At the end of v 7 Jude speaks of the "punishment of eternal fire"; at the end of v 10 he declares their wicked deeds will "destroy them"; at the end of v 11 he says they will be "destroyed." The theme of punishment and judgment appears again at the end of v 13. The false teachers' fate is **blackest darkness.** No doubt doomed destruction awaits these immoral intruders.

FROM THE TEXT

Abused Sacraments. The *agapē* meal was a communal supper shared by early believers (Acts 2:42-46). The celebration of the Eucharist was an integral part of this gathering. Participation in Communion was a significant event within the corporate worship of the church. As Paul discovered (1 Cor 11:17-34), this meaningful celebration could fall victim to abuse if it was used only to satisfy hunger or to display wealth and status (Watson 1998a, 493). Jude reminds us that even the most sacred of activities can be compromised by selfish attitudes or errant motives. These often-concealed attitudes and motives were like "hidden reefs" (v 12) that threatened to batter and destroy the Christian community.

Sermonic Illustrations. Jude is a master illustrator and communicator. He argues his case with vigor and creativity. He does not merely thrust his message in the face of his readers, but he clarifies his point by probing the OT for the examples of Cain, Balaam, and Korah (v 11). He alludes to popular stories of Jewish tradition familiar to his readers to emphasize his point (v 9). He finds analogies in the natural world to illuminate his discussion (vv 12-13).

Considerable attention has been given to Jude's use of extrabiblical sources in the communication of his message. Jude has only done what Jesus, Paul, and every other effective communicator has always done: he clarifies and illustrates his lessons with vivid examples and stories familiar to his audience.

Despite the concerns of some readers, the message and authority of Jude are not compromised by his appeal to extrabiblical sources and examples in this sermonic letter. On the contrary, the effectiveness of his message to his readers is greatly enhanced. As good preachers know, a good and relevant illustration always improves a message.

C. Prophecies Against the Ungodly (vv 14-19)

BEHIND THE TEXT

Jude concludes his denunciation of the false teachers with two prophecies against them. Each prophecy is followed by an application to the false teachers who are identified once again as **these men** (*houtoi;* vv 16, 19).

The first prophecy quotes from *1 En.* 1:9 (in Jude 14-15). This extrabiblical passage was undoubtedly selected because of its repeated use of the term **ungodly** (*asebeia*) and God's judgment against them. The familiarity of Jude's readers with this apocryphal writing is almost certainly his reason for using it. He need not have considered *1 Enoch* to be Scripture or its message authoritative to quote it. Paul similarly quoted noncanonical writers' statements he considered true. For instance, he quotes from Cleanthes and Aratus (Acts 17:28), Menander (1 Cor 15:33), and Epimenides (Titus 1:12). Likewise, Jude quotes from *1 Enoch* because it provides a fitting illustration of the certain punishment awaiting the ungodly teachers who had infiltrated the congregations of his readers.

The structure of these verses is straightforward: Jude cites two prophecies and then applies them specifically to the false teachers. Accordingly, he quotes first a prophecy from *1 Enoch* in vv 14-15, and then applies it to his opponents in v 16. Second, he reminds his readers of an apostolic prophecy in vv 17-18, and he provides its application in v 19.

IN THE TEXT

I. Prophecy of Enoch (vv 14-16)

■ **14-15** Jude quotes a prophecy recorded in *1 Enoch*, an extremely popular apocryphal book during this time period. The prophecy is introduced as from **Enoch, the seventh from Adam.** When Adam is counted first, Enoch represents the seventh generation (Gen 5:3-18; 1 Chr 1:1-3). **Enoch** stands out
14-15 among OT characters because the Bible says he "walked with God; then he was no more, because God took him away" (Gen 5:24; Heb 11:5).

This enigmatic description accounts for the fascination of Jewish tradition with Enoch. "Since it was assumed that Enoch was taken up into heaven, he became the recipient of revelations about the heavenly realm and about the future" (Harrington 2003, 214). As a result, several "prophetic" writings appeared in Enoch's name during the so-called intertestamental period. These purported to contain insights and revelations about the end times. Among these writings is *1 Enoch*. One prevailing theme of *1 Enoch* is the coming of God to judge the wicked. Jude uses this theme to corroborate his proclamation of certain punishment for the immoral teachers.

According to Jude's paraphrase of *1 En.* 1:9, Enoch declares, **See, the Lord is coming with thousands upon thousands of his holy ones to judge everyone, and to convict all the ungodly of all the ungodly acts they have done in the ungodly way, and of all the harsh words ungodly sinners have spoken against him.**

This prophecy fits Jude's denunciation of the false teachers extraordinarily well. Like Jude, *1 Enoch* speaks about the **ungodly** (v 4), the insults of the ungodly against the Lord and his "holy ones" or angels (vv 8-10), the

Lord's coming (v 21), God's judgment (v 6), and the punishment of sinners (vv 7, 10, 11, 13). The relevance of this prophecy to his own struggle against the false teachers undoubtedly explains Jude's quotation of this apocryphal writing.

According to the prophecy, the purpose of the Lord's coming is **to judge everyone.** But the punishing of the **ungodly** was Jude's main point. This is almost awkwardly overemphasized with the threefold repetition of **ungodly** in the last clause of the prophecy (**ungodly acts, ungodly way, ungodly sinners**).

In the last phrase Jude alludes to **the harsh words ungodly sinners have spoken against him.** This phrase is noteworthy because it is not in *1 En.* 1:9.

> That a reference to the sins of speech was probably not in the original text Jude quoted suggests that the idea was an important one for Jude. Presumably he added it because the false teachers were erring especially in this way (see vv 8 and 10). (Moo 1996, 270)

In the application of this prophecy in v 16, Jude pays special attention to the sins of speech. This undoubtedly alludes to the intruders' false and misleading teaching.

■ **16** Jude applies the prophecy of *1 Enoch* to the false teachers, whom he pejoratively identifies as **these men** (see comments on v 8). Focusing on their sins of speech, Jude calls them **grumblers and faultfinders.**

Grumblers is found only here in the NT. But Paul uses a verbal derivative of this noun to describe the persistent complaints of the Israelites toward God and Moses in the wilderness (1 Cor 10:10).

Faultfinders is an adjective meaning "complaining of one's fate" (Earle 1984, 118). This adjective was probably meant to modify the noun **grumblers.** Together, these words mean something like ***disgruntled grumblers***. They complain about the restrictions God's rules and laws placed on their freedom to behave as they wanted.

These faultfinding grumblers **follow their own evil desires. Evil desires** (*epithymias:* ***desires***) frequently carries the negative connotation of lustful desires in the NT (e.g., Rom 13:13-14; Gal 5:24; 1 Pet 4:3; 2 Pet 2:18). Thus, the phrase **follow their own evil desires** probably alludes to their sexual immorality (vv 4, 8, 10, 12). But this phrase also highlights their preference for their *own* desires instead of *God's* desires. Self-discipline or self-sacrifice for the sake of others is repulsive to them. They **follow their own evil desires,** while they criticize the moral restraints they have tossed aside.

Additionally, *to stoma autōn lalei hyperongka:* ***their mouth speaks excessive things.*** The exact meaning of this phrase is uncertain. The last word (*hyperongka;* ***excessive things***) is derived from *hyper* (***above***) and *ongkoō* (***to swell***). It means literally, "of excessive size, puffed up, swollen" (Harrington

2003, 215). Thus, the expression could mean the false teachers use excessive or *puffed up* words about themselves—**they boast.**

But the expression could also convey a sense of arrogance and haughtiness against God. A form of the same word in Daniel describes the evil king's boastful language against God: "[he] will say unheard-of things against the God of gods" (11:36 LXX). Thus, the expression ***their mouth speaks excessive things*** probably means their boastful speaking takes the form of speaking arrogantly about God or against God. "They express their arrogant presumptuous attitude toward God, their insolent contempt for his commandments, their rejection of his moral authority which amounts to a proud claim to be their own moral authority" (Bauckham 1983, 99).

Jude's final criticism focuses on the greed of his opponents (see v 11). They **flatter others** (*thaumazontes prosōpa:* ***admiring faces***) **for their own advantage.** The underlying imagery from the Hebrew idiom, ***lifting/having regard for the face,*** was used in the OT to refer to partiality (e.g., Gen 19:21; Lev 19:15; Deut 10:17). Jude accuses the false teachers of using flattery **for their own advantage,** for personal gain (see Hillyer 1992, 258).

The false teachers' flattery probably expressed itself in their willingness to teach whatever their audience wanted to hear. Claiming spiritual enlightenment, the intruders cast aside traditional Christian moral restraint. They smoothly flattered their hearers with the morally lax message they longed to hear. They did this to win favor with those members of the community on whose generosity they depended for financial support. Jude predicted that this exploitive and self-serving behavior would reap certain condemnation.

2. Prophecy of the Apostles (vv 17-19)

■ **17** In vv 17-19 Jude turns his attention to his faithful readers, whom he addresses as **dear friends** (*agapētoi*: ***beloved;*** see vv 3-4). The emphatic adversative, *hymeis de*, ***but you,*** highlights the stark contrast between Jude's opponents ("these men") and his readers (**dear friends**). In the final verses of this letter, this contrast can be graphically portrayed as follows:

these men	***dear friends***
1. "scoffers," who reject the tradition (v 18)	1. "rememberers," who are faithful to what they were told (v 17)
2. they create "division," tearing down the group (v 19)	2. they "build themselves up," in unity of faith (v 20)
3. they go "the way of godless desires" (v 16)	3. their way is "the most sacred faithfulness" (v 20)
4. they are "physical" (v 10)	4. they "hate even the garment stained by the flesh" (v 23)

5. they "have no Spirit" (v 19)	5. they "pray in the Holy Spirit" (v 20)
6. they are "proscribed for judgment" (vv 4, 15)	6. they "await the mercy of our Lord Jesus Christ" (v 21)

(Neyrey 1993, 85)

Jude introduces this prophecy by urging his readers to **remember what the apostles of our Lord Jesus Christ foretold. Remember** recalls the opening of this section where Jude tells his readers, "I want to remind you" (v 5). Jude's letter is a reminder that the false teachers' existence and future destruction have been foretold (v 4). There is nothing about the apostasy of the intruders that could not have been expected.

Some interpreters contend that the phrase **the apostles of our Lord Jesus Christ** reveals that the apostles belonged to an earlier generation (see Kelly 1969, 281). Thus, the letter must have been written after the first century. This is not necessarily true. The prophecy certainly originated in the past, but this need not have been the distant past. Furthermore, the reference to **the apostles** does not necessarily include all the apostles. Jude probably refers to those apostles who planted the churches to whom he wrote. Nothing in the language of this verse precludes a date within the apostolic age (A.D. 50-85).

■ **18** Jude introduces the prophecy with the words **they said to you. To you** reinforces the idea Jude is not merely alluding to an apostolic tradition of an earlier generation. Rather, he refers to a message delivered to Jude's readers personally. The source of this prophecy is the teaching of the specific **apostles** who first brought the Christian message to Jude's audience.

The prophecy is virtually identical with 2 Pet 3:3. Outside of Jude and 2 Peter, there is no written record of this prophecy from any apostle. Is Jude quoting the prophetic words of Peter in 2 Pet 3:3?

According to the prophecy, **in the last times there will be scoffers.** In the NT **scoffers** is found only here and in 2 Pet 3:3. Jude's opponents may also have scoffed at the hope for Christ's return, but Jude does not mention this. The **scoffers** are simply those **who will follow their own ungodly desires.** Hence, the focus of the prophecy pertains to their mocking of God and his moral requirements.

Ungodly (*asebeia*) recalls the prophecy of *1 Enoch* with its fourfold repetition of this word in v 15. *Asebeia* describes those who have no reverence for God. It usually carries an ethical undertone that points toward an immoral or unethical lifestyle. For Jude the prophecy of the apostles is fulfilled in the disgraceful behavior of the intruders.

In the last times is used frequently to refer to the day of messianic salvation and judgment (e.g., Isa 2:2; Jer 49:39; Hos 3:5; John 12:48; Acts 2:17; 1 Pet 1:20). Jesus warned his followers there would be apostasy in the final age (Matt 24:9-14; Mark 13:5-13). Jude and his readers believed they were living in the **last times** for a variety of reasons. The fulfillment of this prophecy through the false teachers only reinforced this conviction. It is uncertain precisely what this perception of the **last times** entails. Did they anticipate the imminent return of Christ? Or did they merely perceive themselves as living in the final age between the resurrection and return of Christ?

■ **19** Jude applies the prophecy to the false teachers. He asserts **these are the men who divide you** (*apodiorizontes*). The verb **divide** (*apodiorizō*) means "mark out boundaries in order to separate" (Hillyer 1992, 261). The intruders are splitting the church. They are still participating in the fellowship meals (v 12). So the schism has not caused them to separate into their own community. But they undoubtedly identified themselves as an elite group, superior to other Christians, especially to those who limited their freedom to the moral standards of traditional Christian teaching.

Despite their claims of spiritual superiority, Jude maintains they **follow mere natural instincts** (*psychikoi: **souls***) **and do not have the Spirit. Follow mere natural instincts** translates a single Greek word, which literally means ***soul.*** Although ***soul*** usually possesses a positive meaning in the NT, Paul uses *psychikoi* to contrast the *natural* people (*psychikos*) with the *spiritual* people (*pneumatikos;* see 1 Cor 2:14; 15:44). Similarly, Jude uses *psychikoi* with a negative sense. The ungodly intruders are concerned only with what is *natural* to life instead of what is *spiritual* to life. They are "worldly people" (NRSV) or "worldly-minded" (NASB).

Moreover, they **do not have the Spirit.** There is a strong sense of irony in this accusation. The **scoffers** undoubtedly claimed greater spiritual insight than other believers, probably through their experience of dream visions (v 8). But their immoral and shameless behavior demonstrates they are merely physical (*psychikoi: **soulish***) in their orientation. They pursue mere physical stimuli, like unreasoning animals (v 10). Far from superspiritual, the intruders do not even possess the Spirit.

FROM THE TEXT

Use of the Apocrypha. Many readers are surprised that Jude quotes a passage from an apocryphal writing as a fulfilled prophecy. Jude certainly understood the prophetic passage in *1 Enoch* to be true and relevant for his readers. But he never refers to this writing with the word "Scripture" (*graphē*). The canon of the OT was not formally closed until late in first century A.D. The NT canon of Scriptures was not established closed until the late fourth century A.D. "Both Jewish and early Christian communities valued literature that was held to be authoritative, but not all such works eventually were judged to be canonical" (Harrington 2003, 494).

Jude used *1 Enoch* because he knew his audience revered it (Moo 1996, 273). Jude's specific reference to *1 Enoch* is striking. But he says nothing of it being divinely inspired or authoritative Scripture. Jude quoted from this writing as an effective means of motivating his readers to recognize the danger and ultimate destruction of the intruders within their churches.

True Spirituality. Just because someone claims to be spiritual does not make it so (vv 14-19). True spirituality is not proven by words alone. It must be demonstrated in one's upright and holy behavior. Too many believers are deceived by self-appointed "spiritual" leaders who, with an overabundance of personal charisma, preach a tempting message of flattery and personal convenience to gain a following. Despite their boastful claims of spirituality, these charlatans do not possess the Spirit at all. Rather, they are motivated by the most basic physical instincts of greed and self-indulgence. True spirituality is always evident in the consistent coherence between one's words and one's deeds. As Jesus taught his disciples, you can recognize a tree by its fruit (Matt 7:16-20).

IV. EXHORTATION TO KEEP THE FAITH: JUDE 20-23

BEHIND THE TEXT

Jude returns his focuses to his **dear friends.** In the beginning of the letter, he urged his readers to "contend for the faith" (v 3). Now he articulates what this actually means. Jude gives commanding instructions his readers must follow to protect themselves from dangerous intruders.

The instructions are short but far-reaching in their scope. In vv 20-21, Jude's exhortation consists of a succinct description of the essentials of Christian theology, including specific references to the Father, Son, and Holy Spirit. He also describes the essentials of the Christian life, including prayer and the important triad of faith, love, and hope. Additionally, he issues a plea for the pastoral care of those who are swayed and tempted by the influence of the intruders (vv 22-23). In this way, these verses provide a powerful and instructive climax to the entire letter.

The structure of vv 20-23 is quite simple. First, Jude commands his readers to remain spiritually strong (vv 20-21). Second, he commands them to help others (vv 22-23).

A. A Command to Remain Spiritually Strong (vv 20-21)

BEHIND THE TEXT

These verses represent one Greek sentence. It consists of one imperative main verb and three subordinate clauses that assume the force of commands because of their relationship to the main verb:

Subordinate clause 1:	"build yourselves up on your most holy faith"
Subordinate clause 2:	"praying in the Holy Spirit"
Main verb:	"keep yourselves in the love of God"
Subordinate clause 3:	"waiting anxiously for the mercy of our Lord Jesus Christ to eternal life" (all NASB)

In this way, vv 20-21 contain a four-pronged command to remain spiritually
20-21 strong. Each command focuses on the necessity of believers to maintain their faith. "Here is the first requirement when false teaching arises: to secure one's own spiritual position" (Moo 1996, 283). The need to help others who are threatened will be addressed in vv 22-23. But the first step believers must take is to ensure their own spiritual strength and foundation.

IN THE TEXT

■ **20-21** Jude commands his readers: **build yourselves up in your most holy faith.** The image of building the Christian community is a widely used metaphor in the NT (1 Cor 3:9; 1 Pet 2:5). The reflexive pronoun **yourselves** (*heautous:* ***each other***) indicates that "Jude does not mean that each believer should build himself up . . . but that all should contribute to the spiritual growth of the whole community" (Bauckham 1983, 112-13). While false teachers "divide" the church (v 19), true believers unite and strengthen the church as they **build** each other **up.**

The phrase **your most holy faith** might indicate how believers should build up each other—**build yourselves up** ***by means of*** **your most holy faith.** But it probably identifies the foundation upon which believers should build.

As in v 3, **faith** refers to what Christians believe—"the orthodox body of truth and practice from the apostles" (Blum 1981c, 395). Jude's appeal is twofold: his readers are to seek "an ever deepening grasp of what God in Christ has done for them as handed down by the apostles (v. 3)" (Hillyer 1992, 363). The lawless teaching of the false teachers leads to godless and immoral behavior. And so, by contrast, true believers build each other up on the solid foundation of the moral instruction of the faith. The Christian faith is **most holy** because it is not derived from human reasoning, but from the holy God who has revealed himself to believers through the holy one, Jesus Christ.

Second, along with and as a means of ***building*** themselves **up** in their **faith,** Jude enjoins his readers to **pray in the Holy Spirit. Pray** is in the present tense, indicating that prayer needs to be a constant activity of Christians.

Prayer **in the Holy Spirit** takes place in the control of as well as under the inspiration of the Holy Spirit (Bauckham 1983, 113). Prayer **in the Holy Spirit** is not in a special prayer language. Regardless of how believers pray, their prayers should be continual and they should be offered in submission to and in dependence on the Holy Spirit (see Rom 8:26-27). It was undoubtedly Christ's prayer **in the Holy Spirit** that enabled him to pray to the Father, "Yet not as I will, but as you will" (Matt 26:39).

Third, Jude commands his readers: **keep yourselves in God's love.** This phrase represents the main imperative of vv 20-21. Jude described his readers as "kept by Jesus Christ" in v 1. But now he urges them to **keep yourselves in God's love.**

The juxtaposition of these two statements encapsulates the NT approach 20-21
to the Christian life. The NT teaches that God has done everything that is needed for salvation through the life, death, and resurrection of Christ. Yet, a person must respond obediently to God's offer of salvation through Christ in order to realize this salvation personally. "God 'keeps' us, but we also need to 'keep ourselves.' Both are true, and neither can be sacrificed without missing something essential to the Christian pursuit of godliness" (Moo 1996, 285).

Keep yourselves in God's love is strikingly similar to Jesus' instruction to his disciples to "remain in my love" (John 15:9). Jesus explains to his disciples that they remain in his love by obeying his commandments (15:10). It is precisely in the area of obedience to Christ's commands that the false teachers erred so miserably. Jude reminds his readers that those who truly love God will **keep** themselves **in God's love.** One of the ways believers **keep** themselves **in God's love** is by obeying his commands (John 15:1-17).

The last command focuses on the future. Believers must **wait for the mercy** (*eleos: **compassion, pity***) **of our Lord Jesus Christ to bring you to eternal life. Mercy** is "the emotion that arises when one sees another person's affliction" (Verbrugge 2000, 179). It is frequently used in Scripture to refer to the eschatological hope of God's people (e.g., Matt 5:7; 2 Tim 1:18). The

mercy of God as revealed through Jesus Christ enables believers to have hope for the future. "Not even the faithful Christian escapes condemnation except by the Lord's mercy" (Bauckham 1983, 114). Our hope of salvation is based solely on mercy.

Wait for (*prosdechomenoi*) is also used in eschatological contexts to describe the expectation of believers for the last day (e.g., Mark 15:43; Luke 2:25; 12:36; Acts 24:15; Titus 2:13). It "connotes eager yet patient expectation and the kind of lifestyle that should accompany such hope for deliverance" (Moo 1996, 285).

Believers have hope for the future because the Christian life has **eternal life** as its goal and **the mercy of our Lord Jesus Christ** as its basis. Jude enjoins his readers to focus their attention beyond the disruption of the intruders to the glorious day of Christ. On that day, the Lord will return bringing judgment to the false teachers and **eternal life** to the faithful believers.

B. A Command to Help Others (vv 22-23)

BEHIND THE TEXT

Because of the many textual variants in Jude's letter, it has been called "the most textually corrupt book of the NT" (Allen 1998, 133). This is especially evident in vv 22-23. The text of these verses has been preserved in
22-23 a variety of forms. It is no longer possible to determine with certainty which is the original. The precise text is so uncertain that four of the major English versions (KJV, NEB, NIV, and RSV) provide significantly different translations, and a fifth translation is preferred by several influential commentaries.

One significant point of difference in the manuscripts concerns who is to be helped. Some point to three classes of people who need to be helped; others point to just two classes of people (Metzger 1994, 658). The different textual options are illustrated in the following translations:

The two-clause option		
"On the one hand, snatch some from the fire. On the other hand, have mercy with fear on those who dispute." (Neyrey 1993, 84; see Bauckham 1983, 108)	"And of some have compassion, making a difference: and others save with fear, pulling them out of the fire." (KJV)	"Show mercy toward those who have doubts; save others by snatching them out of the fire; and to others show mercy mixed with fear." (GNT; see NEB)

The three-clause option

Be merciful to those who doubt; snatch others from the fire and save them; to others show mercy, mixed with fear. (NIV; see NRSV, NASB, REB, NJB)	"And convince some, who doubt; save some, by snatching them out of the fire; on some have mercy with fear." (RSV; see JB)

Each of these translations is derived from different Greek manuscripts. The table reveals that the three-clause options are most preferred among recent translations. Two factors favor the adoption of the three-clause option. First, Jude has a preference for presenting ideas, words, and images in groups of three. The three-option clause reflects this tendency. Second, the three-option clause is the reading that best explains the other readings. Therefore, I follow the three-clause option suggested by the NIV (see the discussion in Bauckham 1983, 108-11).

IN THE TEXT

■ **22-23** After securing their own salvation, believers must help those whose spiritual condition is uncertain. Jude commands his readers to reach out to three different groups of people.

1. First, they must **be merciful to those who doubt** (*diakrinomenous:* ***dis-*** 22-23
pute). Jude uses the same Greek word to describe the archangel Michael who was "disputing" with the devil (v 9). The translation **doubt** is the more usual meaning. Within the context, Jude is more likely to have urged his readers to be merciful to those who **doubt** than to those ***who are disputing.***

Those who doubt probably refers to believers who were influenced by the false teaching of the intruders. Just as Jude's readers have set their hope on the **mercy** (*eleos*) of the Lord Jesus Christ (v 21), they are now urged to **be merciful** (*eleate*) to believers wavering in **doubt.**

2. Second, some people need to be helped directly and vigorously. Thus, Jude's dear friends must **snatch others from the fire and save them. Fire** is used frequently in the Bible as an image of everlasting punishment (e.g., Matt 5:22; Mark 9:43, 48). The appeal is probably influenced by Zech 3:2, where Joshua the high priest is described as "a burning stick snatched from the fire." Wesley understands **fire** as imagery for "sin and temptation" (1981, n.p.). These lead people to the **fire** of final judgment.

Those snatched from the fire are probably believers who have fallen into sinful behavior under the influence of the false teachers. They have not already fallen into the fires of hell through their sinful behavior. But "they are on the brink of it and can be snatched back before they fall into it" (Bauckham 1983, 115).

Snatch is a vivid word. It means "to seize upon with force" (Zodhiates 1992, 257). The word suggests that an aggressive and direct path of action is required for the salvation of some people. The faithful Christians of the community were to **snatch** and **save them** before it was too late.

3. Third, Jude gives the command: **to others show mercy, mixed with fear—hating even the clothing stained by corrupted flesh.** The strong language suggests that Jude has the false teachers themselves in mind here. "They are to have pity upon even the most abandoned heretic, but to exercise great care while getting alongside him lest they themselves become defiled" (Green 1987, 204). Although they should be shown **mercy,** their mercy must be **mixed with fear** (*en phobōi*). In the NT, **fear** (*phobos*) typically "denotes that reverential awe with which believers should view the holy and majestic God" (Moo 1996, 289).

The idea of "stained clothing" is borrowed from Zechariah again. In Zech 3:3-4, Joshua the high priest is described as "dressed in filthy clothes." In Zechariah, the term "filthy" is related to two Hebrew words connected to human excrement (2 Kgs 18:27; Isa 36:12) or to a drunkard's vomit (Isa 28:8).

Clothing refers to the garment worn next to the skin. "Jude pictures the sinful teaching and practices of these people as underclothes fouled by feces" (Moo 1996, 289). These words create a vivid and intentionally unpleasant image. Jude suggests that whatever comes in contact with these people is contaminated by their sins. Because of the awful threat of contamination, believers should **show mercy** on them, but they should be careful. Their **mercy** should be **mixed with fear** lest they be tempted and drawn into the same awful contamination of the false teachers.

Various NT passages forbid believers from having personal contact with fallen believers or false teachers who have abandoned the Christian faith (see Matt 18:17; 1 Cor 5:11; Titus 3:10; 2 John 10-11). Because of the danger posed by the false teaching, Moo suggests that the mercy Jude has in mind is to be exhibited in prayers for them (1996, 288-89). This suggestion is credible. "Even, then, as they act in mercy toward these who have fallen, praying that the Lord may bring them back, they must not overlook in any way the terrible and destructive behavior these people are engaged in" (Moo 1996, 289).

FROM THE TEXT

Theology. In two short verses (vv 20-21), Jude provides a brief but vital portrayal of the essentials of Christian life and theology. In terms of theology, Jude underscores the interconnected work of God the Father, Jesus Christ the

Son, and the Holy Spirit in the salvation of believers. Accordingly, **God's love** provides the foundation for believers' salvation. The **mercy of our Lord Jesus Christ** is the means and agency of that salvation. And the **Holy Spirit** guides and empowers the prayers of believers as they pursue this salvation. In terms of the Christian life, Jude employs the Christian triad of faith, love, and hope to encourage his readers (see 1 Cor 13:13). In addition, believers should be constant in prayer. Although brief in words, Jude's instructions are powerful in scope.

Christian Hope. Believers must keep aflame the fire of Christian hope. It is often difficult for believers to maintain the correct balance between hope for the future and preoccupation with the present. "If too great attention is paid to the future hope, the Christian tends to become so other-worldly that he is not much use in this world. If, however, as is the greater danger today, the future element is soft-pedaled, Christianity becomes a merely religious adjunct to the social services" (Green 1987, 200-201).

Prayer. Perhaps prayer **in the Holy Spirit** is the only way to maintain a healthy balance. Through ongoing, Spirit-inspired prayer, Christians surrender their wants, needs, and desires to God. Only then can the Spirit guide and mold their hearts into a perfect balance of faith, hope, and love.

Evangelism. Believers must examine the passion and determination they exhibit in their evangelistic and outreach efforts. Our efforts should be characterized by more than perfunctory and nonconfrontational hints about the path of salvation through Jesus Christ. Jude urges his readers to aggressive action—to **snatch others from the fire** (v 23). The imagery is forceful. Calvin writes of the vivid imagery of this metaphor:

> When there is danger of fire, we hesitate not to snatch away violently whom we desire to save; for it would not be enough to beckon with the finger, or kindly to stretch forth the hand. So also the salvation of some ought to be cared for, because they will not come to God, except when rudely drawn. (Calvin 1948, 448)

Jude exhibits a deep concern about the contagious nature of sin and the difficulty of remaining pure from its stain (vv 12, 23-24). The NT affirms that believers must prepare themselves for the coming of Christ by being holy, spotless, and blameless (Eph 1:4; Phil 2:15; 2 Pet 3:14). Jude reminds believers of their responsibility to reach out and help those who have been drawn away from the faith by the seductive influence and teaching of false teachers. But he is careful to warn believers not to become contaminated by sin themselves (v 23).

Jude's words are obviously not a license for employing rude and insensitive methods to reach out to the lost. But many will be eternally lost unless some caring Christians are willing to risk misunderstanding or rejection to

snatch them from the fire. The words **snatch others** imply that not *all* evangelistic efforts should be aggressive and confrontational. *Some* must be. Otherwise, an entire group of people run the risk of being eternally lost.

Sin's Pull. Sin appeals to the strong forces of humanity's natural drives and passions. Therefore, Christians must never underestimate the power and pull sin can exert upon people. Even mature and healthy Christians must watch themselves, or they may also be tempted (see Gal 6:1). Through dependence on Christ, however, temptation can be overcome (1 Cor 10:12-13; Heb 2:14-18).

V. CONCLUDING DOXOLOGY: JUDE 24-25

BEHIND THE TEXT

Most NT letters end with personal greetings, prayer requests, or a final benediction pronounced upon the readers. Jude's letter omits this customary conclusion and uses a doxology instead. Doxologies were often used in Jewish services to conclude prayers and sermons (Bauckham 1983, 121). Thus, the doxological conclusion lends to it the flavor of a sermon.

Doxologies usually have four distinctive parts: (1) the person praised, (2) the word of praise (usually *doxa*, ***glory***), (3) the indication of time, and (4) the word *Amen* (***so be it, may it be done***), as an indication of the hearers' appropriate response (Bauckham 1983, 119). Jude follows this typical format precisely. But he expands the form significantly. As a result, Jude contains one of the longest and most beautiful doxologies in the NT.

■ 24 Jude's lengthy description and warning of the false teachers must have cast a dark and dreadful cloud over his readers. But his doxology lifts their attention to the triumphant One: **To him who is able.** The focus of the doxology is on God (see v 25). Jude directs his readers' attention to two things God **is able** to do:

First, God is able **to keep you from falling**. The theme of "keeping" is prominent throughout the letter. Positively, Jude affirms that believers are "kept by Jesus Christ" (v 1). In response, believers must also "keep" themselves "in God's love" (v 21). Negatively, Jude uses the same verb (*tēreō*) to underscore the certainty that God ***keeps*** sinners for judgment (vv 6, 13). In his doxology, Jude reiterates God's positive ***keeping*** power with a new verb that affirms the power of God to **keep** (*phylaxai:* ***guard***) believers from falling. *Phylaxai* conveys the image of "standing guard," kept in protective custody (Hillyer 1992, 267). **Falling** (*aptaistous*) refers to falling into sin (Jas 3:2).

The metaphor **to keep you from falling** is probably derived from the psalmist, who often describes the disasters that would befall believers if God did not prevent their feet from stumbling or slipping (Pss 38:16; 56:13; 66:9). God is powerful enough to protect Christians from falling into the sinful ways of the false teachers. God keeps them so that they may attain final salvation.

Second, Jude affirms God's ability **to present you before his glorious presence without fault and with great joy. His glorious presence** refers to the day of judgment when all people will stand before God to give an account of their lives. Jude assures his readers that God is able to protect them from sin so they can stand before him **without fault** (*amōmous*). *Amōmous* was originally used to describe acceptable sacrifices (Heb 9:14). But it came to be used generally to describe moral purity. Peter uses this word to describe Jesus as the perfect sacrificial lamb (1 Pet 1:19). God's ability **to keep you from falling** will be abundantly evident when believers stand before his throne **without fault.** As a result, the day of judgment will not be a time of fear or dread for believers. Because of "him who is able," believers will celebrate that day **with great joy.**

■ 25 Jude clarifies who is able to keep believers secure and to whom glory should be given: It is **to the only God our Savior.** The KJV uses the reading "to the only wise God." But the word "wise" is found only in a few later, less reliable manuscripts. "Wise" was probably assimilated into these manuscripts under the influence of the doxology of Romans, which gives glory "to the only wise God" (Rom 16:27; see Metzger 1994, 661).

The description of God as **Savior** (*sōtēr*) is rare in the NT (only eight times including this verse). Typically, the title **Savior** is reserved for Jesus Christ (fifteen times). But God is consistently identified in the NT as the initiator of the process of salvation made possible through Jesus Christ (e.g., Rom 5:8). Thus, it is not surprising God may also be identified as **Savior.**

Four virtues are attributed to God: **glory, majesty, power and authority. Glory** (*doxa*) describes the overwhelming radiance inherent to God's being. The virtue of **glory** is present in virtually every doxology in the NT (except for 1 Tim 6:16 and 1 Pet 5:11). The English word doxology (= ***a word of glory***) is actually derived from the Greek word *doxa* (**glory**). **Majesty** (*megalōsynē*) is used only of God in the Bible. It describes God's kingly status and greatness. **Power** (*kratos*) denotes "that absolute power of God which ensures Him ultimate victory" (Kelly 1969, 293). **Authority** (*exousia*) is closely connected with the idea of God's **power.** It portrays God's "intrinsic right to rule all things" (Moo 1996, 301). All four attributes are commonly associated with God.

The phrase **through Jesus Christ our Lord** can be interpreted in two ways: (1) God saves people through Jesus Christ (NASB, NRSV). Or (2) glory can only be properly given to God through Jesus Christ (NIV). Both interpretations make sense. However, since the phrase immediately follows **our Savior** in Greek, it probably identifies the means by which salvation is attributed to God. God has become the **Savior** of believers through the life, death, and resurrection of Jesus Christ.

The duration of God's glory is **before all ages, now and forevermore.** This is a picturesque idiom for eternity. Literally, the phrase can be translated ***before all the ages and now and into all the ages.*** Jude asserts that **glory, majesty, power and authority** belong to God in all three realms of time. These virtues have belonged to God since ***before*** the beginning of the created order. They belong to God ***now*** in the present age. And they will continue to belong to God ***into*** and through the end of the coming ages. These attributes of glory and praise are his forever!

Most doxologies conclude with the word **Amen. Amen** was often used in the OT at the end of a sentence as an adverb meaning ***truly, surely,*** or ***certainly.*** It "confirms the preceding words and invokes their fulfillment" (Zodhiates 1992, 134). Therefore, **Amen** seals the truth and certainty of Jude's praise to God and invokes the affirmative response of his readers to his message.

FROM THE TEXT

God, Our Savior. Jude's doxology attributes the salvation of believers completely to God. God is described as **Savior** through Jesus Christ. He is the One who is able to keep believers from falling into sin. Not only is he able to help believers *survive* the impending scrutiny of the day of judgment, but he helps them pass with *flying colors* and **with great joy.**

Jude has impressed the dangers of the false teachers upon his readers. He has candidly outlined the moral requirements of believers and their obligation to help other struggling Christians. The risks and challenges that face them are real and sobering.

But in these final words of triumph and glory, Jude reminds believers that their hope of victory and salvation is founded upon **him who is able.** God is the One who has *kept* them so far through Jesus Christ (v 1). And he is the One who will continue to *keep* them from falling (v 24), as they *keep* themselves in his love (v 21).

Because of these assurances and promises, Jude can conclude his sobering letter with this magnificent exclamation of praise and glory **to the only God** who is able to accomplish these things. And so, with this beautiful doxology, Jude declares with certainty that to God alone belong the **glory** and the **majesty** and the **power** and the **authority,** both **now and forever**!

And all God's people said: **Amen!** May it be so!